W9-ACV-078

The Culture of Sentiment

THE CULTURE OF
Sentiment

Race, Gender, and Sentimentality in Nineteenth-Century America

Edited by
SHIRLEY SAMUELS

New York   Oxford
OXFORD UNIVERSITY PRESS
1992

Oxford University Press

Oxford   New York   Toronto
Delhi   Bombay   Calcutta   Madras   Karachi
Kuala Lumpur   Singapore   Hong Kong   Tokyo
Nairobi   Dar es Salaam   Cape Town
Melbourne   Auckland   Madrid

and associated companies in
Berlin   Ibadan

Copyright © 1992 by Oxford University Press, Inc.

Published by Oxford University Press, Inc.,
200 Madison Avenue, New York, New York 10016

Oxford is a registered trademark of Oxford University Press

Library of Congress Cataloging-in-Publication Data
The Culture of sentiment:
race, gender, and sentimentality in, nineteenth-century America /
edited by Shirley Samuels.
p. cm. Includes index. ISBN 0-19-506354-6
1. American literature—19th century—History and criticism
2. Slavery and slaves in literature.
3. Feminism and literature—United States—History—19th century.
4. Women and literature—United States—History—19th century.
5. American literature—Women authors—History and criticism.
6. United States—Popular culture—History—19th century.
7. Sentimentalism in literature. 8. Afro-Americans in literature.
9. Sex role in literature. 10. Race in literature.
I. Samuels, Shirley R.
PS217.S55C85 1992   810.9′003—dc20   91-44238

2 4 6 8 9 7 5 3 1

Printed in the United States of America
on acid-free paper

Acknowledgments

Many of the contributors to this volume, especially Lauren Berlant, Susan Gillman, Harryette Mullen, and Lynn Wardley, have discussed its concepts with me over the past several years, and I am grateful to them. For ongoing encouragement and support I am grateful to Mark Seltzer. For other helpful suggestions and timely assistance I would like to thank Mary Ahl, Linda Allen, Phillis Molock, and Aggie Sirrine; and Colin Bailey, Phil Barrish, Mary Chapman, Susan Gilmore, Jillian Hull, Isabelle Lehuu, Laura Murray, Liz Petrino, Katheryn Rios, Francesca Sawaya, Cathy Tufariello, and Tim Young. Thanks also to Susan Chang, Liz Maguire, and Paul Schlotthauer at Oxford University Press for much needed patience, persistence, and enthusiasm. Versions of the following chapters have appeared previously and are reproduced here with the permission of the publishers.

Chapter 1 appeared in *Yale Journal of Criticism* 5 (Fall 1991).

A preliminary version of Chapter 3 was published in *Women's Studies International Forum* 9 (1986).

Chapter 5 first appeared in *Representations* 24 (Fall 1988), and is reprinted by permission of the Regents of the University of California.

Chapter 6 appeared in *American Literature* 63 (1991), copyright © 1991 by Duke University Press.

A different version of chapter 8 appeared in Ann Fabian, *Card Sharps, Dream Books, and Bucket Shops: Gambling in Nineteenth-Century America* (Ithaca, N.Y.: Cornell University Press, 1990).

Chapter 10 was published in different form in Joy Kasson, *Marble Queens and Captives: Women in Nineteenth-Century American Sculpture* (New Haven: Yale University Press, 1990).

Part of chapter 11 appeared in Dana Nelson, *The Word in Black and White: Reading "Race" in American Literature, 1638–1867* (New York: Oxford University Press, 1992).

Chapter 12 appears in *Yale Journal of Criticism* 5 (Fall 1992).

Chapter 15 was published in *American Literary History* 3 (1991).

Contents

The Culture of Sentiment

Introduction

Shirley Samuels

In the search for tears we soon encounter the book.
                    Anne Vincent-Buffault, *The History of Tears:*
                    Sensibility and Sentimentality in France¹

This brief introduction presents a guide for reading the book—or perhaps a road map, since it points out locations rather more than it describes them in detail. Such details are amply provided by the chapters included here. What I want to set out are some provisional possibilities concerning the use of words like "culture" and "sentiment" and phrases like "race, gender, and sentimentality in nineteenth-century America." I want to argue that in nineteenth-century America sentimentality appears as a national project: in particular, a project about imagining the nation's bodies and the national body.

In *The Sentimental Novel in America* (1940), Herbert Ross Brown recounts the "stirring scenes in a great national drama," scenes which include "the conquest of a continent" and the "rise of the common man on the wings of the new democracy." This national drama of manifest destiny and a rising middle class has been, he argues, inadequately confronted by sentimental writers. These writers, who should have been concerned with "the realities of this raucous period in which were being fashioned the sinews of a new nation," were not up to the project of nation building as male body building; they were not, he declares, "fitted to enlighten their readers as to the real nature of their civilization." As a prominent example, he finds that the "most conspicuous failure of the sentimentalists was their inability to solve the irrepressible problem of slavery."² It may be too easy to dismiss this criticism on the grounds of its eager imperialism, figured by the masculine "sinews" of an expanding nation. Yet the responsibility that the writer has found the sentimentalists remiss in upholding—to represent the "real nature" of America and to resolve the "irrepressible conflict" of slavery—is an extraordinary one: he both indicts them for their powerlessness and accuses them of not exercising power. How does this double sense of power and powerlessness continue to inform criticism of the nineteenth-century American project of sentimentality?

If the "irrepressible problem of slavery" was there to be "solved" by senti-

3

mentalists, this indicates at once the intimate association of their project with
the upheavals over slavery and abolition—an association in which the idea of
nation excludes both women and slaves, one hidden behind the other, in the
most political issue of nineteenth-century America—and, paradoxically, a
separation of the sentimentalists from the possibilities of "real" power, the
"real nature of their civilization." In this view the masculine national body,
the "sinews of a new nation," is opposed to the feminine—and to slavery. But
at the same time women were responsible for managing the relation between
national embodiment and national bodies. These contradictory relations, the
nineteenth-century managing of associations between the body and the nation, indicate an involution of gender and nationalism that has been explored,
for example, by the historian George Mosse, who asserts: "Woman as a
national symbol was the guardian of the continuity and immutability of the
nation, the embodiment of its respectability."[3] The paradox of sentimentality,
like the paradox of the "separate spheres" ideology with which it is often
associated, is this combination of the national symbolic and particular embodiments, an obligation at once to national respectability and to a private virtue
removed from national power.[4] This double logic of power and powerlessness
meant, in the case of separate spheres, that a separation from the world of
"work" (and economic power) was compensated for by the affective power of
the "home"; in the case of sentimentality, separation from political action
nonetheless meant presenting an affective alternative that not only gave political actions their emotional significance, but beyond that, intimately linked
individual bodies to the national body. The imagination of national embodiment nonetheless repeatedly excluded the racial and gendered body.

Critics of sentimentality continue to take it to task for not fulfilling national
and political responsibility. Announcing that its "exhibition and commercialization" stand in place of a "genuinely political and historical sense,"[5] this
criticism typically finds that the commercialization of sentimentality (the commerce in sentiment), offering artifacts overloaded with emotional values for
sale to an audience shaped by their consumption, prevents what is imagined as
a "genuine" engagement with politics and history. Celebrations of sentimental
fiction similarly conceive of an audience reciprocally shaped by its "sensational designs." Avowing its engagement with "the brute facts of political and
economic oppression,"[6] such an analysis finds that the production of a sentimental consumer means the alteration of political as well as emotional values.
Yet if this second view indicates the strategic effects of sentimentality on the
national public sphere, it rarely addresses the often conservative results of
such polemical intervention.

Sentimentality is literally at the heart of nineteenth-century American culture. These essays show the process through which that culture is both produced and contested, focusing, for example, on the particular circumstances
of policies concerning gender, race, and ethnicity, and often on the involvement of women as objects or agents of these policies. As a set of cultural
practices designed to evoke a certain form of emotional response, usually
empathy, in the reader or viewer, sentimentality produces or reproduces spec-

tacles that cross race, class, and gender boundaries. Specifically, some of the chapters here address how, while frequently operating as social commentary or critique, sentimentality acts in conjunction with the problem of the body and what it embodies, how social, political, racial, and gendered meanings are determined through their differential embodiments. Perhaps the most power-ful instance of sentimental work thus appears in the midnineteenth-century conjunction of feminist and abolitionist discourse. This crossing point of femi-nism and abolition foregrounds the problem of the "body politic" in American culture and, centrally, the crucial position of sentimental aesthetics in redefin-ing a politics of the American body.

To take one example of the particular bodies discussed here, the notorious bodies of Uncle Tom and Little Eva: Stowe presents, on the one side, the suffering female child whose potentially grotesque death is radically spiritual-ized (the child's suffering body operating as an agent of moral reform), and on the other, the brutally beaten slave whose triumph is shown to be an escape from or transcendence of the body which has been the cause of his suffering. The critical controversies raised by these texts, and by this instance, involve a debate between a *dismissal* of the sentimental move outside or beyond the boundaries of a gendered or racialized body—a move seen as a *betrayal* of the specific embodiment figured—and, alternately, a celebration of the emancipa-tory strategies of a sentimentality that *rescues* subjects from the unfortunate essentializing that the fact of having a body entails. Stowe's "solution" of Heaven and the Afterworld, for instance, can appear alternately a utopian projection and an inadequate remedy, at once honoring and disowning the embodied subjects of the nation in the making. Such a transcendence of the body both foregrounds the natural body and understands the body as an abstract embodiment of the values that it transcends. The charge against sentimentality, in this view, is its undercutting of political potential; the ideal-ized body removes the political from critique.

The reform literature associated with sentimentality works as a set of rules for how to "feel right," privileging compassion in calibrating and adjusting the sensations of the reader in finely tuned and predictable responses to what is viewed or read. The discomfort of sentimentality comes from what can be a coerced or artifactual emotional response—being forced to feel what it feels like—a response that raises questions about the moral or political status of the works, or produces an uneasiness regarding what borders on the prurient or salacious aspects of the texts' subjects.

In short, the texts examined here expose bodies. One question about how the critical gaze constitutes but also appropriates and controls its objects of scrutiny involves whether the sentimental gaze acts to conservative ends (what can even appear as a form of social control) or seeks to produce radical reform. The sentimental response of passive sympathy, caricatured (by Wil-liam Dean Howells) as "tears, idle tears," may appear as a retreat into the privacy of the body; action, in contrast, functions as the body mobilized by sympathy to reform efforts. Yet the bodies for whom such reform efforts are enacted are only to a limited extent culturally and critically malleable, and these essays also examine their potential or actual recalcitrance or resistance. The reassurance that the critical position is not contaminated by the object or the action of its interrogations is a reassurance that sentimentality, clearly the site of multiple contaminations, frequently refuses.

Sentimentality in nineteenth-century America, then, appears not so much a genre as an operation or a set of actions within discursive models of affect and identification that effect connections across gender, race, and class boundaries. What might be called the aesthetics of sentiment appear in advice books, statues, photographs, pamphlets, lyric poems, fashion advertisements, and novels, this last the category most frequently examined for its signs and registers. The sentimental complex also situates the reader or viewer: that is, the act of emotional response the work evokes also produces the sentimental subject who consumes the work. This production crucially involves a movement of sympathy, in all its anxious appeals, across race, class, and gender lines. These papers explore, for instance, the intersections of "women's culture" and changing racial conflicts, ranging from issues of slavery, abolition, and Indian policy in the antebellum years, to those of disfranchisement, segregation, and racial violence in the post-Reconstruction years. The essays address not only the classic moment of sentimentality in the antebellum period, but also less familiar genres and modes of sentimentality constructed throughout the nineteenth century. The volume thus seeks to redefine both the formal and political boundaries of "sentimentality." It traces a genealogy of the culture of sentiment that mobilizes both a rhetorical configuration of emotional excess and a problem of the body and what it embodies: its gendered, racialized, or national affiliation, and what, following Pierre Bourdieu, might be called the position or disposition of the sentimental subject, the "habitus" of sentimentality.[7]

The double logic of sentiment, and its cultural work, is richly articulated in the chapters that follow. Sentimental education in late nineteenth-century America, according to Laura Wexler, used "tender violence" to induce accommodation to middle-class culture; focusing on contemporary stories of young Native American girls at the Hampton Institute, she reveals the aesthetic and ideological effects of transplanting them into "white" America. In the alternately sensational and sentimental courtroom language of an early nineteenth-century murder trial, Karen Halttunen discovers a vivid opposition of the demonic and the domestic woman. With the jury as audience, rival attorneys pitted two competing visions of the nineteenth-century woman against each other: Angel in the House or Destroying Demon. Carolyn L. Karcher contends that a desire to circumvent the limitations of sentimental fiction by providing an alternative to the tragic mulatto archetype inspired Lydia Maria Child's "Slavery's Pleasant Homes." As a socially marginalized work too radical to be published outside antislavery circles, Karcher argues, this story offers an ideal site for exploring the relations between sordid details and sentimental tastes in polemical literature. These sentimental tastes are illustrated in the fashion plates of *Godey's Lady's Book,* the most popular nineteenth-century American woman's magazine, yet Isabelle Lehuu proposes that *Godey's* images of fashionably dressed women staged a potentially subversive culture.

That reading sentimental fiction is a "bodily act" in which the tears of the reader are "pledged" for the bodies of slaves is the subject of Karen Sánchez-Eppler's chapter. Concentrating on texts in which the rhetorical crossings of women and slaves predominate—feminist-abolitionist pamphlets, the sentimental novels and gift-book stories that supported the antislavery cause, and the more conservative Sunday school primers—she argues that, in trying to domesticate slavery, such literature often exposes the contradictions and asymmetries inherent in the comparison or equation of woman and slave. Interpreting bodies also centers Lora Romero's discussion of precipitous "prodigies" in *The Last of the Mohicans;* she implicates the practices of New Historicism in Cooper's ethnographic celebration of "the perfection of form" he assigns to the vanishing American. In her reading of *Uncle Tom's Cabin* and *Life in the Iron Mills,* Amy Schrager Lang at once questions why gender and race substitute for class in this fiction and, contrasting the "malleable" Uncle Tom to Hugh Wolfe, who must be "hewed and hacked" out of recalcitrant korl, examines how bodies are produced for the sentimental reader.

The alliance between the commercial and the sentimental that middle-class culture promoted recurs throughout these accounts. Ann Fabian finds that this alliance was ineptly managed by Jonathan Harrington Green, an antebellum gambler turned writer and reformer; his failure to make a profit by trafficking in sentiment exposes important contradictions in the social and imaginary geography of the sentimental culture of the 1850s. The nexus of bodily and economic concerns also determines my rendering of antebellum discourses on slavery; I see in both abolitionist and proslavery accounts a panic about *identity* (social, bodily, personal) that repositions the terms of national identity and a national culture. As Joy Kasson traces them, American anxieties about the integrity of the body can be elucidated through the subject of a woman in bondage, a subject that provided a kind of pornographic excitement for nineteenth-century male spectators. Focusing on Hiram Powers's *The Greek Slave,* a life-sized female nude sculpture viewed by more than a hundred thousand spectators during the 1840s, Kasson argues that, in their "reading" of the sculpture, audiences made visible conflicting attitudes toward slavery, sexuality, the family, and the female body. Dana Nelson discovers in the bitterly ironic portrayals of *Hope Leslie,* Catherine Sedgwick's history of the last of the Pequods, a political commentary on the patriarchal assumptions of both the Puritans and her contemporary reading audience.

The sentimental complex provides the terms, the conflicted terms, of a female public culture. Lynn Wardley looks at the animated "fetish" in *Uncle Tom's Cabin,* proposing in part that surviving West African perceptions of the spirit in objects, and of death as a homecoming, inform the nineteenth-century American domestication of death. Novels drawing on melodramatic conventions, such as the revelation of hidden identities, form the basis of what Susan Gillman calls the American race melodrama. Reading paradigmatic texts by Mark Twain, Pauline Hopkins, and W. E. B. Du Bois, she locates an erotics mediated through gender and nationalism that fuses the crisis of race with melodramas of familial love disrupted and restored. Harryette Mullen argues that the trope of "resistant orality" allowed nineteenth-century black women writers like Harriet Jacobs to "talk back" to Stowe and to the male-centered slave narrative tradition personified by Frederick Douglass; such a tradition inspires the competing voices in the work of novelists like Toni Morrison. What Lauren Berlant calls the "female complaint" appears as an important aesthetic "witnessing" of injury in Fanny Fern, a journalist and social critic with extraordinary talents for sentimentality and complaint. Situated in the space between a sexual politics that threatens the structures of authority, and a sentimentality that affirms the inevitability of the speaker's powerlessness, the female complaint serves as a collective social practice for bourgeois American women, conjoining the dual sentimental aims of social containment and social change.

Together, these chapters are part of the process of acquiring practices and vocabularies with which to approach some newly opened areas of inquiry in the understanding of American national culture. Such a process calls for both flexibility and attentiveness, and incorporates a range of critical vocabularies, including the often intersecting idioms of feminism, psychoanalysis, Marxism, and New Historicism. We hope to gain from this process a more thoroughly situated and engaged sense of how sentimental texts produce effects and how social and cultural meanings are embodied. Such considerations of the embodiment of social and cultural meanings not only reclaim both noncanonical and canonical works by testing them in new systems of analysis; they also crucially reinterpret the tension between the pleasure of sympathy and the power of sympathy—between relations of sympathy and relations of power.

1

Tender Violence:
Literary Eavesdropping, Domestic Fiction, and Educational Reform

Laura Wexler

I

Upstairs, a long time ago, she had cried, standing on the bare floorboards in the front bedroom just after we moved to this house in Streatham Hill in 1951, my baby sister in her carry-cot. We both watched the dumpy retreating figure of the health visitor through the curtainless windows. The woman had said: "This house isn't fit for a baby." And then she stopped crying, my mother, got by, the phrase that picks up after all difficulty (it says: it's like this; it shouldn't be like this; it's unfair; I'll manage): "Hard lines, eh, Kay?" (Kay was the name I was called at home, my middle name, one of my father's names).

And I? I will do everything and anything until the end of my days to stop anyone ever talking to me like that woman talked to my mother. It is in this place, this bare, curtainless bedroom that lies my secret and shameful defiance. I read a woman's book, meet such a woman at a party (a woman now, like me) and think quite deliberately as we talk: we are divided: a hundred years ago I'd have been cleaning your shoes. I know this and you don't.

Carolyn Kay Steedman, Landscape for a Good Woman

The widely influential Douglas-Tompkins debate on the literary value of American domestic fiction attributes a broad range of cultural effectiveness to nineteenth-century sentimental novels. Ann Douglas began *The Feminization of American Culture* by asserting the moral primacy of Puritan culture in the northeast United States and the tragedy—rather than merely the melodrama—of the terms under which it gave way. The Edwardsean Calvinist school of ministers was the "most persuasive example of independent yet institutionalized thought to which our society has even temporarily given credence," and its members "exhibited with some consistency the intellectual rigor and imaginative precision difficult to achieve without collective effort, and certainly rare in

9

more recent American annals." The invaluable intellectual "toughness" of this theological establishment, however, was disastrously undermined by, among other things, the "sentimental heresy" of the cult of the victim perpetrated by "literary men of the cloth and middle-class women writers of the Victorian period." "Feminization" of American culture encouraged the idea that appropriate notice of the painful social dislocations of nineteenth-century capital and urban industrial expansion could be given symbolic expression in literary rather than theological works. The ultimate effect of this change of venue to literary representation was not, as the writers of these works often alleged, to foreground and correct social inequities, but rather to provide an emergent middle-class readership with permission for a kind of aesthetic and emotional contemplation that was underwritten precisely by its refusal actively to "interfere" in civil life. Sentimentality became a way to "obfuscate the visible dynamics of development." It also functioned as an "introduction to consumerism" and as the herald of a "debased" American mass culture through which we have learned to "locate and express many personal, 'unique' feelings and responses through dime-a-dozen artifacts." The principal literary exemplum of the Douglas thesis was the death of Little Eva in Harriet Beecher Stowe's *Uncle Tom's Cabin,* a "beautiful death, which Stowe presents as part of a protest against slavery [which] in no way hinders the working of that system." Adherence to nineteenth-century sentimentalism's "fake" standards had "damage[d] women like Harriet Beecher Stowe." Even just from studying sentimentalism, Douglas herself "experienced a confusion" of identity that separated her painfully from the "best of the men [who] had access to solutions" and associated her uncomfortably with the women writers, whose problems "correspond to mine with a frightening accuracy that seems to set us outside the processes of history." American Victorian sentimental fiction was, she concluded, "rancid writing"; it was her duty as a feminist to be "as clear" as possible about that fact.[1]

Jane Tompkins, in *Sensational Designs,* vigorously attacked Douglas's thesis that the spirit of nineteenth-century domestic fiction was destructive, and opened an expansive alternative perspective. Instead of mourning the "vitiation" of a rare, tough-minded, communal, Calvinist "male-dominated theological tradition,"[2] Tompkins took the ideological and commercial ascendency of nineteenth-century women's writing as a mark of "the *value* of a powerful and specifically female novelistic tradition."[3] Turning the tables on the Douglas scenario, Tompkins argued for the coming-into-being within this literature of a coordinated, specifically female, evangelical tradition, whose principal figures concurred and strategized with much the same serious, socially engaged intention that Douglas's Edwardsean school evinced. It followed that the most consequential difference lay not between the ministerial tradition and the women themselves, but between our own reevaluation of the kinds of social knowledge and goals for reform generated from the perspective of Victorian female engenderment and those of the contemporary intellectual establishment. "The very grounds on which sentimental fiction has been dismissed by its detractors," Tompkins wrote, grounds which have come to seem universal standards of aesthetic judgment, were established in a struggle to supplant the tradition of evangelical piety and moral commitment these novelists represent. In reaction against their world view, and perhaps even more against their success, twentieth-century critics have taught generations of students to equate popularity with debasement, emotionality with ineffectiveness, religiosity with fakery, domesticity with triviality, and all of these, implicitly, with womanly inferiority.

In other words, what Douglas saw as the usurpation of the chief source of serious social criticism in the northeastern United States prior to the Victorian period by a sentimentalism that was a passive and hypocritical "rationalization of the economic order," Tompkins scripted as a move toward greater scope and democratization by a sentimentalism that was profoundly "a political enterprise, halfway between sermon and social theory, that both codifies and attempts to mold the values of its time."[4]

For Tompkins, this "sentimental power" spoke to and of the interests of the "large masses of readers," at least some of whom were, presumably, the same persons who were suffering under the new urban industrial regime. Tompkins developed a provocative reassessment of the social function of literary stereotypes, whose "familiarity and typicality, rather than making them bankrupt or stale, are the basis of their effectiveness as integers in a social equation." The contemplation of such literary moments as Little Eva's death, she postulated, provides readers with comprehensible examples of "what kinds of behavior to emulate or shun" and thereby "provide[s] a basis for remaking the social and political order in which events take place." Sentimental fiction, in this view, offered a practical, quotidian, grass-roots politics that the more abstract, theological, patriarchal Calvinist tradition tended to disdain. Nor were the authors of this literature simply apologists for the corruptions of the capitalist order. They reached down to the "prejudices of the multitude," which those who stood upon the Yankee Olympus wanted only to "uplift," and spoke words of resistance and encouragement in the mother tongue. Interestingly, as a result of her study, Tompkins, like Douglas before her, found herself surprised to be allied with "everything that criticism had taught me to despise: the stereotyped character, the sensational plot, the trite expression."[5] But the recognition of her bond with the women did not provoke the same identity crisis it produced in Douglas, whose preference for "the best of the men" made her afraid that her empathy with the women could be seen as "siding with the enemy."[6] Rather, as a "woman in a field dominated by male scholars," Tompkins decided strategically to discuss "works of domestic, or 'sentimental,' fiction because I wanted to demonstrate the power and ambition of novels written by women, and specifically by women whose work twentieth-century criticism has repeatedly denigrated." In *Uncle Tom's Cabin* and *The Wide, Wide World*, Tompkins found intellectual nourishment that was not "rancid" but "good."[7]

Clearly, to decide the merits of one of these arguments over the other is simultaneously to arrive at a position on such a large number of nineteenth-

and twentieth-century social, economic, cultural, and critical practices that the task is beyond the reach of a single essay, and even, perhaps, beyond the wishes of any relatively more modest reader who feels prepared at this juncture only to form an opinion on literary sentimentalism. Exactly this enlargement of the notion of what it would take to fully understand nineteenth-century American sentimentalism or to write its history is, however, one of the chief accomplishments of Douglas's and Tompkins's scholarship, as well as the early supporting work by Alexander Cowie, Barbara Welter, Henry Nash Smith, Helen Papashvily, Gail Parker, Dee Garrison, Nina Baym, Mary Kelley, and Judith Fetterly, among others, which prefigures, surrounds, and amplifies the basic insights codified by the more famous exchange. Jane Tompkins recognized the primary and essential contribution of this dilation herself, when she wrote of her interlocutor that

> although her attitude toward the vast quantity of literature written by women between 1820 and 1870 is the one that the male-dominated tradition has always expressed—contempt—Douglas's book is nevertheless extremely important because of its powerful and sustained consideration of this long-neglected body of work. Because Douglas successfully focused critical attention on the cultural centrality of sentimental fiction, forcing the realization that it can no longer be ignored, it is now possible for other critics to put forward a new characterization of these novels and not be dismissed. For these reasons, it seems to me, her work is important.[8]

A revision of the traditional critical contempt was what Tompkins was attempting, but for writing that Douglas had put on the map. It is evident, therefore, that in one crucial respect both Douglas and Tompkins are in absolute agreement. This is on the issue of the active and productive social function of domestic literature—the "cultural work within a specific historical situation" that Tompkins values, and the "intimate connection between critical aspects of Victorian culture and modern mass culture" that Douglas castigates.[9] For both critics, sentimental fiction is a "power" and a political "force" too considerable to be neglected; it is a "protest" (Douglas) and a "means of thinking" (Tompkins).[10] Both critics see the task at hand as a readjustment of our notions of cultural history by way of reexamining this particular literary material and its effect upon its readers.

It bears recalling, however, that this mutual vision of cultural history as centered in literary history itself has roots in the Victorian era, in the birth of the critical profession, and that, whatever evaluation of the productions of domestic culture the critics holds, their methodology equally prioritizes a particular segment of white, middle-class, Christian, native-born readers and their texts as the chief source of information about the culture. "This book," wrote Douglas, "while focused on written sources, might be described in one sense as a study of readers and of those who shared and shaped their taste."[11] Tompkins, who had earlier edited an important collection of essays on reader-response criticism, might easily have said the same. But what is meant by a "reader"? The readers Tompkins invokes in *Sensational Designs* are both "the widest possible audience" in the nineteenth century and "twentieth-century critics."[12] Douglas has in mind "American girls socialized to immerse themselves in novels and letters."[13] What this emphasis on "readers" suggests is the presence of a historically determined agreement between Douglas and Tompkins more essential and more important even than their mutual choice of material or the joint perception of its moral urgency and social consequence: an agreement on how it is and to whom it is that reading matters; an agreement that instruction of the literate middle class is the chief object as well as the chief subject of domestic narrative. It seems evident that this agreement operates within the Douglas-Tompkins debate to focus, and also to circumscribe, the material that it can coordinate. The direct and indirect effect of the widespread reading of midnineteenth-century sentimental fiction upon those who were *not* either critics or white, middle-class, Christian, native-born readers is by and large left out. This omission makes for a kind of repressed margin even within a critical discourse whose impulse it always was to examine seriously the composition and function of the fringe.

Lest it seem that such an agreement bears only a general relation to the issues, I want to point out its material function in the coincidence of two anecdotes that both Tompkins and Douglas independently offer their readers— two strikingly intimate stories about reading *Uncle Tom's Cabin* which are in themselves attempts to represent, each in a fine, vivid, domestic style, the impact of this "power" and "force" on their own personal lives as readers. Without in any way softening the edge of the disagreement between the two critical positions, I would like to propose that the coincidence of these reflections on reading Stowe is important to the debate on sentimentalism beyond their decided narrative value and the generally helpful, concretizing effect they have on the clarity of the critical arguments. As specific representations of the scene of the incorporation of domestic fiction and its social effect, these anecdotes exemplify the homology of the two critics' assessments of how such fiction functions in the real world, in actual people's lives. They indicate both the range and the limitation of the debate as it has so far been staged.

For her part, Ann Douglas asserted that "today many Americans, intellectuals as well as less scholarly people, feel a particular fondness for the artifacts, the literature, the *mores* of our Victorian past. I wrote this book because I am one of those people." She recalled that

> as a child I read with formative intensity in a collection of Victorian sentimental fiction, a legacy from my grandmother's girlhood. Reading these stories, I first discovered the meaning of absorption: the pleasure and guilt of possessing a secret supply. I read through the "Elsie Dinsmore" books, the "Patty" books, and countless others; I followed the timid exploits of innumerable pale and pious heroines. But what I remember best, what was for me as for so many others, the archetypical and archetypically satisfying scene in this domestic genre, was the death of Little Eva in Harriet Beecher Stowe's novel, *Uncle Tom's Cabin*.

Douglas amplified the confessional thrust of this memory:

> Little Eva is a creature not only of her author's imagination but of her
> reader's fantasy; her life stems from our acceptance of her and our involve-
> ment with her. But Little Eva is one of us in more special ways. Her admirers
> have always been able to identify with her even while they worship, or weep,
> at her shrine. She does not demand the respect we accord a competitor. She is
> not extraordinarily gifted, or at least she is young enough so that her talents
> have not had the chance to take on formidable proportions. If she is lovely
> looking and has a great deal of money, Stowe makes it amply clear that these
> attributes are more a sign than a cause of her success. Little Eva's death is not
> futile, but it is essentially decorative; and therein, perhaps, lay its charm for
> me and for others.

Finally, she felt forced to admit that her beloved Little Eva did not rest innocu-
ously within the pages of an old-fashioned book but reappeared as the figure
"of Miss America, of 'Teen Angel,' of the ubiquitous, everyday, wonderful girl
about whom thousands of popular songs and movies have been made." Thus
her "pleasure" in Little Eva was "historical and practical preparation for the
equally indispensable and disquieting comforts of mass culture." To describe
Little Eva's Christianity as "camp," which Douglas had done one page earlier,
was really a way to "socialize" her "ongoing, unexplored embarrassment" at
the strength of a persistent emotional attachment to such figures.[14]

Jane Tompkins also referred to a scene from her younger days when, "once,
during a difficult period of my life, I lived in the basement of a house on
Forest Street in Hartford, Connecticut, which had belonged to Isabella
Beecher Hooker—Harriet Beecher Stowe's half-sister. This woman at one
time in her life had believed that the millennium was at hand and that she was
destined to be the leader of a new matriarchy." And her memory also quickly
turned confessional, although for the opposite reason from that of Douglas.
What Tompkins felt defensive about was not the length and durability of her
connection to the writers of nineteenth-century domestic fiction but the over-
long *absence* of that connection, prior to the entry of feminist criticism into
the academy:

> When I lived in that basement, however, I knew nothing of Stowe, or of the
> Beechers, or of the utopian visions of nineteenth-century American women. I
> made a reverential visit to the Mark Twain house a few blocks away, took
> photographs of his study, and completely ignored Stowe's own house—also
> open to the public—which stood across the lawn. Why should I go? Neither I
> nor anyone I knew regarded Stowe as a serious writer. At the time, I was giving
> my first lecture course in the American Renaissance—concentrated exclu-
> sively on Hawthorne, Melville, Poe, Emerson, Thoreau, and Whitman—and
> although *Uncle Tom's Cabin* was written in exactly the same period, and al-
> though it is probably the most influential book ever written by an American, I
> would never have dreamed of including it on my reading list. To begin with, its
> very popularity would have militated against it; as everybody knew, the classics
> of American fiction were, with a few exceptions, all succès d'estime.[15]

Where Douglas betrayed her scholarship by responding to the women, Tompkins betrayed her womanhood by siding with the men.

Notable in both stories is the engaging particularity and lively individuality of the speakers. They respond to the literary and sociological problems raised by Harriet Beecher Stowe in the well-trained, observant, mildly ironic, and self-confident voices that are characteristic of our educated middle class. Personal anecdotes embedded within critical discourse are a form akin to gossip in the "function of intimacy" that Patricia Meyer Spacks has described.[16] This means that even the rhetorical register of the stories communicates how the social legacy of sentimentalism is something that may be explored in a private, personal space between readers who are middle-class and their books, which either do or do not incite them to ideas, actions, and loyalties of one sort or another. The problem of reading and responding to sentimentalism takes shape largely as an intimate matter, a question of the individual's training and sensitivity. It becomes, by extension, a question for us even of our own particular taste, rather than our historical positioning. The theater of operations in which the act of reading is depicted in these anecdotes as occurring and having its effect is only either private or professional life, as inflected by personal ambition. Alternative perceptions of the social action of literature, different class orientations, or other points of connection that map a differently organized social formation than the tightly knit circuit between the individual middle-class reader, the critical profession, the book, and the shifting vogue of the literary marketplace are not illustrated or implied. It is in both cases as if the issue of the moral stimulation of sentimentalism raises questions for a literary consciousness alone, more or less observant, more or less well educated, more or less discriminating.

II

But this picture neglects, and the Douglas-Tompkins debate as a whole has tended to elide, the expansive, imperial project of sentimentalism. In this aspect sentimentalization was an *externalized* aggression that was sadistic, not masochistic, in flavor. The energies it developed were intended as a tool for the control of others, not merely as aid in the conquest of the self. This element of the enterprise was not oriented toward white, middle-class readers and their fictional alter egos at all, either deluded and hypocritical *or* conscious and seriously committed "to an ethic of social love," as Nina Baym characterizes the theme of domestic fiction.[17] Rather, it aimed at the subjection of different classes and even races who were compelled to play not the leading roles but the human scenery before which the melodrama of middle-class redemption could be enacted, for the enlightenment of an audience that was not even themselves. While sentimental pietism most certainly did "cripple" numerous ministers and lady writers, as Ann Douglas contends, and make them servants of their own oppression, it is arguable that it disabled other people more.[18] If sentimentalism is, as Nina Baym usefully defines it, a domestic ideal set forth "as a value scheme for ordering all of life, in competition with the ethos of money and exploitation that is perceived to prevail in

American society," then those who did not have, could not get, or had been robbed of their "homes" would be, of necessity, nonparticipants in the pursuit of this ideal.[19] This fact would irredeemably dehumanize them in the eyes of those who came from "homes" and leave them open to self-hatred and pressure to alter their habits of living in order to present themselves as if they too might lay claim to a proper "domestic" lineage in the way that the nineteenth century understood that genealogy. "In the abolitionist movement," writes Dorothy Sterling in *We Are Your Sisters: Black Women in the Nineteenth Century,*

> the black women who worked with whites were caught between two worlds. Only a generation or two removed from slavery themselves, hemmed in by the same discriminatory laws that poor blacks faced, they nevertheless strove to live up to the standards of their white associates. No one's curtains were as starched, gloves as white, or behavior as correct as black women's in the antislavery societies. Yet the pinch of poverty was almost always there. Light-skinned Susan Paul, an officer of the Boston Female Anti-Slavery Society and a welcome guest in white homes, did not tell her white friends of her desperate struggle to support her mother and four orphaned children until she was on the verge of eviction from her home.[20]

It is demonstrable that the progressive educational reform movements for blacks, Indians, and immigrants in the later nineteenth century built lavishly on this kind of social disparagement, while attempting to elicit from all students a concession of the universal superiority of the middle-class, white, Christian "home" that erased the history and the recent defeat of their own alternative modes of living. In "Sparing the Rod: Discipline and Fiction in Antebellum America," Richard Brodhead has traced that complicated interfiliation of sentimental values and educational policy at midcentury. What he terms "disciplinary intimacy" is a dense cross-wiring of "bodily correction . . . the history of home and school . . . and the field of literature" that develops in the writings of Horace Bushnell, Catherine Beecher, Mary Peabody Mann, Lyman Cobb, Lydia Sigourney, Catherine Sedgwick, Lydia Maria Child, Horace Mann, and Harriet Beecher Stowe. This set of texts sets forth an argument for the replacement of the corporal discipline of children at school and at home by an internalized model of loving, middle-class parental authority which the child would be loathe to disobey. We may think of the novel and of disciplinary intimacy together, Brodhead writes, "as being taken up inside a certain formation of family life in the early nineteenth century, [as] . . . being placed as another of those adjacent institutions (like the public school) that the middle-class family recruited in support of its home-centered functions." "Sparing the Rod" significantly enlarges the parameters of the debate on sentimentality by recognizing the ways in which the ideology of domesticity infiltrated precisely those public institutions that are gatekeepers of social existence. But Brodhead is principally interested in pointing out how this "theory of discipline through love had its force," through the medium of novels, in the establishment of the middle class, rather than in the disestablishment of others. In Brodhead's analysis, what this literature did was to supply "an emerging group with a plan of individual nurture and social structure that it could believe in and use to justify its ways." He adds that "it helped shape and empower the actual institutions through which that group could impress its ways on others," but this is not the history he chiefly studies. Although he recognizes its aggressive potential, Brodhead focuses on the majority: "At a time when it was in no sense socially normal the new middle-class world undertook to propagate itself as American 'normality'; and it is as a constituent in this new creation of the normative that the complex I have traced had its full historical life."[21]

Therefore, it needs to be further investigated how the fierce devaluation of the extradomestic life implicit within the terms of this monitory framework was just as productive as the cult of domesticity, except in another way. In his elegant study *Hard Facts: Setting and Form in the American Novel*, Philip Fisher has shown that the politically "radical methodology" of sentimentality is that it "experiments with the extension of full and complete humanity to classes of figures from whom it has been socially withheld. The typical objects of sentimental compassion are the prisoner, the madman, the child, the very old, the animal, and the slave." This extension of the self is "experimental, even dangerous," Fisher writes, convincingly, from the perspective once again of the white, middle-class critic. But mustn't we ask, radical and dangerous for whom? The prisoner, the madman, the child, the very old, the animal, and the slave already have selves that are poised over the social void. Self-recognition is not dangerous for them; to themselves, they are not "novel *objects* of feeling," as Fisher puts it, but *customary objects* of feeling. The extension toward them by others of newly perceived "normal states of primary feeling" can only make for bewilderment since primary feeling *is* their normal state, though its style will not necessarily match up with the new offering. The conclusion must be that the full and complete extension of "humanity" that facilitates sentimental politics is dangerous for the sentimental reader. And in addition, that it is the sentimental reader who is dangerous for his or her "novel" object, precisely *because* he or she newly discovers in that object the possibility of a primary relation to itself that has been there all along, but must then be denied its history so that the discovery can be made. Furthermore, any meaningful enlargement by sentimentality of the percentage of the population who can come "inside" this magic circle still leaves behind the vast numbers who cannot qualify for entry under moral standards determined by arbiters who remain in power. Sentimentalism encourages a large-scale imaginative depersonalization of those outside its complex specifications at the same time that it elaborately personalizes, magnifies, and flatters those who can accommodate to its image of an interior.[22]

In the nineteenth century this construct did social work. It supplied the rationale for raw intolerance to be packaged as education. Without the background of the several decades of domestic "sentiment" that established the private home as the apotheosis of nurture, the nineteenth-century interracial boarding school could probably not have existed, since it took as its mission the inculcation of domesticity in former "savages" and slaves. It is furthermore a matter of record that in at least some of these schools the Indian and black children who were the students received domestic training not as the future householders and sentimental parents they were ostensibly supposed to become, but as future domestic servants in the homes of others. Such a vast institutionalized pandering to middle-class domestic labor requirements obviously extends far beyond whatever hypocrisy or naiveté the single middle-class, feminized, literary imagination, working intimately on perfecting its own image, may or may not have adopted. It may be useful to speak in this connection of sentimental fiction not only as a literary genre, but as a generic cultural category on its own—that is, as *the* sentimental fiction. It would designate the alliance of the double-edged, double-jeopardy nature of sentimental perception with the social control of marginal domestic populations. The sentimental fiction, then, would be the myth that widespread instruction in domesticity, and vigorous pursuit of social reform based explicitly and insistently on affective values, were ever really intended to restore the vitality of the peoples that domestic expansion had originally appropriated.

How can we begin to reclaim this territory? To start, it should be remarked that along with the democratization of literacy, the expanded market framework, and the heightened interest in fiction characteristic of American mid-Victorian culture necessarily came the "unintended reader." By this term I mean to identify readers who were *not* the ones that sentimental authors, publishers, critical spokesmen, or the nascent advertising industry had in mind. They were readers who read material not intended for their eyes and were affected by the print culture in ways that could not be anticipated, and were ungovernable by the socioemotional codes being set forth within the community-making forces that literature set in motion. Occasionally in the nineteenth century, although more commonly in the twentieth, the unintended reader has left testimony to the effect that such an experience of reading has had on him or her. One such is the young Federick Douglass, whose chance encounter with a popular anthology called *The Columbian Orator,* in which he found an invaluable dialogue between a master and a slave and "one of Sheridan's mighty speeches on and in behalf of Catholic emancipation," was a piece of great good fortune "[that] gave tongue to interesting thoughts of my own soul, which had frequently flashed through my mind, and died away for want of utterance."[23] Another is Margaret Fuller, a voracious reader of masculine texts whose classical education and intellectual appetite were carefully orchestrated by her father but contradicted the expectations and desires of her society. Reading adventurers like these, a woman and a slave, did not necessarily harbor a deluded faith in middle-class values. Literary eavesdropping could lead to stunningly vibrant political insights into the nature of class distinctions, when the unintended reader compared his or her life and even habits of reading to the situation of the reader who was deliberately being addressed. We can see from the syncopated experience of the unintended reader how the range of social practices surrounding the reading of sentimental fiction precipitated not merely class formation but class conflict. These experiences illustrate how any instrumental role played by the sentimental genres of poetry, short fiction, inspirational essays, journalism, and the domestic novel in the formation of the new middle-class self-consciousness might have a no less forceful corollary in the culture's disregard and disorganization of the people who were displaced by the ingathering of this new class formation. Ultimately, it was against their humanity, or out of the raw material of their right to information, self-esteem, and possible life choices, that this new identity was furnished and then maintained.

In addition, as fiction supplied the increasing demand for accessories to self-absorption throughout the middle period of the century, and underwrote other mechanisms of middle-class consolidation and domination such as educational theory, sentimental ideology continued to mature in power past midcentury, even while the sentimental mode itself was waning. The last quarter of the nineteenth century has generally been avoided in studies of literary sentimentalism, which conscientiously stop around the 1870s when the production of texts is perceived to have slowed down.[24] But if one excludes from the theory of the cultural work of domestic fiction the afterglow of sentimentalization—on the grounds that the literary genre had by then run its course—one distorts the history of its concrete social institution-alization in schools, hospitals, prisons, and so on, whose building, staffing, and operation quite naturally had to lag behind the literary imagination. This foreshortened periodization is especially ironic, given that the question of social and institutional productivity was the reason advanced in the first place for expending serious attention on the sentimental aesthetic. To begin to recover its submerged lineaments, then, it seems that a more liberal understanding of the extent and solid permanence of the consequences of the sentimental campaign must be sought.

III

The evidence for these wider effects of sentimental fiction often lies outside the purely literary realm, or even the material world of the middle-class sentimental reader as it has been defined and investigated by literary historians. There is a rich and largely untapped source in visual form, in the many photographs that were made during this period of black, Indian, and immigrant students and readers. These have come down to us sometimes with documentary testimony attached, sometimes with literary referents, sometimes without. Ethnic (as distinct from simply regional) writing, which began in earnest during this period, is another such source. Together they make it possible to envision the scene of the imposition of sentimental modalities on people who were in no sense the intended beneficiaries of domestic fiction, but who were nonetheless as powerfully directed by its dictates as its most highly preferred audience. What I am suggesting, then, is the usefulness of elaborating the debate on the consequences of nineteenth-century sentimental fiction even beyond the extended borders that have come only recently, in the aftermath of the Douglas-Tompkins exchange, to seem both appropriately strenuous and natural to the subject at hand. To map the power of the word in the hands of nineteenth-century, middle-class literary women and their retinue, it is helpful not only to develop new theories of language and a fresh sense of the sociology of literature, but to leave even writing itself temporarily, if strategically, behind.

Two photographs, made in the 1880s at the Hampton Normal and Agricultural Institute in Hampton, Virginia, by an unknown photographer, will begin to illustrate this point. The Hampton Institute was an agricultural and mechanical trade school, as well as a teachers' training school, that was founded in 1868 by the American Missionary Association and by Northern Quaker philanthropists. It was headed throughout much of the nineteenth century by Colonel Samuel Chapman Armstrong, who had been the white commander of the 8th and 9th U.S. Colored Troops during the Civil War. Armstrong had a decided vision of the education of the freedmen; under his control, the Hampton curriculum was to emphasize the trade over the academic curriculum, despite the fact that spokesmen like William Roscoe Davis, a leading black citizen in town, had called it the "height of foolishness" to teach a people who had been slaves all their lives how to work.[25] Originally charged only to serve the former slave population, in 1878 Hampton began admitting Indian students, in keeping with the rising enthusiasm throughout the country for enforced assimilation of that part of the Indian population who had failed to vanish. Armstrong's paternalistic approach to the school, his disciplinary policy, and his educational vision fit exactly the requirements of the new middle-class pedagogy described by Brodhead. Historian Robert Francis Engs remarks in *Freedom's First Generation: Black Hampton, Virginia, 1861–1890* that, according to the catalogue,

> the Hampton student's life was programmed from "rising bell" at 5:15 a.m. to "lights out" at 9:30 p.m. They attended chapel twice daily. Male students were organized into a cadet corps. Uniforms were required of all male students, which was a boon to most of them as they could not afford other decent clothing. The corps marched to classes and meals: inspection of each student and his room was performed daily. Women students were not as regimented, but were as closely supervised their teachers and dormitory matrons. The girls were taught to cook and sew, to set a proper table, to acquire all the graces that would make a good housewife—or housekeeper. Habits of neatness and cleanliness, never required of many slaves, were insisted upon for both sexes.

Colonel Armstrong himself taught a course in moral philosophy in a series of "Talks" after Sunday evening chapel which emphasized the "practical conduct of life." He even supported coeducation because he believed the "home aspect" of the school to be its most important function, since "those on whom equally depends the future of their people must be given an equal chance," and "the interest in schools like this is that the teacher has a far more decisive formative work to do than among more advanced races." Engs concludes that the Hampton Institute was to be a "little world" in which all the proper attitudes of morality, diligence, thrift and responsibility were to be assiduously cultivated. Among the factors which made Hampton unique was the school's intensive program to indoctrinate its students in the proper way of life. The teachers at Hampton were educated, middle-class Northerners; naturally their concept of the "proper way of life" was the way that they lived themselves. Thus, they stressed to their pupils the need to acquire middle-class styles of behavior, perhaps more intently than they emphasized middle-class goals and aspirations.

Armstrong's own formulation of what was needed was a "tender, judicious and patient, yet vigorous educational system" for the black man. The "darky" (as Armstrong habitually referred to his students) needed an experience of "tender violence" to "rouse him" from the passivity of his race. The program for Indians seems to have been oriented no differently.[26]

Despite its obvious constrictions and condescensions, Hampton benefited the black community in a number of ways and was very successful in equipping and certifying large numbers of Southern blacks to educate their own race. Almost ten thousand Southern black children were being taught by Hampton graduates by 1880. The outcome was dramatically different for the Indian graduates, because the Bureau of Indian Affairs and the reservations to which they eventually returned made much more erratic provision for schools even than the rural South, and jobs on the reservation for trained teachers were brief and few. Indian Hampton graduates were often not employed in the field for which they had trained. Nevertheless, the Hampton administration, the trustees, and the U.S. government considered its Indian training program a success precisely because of its indoctrination in the middle-class, Christian, domestic life-style. Apparently it was a patriotic service just to intervene between an Indian and his or her tribe.

The two photographs (Figs. 1.1 and 1.2) made by the anonymous photographer sometime in the 1880s were intended to advertise that capacity to intervene, for publicity and fund-raising purposes. They follow the common formula of the "before" and "after" shot. (This had been a staple of Victorian charitable and educational institutions at least since Dr. Thomas John Barnardo experimented with similar sets of photographs of the street urchins taken into his "Home for Destitute Lads" in Stepney Causeway, England, in the 1870s.) The first photograph is entitled "On arrival at Hampton, Va.: Carrie Anderson—12 yrs., Annie Dawson—10 yrs., and Sarah Walker—13 yrs." The second is entitled "Fourteen months after." In the first photograph, three little girls huddle close together. They sit on a bare tile floor and lean against a wall, keeping their plaid blankets gathered closely about them. Carrie Anderson, Annie Dawson, and Sarah Walker are Indian children who have just arrived at Hampton from the West for a term of education that, given the then current thinking of the Bureau of Indian Affairs, was likely to last for several years without respite or visits home. "The policy of the Bureau of Indian Affairs [was] that Indian children would more rapidly assimilate into

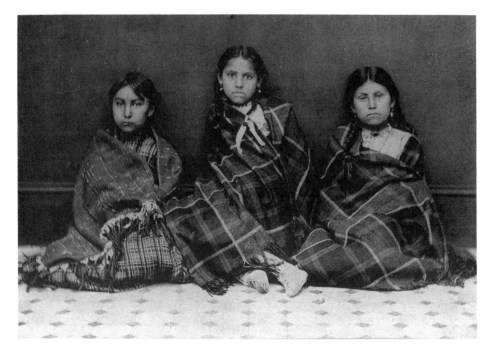

Fig. 1.1. "On arrival at Hampton, Va.: Carrie Anderson–12 yrs., Annie Dawson–10 yrs., and Sara Walker–13 yrs." When children arrived at an Indian school after the long train ride east from the reservation, a photograph would be made of "before." (Photographer unknown, ca. 1880s. Reprinted by permission of the Peabody Museum, Harvard University.)

American society if they were kept away from the reservation for long periods of time," writes Dexter Fisher, an Indian historian and literary critic.[27] The children probably did not yet know at this point how long they were likely to be separated from their families and the customs with which they were familiar, but they look glum and fairly suspicious, if not exactly frightened of their new environment. It is quite possible that they are not able to understand a single word of English. The smile has not yet appeared in American popular culture as a necessary facial arrangement for getting one's photograph taken, but the deep, downward turn of the three mouths is quite pronounced, even in comparison to the stoic expressions then elicited in portraits of members of all races.

The photograph is exceptional in the individuality and distinct personality it suggests for each girl. Carrie Anderson, the smallest though not the youngest, wears her blanket like a Victorian shawl; a certain angle of the head and glimmer of the eye might portend a less defensive interest in what is happening to her than the others indicate. Annie Dawson, the youngest and the tallest, has the long, straight limbs of the strong, free Indian girls made fa-

Fig. 1.2. "Fourteen months after." The "before" and "after" shots were collected to be sent to recruiting agents, benefactors and potential benefactors, political figures, and federal bureaucrats; they were sold also as part of stereographic slide collections used for popular and family entertainment. (Photographer unknown, ca. 1880s. Reprinted by permission of the Peabody Museum, Harvard University.)

mous by sentimental poets like Longfellow. Her wide eyes stare directly at the camera; her moccasined feet are held to the front, which gives her a fight/ flight capability. Of the three, she seems the readiest to be openly confrontational, but she is clearly puzzled. Sarah Walker looks the least like a little white girl. Her broader cheeks and narrower forehead fit more closely her racial stereotype; perhaps, though not necessarily, she has the most Indian in her background. Whatever the genetic truth, if she retained this aspect in person, it would almost certainly have distanced her somewhat from her racialist white supervisors, guaranteeing an extra measure both of loneliness and of privacy. All three girls have the long, plaited hair that, more than anything else, emblemized their social condition.

In the "after" photograph much has changed and much remains the same. The challenge is to figure out what has done which, and why. It is the same floor, for instance, and the same wall, but now the children sit like civilized beings on chairs around a table that holds a game of checkers. Or rather, Annie Dawson and Carrie Anderson sit. Sarah Walker is displayed standing behind the table, one hand on the back of Annie's chair and one shoulder of her white pinafore slipping down over the other arm. It is obvious that all three have been carefully posed. The spontaneous and revealing postures of the first image are long gone; they have been overridden by the imperative to dress up the Indian children in white children's outfits, place their hands upon white children's games, set their limbs at white children's customary angles. A decidedly informative balance has been achieved between the awkward symmetry of the seated figures, the rigid, standing girl, and the doll tossed into the crook of the miniature rocking chair. The picture fairly shouts that, in the most crucial respect, the Indian children are just like the white doll: they are malleable to one's desires. Dressed in tightly fitting Victorian dresses with lace collars, lacking their blankets, wearing leather boots in lieu of their old soft moccasins and, perhaps most important, having had their plaits cut off and their hair arranged to flow freely down their backs like a Sir Arthur Tenniel illustration for *Alice in Wonderland,* Carrie Anderson and Sarah Walker replicate exactly the ideal image of Victorian girlhood. The only contradiction is their darkness, which one might easily pretend could have come from the underexposure of the photographic plate. Annie Dawson has somehow managed to retain a braid, but except for this she is similarly transformed.

Annie, Carrie, and Sarah simultaneously collaborate with all of this and resist. The hands go where they are told but the shoulders, heads, and eyes refuse the pantomime. The book lies on Carrie's lap like a stone or like the handwork that Huck Finn didn't know what to do with when he was masquerading as a girl. Her left hand lies across her lap, not even touching the pages that might close, except that she holds the book in a valley of her skirt that she makes by awkwardly opening up her legs. Absurdly, her right hand pretends all the while to be playing checkers. Only Annie Dawson looks at all like she could be considering the checkers game with comprehension and some authentic interest in its strategy. By a remarkable historical coincidence, it was Annie

Dawson who was reported by the Hampton newspaper, *The Southern Work-man,* some twenty-odd years after these photographs were taken, to be "a leader upon the reservations and in the schools. Such an one is Anna Dawson Wilde, an Arickaree, field matron at Fort Berthold, whose work among the Indian women has made for their progress in wholesome living."[28] The long-legged, ten-year-old girl in the blanket, balanced on a hair trigger between resistance and restraint, turned out to be able to play the game and make the system work for her when many others failed.

The second photograph was taken fourteen months after the first. The school authorities are so proud of this fact that it alone is given as the title of the image—"Fourteen months after." No longer are the children named or any information transcribed about their lives, as it had been upon entry. The important point is now only that they have successfully completed a process: they are the picture of "after." Fourteen months is a very brief time to make a change of the magnitude of this pantomimed journey from aboriginal to indus-trial life; it is of this speed, as well as of thoroughness, that the school is boasting in the photograph and its caption. Whereas many believed that the "red man" was simply incapable of making the change to civilized life, Hamp-ton was able to raise a great deal of money on the more enlightened premise that not only did it know how to bring this change about, but it knew how to do it quickly. It is of great importance that the symbols of this change are, without exception, also the chief symbols of nineteenth-century, middle-class children's lives—hair, dress, doll, game, and book. The Indian girls are being reconstituted not just as imitation white girls but as white girls of a particular kind. They are being imprinted with the class and gender construction of the future sentimental reader. Given this, it is probably the book that is the most crucial symbol of enforced acculturation in the photograph. Ann Douglas reports that

> numerous observers remarked on the fact that countless young Victorian women spent much of their middle-class girlhoods prostrate on chaise longues with their heads buried in "worthless" novels. Their grandmothers, the critics insinuated, had spent their time studying the Bible and performing useful household chores. "Reading" in its new form was many things, among them it was an occupation for the unemployed, narcissistic self-education for those excluded from the harsh school of practical competition. Literary men of the cloth and middle-class women writers of the Victorian period knew from firsthand evidence that literature was functioning more and more as a form of leisure, a complicated mass dream-life in the busiest, most wide-awake society in the world. They could not be altogether ignorant that litera-ture was revealing and supporting a special class, a class defined less by what its members produced than by what they consumed.[29]

Through teaching reading, intimates the photograph, institutions like Hamp-ton would be able to do what the persuasive powers of the entire U.S. Cavalry had tried and failed to do: to persuade the Western tribes to abandon their communal, nomadic way of life, adopt the prizes, mores, and values of con-sumer culture, and turn their little girls into desirable women on the middle-class commodity plan. Girls should read, as Ann Douglas put it, because "a love of reading [w]as an unmistakable blessing for the American female." Lydia Maria Child "explained ominously, if honestly," Douglas continues, that "[reading] cheers so many hours of illness and seclusion; it gives the mind something to interest itself about."[30] Now Hampton was offering Carrie Anderson, Annie Dawson, and Sarah Walker equal opportunity.

The real travesty pictured here, however, is not truly the game of dress-up, no matter how intense a matter it became for the girls and the school. It is not even the fear and the regimentation of the body that are so painful to behold. For Annie, Carrie, and Sarah were at Hampton in the 1880s because they wanted to get a white education, they wanted and needed to be able to function in the white man's world. The ambivalence they radiate is exactly that—ambivalence—not rejection of what Hampton had to offer. Most of all, being able to read was an absolute prerequisite both for protecting themselves and their families from the legal swindles that enmeshed the Western tribes and also, maybe even more urgently, for gaining entry as socially recognizable beings into the new world they now had to face. Thus the book that is placed on Carrie's lap is not simply a public relations device depicting the job the school can do. It is not even purely a logo of the respectable veneer that the school is committed to conveying. In its most important aspect, that book is a promise to the girls themselves that what they have come so far and suffered so much to get will, with hard work, be theirs. Yet here is where the photograph lies. Fourteen months is not long enough for an illiterate, unintended reader even to begin to read such a book, much less to manipulate the many cultural codes it embodies. And chances were that a lifetime of reading would not be long enough to transform the social chances of an Indian in white society in the late nineteenth century. There is nothing casual about the book's placement in the lap of the little girl. Neither is there anything casual in her perplexity about what to do with it. On one side the callousness, and on the other side the need, are beyond measure.

IV

Despite the fact that it underwent, and survived, a major federal investigation in 1888 on charges that its treatment of Indian students was inadequate and inhumane, the Hampton Institute was not the only or necessarily the most authoritarian of the nineteenth-century Indian boarding schools. Hampton was distinguished by being an interracial institution; indeed, it was one of the country's earliest large-scale experiments in interracial education. This, in turn, gave it a distinct atmosphere. The multiethnic composition of the student body made for the presence of a vocal, internally generated critique. In general, the black students were eager and willing to demonstrate the degree to which they could cleave to Victorian social standards and leave the imprint of their recent past behind, while the Indian students showed a greater reluctance to forsake traditional patterns. In practice this meant that black and Indian

students were educated together in a program that made little distinction between the differing desires and abilities of each group, so that Hampton had a
continual struggle to maintain an equilibrium between them. The Carlisle Indian Industrial Training School in Carlisle, Pennsylvania, founded in 1879 on
the Hampton model by Richard Henry Pratt (a longtime friend and former
army associate of Colonel Armstrong), is perhaps the most famous of the other
schools, although there were many more, in both the East and the West, that
adhered to the policy of enforced acculturation with an equal if not greater
exactitude. Carlisle was a flagship school for the Bureau of Indian Affairs
policy; like Hampton, it was well funded, well attended, and closely super-
vised. But it was not explicitly interracial unless, of course, one considers
students and faculty together; the distinctions between students of different
Indian nations did not reach the same level of official concern as did those
between Indians and blacks. "Indians from more than seventy tribes have been
brought together and come to live in utmost harmony, although many of them
were hereditary enemies," the 1902 catalogue blithely stated. "Just as they have
become one with each other through association in the School, so by going out
to live among them they have become one with the white race, and thus ended
the differences and solved their own problems."[31] Carlisle historian Lorna M.
Malmsheimer has pointed out the human implications of such an ideology: "It
involved first of all an education in white racial consciousness."

> The children of culturally diverse tribes had to learn that they were Indians,
> the very same kind of people as their "hereditary enemies." Concurrently
> they learned that by white standards they were an inferior race, which led in
> turn to the cultivation of race pride to spur competition with whites. One of
> Pratt's most important reasons for the development of Carlisle's famous ath-
> letic program was to prove that Indians were not inferior. Finally, they
> learned that the ideal white man's Indian would "become one with the white
> race . . . solving their own individual problems." That such problems may
> have required Indians to become far more individualistic than any of their
> middle-class white contemporaries never seems to have occurred to Pratt.[32]

The other schools usually enjoyed fewer material resources and a lower
level of visibility and evinced more circumscribed pedagogical goals tailored
to their more local identities. Nevertheless, it would be a mistake to imagine
that comparative shelter from the spotlight in Washington resulted in an ethos
substantially different from that of the leaders. Rather, smaller and relatively
more homogenous student populations probably provided less of an opportunity to stage or imagine the politics of difference. In all, the numerous Indian
schools across the country (Pratt had recommended five hundred, but there
were fewer than that) accounted for a major strain in the orchestration of late
Victorian Anglo-Saxon racist theory and domestic virtues into a truly national
hegemony. Hundreds of Easterners took jobs as teachers and administrators
in the system; thousands of Indians from the Western tribes—including the
families of the children, if and when they returned home—were exposed to
their teachings; and millions of taxpayers and private donors applauded the
results.

A series of remarkable autobiographical essays published between 1900 and 1902 by Gertrude Bonnin, a Dakota Sioux of the Yankton band, whose Indian name was Zitkala-Ša, or Redbird, shows the degree to which a provincial school—White's Manual Institute in Wabash, Indiana—enforced the same, or even a greater, conformity to sentimental culture, despite its distance from Eastern social centers. It is essays like these, taken along with the hundreds of available photographs, that help to make plain the scope of the cultural reorganization and consolidation then underway. Lacking such supplements, it is difficult for a twentieth-century reader of nineteenth-century fiction to grasp how vast was the interlocking chain of sentimental influence, and how hard people were trying on many fronts to name its multiple functions. For her part, Bonnin's writing covers so exactly the kind of situation dramatized in the before and after photographs at Hampton that it seems almost uncannily to be the experience of Carrie, Annie, and Sarah themselves, revealing what the captions hide concerning what they have just gone through. It is an authentic voice of the Indian's history. But it is narrated in a distinctly gendered, individualistic, emotionally luxuriant, and acculturated idiom more reminiscent of Ellen Montgomery in Susan Warner's *The Wide, Wide World* than of the great, terse speeches by the defeated Indian chiefs of the era, such as Chief Joseph. Zitkala-Ša was one of the first American Indians to begin to write personal narratives, as well as to record some of the oral tradition of their tribes, in an attempt to preserve their history and what remained of their culture. "By the end of the nineteenth century," writes Dexter Fisher, "a written literature based on tribal oral traditions was beginning to emerge that would reach fruition in the 1960's and 1970's in the works of contemporary American Indians."[33] If so, it is probably some kind of unutterably triumphant index of the absolute penetration of the middle-class culture disseminated by these schools and represented by the genteel tradition in American letters that these very early writings by a Native American were suitable to be—and were—published in *Harper's* and the *Atlantic Monthly*. When children arrived at an Indian school after the long train ride east from the reservation, the local newspapers were apt to report the event in terms like these:

> About twelve o'clock on Sunday night Captain Pratt arrived at the junction with eighty-six Sioux children . . . varying in age from ten to seventeen. Their dress was curious, made of different cheap material and representing all the shades and colors. Cheap jewelry was worn by the girls. Their moccasins are covered with fancy bead work. They carry heavy blankets and shawls with them and their appearance would not suggest that their toilet was a matter of care. Some of them were very pretty while others are extremely homely. All possessing the large black eye, the beautiful pearl white teeth, the high cheek bone, straight-cut mouth and peculiar nose. The school is made up of 63 boys and 23 girls. The reason that there were more boys than girls is that the girls command a ready sale in their tribes at all times, while no value is attached to the boys. About 3000 savages assembled at the agency the night previous to the departure of the party and kept up a constant howling throughout the night. On the cars and here they have been very orderly and

quiet. . . . The majority of the party are made up of the sons and daughters of chiefs. . . . The boys will be uniformed in gray material similar to that worn by the two Indians and instructors who have been here for some time. The girls will wear soft woolen dresses.[34]

This particularly bizarre combination of society page, fashion report, and outright racist fantasy can only be accounted for as an amalgamation of semiotic traditions plundered from the women's sections of the newspapers and the periodical press. The writer, strained beyond original expression by the idea as well as the appearance of the children, has resorted, as if by some lucky instinct, to the very traditions of sentimental domestic representation that are about to have such a major political role in the children's actual lives. But of course, the conjunction of these terms is not arbitrary. Rather, this initial representation marks the exact social space into which the children are going to have to learn to fit. It bears only one major difference from the social space of sentimental characters. When children are torn from their parents in domestic fictions, from Charles Dickens to Kate Wiggin, it is the occasion of nearly unbearable grief; but here the same grief is not unbearable—it is, literally *unhearable,* as in the "constant howling" of "3000 savages."

At this point, also, a photographer would make a picture of "before," such as the one we have examined. These pictures, and the "after" shots, were collected to be sent to recruiting agents, benefactors and potential benefactors, political figures, and federal bureaucrats; they were also sold as part of stereographic slide collections used for popular and family entertainment. Once, from Carlisle, an especially vivid set of three pairs was sent "as a complimentary gift to each contributor who donated enough money to 'pay for one brick' in a new dormitory at the school."[35] The pictures were also sometimes sent to the children's parents back home in an attempt to allay their anxiety. They were, however, unlikely to accomplish this last purpose.

V

In her autobiographical "Impressions of an Indian Childhood," Zitkala-Ša's most vivid accomplishment is the representation of the depth of pain that it caused her mother to part with her to the recruiting agents of White's Manual Institute, and that it caused her to go. She was eight years old; the missionaries promised her "all the red apples [she] could eat" and "a ride on the iron horse." Prior to their appearance, she recalls, she and her mother lived a closely united although far from simple life. Their straightforward daily routines of cooking, fetching water, sewing beadwork, watching the plants and animals around them, telling and retelling the old stories, sporting, and ministering to their neighbors were punctuated by moments of memory so terrible for the mother that they must never be spoken of. "My little daughter must never talk about my tears." Years earlier, during an enforced removal of the tribe to a remoter location, Zitkala-Ša's little sister and uncle had died, a direct casuality of the move and a constant personal reminder of the cruelty of "the paleface." Her mother had not ceased to mourn, nor was she able to feel secure where they had now made their home. Zitkala-Ša's lighthearted predictions about the future were sometimes answered by the worried proviso, "if the paleface does not take away from us the river we drink."[36]

Nevertheless, her life inside and outside the tepee was full of pleasant moments and a special kind of linguistic tenderness between mother and daughter that epitomizes the broad differences in child-raising practices between the Indian tribe and the conquering white culture. Zitkala-Ša reports many incidents which convey the extraordinary forbearance and gentleness of her mother's customary use of words. To use the terms that Margaret Homans has illuminated in *Bearing the Word,* Zitkala-Ša portrays herself and her mother as inhabiting a virtually limitless domain of literal, pre-Oedipal, prefigural speech. "At this age I knew but one language, and that was my mother's native tongue." Other members of the tribe reinforced this rich, essentially linguistic security; the old ones called her "my little grandchild" and "little granddaughter." Her aunt "dried my tears and held me in her lap, when my mother had reproved me." Even the pace of speech was slow enough for many tones and the implications of many kinds of silence to be heard, as people measured their requests and waited patiently for replies. The most important social rule that the child was taught was not to impose herself upon others but to "sense the atmosphere" into which she entered. "Wait a minute before you invite anyone," her mother would caution her. "If other plans are being discussed, do not interfere, but go elsewhere."[37]

With their promise of apples, the missionaries spoiled this paradise and came between mother and child. Zitkala-Ša wanted to go with all her friends to the "wonderful Eastern land" that she had not seen, to the place of knowledge where she would forfeit this garden. "This was the first time I had ever been so unwilling to give up my own desire that I refused to hearken to my mother's voice." Yet even so, the mother was required to give her consent, and she eventually did so, apparently with all the foreknowledge that the child herself was unable to command. "Yes, my daughter, though she does not understand what it all means, is anxious to go. She will need an education when she is grown, for then there will be fewer real Dakotas, and many more palefaces. This tearing her away, so young, from her mother is necessary, if I would have her an educated woman. The palefaces, who owe us a large debt for stolen lands, have begun to pay a tardy justice in offering some education to our children. But I know my daughter must suffer keenly in this experiment."[38]

Without thought, the child "walked with my mother to the carriage that was soon to take us to the iron horse. I was happy. I met my playmates, who were also wearing their best thick blankets. We showed one another our new beaded mocassins, and the width of the belts that girdled our new dresses." The mother's state of mind as the carriage departs is not directly represented, but that does not mean that it is simplified or slighted. Instead, too distressed to find words, the silent child mirrors the magnitude of the loss in miniature.

When the little girl "saw the lonely figure of my mother vanish in the distance, a sense of regret settled heavily upon me." She continues:

> I felt suddenly weak, as if I might fall limp to the ground. I was in the hands of strangers whom my mother did not fully trust. I no longer felt free to be myself, or to voice my own feelings. The tears trickled down my cheeks, and I buried my face in my blanket. Now the first step, parting me from my mother, was taken, and all my belated tears availed nothing . . . We stopped before a massive brick building. I looked at it in amazement, and with a vague misgiving, for in our village I had never seen so large a house. Trembling with fear and distrust of the palefaces, my teeth chattering from the chilly ride, I crept noiselessly in my soft moccasins along the narrow hall, keeping very close to the bare wall. I was as frightened and bewildered as the captured young of a wild creature.[39]

But she wasn't, of course, the young of a wild creature; she was simply a small child who was being treated like an animal. Inasmuch as this account is mythic, it is the self-congratulatory myth that modern Western culture has been telling itself about language since its inception: that educated speech begins when the bond with the mother is broken. With reason, then, after this "first step," the narrative turns entirely to Zitkala-Ša's accommodation to school. As a sentimental writer, she will learn her literary lessons well. On the other hand, this is not merely myth but trauma, barely achieving years later the delineation of speech. The "howling" of three thousand "savages" on another of these occasions is yet another rendition of the same literary intention: to pursue the semiotic of physical closeness and mental connection even into where the law of the great white father has made its terrible cut. It was the destiny of Zitkala-Ša as a real, live, nineteenth-century Indian child to play out this constitutive Wordsworthian drama in the most literal of ways. It would be three years before she saw her mother and her home again.

On the train she writes in "The School Days of an Indian Girl," further violation followed, this time not only of verbal but also of visual space:

> Fair women, with tottering babies on each arm, stopped their haste and scrutinized the children of absent mothers. Large men, with heavy bundles in their hands, halted near by, and riveted their glassy blue eyes upon us. I sank deep into the corner of my seat, for I resented being watched. Directly in front of me, children who were no larger than I hung themselves upon the backs of their seats, with their bold white faces toward me. Sometimes they took their forefingers out of their mouths and pointed at my moccasined feet. Their mothers, instead of reproving such rude curiosity, looked closely at me, and attracted their children's further notice to my blanket. This embarrassed me, and kept me constantly on the verge of tears.

But by far the worst moments had to do with sound, so different from her quiet mother's world. On arrival, "[t]he strong glaring light in the large whitewashed room dazzled my eyes. The noisy hurrying of hard shoes upon a bare wooden floor increased the whirring in my ears. My only safety seemed to be in keeping next to the wall." Just at this point, the regime of sentiment made its dreadful entrance:

As I was wondering in which direction to escape from all this confusion, two warm hands grasped me firmly, and in the same moment I was tossed high in midair. A rosy-cheeked paleface woman caught me in her arms. I was both frightened and insulted by such trifling. I stared into her eyes, wishing her to let me stand on my own feet, but she jumped me up and down with increasing enthusiasm. My mother had never made a plaything of her wee daughter. Remembering this I began to cry aloud.

Zitkala-Ša, doubtless an exceptionally pretty girl by Anglo-Saxon standards, had just become, though she did not know it yet, an ersatz Victorian child, the doll-baby of the Hampton photographer, the toy of her female tamer. It would take her many years to figure out what had happened, and more to learn how to respond. At the time, all she understood was that "I pleaded; but the ears of the palefaces could not hear me." At night when she climbed "the upward incline of wooden boxes, which I learned afterward to call a stairway," she was "tucked into bed with one of the tall girls, because she talked to me in my mother tongue." But to no avail: "I fell asleep, heaving deep, tired sobs. My tears were left to dry themselves in streaks, because neither my aunt nor my mother was near to wipe them away."[40]

Meanwhile, no violence against her sense of personal integrity passed unreckoned. One recalls the dresses in the "after" photograph of Carrie, Annie, and Sarah with greater comprehension for having read Zitkala-Ša's initial reaction to the school code: "The small girls wore sleeved aprons and shingled hair. As I walked noiselessly in my soft mocassins, I felt like sinking to the floor, for my blanket had been stripped from my shoulders. I looked hard at the Indian girls, who seemed not to care that they were even more immodestly dressed than I, in their tightly fitting clothes." She became a bright but rebellious pupil. Sometimes she managed a small revenge that gave some satisfaction. Once she broke a jar in which she had been ordered to mash turnips for the students' supper. Once, after a nightmare inspired by vivid religious instruction about the danger of the devil, she scratched a hole in *The Stories of the Bible* where his frightening picture had appeared. But in general, the pain of that period was unmitigated and enduring; it eluded, she felt, even her considerable later powers of expression. "The melancholy of those black days has left so long a shadow that it darkens the path of years that have since gone by. Perhaps my Indian nature is the moaning wind which stirs them now for their present record. But, however tempestuous this is within me, it comes out as the low voice of a curiously colored seashell, which is only for those ears that are bent with compassion to hear it." This failure, I think, is debatable, for the haunting low voices of these tales not only speaks her own story but tells the sorrow of a hundred silent pictures, of which the "before" and "after" Hampton photographs are but two. On the other hand, her voice was certainly now a "shell," for mother and daughter were never to be completely comfortable together again.[41]

Clearly, by the time that she came to write these autobiographical stories, Zitkala-Ša's self-conception had been so effectively ensnared within the codes of sentiment that there was no Indian in them that was left untouched by

Western codes. Even her own increasing inability to straddle the contradictions between the two societies is figured within her autobiography again and again as nothing more or less middle-class than an increasing inability to *read*. To take a single instance, when she returned home on a visit:

> My mother was troubled by my unhappiness. Coming to my side, she offered me the only printed matter we had in our home. It was an Indian Bible, given her some years ago by a missionary. She tried to console me. "Here, my child, are the white man's papers. Read a little from them," she said most piously.
>
> I took it from her hand, for her sake; but my enraged spirit felt more like burning the book, which afforded me no help, and was a perfect delusion to my mother. I did not read it, but laid it unopened on the floor, where I sat on my feet. The dim yellow light of the braided muslin burning in a small vessel of oil flickered and sizzled in the awful silent storm which followed my rejection of the Bible.[42]

Nonetheless, even at this early point in her development, the memories she nourished of her childhood show an acute sensitivity to the devoured territory outside of reading, as well as an awareness of her mother's (in addition to her own) personal struggle and rebellion against the social renunciation exacted by submitting to the dictates of a sentimental education, and to the gratuitous cruelty of those who used force to encourage her and her companions to comply. Although the moral structure and often the melancholy of the stories merge with that of the sentimental heroine, and many of the remembered incidents with those of the blond girls of popular fiction, their tendency is nevertheless iconoclastic. Unlike Ellen Montgomery, Zitkala-Ša was able to find through her tears no virtue or transcendence in the Bible, no soul sister in the kitchen where she must labor, no dashing suitor in the dazzling institutional halls. Whereas the white heroine gains much, eventually, by subscribing to a program of inspirational reading and the "tender violence" of her rather sadistic and didactic mentor, the red heroine nearly loses her health and her spiritual footing by her determined and lonely adherence to the lessons of her books.

At enormous personal cost, Zitkala-Ša graduated from White's Manual Institute, completed two years of Earlham College in Richmond, Indiana, taught at Carlisle, and studied violin at the Boston Conservatory of Music. She even embarked on a literary career, writing these sketches and short fiction that spoke within and to sentimental forms. She received reviews like the following "Persons Who Interest Us" column in *Harper's Bazaar:*

> A young Indian girl, who is attracting much attention in Eastern cities on account of her beauty and many talents, is Zitkala-Sa. . . . Zitkala-Sa is of the Sioux tribe of Dakota and until her ninth year was a veritable little savage, running wild over the prairie and speaking no language but her own. . . . She has also published lately a series of articles in a leading magazine . . . which display a rare command of English and much artistic feeling.[43]

But following an extraordinarily successful three-year period as the beautiful and famous Indian authoress and "the darling of a small literary coterie in

Boston,"[44] having given public, oratorical recitations of Longfellow's poem "Hiawatha" and having had her portrait made with her book on her lap by the famous Fifth Avenue photographer Gertrude Kasebier, Zitkala-Ša quite suddenly rejected the slippery pathway of white women's style of achievement and white men's style of praise. Forsaking New York and literature, she married Capt. Raymond T. Bonnin, also a Dakota Sioux, moved to the Uintah and Ouray reservation in Utah, and eventually became an early and pugnacious Indian activist lobbying in Washington, D.C., for the rights of her people.

The coming-to-consciousness that underlay this eruption is foreshadowed in the last of the early autobiographical stories (entitled "An Indian Teacher"), where Zitkala-Ša, by then herself a teacher at Carlisle, literally forsakes the pseudoliteracy of "the white man's papers" and rebels against her years of sentimental indoctrination. Here, I think, she is finally ceasing to apply the ill-fitting model of domestication and beginning to seek another, sterner tongue. And so ends the extraordinary account of the struggle of one unintended reader who was later to become, in marked contradiction to the quiescent, feminized, and assimilationist standards in which she had been trained, a quite unintended kind of success. She writes:

> In the process of my education I had lost all consciousness of the nature world about me. Thus, when a hidden rage took me to the small white-walled prison which I then called my room, I unknowingly turned away from my one salvation.
>
> Alone in my room, I sat like the petrified Indian woman of whom my mother used to tell me. I wished my heart's burdens would turn me to unfeeling stone. But alive, in my tomb, I was destitute!
>
> For the white man's papers I had given up my faith in the Great Spirit. For these same papers I had forgotten the healing in trees and brooks. On account of my mother's simple view of life, and my lack of any, I gave her up, also. I made no friends among the race of people I loathed. Like a slender tree, I had been uprooted from my mother, nature, and God. I was shorn of my branches, which had waved in sympathy and love for home and friends. The natural coat of bark which had protected my oversensitive nature was scraped off to the very quick.
>
> Now a cold bare pole I seemed to be, planted in a strange earth. Still, I seemed to hope a day would come when my mute aching head, reared upward to the sky, would flash a zig-zag lightning across the heavens. With this dream of vent for a long-pent consciousness, I walked again amid the crowds.
>
> At last, one weary day in the schoolroom, a new idea presented itself to me. It was a new way of solving the problem of my inner self. I liked it. Thus I resigned my position as teacher; and now I am in an Eastern city, following the long course of study I have set for myself. Now, as I look back upon the recent past, I see it from a distance, as a whole. I remember how, from morning till evening, many specimens of civilized peoples visited the Indian school. The city folks with canes and eyeglasses, the countrymen with sunburnt cheeks and clumsy feet, forgot their relative social ranks in an ignorant curiosity. Both sorts of these Christian palefaces were alike astounded at seeing the children of savage warriors so docile and industrious.
>
> As answers to their shallow inquiries they received the students' sample work

to look upon. Examining the neatly figured pages, and gazing over their books, the white visitors walked out of the schoolhouse well satisfied: they were educating the children of the red man! They were paying a liberal fee to the government employees in whose able hands lay the small forest of Indian timber.

In this fashion many have paused idly through the Indian schools during the last decade, afterward to boast of their charity to the North American Indian. But few there are who have passed to question whether real life or long-lasting death lies beneath this semblance of civilization.[45]

In this story Zitkala-Ša has presented as finally finished what previously, as a sentimental reader, she could not accomplish or even imagine. Her long slavish education is over; she has escaped from the schoolroom. "It was a new way of solving the problem of my inner self. I liked it." She has set herself a whole new course of reading which, it is implied, is of a different order. And her myth of origin has also undergone a subtle but crucial change: in recognizing how falsely "figured" were the students' "pages," how superfluous "their books," and how unnecessarily she has forfeited her mother, nature, and God, she renounces, at least experimentally, the treacherous dream of Western Romanticism, of restoration through literature to the prelinguistic garden of authentic expression that, apparently, was what had been taught to her to motivate her studies and offer restitution for her loss. Newly, she can bear to recognize not only how thoroughly she has been "uprooted" but also how small were her chances this way of getting replanted in any good earth. Henceforth, in the city, armed with this perception, her clearer vision can become truly historical for the first time, and redemptive so that she can now "look back upon the recent past [and] see it from a distance, as a whole." That this new center, also, will not hold is knowledge buried in the future. In her "hidden rage" she is potent and prophetic. Given the time at which she wrote, her renunciation of sentimental fiction—and that in many senses—was clearly a precondition of "real life" over "long-lasting death." But given the time in which we now must read, the almost total disappearance from our literary history of the achievement of antisentimentalism in women writers like Zitkala-Ša can only propel us deeper into illusion.

VI

By the turn of the century, the enabling partnership sketched out in the antebellum era between reading and household moral training on the one hand, and educational and rehabilitative theory on the other, could be taken for granted. Furthermore, it was finding an unexpectedly effective adjunct in new state-of-the-art techniques of visual demonstration whose verisimilitude left even the persuasive capacities of "sensational" fiction, as Jane Tompkins terms it, behind. Especially important in terms of public instruction were the related uses of the living diorama and the documentary photographic display. These exhibitionary practices had evolved since the mid-1880s from earlier, simpler forms into veritable mass-market media. They entailed prodigious feats of technologi-

Fig. 1.3. "Zitkala-Sa." Following an extraordinarily successful three-year period as the beautiful and famous Indian authoress, and having had her portrait made with her book on her lap, Zitkala-sa quite suddenly rejected the slippery pathway of white women's style of achievement and white men's style of praise. (Gertrude Kasebier, ca. 1898. Reprinted by permission of the Division of Photographic History, National Museum of American History, Smithsonian Institution.)

cal and social engineering. Native Americans, for instance, whose genocide during the nineteenth century paved the way for the fin de siècle "revival" of their traditions, were recruited at that time to convene a spectacular simulacrum of Plains culture known as Buffalo Bill Cody's Wild West. Buffalo Bill toured this country and Europe, regaling millions with an "educational" message about the noble defeat of the Indian way of life that rivaled any production of sentimental fiction for either righteous passion or bad faith. Filipino peasants, whose status as objects of exchange between U.S. and Spanish imperial forces in 1898 obliterated their own recent attempt at self-determination and overrode any vision of their suffering in American eyes, were sanctimoniously imbued with an aura of domestic exoticism, which climaxed when authorities set up a forty-seven acre reservation at the St. Louis Exposition of 1904; the reservation was populated by nearly one thousand two hundred temporarily imported tribal Filipinos, in an effort "to illustrate to the American public the islands' rich natural resources and many native types, who had reached varying stages of 'civilization.' "[46] Images of Eastern European and Asian immigrants living in the tenements of New York and other major cities, whose "crime and misery" formed the subjects of "humorous or adventuresome anecdotes" described in slide lantern shows, were exhibited to genteel native-born audiences in simulated educational "tours" of the slums led by the photographer Jacob Riis. The purpose of the tours was to recall the duty of domestic instruction and settlement house "reform" to the "benevolent, propertied middle class" of landlords, who needed to be reached (although Riis did not say this in so many words) before the immigrants themselves rose up and destroyed both the opportunity and the property.[47] In all these spectacles and numbers, more consciousness of the social and historical reciprocity of those who see and those who are seen is effaced precisely along the lines of deflection that sentimentality had entrenched.

Ann Douglas, then, was not wrong in linking Victorian domestic literary pietism causally to the depredations of mass culture, but was merely misguided in her animus against Victorian women as women. The women's culture of 1820–1870 that she derides was dangerous not because it was *feminine* but because it was *racist,* just like the culture of the men. This point was often made by the black women intellectuals of the time. Successful appeal to the bipartite structure of (1) impoverishment of the sense of history, and (2) purely emotional remediation that characterizes the sentimental reflex, relies not only on the years of private behavioral tutoring absorbed by individual readers at the hands of the authors of domestic novels, but equally on the predictability of the widespread cultural acceptance of that evoked response as the normative, public disposition toward the socially stigmatized. Sentimentalization is a communal, not just an individual, disposition. It expands within the group to make individual awareness in fact unlikely, just as if our whole society without comment encouraged our children blithely to play "concentration camp" or "gas chamber"—or indeed "cowboys and Indians"—in the quiet twilight streets after dinner, with Indians and Holocaust survivors alongside our fond selves to witness. As long as the arena of the sentimental encounter is imagined mainly as a private, contained, bookish, housebound space, typified either by "the basement" of Jane Tompkin's anecdote or the figurative attic of "a legacy from my grandmother's childhood," as in Ann Douglas's confession, the deeper tracings of its terrorism against nonreaders and outsiders cannot be conceived.[48]

Sentimental "power" struck its outright victims differently from its middle-class audience. We are fortunate to have some record of the reactions of those on the receiving end of the racially instrumental side of a nineteenth-century domestic education, in both written and photographic form. From this record we can at least partially assess both the disarray produced on impact and the strategies of resistance that appeared in its wake. In *Desire and Domestic Fiction,* a major reconsideration of the political history of the domestic novel in England, Nancy Armstrong reasons that "as the official interpreters of the cultural past, we are trained, it appears, to deny the degree to which writing has concealed the very power it has granted this female domain. It is no doubt because each of us lives out such a paradox that we seem powerless to explain in so many words how our political institutions came to depend on the socializing practices of household and schoolroom."[49] How can we tell a "good woman" from another kind? What kind of house is "fit for a baby"? How should a "good woman" raise her child? Armstrong demonstrates that it is a notable feature of English-speaking culture over the past two centuries that not only has it been bent on supplying definitive, professional, and prestigious answers to these questions, but that it also has produced and sustained an enormous imaginative literature designed to keep the urgency of these always already answered puzzles in the forefront of consciousness. This is the tradition of domestic fiction.

But it would be imperceptive to maintain that this tradition concerns domestic matters "merely." Since the late eighteenth century, many of the most central political engagements of our society have been shaped and even fought upon that ground, all the while passing themselves off instead as romantic engagements, private affairs of kith and kin, heart and hearth. The development of an aesthetic of sentiment, therefore, is largely the story of how the values of middle-class women came to occupy both the "private women" and the "public stage" of popular consciousness, to borrow Mary Kelley's terminology.[50] It is the story of how one specific social formation, composed of men as much as women, learned to use a wide variety of representations of the "good woman" to identify, enlarge upon, and then protect its interests. It is additionally, I have been arguing, the story of how such representations actively and materially empowered the many "massive" and "amazing" brick buildings where the curriculum of race was the subject of merciless indoctrination, in the last quarter of the nineteenth century, and reading, its vehicle.

Armstrong closes her study of the English tradition by reminding us that "if one stresses the particular power that our culture does give to middle-class women rather than the forms of subordination entailed in their exclusion from the workplace and confinement to the home . . . then there is clearly a great deal of work to do."[51] It is also to be hoped that some of this work will be a corrective to the violence that we, as twentieth-century feminist reconstructionists—despite *our* instincts of tenderness and good will—may be doing to the full story of reading, writing, and domestic fiction in the United States, for the purposes for our own partial notions of educational reform.

2

"Domestic Differences": Competing Narratives of Womanhood in the Murder Trial of Lucretia Chapman

Karen Halttunen

At twilight on 9 May 1831 a young stranger appeared at the home of William and Lucretia Chapman in Andalusia, Pennsylvania, to request lodgings for the night. Dirty, poorly dressed, and with a limited command of English, he identified himself as Lino Amalia Espos y Mina, son of the governor of California. William Chapman tried to send him to a nearby public house, but when Mina explained that he had been turned away for want of money, Lucretia Chapman urged that he be admitted to their home for the night. During the days that followed, Mina told his hosts that he was a man of wealth and distinction in Mexico, where his family owned gold and silver mines and a trunk full of diamonds. He had recently traveled to France with a companion, upon whose sudden death the authorities had confiscated a trunk containing over $30,000 of Mina's own money, so he had borrowed money to travel to the United States to seek help from a friend named Casanova whom he had not yet located. Lucretia Chapman soon announced that Mina was to be a pupil at the Chapmans' school, which specialized in speech training, and that she herself would spend three years teaching him English for the handsome fee of $6,000.

Over the next few weeks, the fortyish matron and the twenty-two-year-old "Spaniard" spent considerable time alone with each other: they rode together, shut themselves up in Mina's room during his periodic "fits" of illness, and on one occasion traveled into Philadelphia for a three-day stay. They were seen kissing, and one servant who accompanied them on a visit to a neighbor's reported that Mina had lain his head in Mrs. Chapman's lap, while she placed her arms around him and they sang love songs. On two or three occasions, Lucretia accompanied Mina to a Philadelphia tailor and ordered suits of clothes for him on the Chapmans' account. Lucretia and her husband became increasingly quarrelsome. When William, a man of a retiring and scholarly bent, complained of her conduct, she spoke back harshly, calling him a fool,

39

saying that she wished to God he was gone since she was tired of him; on one occasion she kicked him. According to the maid servant, "She said she was mistress of her own house, and would do as she pleased."

On Friday, June 17, William Chapman fell ill; two days later his physician prescribed treatment for what he considered a mild case of cholera morbus. On Monday, Lucretia prepared chicken soup for her husband, salted it in the kitchen, then took it into the parlor, where Mina was present, to "season" it before delivering it to her husband's sickroom. That same day William took a turn for the worse, complaining to visiting bookpeddler Edwin Fanning of a burning heat in his stomach, and charging his wife with neglect. Meanwhile a neighbor's chickens that had been feeding in the Chapmans' yard died suddenly; the next day, some twenty or thirty ducks that had been in the yard also died. By Tuesday evening, when a second doctor called, William Chapman was extremely ill, vomiting and purging; his extremities were growing cold and his pulse was feeble. By Wednesday he was occasionally delirious and had lost his sense of hearing, and the first doctor returned to find him near death, his face spotted, his pulse barely perceptible, the skin on his extremities shrunken. At 5:00 A.M. on Thursday, June 23, William Chapman died. The neighbor who had lost his poultry laid out the corpse, which seemed to him to have grown rigid with unusual speed, and the boarder Mina shaved it in preparation for the funeral the next day. When a neighbor suggested to Lucretia Chapman that a relative or friend should walk with her from the carriage to her husband's gravesite, the widow suggested Mina, but the neighbor rejected her choice as inappropriate, since he was a stranger and undersized. So another man accompanied Lucretia to the grave, while Mina walked with Lucretia's oldest daughter, Mary, and William Chapman was duly buried.

Eleven days later, on 5 July 1831, Lucretia Chapman and Lino Amalia Espos y Mina were married in New York City. Immediately after the ceremony Mina returned to Pennsylvania, while Lucretia journeyed to Syracuse to ask her sister and brother-in-law to come live in the house at Andalusia so that Lucretia, Mina, and the five Chapman children might travel together to Mexico. During this early marital separation, Lucretia wrote several love letters to her new husband, addressing him as "*dearest* Leno, so young, so fond, so noble" and "my '*pretty little husband.*' " The couple were reunited in Andalusia on July 13. Five days later Mina went into Philadelphia, purportedly to find his old friend Casanova. But, as he explained in a letter to Lucretia, it seemed that Casanova had died, leaving Mina a bequest which had to be collected in Baltimore. So the newlyweds continued to correspond, Mina's letters easily rivaling Lucretia's for the fervency of his proclaimed love: "I whould [*sic*] first see the sun stop its Carrier [*sic*] through this wide world, and be plunged in the most green or blackest gulphs [*sic*] that demons could invent, than have it said that I should Repay you with ingratitude," he wrote, closing as "your invariable and constant faithful Beloved Husband." Then, on July 25, Mina began to write from Washington, D.C., to say that he had encountered some legal difficulties in securing his inheritance and was seeking assistance directly from the President of the United States, who met with him on three occasions and expressed his eagerness to meet Lucretia.

But even before these latest claims, Mina's new wife had begun to grow suspicious. On July 23 she followed his trail to Philadelphia, where her tailor told her he believed Mina to be an impostor. She spoke with the Mexican consul, whom she had mistakenly understood to have confirmed Mina's claims, and learned that he too knew Mina to be a fraud. Back in Andalusia she searched Mina's room and found a hotel bill for the lodging of Mina and two female companions on July 8 and 9. On July 31 Lucretia Chapman Espos y Mina wrote one last letter to her second husband. Citing all the evidence of his perfidy, she inquired after the fate of her horse and carriage, gold and silver watches, miscellaneous jewelry, and other small treasures; revealed her jealousy of a new female friend in Washington of whom he had written; and enclosed his Philadelphia hotel bill with the comment, "This you left instead of a dagger to pierce me to the heart." Her letter closed, "But no, Lino, when I pause for a moment, I am constrained to acknowledge that I do not believe that God will permit either *you or me* to be happy this side of the grave. I now bid you a long farewell."

This letter never reached Mina; it was intercepted at the post office by a victim of one of Mina's financial swindles, who sent it to the high constable of Philadelphia. Early in August, Mina returned to Andalusia, where Lucretia greeted him by telling her sister that he was an impostor. But after a private conversation with him, she revoked her charge and pronounced him "a clever fellow." A few weeks later she sent him to Massachusetts supplied with letters of introduction, which made no mention of their marriage, to her family in Brewster. To them he told tales of his wealth, boasted of the great house he had built for Mrs. Chapman in Andalusia, and began to court her niece. By this time the Philadelphia authorities had launched an investigation of Mina's activities, and had heard the story of the chicken soup and the dying poultry from the neighbors. On August 28 or 29 the police questioned Lucretia, who expressed doubt that Mina was an impostor, denied that he had plundered her, defended him against the suggestion that he had poisoned William Chapman, and made no mention of her remarriage. Despite her defense, investigators arranged for Mina's arrest in Boston on September 9, catching up with him just in time to prevent his bigamous marriage to Lucretia's niece. During the course of the investigation, it also emerged that Lino Amalia Espos y Mina was actually Celestine Armentarius (also known as Amalia Gregoria Zarrier), who had been serving time in the Philadelphia penitentiary on three convictions of larceny from March 1830 on, until freed by pardon on the morning of 9 May 1831, the day he first appeared on the Chapmans' doorstep.

On September 17 an article in the *Police Gazette* implicated Lucretia Chapman in the murder of her husband, and three days later, accompanied by her oldest child, she left Pennsylvania for New York. On September 21 the body of William Chapman was exhumed and its stomach and duodenum removed for chemical analysis. The opinion of the anatomists who examined the body at the grave site—noting an unusual resistance to abdominal putrefaction, inflammation of the stomach, and a peculiar smell which they likened to pickled herring—and of the two chemists who tested the stomach and duodenum at a laboratory on the following day—producing no visible residue but rather the pronounced smell of arsenic—was that William Chapman's death had probably been caused by arsenic poisoning. The fugitive Lucretia was tracked down and arrested, and at the December sessions of the Bucks County Court she and Mina were jointly indicted for murder. Over the objections of the commonwealth, Mina's counsel moved successfully for separate trials, and the prosecution chose to try the woman first. Three weeks before she came to trial in February 1832, the commonwealth discovered that on June 16, the day before William Chapman fell ill, Mina had purchased several ounces of arsenic from a Philadelphia druggist.

The story as told above is my own reconstruction of events based on the extensive testimony of witnesses at Lucretia Chapman's murder trial, including servants, boarders, pupils, and the defendant's daughter; neighbors, Lucretia's clergyman, and the family's personal physicians; the tailor, the pharmacist, the undertaker, the Mexican consul in Philadelphia, police officers, and sundry medical experts.[1] Such a narrative is of course an artificial construct, for, as Hayden White has observed, the world does not just "present itself to perception in the form of well-made stories, with central subjects, proper beginnings, middles, and ends."[2] Any narrative of the Lucretia Chapman story involves a fictive process that unavoidably imposes some degree of arbitrary ordering upon the chaos of everyday experience. The Chapmans' was a complex household encompassing a married couple with their five children, a minimum of four servants of both the live-in and live-out variety, some four adult boarders seeking assistance from the Chapmans for their speech impediments, one or two children who were also pupils, Mina "the Spaniard," and occasionally an itinerant bookseller. As these and other people successively took the witness stand to testify to the events of the summer of 1831, their stories revealed crucial gaps; none knew, for example, what actually happened in the parlor where Lucretia and Mina were closeted with the soup that was to be administered to William. Their stories also disagreed on key points, such as the nature and significance of Lucretia's and Mina's conduct together before William's death. Did they often ride out alone together, or were they usually accompanied by someone else, and was it Lucretia's usual practice thus to ride with her students? As for the trail through the house of the chicken soup on the Monday before William's death, did Lucretia let the soup sit out on the kitchen table all afternoon after William had partaken of it, and would she thus have left it within reach of her children, had she known it to be poisoned? Adding to the confusion was the central involvement in the case of a confidence man who invested great energy in willful self-misrepresentation, enhancing his physical appearance with expensive new clothing provided by his patroness, forging letters and documents of identity, and generally lying to everyone.

It is the cultural function of narrative to assign meaning to the chaos of human experience largely by defining its shape in time through attention to plot, "the intelligible whole that governs a succession of events in any story."[3] From the mid-eighteenth through the mid-twentieth century, Peter Brooks has argued, Western societies have evinced an extraordinary need for plots which he links to secularization: "The enormous narrative production of the nineteenth century may suggest an anxiety at the loss of providential plots: the plotting of the individual or social or institutional life story takes on new urgency when one no longer can look to a sacred masterplot that organizes and explains the world."[4] Had William Chapman been murdered in 1731, the printed account of the incident would have assumed the form of an execution sermon for the convicted murderer, which would have passed briefly over the sequence of events before and after the assault to concentrate on the spiritual destiny of the convicted criminal about to be launched into eternity at the gallows. But in 1831 the cultural work necessitated by Chapman's violent death assumed the form of a printed transcript of the murder trial, which represented the state's attempt to reassert moral order by uncovering the true narrative of what happened in the Chapman household in the summer of that year, so as to assign legal responsibility for the crime.[5]

The modern American criminal trial is organized around storytelling, which serves at the most elementary level as a communications device. The juror is like someone reading a detective novel "replete with multiple points of view, subplots, time lapses, missing information, and ambiguous clues. . . . Without the aid of an analytical device such as the story, the disjointed presentations of information in trials would be difficult, if not impossible, to assimilate."[6] But it is the peculiar nature of courtroom storytelling that it is competitive: first the prosecution and then the defense takes up the chaos of details provided by witnesses and shapes it into as coherent and compelling a narrative as possible, in an effort to persuade jurors to choose that side's plot line. This structuring has been the central feature of the Anglo-American criminal trial since the mideighteenth century, when the adversary system was shaped into its present format, in which the prosecution first delivers its case, the defense responds, and then both sides offer narrative summations of the events in question.[7] The judicial ritual of dueling storytellers thus emerged historically at about the same time as the secular narrative tradition, and has proved to be a crucial expression of that tradition.

In his summation for the Commonwealth in the murder trial of Lucretia Chapman, Mr. Reed announced his "intention to present such a narrative as will recall to the mind of the Court and Jury, all the material facts of the case" (100). Though a significant degree of implicit plotting went on in the choosing and ordering of witnesses by both prosecution and defense, it was in their summations that they explicitly and didactically set forth their competitive narratives of what had taken place. There they shaped chaos into plotted narrative through a close attention to sequence and consequence, characterization and motivation, plausibility and point of view. Sometimes their narratives were positive, articulating what did happen; sometimes, usually in the case for the defense, they were negative, aiming to undermine the opposition's tale by impugning the credibility of major witnesses, and exposing internal contradictions and logical and informational gaps. Most broadly, the summations of the Chapman trial pursued two different lines of narrative. The first line, which will not be treated here, addressed the medical question: did William Chapman die of arsenic poisoning or of natural causes? (Though the medical and chemical testimony tended to affirm that he had been murdered, this issue was by no means uncontested.) The second line of narrative, which will be explored in the remainder of this chapter, addressed the social question: did Lucretia Chapman play a role in her husband's murder?

On this question, both prosecution and defense told stories that drew extensively on the conventions of sentimental fiction. In narrating their plots, they employed an emotionally inflated rhetoric that made reference whenever possible to the feelings of their various characters, represented their own emotions in recounting the tale, and appealed directly to the sentiments of their primary readership, the jury. They presented stock characterizations— the woman seduced and abandoned, the heartless seducer, the trusting husband, the faithful or, alternatively, scheming family retainer—and staged dramatic vignettes such as Mina's first entrance into the Chapman household, and Lucretia's horrified discovery that he was a fraud. They explored at length such sentimental issues as sincerity and hypocrisy, confidence and betrayal, and debated the reliability of outward signs of the inner state of the heart, such as Lucretia Chapman's choice of mourning attire and her facial expression upon learning that the police suspected Mina of murder. And they exploited a sentimental fascination with the private vices that might lie hidden behind the public façades of respectable middle-class homes.

In adopting sentimental literary conventions for their narratives, attorneys on both sides of the case revealed the extent to which sentimentalism served as the dominant cultural framework for interpreting domesticity in the first half of the nineteenth century. But within that common framework, the prosecution and the defense came to dramatically different conclusions about what both sides recognized as the critical question in the case: what was the true nature of Lucretia Chapman and, more broadly, of the Womanhood she represented? The Lucretia Chapman murder trial is a case study in the cultural contest over the nature of womanhood that shaped Anglo-American gender ideology throughout the nineteenth century.

The prosecution's narrative of what happened in the Chapman household in the summer of 1831 was an Edenic myth of domestic paradise lost.[8] The Chapman family before the arrival of Mina had been "the abode of harmony and domestic peace" (113) where Lucretia Chapman was wife to a husband "whose honest affection was worth possessing" and mother of children "worthy of a mother's love" (112). But one evening, "[a]t the threshold of this home of innocence and prosperity" where William Chapman sat rocking his youngest child, a stranger appeared. "In one month from that time, that kind father . . . was slumbering in his bloody grave, and his place was usurped by the author of his ruin" (113). The prosecution professed reluctance to characterize Mina "as the destroyer only," as the defense had called him: "It was rather the tempter that came. Yes! Sir. The tempter who was to extend his subtle wiles over all about him, and, using as his ready instrument, the wretched being now before you [i.e., Lucretia Chapman]" (113). To "this mysterious stranger" (117) the prosecution attributed a "necromantic influence," "a magical power of as unbounded sway" as that exercised by a fairy-tale magician who could "enforce instantaneous submission to his will" (125). But in explicitly labeling him as *tempter* rather than *destroyer,* the prosecution positioned itself to implicate Lucretia Chapman in her own Fall.

Within days of his appearance, the satanic Mina had initiated the seduction of Lucretia Chapman. He began by appealing to her avarice: "Money, immense wealth, was the burthen of every tale the tempter told—his trunk of diamonds, and his mines of silver, his thousands in this country, and his millions in Mexico—his rank, his titles, his great connexions—these were his chosen themes" (113)—all of which tales she "heard with a listening and credulous ear" (193). Then, when the love of gold had "effaced from her mind the last vestige of moral principle and virtuous feeling" (193), she fell prey to "the additional impulse of licentious passion" (115). The prosecution openly sneered at the defense's explanation that Lucretia and Mina's conduct together before William Chapman's death—"this kissing and fondling, this daily, hourly, habitual indecency, this actual corporeal prostitution, this shameless indulgence of appetite"—involved "the mere 'indiscretion and imprudence' of unsuspicious purity" (115).[9] Lucretia Chapman, the prosecution assured the jury, had committed adultery. Then, "having sacrificed on the altar of passion her own honour, and the honour and happiness of her husband, she was ready to the same relentless idol to make a bloody offering. More fiends than one were busy in her breast—more than one disordered passion had its refuge there" (117). In view of her adulterous abandonment of "all her sacred obligations" to her husband and children, the prosecution asked, "is it a wonder that her moral sensibility, indurated and deadened by this wear and tear of profligacy, did not revolt at the suggestion or perpetration of the crime of which she is now accused?" (118).

The prosecution thus conceded that Lucretia Chapman had initially fallen prey to Mina's confidence game—"Incredible, monstrous, as those fictions now appear, she believed them!" (112)—and acknowledged that "[i]t is among the mysteries of this dark transaction, that this gilded bait was so readily swallowed" (114). The fisherman, after all, was a ragged, dirty, ill-spoken beggar, and the fish was an intelligent woman of substance. In the context of a modernizing culture haunted by the specter of the confidence man, the prosecution conventionally invoked "the art of the tempter, and the credulous facility of his victim" (114) as almost self-evident explanations of her conduct.[10] But the prosecution had no intention of affirming Lucretia Chapman's original innocence before her contamination by the satanic Spanish stranger. They contended that Lucretia Chapman suffered from "a moral temperament radically diseased" (112), a "tainted fancy" (113) which made her victimization anything but innocent. She readily swallowed the tempter's

bait because she suffered from a "morbid appetite" (115) for material possessions, and a "licentious appetite" (112) for illicit sex.

The key to Lucretia Chapman's depraved appetite, according to the prosecution, was her sexuality. That passion "which, when refined, burns in the
purest bosoms" as love, developed in her as an "uncontrolled indulgence" of
"sensual and animal passion" (98). The prosecution addressed Lucretia Chapman's sexual misconduct by staging a kind of verbal peep show: "For the
honour of human nature, as well as for the honour of the female character, I
would willingly drop the curtain over a scene disclosing so much profligacy
and licentiousness as the testimony in this cause has presented to our view"
(193); but since the defense had tried to undermine that testimony, the prosecution felt compelled to "lay aside all feelings of delicacy" and discuss at
length the evidence of "illicit intercourse" (194). And so they did, referring
repeatedly to Lucretia Chapman's "gross depravity and wantonness," her
"open and shameless exhibition of vice" (195), her "glaring outrages upon the
laws of decency and of good morals" (194).

The underlying aim of the prosecution was to convince the jury that to find
Lucretia Chapman guilty of adultery was implicitly to convict her of murder.
This strategy was pursued through an ingeniously ambiguous treatment of the
peculiar legal nature of the charge against her. Because murder by poison
necessarily involved premeditation with malice aforethought, the prosecution
explained, the indictment was for murder in the first degree. "There being
under this indictment no alternative to guilt, actual and technical, but innocence, pure, unblemished, untainted innocence. . . . If she is not guilty, she is
perfectly innocent. If not wholly innocent, she is guilty to the full extent of the
dark and ghastly crime laid in this indictment" (100). Technically, the prosecution was saying that it was not possible to convict Chapman of second-degree
murder; implicitly, they were also suggesting that if the jury thought her guilty
of adultery, they should find her guilty of murder, for to acquit her was to
leave her reputation "without a blemish" (100). The argument for the defense, as explained by the prosecution, was that up to a point "the prisoner
was pure in impulse and innocent in conduct," after which point she could be
charged only with "imprudence and indiscretion." "She is, by the softening
tints of this theory, the loving wife, the affectionate mother, and, if I am not
mistaken . . . the broken hearted widow" (111). But if the jury accepted the
prosecution's portrait of Lucretia Chapman as a depraved adulteress, they
should convict her of murder. The two crimes were close allies, the prosecution argued, and "the woman who could perpetrate the one, would commit
the other" (118).

After Lucretia Chapman's diseased appetite for material possessions and
illicit passion had led her into adultery, in the prosecution's tale, she seized
full matriarchal control of the Chapman household. William Chapman,
"though an amiable and a kind hearted man," was "energetic in neither mind
nor body. He was entirely too under the control of the prisoner, whose masculine intelligence and habits gave her an influence in her family which it was
useless to resist" (117). Though Lucretia Chapman had handled most of the

work of the Chapmans' school long before Mina's arrival, the prosecution was suggesting that her unwomanly sexual appetite bred in her a hunger as well for an unnatural dominion within her marriage. Mr. Chapman, who had himself been swayed by Mina's tales of wealth and station, was soon forced to confront "the intimate relation between Mina and his wife with pain and anxiety" (117). For her part, "almost from the very moment of Mina's becoming an inmate of her house, to the hour of her husband's death, she manifested the most deep and loathing hatred [for her husband], and seemed actuated by a brutality of feeling, which could only characterize a woman so base and depraved as she seems to have been" (192). In front of the children, the servants, and an assortment of strangers, she quarreled with him, called him a fool and said she was ashamed of him, forced him to make his own bed or go without breakfast, openly wished to God he was gone, and once kicked him. Could such a wife, asked the prosecution, "be actuated by any other than the feelings of a savage or a demon?" (192). "If the prisoner at the bar had been a household fiend, instead of the wife of the deceased, could she have exhibited greater cruelty and indignity, or could she have exercised a more absolute and tyrannical dominion over the actions and the feelings of her husband?" (193). Lucretia Chapman clearly emerged in this story as more household fiend than wife—specifically, a *"traitress fiend"* who raised "the hand of treason" as well as murder against her husband (192). The prosecution thus invoked an outdated provision of English criminal law which, until 1790, had treated a wife's murder of her husband not as simple homicide but as an act of petty treason for its assault on patriarchal authority.[11]

Much of the prosecution's characterization of Lucretia Chapman was designed to dramatize this portrait of the defendant as a "household fiend" who had outraged the sentimental ideal of womanhood even before the murder. As licentious adultress and as brutal matriarch, they indicated, she had effectively raised a murderous hand against her husband many times before she administered arsenic in his medicinal chicken soup. This was "no ordinary case of homicide" (182), but "a murder of the deepest and blackest dye" (181), "a case where a *wife* has deliberately conspired against the life of her husband, and has thus become the murderess of the father of her children, and the destroyer of him whom she should have comforted and sustained" (182). The prosecution repeatedly contrasted what should have been with what was, as in this melodramatic treatment of the imagined scene in which Lucretia added the poison to William Chapman's soup:

> Go to the room where the preparations for this deed of death were being made—lift the curtain, and behold that wife, who had plighted her faith, and sworn in the face of heaven, obedience and protection to her husband, plotting and conspiring against that husband's life! Behold her, who should have stood by him in the hour of danger and of need, who should have comforted him in his sorrows, and mourned with him in his afflictions, preparing with her own hand the deadly potion, which was to deprive him of his life! Behold her as a mother, violating not merely the laws of God and of man, but trampling under foot the most sacred ties of nature, and becoming the mur-

deress of her children's father—then ask yourself, whether, in the long and dark array of guilt which the depravity of man exhibits, there can be found a crime more revolting to our feelings, or one deeper and blacker in its dye, than that which is now presented to you? (198)

That evening, when William Chapman's condition had worsened, "[w]as she, like a guardian angel, hovering around his couch, and smoothing, with her tender and affectionate kindness, the bed of death?" (202). Not this household fiend. "At the moment when her injured husband was in the helpless agonies of desperate disease, asking and soliciting aid and protection from strangers and servants, when he was dying, and she knew he was dying, this faithful and affectionate wife, this living emblem of fidelity and love was shut up in a dark room with her paramour, careless to those sacred claims which her dying husband uttered" (121).[12]

In its fictive idealization of the Chapman family before the arrival of Mina, and its repeated references to the womanly ideal that was so grossly violated in Lucretia's actions before and after the death of her husband William, the prosecution's narrative worked within a larger framework of sentimental domesticity. The sentimental view of womanhood rested on the bourgeois ideology of passionlessness, initially propounded by late eighteenth- and early nineteenth-century Anglo-American Evangelicals, which declared that woman was morally superior to man because she was less carnal and more spiritual than he: it was her essential passionlessness that enabled her to serve as "guardian angel" to her husband and children. But the prosecution's characterization of Lucretia Chapman points to the survival of a presentimental understanding of the nature of woman into the nineteenth century. In charging her with "a moral temperament radically diseased," the prosecution echoed a premodern view of woman as naturally more evil than man, because of her depraved inheritance from the first woman, Eve, who had introduced sin into the world by succumbing to the blandishments of the satanic tempter. Woman, within the traditional Christian view, was morally weaker than man as descendant of Eve; she was intellectually weaker and thus more susceptible to deception; and she was physically weaker, subject to deeper passions and an insatiable carnal lust.[13] Lucretia Chapman's seduction by Mina clearly identified her as just such a woman, morally diseased by nature even before his arrival, intellectually susceptible—despite her acknowledged intelligence—to his confidence game, and afflicted with an uncontrollable "sensual and animal passion" that led her into adultery.

In fact, the prosecution's narrative of events cast the case against Lucretia Chapman as a witchcraft charge in all but name. As Carol Karlsen has demonstrated in her insightful study, *The Devil in the Shape of a Woman,* witchcraft accusations in seventeenth-century New England revealed striking patterns in their designation of those women particularly liable to the blandishments of the devil. First, the accused witch was often charged with greed, material discontent, and envy of those above her in society—qualities which the devil exploited by offering her wealth, material possessions, and relief from worldly

drudgery; to those women whose discontent extended to their marital situation, he promised marital happiness. Mina's first step in seducing Lucretia
Chapman was to offer her wealth, social honor, and a trip to Mexico that
would have carried her far away from the cares of the Chapman school—all in
the context of a felicitous marriage to himself. Second, the accused witch was
believed to be very carnal in nature, sexually insatiable and uncontrollable—
accused witch Katherine Harrison acknowledged herself to be "a female, a
weaker vessell, subject to passion"[14]—and witchcraft accusations were sometimes coupled with adultery charges. One contemporary explanation for the
disproportionate number of accused witches who were over forty but not yet
sixty was that these were women who were beginning to lose their sexual
attractiveness to men. So in stepped the devil, to offer them sex—just as
Mina, an attractive young Spaniard, offered adulterous sex to Lucretia Chapman, a woman of "licentious appetite," who was some eighteen years older
than he and, as the prosecution observed in court, not notable for physical
attractiveness.[15] A third common charge against the seventeenth-century
witch was a hunger for power that often assumed the form of gender rebellion. Insubordinate women—in 1486 the witch-hunter's manual *Malleus
Maleficarum* had targeted married women with a perverted desire to dominate their husbands—were particularly liable to witchcraft charges, and
Karlsen notes the special susceptibility of women who acted economically on
their own or their family's behalf for husbands somehow disabled or temporarily absent from the home. Enter the tempter, who offered them the ultimate
power of the *maleficium,* the ability to inflict illness or even death upon the
objects of their malignantly rebellious anger, which frequently included husbands. Lucretia Chapman's overbearing ways, her bad-tempered ill-treatment
of William after Mina's arrival, and her central role in the management of the
Chapmans' school, would clearly have exposed her to a witchcraft charge in
seventeenth-century New England, and would have gone a long way toward
establishing that his final illness and death were at her hands, supernaturally
assisted by the satanic Mina.[16]

In stark contrast to the prosecution's representation of Lucretia Chapman
as an aggressively evil "household fiend" was the defense's treatment of her as
a passive victim, "an oppressed fellow creature—a woman—hapless, helpless, friendless, and forlorn" (155). Within the defense narrative she was the
victim of public opinion, "[f]erreted like a beast of prey by a kennel of deep
mouthed calumniators," and "pictured as a very monster formed to adorn a
niche in the gallery of infamy—another Messalina."[17] She was a victim of the
press, "that mighty engine of instruction . . . which reaches every cottage,
and extends its influence to every mansion," lending its aid "to blacken and to
vilify her" (71). She was above all the victim of an overly zealous prosecution
which had put her through "a terrible ordeal," bringing in judgment against
her her "every word and action—the very expression of her features, and the
colour of her dress" (71). Counsel for the defense scoffed at the prosecution's
protestations of concern for the defendant: "this is the kindness of Judas,
kissing to betray,—the tenderness of the tiger, covering to devour—the com-

miseration of the crocodile, mingling his tears with the lifeblood of his expiring victim" (158). This helpless victim of public opprobrium and a savage prosecution was now seeking justice at the hands of the jury, whose sense of justice, the defense prodded, would surely "revolt at the idea of making it the instrument of convicting a wife and a mother of the most enormous atrocity of which human nature is capable" (72). In a word picture straight from Victorian melodrama, the defense appealed to the jury's masculine protectionism by representing Lucretia Chapman as a helpless woman standing on the brink of a precipice "from which I trust it will be your duty as well as pleasure to rescue and deliver her" (75).

Within the defense's narrative of the case, Lucretia Chapman's tragic victimization began with a generous act of Christian charity. On the evening of 9 May 1831, as the Chapman family gathered in their sitting room, "a stranger claimed admittance"; "actuated only by the purest and kindest feelings," Lucretia Chapman welcomed him into her home, "in accordance with the dictates of our blessed religion" to feed the hungry and aid the stranger (73). The ragged mendicant Mina "found a home in the bosom of their family" and "was regarded as a son by both Mr. and Mrs. Chapman" (142), both of whom believed his stories of wealth, position, and recent misfortune, pitied him for his ill health, and agreed to teach him English. As surrogate mother, teacher, and occasional nurse to the young stranger, Lucretia Chapman remained well within the bounds of propriety in spending time with Mina. And when her husband fell ill—of natural causes—her conduct toward him was "kind, tender, attentive, beseeming a wife and a Christian mother towards the father of her children" (148). But the death of her husband threw the defendant and her children "helpless and unprotected, on the broad bosom of the world. It was then that Mina, cloaking the malignity of a demon under the mask of a sacred obligation imposed by a dying man, told her that Mr. Chapman, in his final hour, had enjoined on him to be a protector to her, and a father to his children, and ensnared her into the act which has proved the grand source of all her difficulties" (142). The grieving Lucretia accepted his story and married him a few weeks after William's death, acting not out of wifely obedience alone, but out of maternal concern as well: "Left upon the wide theatre of the world, with a family of tender offspring looking to her maternal hand for protection and support, was she not bound by the most sacred ties of duty and affection, to embrace every honourable means of advancing their interest, and promoting their happiness?" (149). But in the weeks that followed, she learned that Mina "had married but to plunder her—and having accomplished his treacherous and unmanly object, had left her to a second widowhood" (150). Now she lay in a "lonely cell," where "[l]ife presents to her but a barren and a blasted heath. The recollections of how miserably she has been duped, the infamy of this public exposure, the mildew on a once unspotted reputation—these will torment her pillow to the latest hour" (151).

In an effort to emphasize Lucretia Chapman's essential innocence, the defense laid great stress on Mina's extraordinary skills as a confidence man. "So young, yet so accomplished in villany [*sic*]—with a subtlety of genius and fertility of resource that elude every difficulty, with no moral principle to check him in his wild career—deception seems his very element—the ruin of others his pastime and delight" (75). Within their narrative, Mina's "powers of deception, and seductive arts" earned him such titles as "this Prince of Impostors" and "this modern Proteus" (150). The "smooth tongued villain" (151) drew her in with stories of his wealth and social position, lured her into marriage with the lie about William's dying request, and then plundered her and her children, finally abandoning her "to seek new victims, and to find a wider theatre for his comprehensive genius" (150). No one could read his letters to her after his departure "without shuddering to think how this wily serpent had coiled and fastened himself around the defendant" (150). It was only when Mina was arrested on charges on felony "that the veil was completely removed from her vision, and she awoke as from the illusions of a dream to the awful realities of the precipice on whose brink she was standing" (75).

As the unwitting victim of an artful confidence man, Lucretia Chapman had a major failing, a feminine frailty which the defense delicately labeled "infatuation." Mina had cast a "spell" that "enchained the judgment" of the "infatuated" Lucretia (151). With respect to her hasty marriage to Mina, "she pleads guilty, with sincere contrition," to "the charge of folly and indiscretion" (76); on this point, the defense expressly declined to try to vindicate her "character for delicate refinement and scrupulous regard for the decorums of life" (149), wisely conceding the point that their client was not above all reproach. But though guilty of infatuation, indiscretion, and indecorum, Lucretia Chapman was perfectly innocent of that diseased sexual licentiousness with which the prosecution had charged her. Her conduct with Mina before the death of William Chapman was in keeping with the proprieties; her letters to him after the wedding "exhibit nothing that is incompatible with the most entire purity of the heart, or with a judicious exercise of the faculties of the head" (176). Their "exaggerated tone of feeling" characterized references to her children, her sister, and her nephew, as well as her new husband, and was addressed "to a young man of a nation whose characteristic is warmth, and whose language is tinctured with oriental hyperbole" (150), and who would thus expect to hear similar language from her. She was not sexually licentious, according to the defense; neither was she matriarchal. If she was indeed "high tempered," as the prosecution charged, it should be remembered that she had long been a teacher by vocation, and had "acquired something of the authoritative tone and temper" (143) required by that profession. The Chapmans' home life was perhaps not one of unbroken harmony—"Domestic differences will occur in the best ordered families" (143)—but those differences did not add up to that open gender revolt depicted by the prosecution.

But the burden of the defense's argument was not a negative reply to the prosecution's charge that the defendant was sexually depraved and monstrously matriarchal. More positively, the defense made a case for Lucretia Chapman's fulfillment of the sentimental ideal of true womanhood. She was, first of all, a woman of some social standing, the daughter of a respectable citizen of Massachusetts who had fought in the Revolutionary War, a woman whose reputation was "fair and unblemished" (154). "Endowed by nature with no ordinary faculties," she had since age seventeen "been employed in the arduous and responsible duties of forming the morals and the minds of a large number of young persons" (72) as a teacher. She was in addition a woman of great piety, "a regular attendant at God's worship—a communicant at the holy table . . . whose hospitable charity the stranger and the beggar knew" (154). And she was the devoted mother of five children "whom she had taught to worship that God" (141), and whose dependency now provided her with her sole motivation to live: though willing to die to escape her infamy, "[s]he clings to life by those little tendrils that twine around a mother's heart, with force divine and irresistible" (151). The daily presence of the Chapman children in the courtroom was no doubt intended to dramatize before the jury the defendant's sentimental status as mother.

Finally, Lucretia Chapman was a devoted wife. She had been "kind, tender, attentive" (148) to William Chapman during his final illness, and had mourned his passing with true sentimental sincerity, whatever the prosecution might say. The Commonwealth had brought forth a witness who testified that Lucretia Chapman's mourning attire had been inappropriate to her loss: on the day after William's funeral, she appeared in a properly black dress, but wearing a white turban with a lilac border. To this charge, the defense sentimentally countered: "It is not in 'customary suits of solemn black' alone, that the heart exhibits its afflictions. . . . Her dress was not affected, her agonies were not eloquent, but they were not the less poignant or sincere." Had she in fact murdered her husband, they assured the court, "there would have been no deficiency in what may be called dramatic effect; her error would have been in *excess:* like the Ephesian dame, she would have swept the very earth with her widowed weeds, and veiled her face in sorrow" (178).[18] Her devotion to her first husband was furthermore demonstrated in her dutiful obedience to his alleged dying wish that she marry Mina. And having married Mina, she proved once again her wifely fidelity by refusing, at her first police interview, "to tear asunder the sacred bond of union" by supporting the charge that "the person to whom she has pledged the most solemn vow, is an impostor, a robber, and a plunderer" (152). On this point, both attorneys for the defense waxed eloquent: "Fidelity is the brightest jewel that adorns the female character; it is the *last* that woman loses;—and it would have been an eternal reproach to her *sex*—it would have been perdition to *her,* when her vile husband's fate was poised before her, if the whole police of the city, with all their mental racks and tortures, could have extracted from her heaving bosom, a single groan to guess at" (178).

It was the genius of Lucretia Chapman's defense thus to transform all her apparent vices into virtues. Did she prove inattentive to the prescribed social forms for mourning a dead husband? It was because she eschewed "the studied forms and ceremonies of wo [*sic*]" (178) for a purer expression of a deeper grief. Did she remarry twelve days after his death? She was merely complying with what she believed to be his dying wish. Did she lie to the police officer who came to inquire into Mina's fraudulent activities? That lie was a heroic act of wifely fidelity. Even Lucretia Chapman's eleventh-hour flight from justice was represented by the defense as a natural feminine shrinking from public exposure; she was "[a] woman—whose sex the milder and the gentler virtues adorn and characterize—to whom the rude exposure of a court room is worse than the worst of deaths" (153). Her flight was simply one more proof of her feminine virtue.

If Lucretia Chapman had to be innocent as charged on the grounds of her virtuous womanhood—a defense that rested more on her status as respectable wife and mother than on her actual conduct during the period in question—other women whose stories were central to the defense's narrative did not fare so well. Essential to this tale of the victimization of a true woman was the destruction of the credibility of those servants who testified to Lucretia Chapman's adultery and her ill-treatment of William Chapman. In destroying that credibility, the defense managed to project onto women of lower social caste the charges of evil leveled against Lucretia Chapman by the prosecution. "It has been the melancholy fate of the defendant," her counsel lamented, "to nurse vipers in her bosom; to warm them into life, and to be the victim of their venom" (168). Heading the list of vipers was Ellen Shaw, the live-in maid servant who had left the household shortly before William Chapman's death because, as she explained, she could no longer tolerate Lucretia's sexual misconduct with Mina. The defense designated Shaw's story of their sexual alliance as "a fancy, unrivalled in all the legendary lore of outrageous fiction. The Libertines, the Monk, the Black Forest, the Mysteries of Udolpho, and all the other mysteries that the world ever heard of, saw, or wondered at, never presented to the human mind so shocking a monstrosity as this" (169). They went on to ridicule on its face the idea that a woman such as Ellen Shaw might evince "delicacy": "This virtuous maid would have you believe that in the short space of one month after Mina's arrival, the defendant's conduct had reached to such a height of bloated wantonness, that she was actually compelled to leave the house to save her own blushes. Extraordinary delicacy! I fear the age has become too gross for such refinement" (141–42). The real indelicacy, they suggested, resided in Ellen Shaw herself: why, the defense asked suggestively, had she paid a nighttime visit to the bedchamber of the Spanish boarder and thus come to find Lucretia Chapman in his company? The "redoubtable Ellen Shaw" was the shameless leader of the militant female forces conspiring to destroy Lucretia Chapman: "*dux faemina facti*—an Amazonian Queen—a modern Penthesilea [the Amazon queen killed by Achilles at Troy]" (168). Her feelings toward Lucretia, the defense charged, "were of the most hostile and malignant character," as evidenced by her playing a "female Iago" (169), falsely informing William Chapman that his wife planned to elope with Mina to Mexico. And her hostility had been exacerbated by her dismissal from employment in the Chapman household. "Can you have any doubt, gentlemen, after this, that her malice, thus engendered, has for the last twelvemonth been confined like subterranean fires within her bosom, at last thus to burst forth and spread a ruin around. She presents before you the shocking anomaly of a human volcano, breathing nothing but flames, devastation, and death" (170). This volcanic metaphor clearly stamped Ellen Shaw as a member of the lower social orders, whose passions were not subjected to that self-government practiced by respectable middle-class women such as the defendant. Ellen Shaw was a "worthless, discontented, and discarded" servant, and what man on the jury would be satisfied by any account of his own domestic arrangements offered by such a one? "The language—the manner—the matter—when tortured in her intellectual or moral crucible, loses all their value—their gold is turned to dross!" (170).

If Ellen Shaw was ridiculed by the defense for claiming to blush in the face of Lucretia Chapman's misconduct, a second servant was ridiculed for being "blushless" (168) because of her race. Ann Bantom's presence at the trial invited Mr. Brown to refer contemptuously to "the party-coloured crew, drawn by the prosecution from the prisoner's household" (164), and to pun crudely that she "has been brought forward to give some *colour* to their case" (170). An outdoor servant who occasionally assisted the Chapmans with Monday washing, Bantom had provided very damaging testimony concerning not only Lucretia's and Mina's dalliance, but also the sudden deterioration in William Chapman's condition after he ate the chicken soup. Much of the defense's counternarrative aimed at undermining Bantom's factual credibility on both these points. But as with Ellen Shaw, the defense attorneys also launched an *ad feminam* attack on the witness herself, targeting both her race and her social class: "Thus it is, gentlemen of the jury, black spirits and white are conjured and raked up, from the vile recesses of the kitchen and the garret—and arrayed here before you upon this trial, like Milton's devils— 'fierce as ten furies, terrible as hell.' The day darkens at their approach, and the radiant smile that beams from the brow of innocence, fades away beneath their withering and demoniac charm" (170–71).

In representing Ellen Shaw and Ann Bantom as subterranean creatures "conjured and raked up" from the kitchen like devils from domestic hell to torment the lady of the house, the defense was symbolically exorcising the accused "household fiend" Lucretia Chapman but casting her imputed evil into women from the lower social and racial orders, much as Christ had cast out devils into a herd of swine. It is significant that a third servant, Mrs. Esther Bache, fared better at the hands of the defense. A seamstress who had been in attendance at the Chapman home on one or two occasions, she too testified to Lucretia's impropriety with Mina, but her testimony was merely dismissed as trivial and ridiculous; her chief offense was that "she is one of those ladies with whom Ellen Shaw, and Ann Bantom have been talking." What distinguished Bache from Shaw and Bantom was that she had "every appearance of a respectable woman" (170), a claim to which her title of "Mrs." bore testimony; Ellen Shaw, herself a married woman, was never awarded that title. Social respectability shielded Esther Bache's reputation for virtue much as it did Lucretia Chapman's—at the moral expense of the lower-class Ellen Shaw and Ann Bantom.[19]

Within the characterization proffered by the defense, Lucretia Chapman essentially conformed to the model of sentimental womanhood: she was a faithful wife and devoted mother, a respected teacher of the young, a devout Christian whose piety was actively demonstrated in frequent acts of charity, and a respectable woman of hitherto unblemished reputation, who now yearned to die rather than endure public infamy. The defense admitted the indiscretion of her hasty remarriage, but vehemently denied she was guilty of adultery, and asserted the purity of her attachment to her second husband, whom she had married out of wifely obedience to William Chapman and motherly devotion to his children. Lucretia Chapman was not sexually licentious but passionless (if somewhat infatuated); she was not matriarchal (if sometimes high-tempered) but dependent, submissive to husbandly authority. She was above all a helpless, and a largely passive, female victim—of public opprobrium and prosecutorial zeal, of a devilishly clever confidence man, and of those household vipers she had taken to her charitable bosom, who now turned their venomous fangs against her.

Female evil was indeed present in the Chapman home, according to the defense, but it did not reside in the lady of the house. It was found in the lower regions—subterranean both socially and geographically (the Chapman kitchen was located in the basement)—of the household, where demonic lower-class servants, black and white, plotted to destroy the middle-class angel of the house. The new ideology of passionlessness served the needs of an emerging bourgeoisie by affirming the moral purity of "womanhood," but excluded from "womanhood" those who were perceived as unwilling or unable to fulfill the ideal. As Carol Karlsen has argued, "Woman-as-evil had gradually taken on not a single but a dual shape—one formed by race, the other by class. By the nineteenth century, black women and poor white women were viewed as embodying many of the characteristics of the witch: they were increasingly portrayed as seductive, sexually uncontrolled, and threatening to the social and moral order."[20] Ellen Shaw and Ann Bantom thus proved eminently exploitable within the defense's counternarrative of female evil in the Chapman household, which was designed to exculpate Lucretia Chapman by sacrificing her servants to the jury's presumed effort— presumed, that is, by counsel for the defense—to "cherchez la femme."

The competing narratives offered by the prosecution and the defense in the murder trial of Lucretia Chapman thus offered two versions of the nature of womanhood: the nineteenth-century sentimental view of (the middle-class) woman as man's moral superior by virtue of her natural passionlessness, and the traditional view of woman as intrinsically more evil than man owing to her descent from that mother of sinners, Eve, and her naturally uncontrollable sexual appetite. As a number of scholars have noted, the premodern view of woman as evil persisted side by side with the newer sentimental ideal throughout the nineteenth century, not simply as a vestigial remnant of an outmoded gender ideology, but as a crucial prop to the doctrine of masculine protectionism that legitimized the separation of spheres. In the artistic works treated by these scholars—novels such as *Jane Eyre,* paintings such as William Holman

Hunt's "The Awakening Conscience," sculptures such as Hiram Powers's *The Greek Slave*—the relationship between these two images of womanhood was most commonly one of tension and ambiguity.[21] But in the murder trial of Lucretia Chapman, the adversary system of justice shaped what elsewhere appeared as an ideological tension into two distinct, oppositional points of view which conflicted on two different levels: within the narrative of womanhood offered by the defense, which differentiated middle-class female purity from lower-class female depravity; and between the defense's narrative of Lucretia's passionlessness and the prosecution's tale of her monstrous hunger for money, sex, and power.

Having sorted out in such starkly oppositional form these alternative images of womanhood, the adversary system of justice went on to require that the jury choose between them. The peculiarly competitive nature of courtroom narrativity meant that the storytelling attorneys at the Chapman trial were at least as self-consciously attuned to reader response, and as explicitly anxious to direct that response along proper channels, as any writer of sentimental fiction. "I now appeal to you," the prosecution addressed the jury, "not merely as men having some knowledge of human nature," but "as husbands and as fathers" (196); in a similar fashion, but toward different ends, the defense instructed the jurors, "Though we decide like fate, let us feel like men" (157). But what was at stake in the jury's verdict was precisely how men do or should feel when confronted with the indictment of a respectable middle-class wife and mother for the murder of her husband. Though jurors are expected to sift through vast quantities of detailed evidence in the effort to determine what really happened, and in so doing to conform to certain legal guidelines for their deliberation, in the end a major factor in their verdict is the relative plausibility of the two stories before them—a plausibility based on the attorneys' appeal to a "common sense" involving a culturally shared set of norms and assumptions about human nature and social interaction.

Unlike the artistic audiences of sentimental literature, painting, or sculpture, whose relative silence often proves highly frustrating to historical investigators of reader response, the primary "readers" of courtroom narratives—those twelve good men and true who sat as jurors—formally voted on their plot line of choice. Attorneys for both the prosecution and the defense assumed that their reader-jurors were best prepared to interpret a domestic situation within a sentimental framework of meaning, broadly conceived. But which side set forth the winning version of woman's nature? The answer is, the defense: Lucretia Chapman was acquitted of the charge of murdering her husband. It is unfortunately impossible to know on what grounds the jury found her not guilty. Perhaps they concluded that the physical evidence was insufficient to demonstrate that William Chapman had died of unnatural causes. It seems significant, however, that on the grounds of the same physical evidence another jury was soon to find Mina the Spaniard—who claimed finally to be Carolino Estradas de Mina, a Cuban—guilty of the murder of William Chapman.[22] Perhaps the jury found grounds for reasonable doubt in the absence of direct evidence linking Lucretia to the arsenic purchased by

Mina on the day before William Chapman became ill. The prosecution had, however, placed Lucretia with Mina in Philadelphia on that day, and the circumstantial evidence linking the arsenic to the soup and the soup to Lucretia was considerable. Perhaps the jurors' masculine protectionism was aroused by the defense's representation of Lucretia Chapman as a helpless female victim, by the daily appearance of the defendant's children in court, or by an unwillingness to find a woman guilty of an offense which, in Pennsylvania in 1831, mandated capital punishment.[23] The prosecution certainly betrayed its concern lest such misplaced chivalry influence the jury's decision, portraying Lucretia Chapman as a monster of aggressive female depravity, cautioning jurors not to be manipulated by the calculated introduction of the Chapman children in the courtroom, suggesting that even if she were found guilty, the governor might set aside the death penalty in her case, and warning the jury not to let her go free in the hope that her accused accomplice—a conveniently foreign scapegoat—would soon be convicted and punished for William Chapman's untimely death.

Nonetheless, the evidence against Lucretia Chapman was considerable, if circumstantial.[24] For the modern reader committed a priori to neither the angelic nor the demonic view of womanhood, the probability of her guilt is compelling. Why, then, did a nineteenth-century jury find her not guilty? It is finally possible that the jury acquitted Lucretia Chapman because its members were more comfortable accepting the defense's story of a sentimental woman—domestic, pious, passive, the helpless victim of evil circumstances beyond her control—than the prosecution's narrative of a "household fiend"—licentious, depraved, matriarchal, the aggressive destroyer of her own family circle. The murder trial of Lucretia Chapman demonstrates how the cult of sentimental womanhood could be employed to contain the ideological threat posed by aggressive, sexual, self-willed, and powerful middle-class women.[25] The sentimental story of Lucretia Chapman was a tale told by men to men about Woman. Haunted by the enduring specter of Woman as demon, they succeeded at last in eluding her by publicly and ritualistically declaring their faith in Woman as angel.

3

Rape, Murder, and Revenge in "Slavery's Pleasant Homes": Lydia Maria Child's Antislavery Fiction and the Limits of Genre

Carolyn L. Karcher

> I could not write the story as he told it. If I were to use the English tongue
> with the nervous strength that he did, when he told the bitterest portion of
> his tale, all the women in the land would tear the pages out of the fair
> volume; yet, alas! if we but knew it, when we mention the word Slavery,
> we sum up all possible indecencies as well as all possible villainies. In the
> cover of its consonants and vowels lie hid all manner of evils, that woman
> dare not name, even though to name were to avert them from half their
> sex.
> Caroline Healey Dall, "The Inalienable Love" (1858)

This lament, which prefaces a story by Caroline Healey Dall entitled "The Inalienable Love," provides an apt introduction to the problematic genre of antislavery fiction—a genre nineteenth-century American women developed as a means of circumventing the obstacles they faced when they attempted to write openly about the sordid realities of slavery.[1] Dall is explaining why she has not transcribed the story in the idiom of the fugitive slave who originally narrated it to her—an idiom she clearly finds more powerful and expressive than the genteel language into which she has translated it. Had she used the words of her slave informant, she points out, her female readers would have recoiled in horror (and her male readers, she might have added, would have stigmatized her as unwomanly). It is the *facts* of slavery that are obscene, she objects—not the uninhibited discussion of them. Indeed, she hints, women are no strangers to the "indecencies" and "villainies" endured by slaves, for "half their sex" fall prey to them. Thus, by uncovering these evils and daring to "name" them, women would be striking a blow against their own enslavement, as well as their black sisters' and brothers'. Nevertheless, Dall realizes, she cannot hope to influence her genteel readers unless she respects their sensibilities. Hence her choice of a literary form and language that reflects their tastes, even though she feels all too keenly how inadequately it conveys the experiences of the slaves for whom she would speak.

In this key passage, Dall articulates the central paradox of women's antislavery fiction. On the one hand, because the genre represented a compromise with the code of gentility which forbade women writers to "name" the wrongs they sought to expose, antislavery fiction imposed severe constraints on them. On the other hand, in the guise of championing the slave woman, whose sexual exploitation became its main focus, antislavery fiction allowed women writers to explore what feminist-abolitionists came to call "the slavery of sex"—the predicament of women in patriarchal society.[2] To that extent, it also proved liberating.[3]

Brilliantly illustrating the strategies that the creators of antislavery fiction devised in their struggle to turn its limitations to their advantage is a buried masterpiece of the genre—"Slavery's Pleasant Homes. A Faithful Sketch" by Lydia Maria Child.[4] No abolitionist had wrestled longer than Child with the difficulties of inducing a hostile public to confront the grim facts of slavery, and few had undergone a more precipitous fall from grace on entering the despised ranks of abolitionist "agitators."

Ironically, controversy had swept Child into prominence at the very outset of her literary career. Her first novel, *Hobomok, A Tale of Early Times* (1824), had doubly violated taboo: it had permitted its genteel Puritan heroine to elope with an Indian and bear him a son; and it had enabled that heroine to divorce, remarry, and reintegrate herself into the Puritan community with her half-Indian child, after her long-lost English lover miraculously returned to claim her. Instinctively, Child had already discovered the pivotal theme of her future antislavery fiction—miscegenation—and recognized it as embodying the vital connection between twin systems of oppression: male dominance and white supremacy.[5]

"Revolting . . . to every feeling of delicacy in man or woman," the critics had stormed,[6] yet *Hobomok* had achieved a succès de scandale, winning its twenty-two-year-old author entrée into Boston's most exclusive literary salons.[7] Moreover, it had emboldened other pioneers of the American historical novel, notably James Fenimore Cooper and Catharine Maria Sedgwick, to tackle the radical question it raised: whether intermarriage and assimilation might not constitute viable alternatives to race war and Indian genocide.[8]

In the next decade Child not only published a novel of the American Revolution, a collection of short fiction, two best-selling housekeeping and child-rearing manuals, and several children's books, including a history of the Puritans' injustices toward Indians. She also founded the first successful children's magazine in the country, *The Juvenile Miscellany*, editing it for eight years, and launched the Ladies' Family Library, a series comprising three volumes of biographies designed to provide women with inspiring role models, and an ambitious two-volume *History of the Condition of Women, in Various Ages and Nations*, which laid the groundwork for later feminist theory.

Every genre Child tried out—or invented—served her as a vehicle for experimenting with rhetorical strategies aimed at winning broad support for avant-garde ideas about race and gender. Thus, no sooner did Child begin investigating the issue of slavery than she started using *The Juvenile Miscellany* as an outlet for tales dramatizing the cruelty of slavery and preaching racial equality. Among the earliest specimens of antislavery fiction I have been able to locate, her stories "The St. Domingo Orphans" and "Jumbo and Zairee"[9] apparently slipped past parental censors, who reacted with outrage when, in 1833, Child issued the manifesto that publicly identified her as an abolitionist: *An Appeal in Favor of That Class of Americans Called Africans.*

This time the controversy that swirled around her plunged Child from the pinnacle of popularity into total ostracism. Her fashionable patrons slammed their doors in her face; the Boston Athenaeum abruptly revoked the free library privileges it had granted her (privileges only one other woman in its history had received); indignant parents canceled their subscriptions to the *Miscellany* en masse, forcing Child to abandon the magazine; and the sale of her vast body of works plummeted.

The problem was not that Child had changed her rhetorical tactics—quite the contrary. The very title *An Appeal in Favor of That Class of Americans Called Africans* struck a conciliatory note, and nothing could have been more disarming than the plea with which Child prefaced the book:

> Reader, I beseech you not to throw down this volume as soon as you have glanced at the title. Read it, if your prejudices will allow, for the very truth's sake:—If I have the most trifling claims upon your good will, for an hour's amusement to yourself, or benefit to your children, read it for *my* sake:— Read it, if it be merely to find fresh occasion to sneer at the vulgarity of the cause:—Read it, from sheer curiosity to see what a woman (who had much better attend to her household concerns) will say upon such a subject:—Read it, on *any* terms, and my purpose will be gained.[10]

But the American public of the 1830s simply would not tolerate controversy over slavery. The economic prosperity of the nation rested on the partnership between Southern cotton planters and Northern textile manufacturers, merchants, and financiers. These elites governed public opinion and, in the years following the publication of Child's *Appeal,* used every means at their disposal to quash "agitation" of an issue that threatened their interests: mob attacks against abolitionist lecturers and editors, the destruction of antislavery presses, censorship of the mails to prevent dissemination of antislavery literature, and even a "gag" law stipulating that antislavery petitions submitted to Congress be tabled without discussion.[11] Such was the climate of opinion Child had to brave in challenging her compatriots' most inveterate prejudices.

Although the *Appeal* cost Child her popularity, it provided the fledgling abolitionist movement with an invaluable resource.[12] The first book to call for the immediate abolition of slavery and to repudiate all forms of racial discrimination, including antimiscegenation laws (a particularly courageous stand for a woman), it surveyed the institution of slavery from a variety of angles—

historical, political, economic, legal, and moral—and marshaled data showing that emancipation was practicable and that Africans were intellectually equal to Europeans. The *Appeal* also initiated exploration of the subject that would soon haunt women's antislavery discourse—the sexual exploitation of slave women and its "degrading effect . . . on the morals of both blacks and whites." "The negro woman is unprotected either by law or public opinion," Child explained:

> She is the property of her master, and her daughters are his property. They are allowed to have no conscientious scruples, no sense of shame, no regard for the feelings of husband, or parent; they must be entirely subservient to the will of their owner, on pain of being whipped as near unto death as will comport with his interest, or quite to death, if it suit his pleasure.
>
> Those who know human nature would be able to conjecture the unavoidable result, even if it were not betrayed by the amount of mixed population.[13]

Ten years later Child would dramatize precisely this scenario in "Slavery's Pleasant Homes." By then she could enrich her story by building on the insights other women had achieved into the "slavery of sex," especially as it affected the white mistresses of these "unprotected" slaves. Among the women Child knew who had viewed the dynamics of the slave system at first hand and had unflinchingly exposed the white mistress's complicity in it were the South Carolina slaveholders' daughters, Sarah and Angelina Grimké, and the famous British Shakespearean actress Fanny Kemble, wife of the Georgia slaveholder Pierce Butler. Their accounts reverberate through "Slavery's Pleasant Homes."

In *American Slavery As It Is: Testimony of a Thousand Witnesses* (1839), the powerful tract the Grimké sisters had compiled in collaboration with Angelina's husband Theodore Dwight Weld, Angelina had painted this chilling portrait of a Charleston mistress identified by one biographer as the Grimkés' mother[14]:

> [A] woman . . . who was foremost in every benevolent enterprise, and stood . . . at the *head* of the . . . moral and religious female society [of Charleston] . . . used to keep cowhides, or small paddles, (called "pancake sticks,") in four different apartments in her house; so that when she wished to punish, or to have punished, any of her slaves, she might not have the trouble of sending for an instrument of torture. For many years, one or other, and *often* more of her slaves, were flogged *every day;* particularly the young slaves about the house, whose faces were slapped, or their hands beat with the "pancake stick," for every trifling offence—and often for no fault at all.[15]

Having unveiled the sexual mores that poisoned family life in the South, Child may well have wondered whether these "young slaves about the house" showed too much resemblance to the master. Grimké Weld left the matter shrouded in silence; her anguish many years later, when she discovered her brother had had children by a slave woman, suggests the subject may have been too painful for her to formulate such a question consciously.[16] Still, the epithets "sluts" and "husseys," which she recalled her mother hurling at slave women, strongly hint at jealousy of their sexuality, as does the punishment inflicted on a young woman sent to the workhouse to be "stripped *naked* and whipped." However reticent about the motives behind the abuses she reported, Grimké Weld graphically described their brutality:

> This mistress would occasionally send her slaves, male and female, to the Charleston work-house to be punished. One poor girl . . . showed me the deep gashes on her back—I might have laid my whole finger in them—*large pieces of flesh had actually been cut out by the torturing lash.* . . . [S]o exceedingly offensive has been the putrid flesh of [slaves'] lacerated backs, for days after the infliction, that they would be kept out of the house—the smell arising from their wounds being too horrible to be endured.[17]

The sexual undercurrents lurking beneath the surface of Grimké Weld's testimony were explicit in Fanny Kemble's *Journal of a Residence on a Georgian Plantation in 1838–1839,* which took the form of letters addressed to her friend Elizabeth Sedgwick, an acquaintance of Child's.[18] Circulated privately among abolitionists (Kemble delayed publishing it for twenty-odd years, in compliance with her husband's wishes), the journal recorded Kemble's initiation into the role of a plantation mistress.[19] Kemble had at first tried to intercede for the slaves, in the hopes that she could at least alleviate some of their misery. After her husband announced that he would "receive no more statements of grievances or petitions for redress" through her, Kemble began to see a parallel, as well as a contrast, between her own condition and that of the slave women she had tried to befriend.[20] In her case, as in the Grimké sisters', the insight impelled her to flee a situation in which she was "powerless to shield the victims," and to assume instead the burden of speaking out against the institution itself.[21] In the case of at least one slave-owning woman Kemble encountered, a Mrs. King, the dim awareness of being almost as much at her husband's mercy as the slave women he pursued turned her into a fury. The scene Kemble sketched of Mrs. King bursting into the dilapidated "hospital" where three slave women were "recovering from their confinements" is one of the grimmest in abolitionist annals. All three of the women had been raped by white men—two by Mr. King himself—yet far from showing any compassion for them, Mrs. King had the three "severely flogged, a process which *she* personally superintended, and then sent them to Five Pound—the swamp Botany Bay of the plantation . . . —with further orders to the drivers to flog them every day for a week."[22]

Despite the ridicule and vilification they had invariably met with, Child, the Grimké sisters, Kemble, and countless other women, black and white, had indeed dared to "name" the "indecencies" and "villainies" of slavery, as Caroline Healey Dall puts it in the passage that so eloquently sums up the woman writer's dilemma.[23] By 1841 Child herself had produced a panoply of tracts and assumed the editorship of the *National Anti-Slavery Standard*—a milestone for women. For their part, the Grimké sisters had broken the taboo against women's speaking in public to "promiscuous" audiences, and others had quickly followed in their wake. After a decade of intensive propaganda work, however, the vast majority of Americans remained hostile to abolitionism and indifferent to the plight of the slaves. It was this exigency that prompted Child to seek new modes of broadening her audience.

The quest led her back to fiction, which she had always found capable of touching the heart and stirring the imagination on a deeper level than "the ablest arguments, and the most serious exhortations."[24] Her faith in the potency of fiction had meanwhile drawn new confirmation from the impact produced by a pioneering antislavery novel published anonymously in late 1836: *The Slave: or, Memoirs of Archy Moore,* by a young lawyer named Richard Hildreth. "People of the dullest minds and the coldest sympathies are thrilled by it, as if their benumbed fingers had touched an electric chain," Child had reported in a letter to William Lloyd Garrison's abolitionist newspaper, *The Liberator.* Praising the novel's unsparing delineation of slavery and its accuracy of detail, she had wistfully avowed, "If I were a man, I would rather be the author of that work, than of anything ever published in America."[25] The qualification "if I were a man" poignantly testifies to Child's sense of the limitations imposed on nineteenth-century women writers. No woman could assume the viewpoint of a rebellious male fugitive and narrate his story in the accents of "fiery indignation" he would naturally use—the device she had most admired in *Archy Moore.*[26] Instead she would have to adapt the conventions of women's fiction to the end of mobilizing women readers against slavery.

The challenge Child faced entailed transmuting the unsavory facts exposed in works like the *Appeal* and *American Slavery As It Is* into fiction palatable enough to attract unsympathetic consumers. It was an enterprise fraught with contradictions: the conventions of romance must serve to dispel readers' romantic illusions about slavery; a language shorn of ugly details must convey the violence of the institution to an audience convinced that abolitionists exaggerated its cruelty; a code of gentility that did not protect slave women against rape or white women against their husbands' philandering must govern fictional treatment of sexuality; above all, a heroine representing a concession to racial prejudice must somehow serve to counteract prejudice.

Child first tried to solve the problem in a story titled "The Quadroons" (*The Liberty Bell,* 1842). There she devised the fictional strategy of personifying the wrongs of slavery in an archetype that has come to be known as the "tragic mulatto."[27] Light-skinned and genteel, the "tragic mulatto" embodies the hypocrisy of the South's sexual code, which dogs her throughout her life. Her tragedy consists in sharing the sensibilities, tastes, and moral standards of the white readers she resembles, yet being subject to the sexual exploitation and abuse endured by the black slave woman whom most readers refuse to acknowledge as their sister. The quadroon Rosalie and her daughter Xarifa exemplify different versions of the "tragic mulatto" 's plight. Both love white men who are barred by law and custom from marrying them. Rosalie dies of grief when her white lover abandons her for a wife of his own race, and Xarifa goes mad when sold to a profligate upon the death of her master.

Child herself found the story embarrassingly sentimental, as she admitted to her friend Maria Weston Chapman, editor of *The Liberty Bell*. "You and Caroline [Chapman's sister] will laugh at it heartily," she conceded ruefully, "but the young and romantic will like it. It sounds, in sooth, more like a girl of sixteen, than a woman of forty; and I can give no rational account how I happened to fall into such a strain. The fact is, I was plagued to death for a subject, and happened to hit upon one that involved much love-making."[28]

Child's comments indicate her awareness of the conflicting demands her fiction had to meet from sophisticated antislavery activists and unconverted general readers. "The Quadroons" might well fulfill the purpose of arousing the latter's "benumbed" sympathies, but it did not reflect the political consciousness the former had sought to promote. Nor did it satisfy Child's aspiration to harness the imaginative power of fiction without softening the indictment of slavery presented in her tracts and editorials. She would reach that goal the following year in a story that ranks among the highest achievements of antislavery fiction. "Slavery's Pleasant Homes. A Faithful Sketch," would feature a darker-hued slave heroine who, unlike Rosalie and Xarifa, rejects the dubious honor of a white gentleman's attentions, chooses a lover from among her fellow slaves, and dies resisting her master rather than mourning the loss of her white lover.[29] It would also fuse the female sexual exploitation narrative Child had developed in "The Quadroons" with the male rebellion narrative Hildreth had pioneered in *Archy Moore*. The two stories' contrasting plots and publication histories neatly illustrate the limits of antislavery fiction as a genre: "The Quadroons" would win popular success, while "Slavery's Pleasant Homes" would remain confined to an antislavery audience.

Child evidently based "Slavery's Pleasant Homes" both on newspaper articles she had read over the years and on personal narratives she had taken from the lips of fugitive slaves. Her skillful use of these sources gives the story an unmistakable ring of authenticity. Two of the articles that inspired her plot date back to the early 1830s. Indeed, Child had cited them in the chapter of the *Appeal* entitled "Moral Character of Negroes." The first, derived from "a Georgia paper," had reported the murder of an overseer by a slave "goaded to frenzy" at seeing his wife whipped. "The Georgia editor viewed the subject only on one side," Child had noted drily, "viz.—the monstrous outrage against the white man—the negro's wrongs passed for nothing!"[30] She would end "Slavery's Pleasant Homes" by similarly quoting from "Georgian papers" and pointing out their one-sidedness. The second article, which had appeared in *The Liberator* in 1832, had explained the circumstances behind the murder of an overseer on a plantation in Santa Cruz belonging to a prominent Bostonian. The murder had been touted by antiabolitionists as evidence of "what diabolical passions these negroes have," and the newspapers had called the perpetrators "negro devils" and "incarnate fiends"[31]—slurs Child would cite in her purported extracts from the Southern and Northern press in "Slavery's Pleasant Homes." As Garrison had reported in *The Liberator*, however, further investigation of the case had revealed that the overseer had taken "a fancy to two of the negroes' wives," chained them to his "bed-post, and flogged [them] unmercifully, to compel them to submit to his orders."[32] The "outraged husbands" had taken "justice into their own hands" and stabbed the overseer to death. In "Slavery's Pleasant Homes" Child would focus on the tragedy of one young slave couple and shift the blame for the wife's rape from the overseer to the gentleman slaveholder—an alteration that made her story a more damning indictment of the slave system than the *Liberator* article on which she founded it.

The aspect of the Santa Cruz incident that had most strongly engaged Child's imagination, leading her to incorporate it into her defense of the African's "Moral Character," had been the murderers' loyalty to their fellow slaves. Although they themselves had escaped detection, they had voluntarily confessed their guilt to save those who had been wrongly charged with the crime from execution.[33] Despite an act of moral heroism surpassing that of Damon and Pythias, Garrison had editorialized, "Not a voice was raised in their favor, and they were shot like dogs"[34]—a comment Child would echo in the final sentences of "Slavery's Pleasant Homes."

What apparently revived Child's memory of the incident and suggested the idea of turning it into a story for *The Liberty Bell* was a new outbreak of "Horrible Events" publicized by the Southern press in 1842, while she was editing the *National Anti-Slavery Standard*. Reprinting the *Natchez Free Trader*'s grisly account of a lynching conducted to punish a gang of slaves for their "unheard-of cruelty" toward two white women, Child had speculated that, as in the Santa Cruz incident, whose particulars she recalled for *Standard* readers, an inquest would prove that the slaves' "demoniac" fury had been "incited by brutal outrages on *their* wives or daughters."[35] Whenever she read of barbarities committed by either blacks or Indians, Child moralized, she always asked herself: "What was *their* side of the story? What long-continued, insupportable wrongs drove human nature to such frightful atrocity, such reckless desperation?" She sought to provide an answer in "Slavery's Pleasant Homes."

Child set her scene not among field slaves—a class about whom she knew little and who were too uncouth to attract the sympathies of genteel readers—but among the house slaves and wealthy owners of an elegant mansion. For details illustrating the intercourse between slaves and masters and blueprinting the household arrangements that lent themselves to sexual intrigues, she relied on the reminiscences of the fugitives she had encountered. Two in particular, "Annette Gray" and "Robert Lee," whose narratives she had published in the *Standard*, supplied her with many of the specifics responsible for the story's unusual realism.[36]

Child had probably invented the main outlines of her plot when an 1842 article about the sequestration that Southern "chivalry" imposed on the upper-class white woman caught her eye. Appearing in the *Portsmouth Journal* and reprinted by Child in the *Standard*, it portrayed Southern ladies as products of a social system that reduced them to denatured harem slaves:

> A seclusion, almost Mahommedan, is demanded of [woman] by the exactions
> of southern fashion. . . . The Odalisque of the harem is delicate as the half-
> opened petals of the rose of the East, and this is all her boast, for when this
> fragile attractiveness is faded, her whole mission in life is over. . . .
>   [T]here is apparent, upon a close observation of southern life, a species of
> lurking and secret jealousy of women—an oriental desire of confining her to
> a state of restriction and surveillance—an overweening anxiety in man to
> engross all her social as well as domestic relations to himself alone.

Shifting to another analogy, the author then compared the "boasted, yet
bastard chivalry of the South" to its medieval prototype. Under both systems
of chivalry, he (or she) asserted, woman is "regarded, in external form, as a
goddess, to be worshipped, but at the same time and in reality, as a child and
plaything, to be allowed no will of her own."[37]

The metaphors of the harem slave and the plaything must have struck Child
as peculiarly appropriate for her purposes. She knew that Southerners liked to
call slavery "the patriarchal institution" and to compare themselves with the
patriarchs of the Old Testament, whose "wives and . . . children, . . . men
servants and . . . maid servants, . . . camels and . . . cattle, were all equally
[their] property."[38] Moreover, she herself had exhaustively researched patriarchal systems in her *History of the Condition of Women, in Various Ages and
Nations* (1835), where she had noted the many cultural practices setting
women "in the light of property," equating them with slaves, subjecting them
to male tyranny, and defining them as sexual objects.[39] Thus she greeted the
Portsmouth Journal's analysis of Southern gender relations with a shock of
recognition. Developing the metaphors of the harem slave and the plaything
into central conceits of her story, she used them to explore the connections
between slavery and patriarchy and to expose slavery's desecration of the
home.

Solidly grounded in Child's twin studies of slavery and the status of
women, based on actual incidents reported in the press or recounted by
slaves, elaborating on metaphors popularized by Romantic literature, and
addressed to the women readers of gift-book fiction, "Slavery's Pleasant
Homes" brilliantly counterpoints fact and fiction as it attempts to re-create
the slave's "side of the story." Its technical virtuosity instantly strikes a modern reader. From the outset, the interplay between the title "Slavery's Pleasant Homes" and the subtitle "A Faithful Sketch" suggests a conflict between
rival literary modes—romance and realism.[40] Readers who want romance, it
hints with self-conscious irony, had better beware of looking for it in a
plantation setting. The deflation of romantic stereotype begins in the very
first sentence:

> When Frederic Dalcho brought his young bride from New-Orleans to her
> Georgian home, there were great demonstrations of joy among the slaves of
> the establishment,—dancing, shouting, clapping of hands, and eager invoca-
> tions of blessing on the heads of "massa and missis"; for well they knew that
> he who manifested most zeal was likely to get the largest coin, or the brightest
> handkerchief.[41]

Immediately afterward, Child introduces the metaphor that defines the plantation not as a Christian home, but as an Islamic seraglio. The bride, she observes, borrowing the language of the *Portsmouth Journal*, "had been nurtured
in seclusion, almost as deep as that of the oriental harem" (148). Through this
metaphor, Child establishes a parallel between Frederic Dalcho's bride Marion
and her slave foster sister Rosa. Both occupy the position of harem slaves to
whom Frederick will claim exclusive sexual access in the tradition of the Oriental despot.

Having intimated that slavery turns the home into a harem, Child proceeds to
examine the resulting perversions of domestic relationships. Marion and Rosa
have "grown up from infancy together," suckled by the same mother, yet
Marion's consciousness of her superior rank warps the affection she feels for
her foster sister: as "soon as the little white lady could speak, she learned to call
Rosa *her* slave" (148). Raised to be nothing more than a "pretty little waxen
plaything," Marion in turn treats Rosa as a plaything, decorating her with
jewels like a doll. Both women suffer diminishment, but of the two, Rosa
suffers more, for nature has actually endowed her with greater beauty and
vitality. Recalling the odalisque to whom the *Portsmouth Journal* had compared
the Southern lady, Marion is "as fragile and as delicate as the white Petunia
blossom." In contrast, Rosa is "beautiful as a dark velvet carnation"—a longer-
lasting and hardier flower. "[L]ike a glittering star," capable of generating its
own light and heat, Rosa has been set "in attendance upon the pale and almost
vanishing moonsickle," whose feeble rays merely reflect the light of the sun.[42]

The violation of nature is equally flagrant in the case of Frederic and his
"handsome quadroon brother . . . and . . . favorite slave," George. As
George remarks bitterly, "[W]e grew up side by side, children of the same
father; but I am his slave. Handsomer, stronger, and more intelligent than he;
yet I am his *slave*" (149, 156).

Reflected in the distorted sibling relationships is the sexual license of the
harem. Inevitably, the marriage of Marion and Frederic will follow the pattern
long since set by Frederic's father, when he indulged in a liaison with a slave
and reared her son alongside his wife's. As if to heighten the difference
between natural and perverted sexual relations, Child makes the unfolding
love between Rosa and George arouse Frederic's lust. The scene pulsates with
dramatic intensity:

> [Rosa] wore about her neck a small heart and cross of gold, which her lover
> had given her the night before. He smiled archly, as he glanced at it, and the
> answer from her large, dark eyes was full of joyful tenderness. Unfortunately,
> the master looked up at that moment, and at once comprehended the signifi-
> cance of that beaming expression. He saw that it spoke whole volumes of
> mutual, happy love; and it kindled in him an unholy fire. He had never
> before realized that the girl was so very handsome. . . . [H]e glanced at his
> young wife. She, too, was certainly very lovely; but the rich, mantling beauty
> of the slave had the charm of novelty. (150–51)

Of course few slaves could have afforded gold ornaments. But by drawing on
romantic convention and depicting Rosa and George in an attitude familiar to

genteel readers, Child is enabling those readers to identify with slaves. The gift itself, moreover—a heart and cross of gold—serves to foreshadow the outcome of the young slaves' love and to symbolize the brute reality beneath the gilded surface of their lives. Their hearts are indeed destined to be cruci-fied in a manner that will shock readers out of their romantic fantasies.

For Rosa and George, a natural expression of "mutual, happy love" finds an unnatural consummation which spells out the meaning of slavery and patriarchy. Pursued by her master, Rosa cannot rely for protection on either her lover or her mistress. George is but a slave, and a revelation that would raise a "storm" in his "proud and fiery" heart would only endanger them both. As for Marion, her own helplessness soon becomes apparent. Noticing her husband's "singularly capricious and severe" treatment of George, she tries to "remonstrate with him," and to learn why he opposes the lovers' marriage; her experience parallels Fanny Kemble's, however—the intercession merely subjects her to a sharp retort that leaves her in tears. At last, events reach their inescapable climax: "One night, Marion was awakened by the closing of the door, and found that Frederic was absent. She heard voices in Rosa's apartment, and the painful truth flashed upon her. Poor young wife, what a bitter hour was that!" (152).

Child's staging of the scene faithfully reproduces the details recounted to her by "Annette Gray" and "Robert Lee," both of whom had described the master's habitual midnight visits to the chambermaid as "distinctly audible" to his wife, as well as to the attendants who slept on the floor of her room.[43] She also patterns the ensuing confrontation between Rosa and Marion on Gray's narrative. Like Gray, who "could not look [her] mistress in the eye" after such visits and "never could help hanging [her] head for shame," Rosa avoids "looking in [Marion's] face, and [keeps] her eyes fixed on the ground." And like Gray's mistress, who was sometimes "violently cross, and scolded me for every thing," but would then try to "make up" for her outbursts, Marion "an-grily" accuses Rosa of "awkwardness" and gives her a "blow," but soon melts into tears, and the two end up weeping in each other's arms (153). If Child follows Gray's narrative in muting the usual consequences of the slave mis-tress's impotence to control her husband's promiscuity—the redirection to-ward her slave of the jealous rage she could not direct toward her husband— she allows no illusions about the Southern mistress's ability or willingness to break the silence that legitimizes the slave system's sexual duplicity and vio-lence.[44] Neither woman, she comments pointedly, "sought any further to learn the other's secrets" (153). After this scene, Marion all but disappears from the story.

Meanwhile, her husband unleashes against Rosa the full fury of his own jealousy. "[E]xasperated . . . beyond endurance" by Rosa's manifest prefer-ence for George, whom she continues to meet secretly in defiance of their master's orders, Frederic swears to "overcome her obstinacy, or kill her": "[O]ne severe flogging succeeded another, till the tenderly-nurtured slave fainted under the cruel infliction, which was rendered doubly dangerous by the delicate state of her health. Maternal pains came on prematurely, and she died a few hours after" (155). The feat Child achieves in this passage is remarkable. With exquisite rhetorical tact she succeeds in evoking a scene whose every element is unmentionable in polite society: a husband's rape of his wife's foster sister; a gentleman's sadistic flogging of a "tenderly-nurtured" woman; a pregnancy resulting from illicit sex; a miscarriage induced by violence.[45]

Adding another dimension to the pattern of disrupted domestic relations that Child exposes in "Slavery's Pleasant Homes" is the connivance of a mulatto slave named Mars, who spies on Rosa and George and informs the master of their stolen interviews. On one level, Mars appears to be a projection of the master, since he too lusts after Rosa and derives his power to injure her from the institution that governs their lives. His name, of course, symbolizes the essence of slavery—war. In this connection, it is noteworthy that Mars originally belonged to Marion rather than to Frederic. Once again, Child refuses to exonerate Marion from responsibility for Rosa's death, or to condone the view that slavery might be tolerable under a kind master or mistress. The god of war, she implies, presides over all forms of slavery alike. On another level, however, Mars represents the fate of human brotherhood under slavery. Just as slavery has falsified the actual sibling relationships between George and Frederic, Rosa and Marion, so it has eroded the potential solidarity of the slaves themselves.

The final phase of "Slavery's Pleasant Homes"—and the most daring for a woman writer—shifts the focus from Rosa's victimization to George's revenge. Here Child's devastating indictment of slavery and patriarchy culminates in the justification of slave revolt. The passage setting the scene for George's retaliation against his master reiterates the motif of violated nature that runs through the story: "But a few months ago, how beautiful and bright was Nature—and now, how inexpressibly gloomy" (156). From this survey of the landscape, George's train of thought, as he stands over Rosa's grave, moves into recollections of the graceful girl whose lacerated body now lies "cold and dead beneath his feet." Significantly, Child leaves unformulated the thought that climaxes this series of associations when George looks toward his master's house and groans, "He murdered my poor Rosa" (157).

Instead, she presents George's ensuing murder of Frederic through Marion's sleeping consciousness:

> On that night, Marion's sleep was disturbed and fitful. The memory of her foster-sister mingled darkly with all her dreams. Was that a shriek she heard? It was fearfully shrill in the night-silence! Half sleeping and half waking, she called wildly, "Rosa! Rosa!" But a moment after, she remembered that Rosa's light step would never again come at her call. (157)

A tour de force, this technique fuses George's murder of Frederic with Frederic's prior murder of Rosa. The effect is to emphasize that the true criminals are Rosa's master and mistress. Symbolically, the dagger found in Frederic's heart when Marion awakens from her troubled sleep turns out to be "the one he had himself been accustomed to wear" (158). The slaveholder's violence, Child shows, has come home to him.

Child does more than exculpate George—she portrays him as a hero. Like his prototypes in the Santa Cruz case, George nobly confesses to the murder, rather than let another man pay for the crime he himself has committed—even though that man is his enemy Mars. Going beyond her source, Child underscores the contrast between George's generosity and the slaveholder's vindictiveness, between George's innate sense of justice and the injustice of a legal system that convicts a slave "with slaveholders for judges and jurors" (158). Whereas George cannot look on unmoved as his enemy is brought forward to be hanged, "[p]lanters rode miles to witness the execution, and stood glaring at their trembling victim, with the fierceness of tigers" (159). Whereas George has compassion for the man whose talebearing has led to Rosa's murder, slaveholders have none for the slave whose wife the master has raped and flogged to death. Echoing Garrison's editorial on the Santa Cruz case, Child comments: "No voice praised [George] for the generous confession. They kicked and cursed him; and hung up, like a dog or a wolf, a man of nobler soul than any of them all" (160).

Child's finest stroke is to end her story by juxtaposing fact and fiction—a technique Melville would later use in "Benito Cereno" and *Billy Budd*.[46] Representing what conventionally passes for fact are newspaper accounts of the story Child has just told. "*Fiend-like Murder,*" announces the headline in the Georgian papers. The article reads: "Frederic Dalcho, one of our most wealthy and respected citizens, was robbed and murdered last week, by one of his slaves. The black demon was caught and hung; and hanging was too good for him" (160). With barbed irony, Child notes that "[t]he Northern papers copied this version; merely adding, 'These are the black-hearted monsters, which abolition philanthropy would let loose upon our brethren of the South.' " The role of the Northern press, as she knew all too well, was not to provide a different perspective on slavery, based on independent investigation, but to subserve the interests of slaveholders and the merchants, bankers, and textile manufacturers constituting their Northern allies.

Child leaves to her readers the task of picking out the obvious discrepancies in these accounts—the implication that the same slave was responsible for both the robbery and the murder, and the assertion that the culprit was "caught." She even lets readers decide for themselves whether the term "fiend-like murder" applies better to Rosa's or to Frederic's murder. She simply reminds them of the crucial facts the newspapers have omitted: "Not one was found to tell how the slave's young wife had been torn from him by his own brother, and murdered with slow tortures. Not one recorded the heroism that would not purchase life by another's death, though the victim was his enemy. His very *name* was left unmentioned; he was only Mr. Dalcho's *slave!*" (160). Through such omissions, Child suggests, the pro-slavery press has succeeded in turning a victim into a criminal, a hero into a monster, a man into a thing.

Thus, having begun by puncturing the illusions of romantic fiction, "Slavery's Pleasant Homes" ironically closes by laying bare the mendacity of factual reportage. In the hands of the master class, both prove equally unreliable as media for transcribing what Child had called the slave's "side of the story." It is doubly appropriate that the story should come back full circle to the question of fiction versus fact, for that was the central question Child faced as an antislavery propagandist. She had tested the limits of the two modes available to her for arousing public sentiment against slavery and had found neither adequate. Tracts, eyewitness testimony, slave narratives, and antislavery newspapers provided a far more accurate view of life under slavery than romantic fiction could pretend to, yet readers first had to be induced to purchase them. And Child, like Caroline Healey Dall, knew that most readers "would tear the pages out of the fair volume" sooner than have their sensibilities harrowed by graphic accounts of "indecencies" and "villainies" that "woman dare not name."[47]

In "Slavery's Pleasant Homes" Child had sought to buttress fiction with the authenticity of fact and to charge fact with the emotional power of fiction. She had also sought to circumvent the objections of "delicate-nerved, ladies" and censorious gentlemen by coding her description of Rosa's rape and flogging.[48] In parallel fashion, when editing Harriet A. Jacobs' *Incidents in the Life of a Slave Girl* seventeen years later, she would "put the savage cruelties into one chapter, entitled 'Neighboring Planters,' in order that those who shrink from 'supping upon horrors,' might omit them, without interrupping [*sic*] the thread of the story."[49] As the publishing histories of both works indicate, however, such expedients were doomed to failure. No amount of rhetorical tact could have made a story that portrayed the slaveholding elite so starkly— much less one that justified a slave's murder of his master—acceptable to readers of the class antislavery fiction sought to reach. Its penetrating insights into the interlocking systems of racial and sexual oppression that turned the home into a harem, and its ardent championship of the slave's right to rebel, condemned Child's masterpiece to burial in a coterie publication. She herself apparently drew the same conclusion. Accordingly, when she reissued her antislavery stories in her commercially published collection of miscellaneous writings, *Fact and Fiction* (1846), she left out "Slavery's Pleasant Homes." As late as 1861, the difficulties Child encountered in getting *Incidents in the Life of a Slave Girl* "into the market" indirectly confirmed her assessment of what a genteel audience and literary establishment would tolerate; despite the phenomenal popularity of Harriet Beecher Stowe's *Uncle Tom's Cabin* (1852), Child still found Boston booksellers and publishers "dreadfully afraid of soiling their hands with an Anti-Slavery book."[50]

By then Child's earlier story for *The Liberty Bell,* "The Quadroons" (1842), had long since set the pattern for women's antislavery fiction, the literary formula it supplied having proved more effective than any other in mobilizing public opinion against slavery. As Child had wryly predicted, her pathetic tale of victimized racial outcasts had captured the sympathies of readers who wanted romance, not dreary fact. Yet its very success had once again shown how utterly the contradictions of antislavery fiction defied resolution. Without dangerous concessions to the prejudices of its intended audience, the genre could not arouse compassion for the slaves; with those concessions, it inevitably perpetuated an ideology relegating people of color and white women to subordinate status.

The archetype of the tragic mulatto, which Child introduced into American literature, made it possible to dramatize the sexual plight of the slave woman in terms that appealed to a genteel audience. The breakthrough this signified is obvious from the long line of works "The Quadroons" inspired, beginning with *Uncle Tom's Cabin* and William Wells Brown's *Clotel* (1853).[51] As a vehicle for protesting against racism, however—and as an instrument for probing the connections between white supremacy and male dominance—the archetype proved highly ambiguous. True, it granted a portion of black women "the right to be 'ladies,' " and portrayed them as "partaking with grace and virtue in the life typically reserved" for upper-class white women.[52] The tragic mulatto archetype also had the potential for challenging the concept of race on a more fundamental level, since a heroine who could pass for white embodied the absurdity of racial classifications. In the long run, nevertheless, the use of the genteel near-white heroine to personify the wrongs of slavery reinforced the very prejudices antislavery fiction sought to counteract. Hardly representative of the field hands who constituted the vast majority of the slave population, the tragic mulatto could not promote the vision needed to address their problems after emancipation. Nor could a figure approximating white standards of beauty and upper-class notions of refinement foster a taste for cultural diversity. Far from encouraging the development of alternative cultural ideals, the archetype of the tragic mulatto, whose tinge of black blood barred her from marrying the white gentleman she loved, implicitly condemned blacks to pursue the hopelessly elusive goal of becoming white. The legacy of "The Quadroons" continues to haunt the culture that could not face the truths encoded in "Slavery's Pleasant Homes."

4

Sentimental Figures:
Reading *Godey's Lady's Book*
in Antebellum America

Isabelle Lehuu

Even though the sentimental stories of *Godey's Lady's Book* have long been forgotten since their heyday in the nineteenth century, the watercolored steel engravings of *Godey's* ladies have survived the wear of time and are carefully cherished by today's collectors. Interestingly, the late twentieth-century taste values the same hand-colored prints which were often torn from women's magazines to decorate homes of antebellum America. Such a legacy suggests the importance of the visual texts both with and without the original verbal texts. Steel-engraved ladies were an intrinsic component and a major commercial feature of nineteenth-century periodicals. Yet scholars have repeatedly neglected them and considered them almost as an anomaly in the narrative of historical progress. As one historian concluded, the fashion engraving represented "a particular wrinkle of early American civilization."[1] It is therefore the central project of this chapter to finally recognize the historical validity of *Godey's* visual representations of gender and to assess their cultural significance in antebellum America.

The ladies of Louis Antoine Godey's magazine, more than the features of other periodicals, illuminate the construction of femininity in antebellum printed material. First published in 1830, the famous Philadelphia monthly magazine continued uninterrupted for over sixty years. Few books about pre–Civil War culture have failed to mention *Godey's* as the epitome of sentimental literature and frivolous taste. Scholars have sometimes cited the magazine's ornaments as part of the style and economic astuteness of women's periodicals. However, most studies have focused on the literary contributions by Edgar Allen Poe, Nathaniel Hawthorne, Ralph Waldo Emerson, Harriet Beecher Stowe, Lydia H. Sigourney, and Catherine M. Sedgwick, among others, as a way of redeeming the triviality of the fashion magazine. More recently, feminist scholars have been concerned with legitimizing sentimental literature and reassessing the protofeminist functions of lachrymose stories for women readers. They have emphasized the role of Sarah Josepha Hale, crusader for female education and editor of *Godey's Lady's Book* from 1837 to 1877. But feminist critics too have chosen to ignore the frivolous ornaments apparently at odds with republican simplicity and the "matriarchy of the kitchen." In their accounts, nineteenth-century magazines were designed for readers, not viewers. Consequently, the visual and frivolous aspects of fashion and pictorial embellishments have rarely been deemed worth mentioning.[2]

The cultural centrality of a ladies' magazine with a national distribution that claimed 150,000 subscribers by the time of the Civil War deserves further attention. *Godey's* icons of femininity and ladyhood also belong to a reexamination of nineteenth-century American culture, because they point to the distinctive character of women's textual emergence. However, the visual texts of the magazine represent not only an additional object of textual inquiry but also a window onto a rereading of nineteenth-century sentimentality and its internal tensions and instabilities.[3]

Godey's Lady Book regularly claimed in its editorials and advertisements to be "literary and pictorial," "useful and entertaining." Therefore this chapter inquires into the complex relationship of images to texts and explores how illustrations both underwrote and undermined the sentimental message of *Godey's* stories and editorials. In addition, the introduction of pictorial texts in a broader discussion of sentimentality offers a way to transcend the ongoing debate between the antisentimentalist critics and the revisionists. Ann Douglas has reiterated the value judgment of nineteenth-century cultural arbiters, seeing sentimental literature not only as a lesser genre, but as a corrupting means of self-indulgence and an epitome of consumerism.[4] At the same time, Douglas's critique of a feminine and mass culture provoked a revisionist approach to sentimental novels. Jane Tompkins, in particular, has convincingly deciphered the "world-shaking" designs of novelists and the empowerment of their readers embodied in popular novels of the nineteenth century.[5] Nonetheless, revisionists have been limited to the private work of popular literature, and skeptical historians still wonder about the success of sentimental power beyond the private realm. In this chapter I argue that the transformative force of popular literature was a public event. Middle-class female readers were not merely passive consumers of sentimental periodicals but rather played an active role in the transformation of American culture.[6] Nineteenth-century reading of sentimental literature led not only to the construction of meaning in individual lives but also to the public transformation of American print culture.

In opposition to Douglas, I argue that women in antebellum America achieved significant cultural gains. They introduced a popular and feminine aesthetic, and forced the traditional print culture to make a space for woman's voice, even if that space was conceived as a "separate sphere." They publicly altered antebellum culture, while contributing to its stratification and categorizing. The antebellum "feminization" of a branch of the periodical press reflected the specificity of its targeted audience, while enforcing the division of gender through the production of separate texts.[7] The nineteenth-century visual and textual representation of women was both progressive and restrictive. The early American republic witnessed the production of publications especially designed for women, while confining them within the boundaries of a feminine aesthetic. Ultimately, even though the formula of ladies' magazines publishing fashion plates as a way to catch the female subscription retained the stigma of popular printed matter, illustrations altogether were increasingly accepted in the world of publishing in the decades preceding the Civil War. In this respect, the white middle-class women readers of *Godey's Lady's Book* contributed to a major change in American culture.

A close analysis of *Godey's* engravings will illustrate the cultural meaning of sentimental figures in antebellum America. For this purpose *Godey's* engravings are considered not so much as direct representations of nineteenth-century white middle-class women's image of themselves, but rather as texts that the reader-viewers were appropriating, enjoying, and approving. It may seem obvious to us that a magazine targeting a female audience would offer fashion plates. However, a careful reading of *Godey's Lady's Book* reveals the historicity of the hand-colored steel engravings that featured duos and quartets of ladies.

The Coming of *Godey's*

To be sure, *Godey's Lady's Book* was not the first illustrated magazine for women. Colored fashion plates had been published in *La Gallerie des modes* in Paris from 1778 to 1787, and several English ladies' magazines of the late-eighteenth century featured discussions of fashion and sometimes a fashion plate next to the literature. The early American republic followed the example of the mother country and witnessed the production of periodical publications specially designed for the "fair sex," in contrast to the absence of women's subjects in newspapers. Even monthly repositories of polite literature such as the Boston *Miscellany* and the Boston *Atheneum, or Spirit of the British Magazines* hoped to increase their circulation by attracting women. Nonetheless, few American magazines imitated English ladies' magazines in publishing a fashion plate as part of a market strategy. For instance, the Philadelphia *Ladies' Magazine and Repertory of Entertaining Knowledge,* which appeared from 1792 to 1793, copied large portions of the London *Lady's Magazine* but apparently lacked money "for such additions as the engravings, patterns, and pages of music" especially attractive to subscribers.[8] Not until the 1820s and 1830s did fashion make an appearance in American magazines for ladies, as though prejudice against fashion was the result of the emancipation of the young and virtuous republic from the influence of corrupt Europe. The first American periodical for women which issued a colored fashion plate was the Philadelphia *Album and Ladies' Weekly Gazette* in June 1827. Its editor, Thomas C. Clarke, also founded the *Ladies' Literary Port Folio* in 1828 with the same attraction of a fashion plate.[9] But soon afterward *Godey's* achieved preeminence with colored fashions and other embellishments. While offering a symbiosis between traditional European fashion publications and American gift books of the late 1820s, *Godey's* set the pattern for a definite genre of magazines soon to be replicated. And *Godey's* success was so persuasive that steel-engraved ladies became a significant feature of the pre–Civil War years.[10]

It is worth noticing that the commercial use of fashion plates was controversial. For the first seven years of its existence, *Godey's* made the fashion engraving and the discussion of fashion a priority. However, when the conservative reformer Sarah J. Hale took charge of *Godey's* editorship in 1837, she vehemently condemned fashion and only reluctantly retained the magazine's famous fashion plates for the sake of the public. Hale had already confronted the question of fashion plates in her own Boston publication, the *Ladies Magazine,* before merging with *Godey's.* She had criticized the display of fashion as a symbol of extravagance and European luxury ever since her publishing beginnings in 1828. Nonetheless, she was forced to compromise with the public's demand because of economic necessity and finally introduced a fashion plate in the November 1830 issue of the *Ladies Magazine.* When she gave up the use of fashion plates for good in 1834, her *Ladies Magazine* simultaneously declined in popularity just at the time of fierce competition in the publishing world.[11]

In effect, even though editors and publishers produced the magazines, they had to reckon with the readers' aesthetic dictates, which made images central to the economy—including production and consumption—of antebellum feminized print culture. While the public's demand was a major force of production, the dissemination of engravings in books and magazines was due in part to the technology available for the reproduction of images by the second quarter of the nineteenth century. Cheaper than copperplates but much finer than woodcut, steel allowed an intensive reproduction of illustrations. It satisfied both the public and the publishers, who aimed at a profit through mass production and lowering of the item price. However, since the steel-engraving plate needed to be printed separately from the text, it was more expensive than a woodcut. The golden age of steel engraving from 1825 to 1845 has been described as the successful period of illustrated publishing for the middle classes, who were particularly fond of "semiluxurious" illustrated books.[12] And *Godey's Lady's Book* was both a product and an agent of that publishing golden age. Yet the experience of *Godey's* contained its own specificity because of the size of its reading public, the duration of its popularity, and the context of American culture that emphasized republican simplicity versus European luxury and elitism.

Interestingly, *Godey's* fashion plates were admired and appropriated by the magazines' subscribers, even though they were juxtaposed to and controlled by stories containing the dress reformers' message, which championed sincerity and condemned the hypocrisy of fashion. Nineteenth-century women readers were probably interested in the fashion of dress exhibited in *Godey's,* but their satisfaction resulted primarily from the portrayal of women in full-page watercolored engravings. The issue, then, is not so much about the character of fashion and its progressive acceptance in American society as about female imaging. Accordingly, the style of the fashion represented in print is historically less important than the very fact that women were represented in print. Dresses, hats, and petticoats did matter for *Godey's* readers, but the analysis of their printed debuts goes beyond mere testimony of dimity and fashion. The publication of feminine and sentimental figures in *Godey's Lady's Book* testifies to the contribution of the reading public in the construction of sentimental culture.[13]

Nineteenth-century readers were buying a synthesis of pictures and narratives when they subscribed to *Godey's*. Potential conflict was embedded in the juxtaposition of visual and verbal texts. For *Godey's* was a composite text in which images were controlled by words and assimilated into the discourse of sentimentality, while possibly undermining the authority of the text and allowing autonomous readings.[14] Images gave a specific character and added value to the magazine. However, while the fashion engravings were as important as, or even more important than, the editorials, in terms of commercial strategy and readers' pleasure, they were integrated into the magazine and assumed the power of the printed word. For instance, images were "telling stories," and fashion plates represented as conversation pictures when labeled with captions such as "it is a secret."[15] Images were reminiscent of a time of oral and visual communication. Such elements of a residual culture long undermined by textualization were incompletely incorporated into print culture.[16] Under a cover of harmony with the written word, images were subversive. They challenged the legitimate culture without representing an alternative culture per se, for they had acknowledged the power of the word. In turn, the written word attempted to dominate images which, once controlled, could serve the instructive function of print. *Godey's* is a vivid example of such a strategy.

Godey's Ladies

Godey's Lady's Book published twelve issues a year. From about 48 pages in the 1830s and early 1840s to about 60 pages in the late 1840s and over 92 pages in the 1850s, with some issues up to 120 pages, the "Book"—to use *Godey's* self–reference—changed shape over time. Any change was presented as an improvement by the editors. With the increase in size, some new features were introduced. The magazine of the 1830s was essentially made up of stories, poems, musical composition, fashion intelligence, and a hand-colored fashion plate every three months. Additional departments were introduced in the 1840s, such as a ladies' work department or health and beauty advice. Woodcuts of needlework, crochet, and hair design increasingly appeared within the text. The constant policy of the magazine was to augment the number of pictorial embellishments at the same rate as the number of pages. In the 1850s *Godey's* doubled its size, and advertisements on back covers emphasized the "immense increase of reading matter without reducing the number of full page steel engravings."[17] Such a strategy is easily explained: illustrations were profitable. Louis Godey told his readers that the illustrations constituted the main expense of the magazine: he could run the magazine at lower cost without the "embellishments." But he would generously continue to satisfy the reader's demand for visual texts. In fact, such a big investment resulted in a secure profit from subscriptions. Therefore, from the very first years of its publication, *Godey's* advertised the quality of the plates and the number of engravings per issue rather than the quality of its literature.

Throughout its existence *Godey's* most distinctive feature was the watercolored fashion plate. The fashion plates were watercolored at home or in the shop by women hired specifically for the purpose. Watercoloring had traditionally been an essential feminine accomplishment.[18] At the same time it seems particularly ironic that the emergence of a female identity in print was made possible by use of cheap female labor at the protoindustrial level. At one point Louis Godey had 150 employees for hand-coloring alone. He informed his readers that "the mere coloring of the prints cost us nearly three thousand dollars per annum."[19] *Godey's* sometimes experimented with other techniques. For example, the first mezzotint fashion plate was published in February 1847. But in general the pattern was set by hand-colored steel engravings of ladies. In sum, the production of *Godey's* plates reflected a historical moment of manual reproduction, one of protoindustry within traditional settings that resisted the shift toward mechanical reproduction already taking place in the printing industry. *Godey's* images retained the unique aura of artisanal labor in the face of commodity production. The female workers of the magazine used another color for a dress when the first ran out, leading sometimes to readers' complaints about the discrepancy between one woman's fashion plate and her neighbor's. The publisher ingeniously justified the variety by arguing for the uniqueness of a lady's complexion and denied mass production: "we now colour our plates to different patterns, so that two persons in a place may compare their fashions, and adopt those colours that they suppose may be most suitable to their figures and complexions."[20] Undoubtedly, the fate of the "Book" was attached to its embellishments, and its success seemed to vanish once its illustrations appeared old-fashioned. After the Civil War, illustrations became essential to most magazines, and *Godey's* vaunted "steel against wood" as proof of luxury and a strategy for survival. However, *Godey's* began to look provincial, and by the late 1880s half-tone electrotypes supplanted the historic *Godey's* engravings.[21]

During its antebellum heyday, *Godey's* displayed fashion engravings in addition to a variety of illustrations recycled from contemporary gift books such as engravings of landscapes, genre paintings, and religious scenes. The fashion plates were not only more valuable but also technically different. They seemed unfinished, more like drawings without volume and body, projections waiting for a finish and color, or just suggestions, models, or prepared canvas awaiting women's own construction of meaning. This should not be surprising, given the specificity of female education, which had long stressed intuitive and emotional qualities at the expense of mental capacities. In contrast, the functional curriculum of female academies in the early republic had little room for an ornamental education, which had traditionally emphasized the "elegant accomplishments" such as drawing and embroidery as a badge of upper-class status. Yet middle-class reformers who promoted functional education for wifehood and motherhood failed to eradicate such decorative accomplishments and could only incorporate them in their moral reform for female improvement.[22] Drawing was based on the skill of reproduction rather than creation. And education in drawing seemed particularly appropriate for working women—supposedly well adapted by nature to the manufacture of articles of taste and fancy—and a safe path away from vice and misery. As one teacher of drawing put it, "the natural refinement and delicacy of the female mind renders it a fruitful soil, that should not be neglected or let run to waste, when its cultivation might realize such rich advantages, not only to themselves, but to their country." The advantages of education in drawing for girls became essential and second only to the formation of religious principles.[23]

Godey's hallmark, the fashion plate, represented ladies rather than just costumes and dresses. The costumed figures were posing against a decorated background, indoors or outdoors, with furniture, wallpaper, and drapery fabrics. The fashion plate itself was a decor for parlor theatricals and intimate staging. Whether standing or sitting, the ladies of *Godey's* engravings kept the same empty expression on their faces. The mouth was closed; the eyes looked down or at another lady. The engraving was a distant spectacle offered to reader-viewers. In contrast to portraits, *Godey's* ladies did not pay attention to the spectator; they looked at each other and were involved in their closed society or separate sphere. In addition to the direction of the eyes, the orientation of the ladies' heads was interesting. *Godey's* ladies held their heads quite artificially, like a sort of mask, as if heads were accessories like hats. They were not supposed to represent the source of female energy, for women's movements were directed not by intellect but by sentiment. More significant were the gentle, clean hands of *Godey's* ladies. They suggested pseudodialogues in the fashion plates. They were directed to other figures, or held objects, most likely flowers or handkerchiefs, but often books or engravings—presumably from *Godey's Lady's Book* (Fig. 4.1). The world of *Godey's* re-presented the "civilization of the hand" as opposed to the machine.[24] The fireplace or home was women's sphere, and presented a haven separate from industry and social evil. *Godey's* fashion plates conformed with the nineteenth-century cult of true womanhood. In addition, the gentle white hand holding an object was a symbol of leisure and property. *Godey's* pictured a world of objects to be possessed and appropriated, and in so doing defined itself as another object in middle-class interiors.[25]

Unlike other objects, however, *Godey's* ladies engendered a new vernacular. Words and images complemented each other and made a whole, an imaginary speaking body. The publication of fashion engravings reconstructed in print an alliance between gesture and voice, simulating an oral performance. And color, the visible component of pictorial signs, gave the fashion plate its "flesh and body."[26] Feminine writing could not exclude feminine imagery,

Fig. 4.1. (July 1845). Godey's steel-engraved ladies, viewing a copy of the fashion magazine, reaffirm the cult of true womanhood. (Courtesy of Olin Library, Cornell University.)

which already incorporated a male-dominated discourse about the female body. While male writing did not presuppose the juxtaposition of pictorial representation of his body, female literary culture was compelled to incorporate images of her physical self. Because of the social sanction against women's speech and writing, silent and gestural women used images in their *prise de parole*. Women as "tongue snatchers" took the word and molded it to their image and likeness, while implicitly surrendering to a female-as-object discourse.[27]

In *Godey's* engravings the details of dress were second to the decor, the situation, the pose. A fashion plate entitled "Taking Tea in the Arbor" was a staged representation of a private scene. The "description of the plate," which had been included in the first article during the early years of the magazine, was moved to the last pages of the issue soon after Sarah J. Hale became the editor. Hale's conservative feminism failed to rid the magazine of its fashion images; but at least frivolous discussions of fashion were relegated to the editor's table, therefore isolating the engraved figures and private scenes from their promptbook. Only the curious reader would discover that one figure was wearing a "morning-dress of white cambric, of exquisite quality, the skirt trimmed with double rows of muslin puffing," while the other had a "walking-dress of rich jasper silk."[28] For most reader-viewers, however, the specificity of the fashion matter was probably less important than the theatricality of the scenes in *Godey's* plates.

The theatricality of social relationships was newly accepted in the late 1840s and 1850s. Parlor theatricals reflected the social representation of middle-class gentility.[29] Similarly, *Godey's* staged theatrical performance directly on the page for its readers. The "Book" was an ersatz of theater for a large audience, and *Godey's* theatrical prints curiously recalled a long tradition of books of theater. The visual effect of theater was communicated through the numerous illustrations of the major scenes of the play. The argument of the engraving as a two-dimensional theatrical stage was confirmed by its presentation through a medallion, which re-created the environment of a theater and projected the stage in the back, while it simulated the intimacy of a performance for the solitary reader.[30] The fashion engraving was conceived as the theatrical exhibition of a domestic scene in which the space was similar to the parlor in nineteenth-century middle-class homes, between the private rooms and the public street. Meanwhile the description was that of a performance, as indicated by a commentary: "apart from its interest as a faithful report of fashion, in the arrangement of the scene and its actors, our artist has displayed unusual good taste."[31]

The fashion plate also standardized female duos and quartets. The repetitious representation of almost identical ladies, like a species, was a pictorial reconstitution of the "sisterhood" of middle-class women.[32] They participated in intimate relationships, sharing secrets or chitchat about fashion. Furthermore, the sequence of repetitive images created a cinematic montage, generating meanings independent from the editorials or adjoining stories. *Godey's* figures thus offered a potential autonomy from the letters. The reader-viewer was then allowed to interact with the freed visual texts, contemplating them silently as icons of a private and domestic religion. At the same time, the visual representation of gender provided all its readers with a shared experience and served as a blueprint for the formation of a group consciousness.

Nevertheless, not all American women had the opportunity to appear in the new print culture. Feminine print culture was molded to the likeness of ladies, not to the likeness of mill girls. The mill girl was not given a voice in the cultural formation of antebellum America; she had to embrace the views of the ladies, whose portrayal appeared in a dream world. Even though the ideology of domesticity was not alien to working women, *Godey's Lady's Book* was designed as a magazine for ladies and claimed the respectability of its audience. Both the style of the stories and the engravings emphasized an air of gentility, with "taste and refinement."[33] To be sure, the magazine also delighted working-class readers. The factory operatives of the Lowell mills, who are often cited by historians for their compliance with the moral values and paternalism of their employers, preferred amusement and entertainment to serious lectures. As their militant publication, *Voice of Industry,* suggested, "the trashy, milk-and-water sentimentalities of the *Lady's Book* and *Olive Branch,* are more read than the works of Gibbon, or Goldsmith, or Bancroft."[34] Certainly, working women were appropriating a magazine which originally targeted leisured women, and in so doing they subordinated class to gender formation.

Godey's confined women within narrow boundaries while providing them with a separate medium for their voices. The female reader-viewer received a "book" of her own and became visible. The reading audience of *Godey's* contributed to the configuration of the female subject while using the language of the female object. Thus the presence of feminine images in antebellum print culture was both conformist and subversive. Even though *Godey's* justified publication of the plates in condescending terms of a traditionally different feminine taste, more sensitive and emotional than intellectual, thus acknowledging the inequality of the female ornamental stratum of literature, the ladies' separate sphere of print culture could also provide a forum for agitation. Just as nineteenth-century women's power originated in the cradle of the family circle, the religious associations, and the community of sisters, so the separate sphere of print culture represented a center of power, a platform for the voiceless, and a channel for the formation of an authentic feminine speech. The intrusion of female vernacular into print culture overlapped with the antebellum crusade for beauty and a softening of American Protestant piety, and was similarly rooted in the empowerment of white middle-class women in the decades preceding the Civil War.[35]

Crusade for Beauty

Sarah J. Hale's editorials provided the "embellishments" of a conventional female miscellany-repository with a moral and conservative frame. After compromising with the public taste for fashion plates, Hale was able to make *Godey's* a commercial success.[36] The complementarity of images and texts drove sales. The valorization of images assured the continuity of the market, while the written texts worked at the legitimation of the magazine. Images added value to the product and made it an expensive commodity. At the same time they represented a didactic means of conveying messages to women. Publishers of illustrated magazines did not admit plainly that they satisfied the public's demand for images, but used the rhetoric of the antebellum crusade for beauty and the appeal to the senses through images. The discourse surrounding the publication of pictures was not about the triviality or idolatry of beautiful images, but about the directness of pictorial messages that served the cause of beauty, piety, and morality.

Publisher and audience emphasized the beauty of the magazine, defining a sensual reading through the pleasure of visual texts. There seemed to be a conflict between the need for enlightenment through books and magazines, and the conception of reading as enjoyment. Reading as mere pleasure was scandalous and immoral.[37] It reinvoked a hedonist class, at odds with the new republic. The editors of *Godey's* were aware of opponents who described the fashion magazine as the amusement of a class, and developed various literary strategies to redeem the visual pleasure of the text. To the argument that periodical reading was leisure and entertainment—in other words, a private vice—reformers and writers cited the need to encourage female literacy and combine it with maternal instruction and public virtue.

Godey's epitomized the nineteenth-century shift from a primarily devotional to an increasingly secular literature, blurring in a single medium the sacred and the profane. And Godey probably intended such an effect by calling his magazine "The Book," often without quotation marks. *Godey's Lady's Book* was meant to be a women's Bible and could complement the large family Bible.[38] The act of reading was presented as a domestic occupation, a private or familial relationship, comforting and feminine, within the intimate space of the home. Images, in particular, were central to the spirituality of nineteenth-century Americans, and altered antebellum practices of piety. Protestantism was progressively renouncing traditional objections to images. The second quarter of the nineteenth century witnessed a definite movement in favor of the fine arts and a growing relation between art, morality, and religion. Art was regarded as a refining instrument for social improvement, and women as the special guardians of artistic riches.

During the three decades before the Civil War, Americans experienced different attitudes toward Catholicism and artistic extravagance in the expression of religious spirituality. Protestants began to consider the possibilities of painting as an appeal to religious sentiments. Belief in the uplifting aspect of aesthetic contemplation became more common, as if beauty could save an increasingly impersonal and materialistic world. The power of art was meant to soften brutish feelings.[39] To a certain extent, American Protestantism accepted as a means to piety artifacts that had been associated with alien faiths. Art also played an important role in nineteenth-century middle-class culture,

once the disestablishment of churches and the development of domestic religion made the family the center of spiritual formation. Art came to decorate
middle-class homes, while visual images were increasingly perceived as symbols and as a religious language.[40]

The issue at stake is the place of a female vernacular in the antebellum
transformation of religion and the evangelical movement. The moral crusade
for beauty was gender-specific. Art was the feminine courtesy and gentility
par excellence, the civilized versus the urban crowd and the savage beasts.
Women and art joined in a civilizing influence. In particular, the female
gentility embodied in the imagery of Mother and Child revealed both the
feminization of American religion and a softening of American Protestantism.
Antebellum Protestant piety was feminized and came to resemble a sensibility
usually associated with Catholicism.[41]

Godey's embellishments were icons for new practices of piety and allowed
contemplative reading. While not a fashion plate, one particular engraving
entitled "The Coquette" deserves our attention, for it reveals the work of
sentiment and the manipulation of pictures in addressing the fashionable. The
pictorial scene remains mysterious in itself and requires the details of the
written story. The practice of reading as the work of a detective deciphering a
message uses the power of the story for unveiling the mystery of the image.
The description holds the attention of the reader late into the text before
presenting clues to the detailed illustration (Fig. 4.2).

According to the narrative, Mrs. Morgan was a beauty but not a good wife.
As the complete opposite of "The Constant" or "true womanhood," she
preferred entertaining a society of admirers to keeping house, and she made
her husband unhappy.

> She sat alone in their own room one morning, after he had gone out, with the
> cold gray light of reality breaking round her. She had gone to a jewel box for
> some trinket, her favorite in girlhood, and had found, beneath half-forgotten
> ornaments, the miniature of her husband, his gift at their betrothal. She had
> drawn a lounging-chair to the table, in an indolent, careless mood, thinking
> to check reproachful thought in the preparation of a dress for the evening.
> Her pet spaniel was watching curiously, from her knee, an intrusive visitor
> from a neighboring apartment. The seductive languor of early spring filled
> the whole atmosphere, and sad, regretful memories came stealing over her
> with its softness.[42]

This enlightening scene led Mrs. Morgan to self-examination, humiliation,
reproach, and finally repentance. In other words, both the commentator and
the illustrator of the story are describing a conversion experience. It does not
matter whether the image or the story was produced first; the nineteenth-
century reader-viewer was in the presence of both. And one cannot avoid
seeing similarities between the miniature of Mrs. Morgan's husband and the
medallion in which she is portrayed for *Godey's* ladies. There was a play
around the power of images, the revelation and potential redemption. The
engraving could well be a religious icon, a pious object of domestic religion.

Fig. 4.2. (March 1851). Images had power to touch a woman's heart. (Courtesy of Olin Library, Cornell University.)

Reformers believed that an image provided a direct, immediate, emotional message. It was meant to touch the heart of every woman and was charged with moral power. An image carried an ideological message and could spread the spirit of domestic love and social peace. "What better lesson could a long story teach?" Pictorial texts were used by sentimental reformers as the embodiment of simplicity and spirituality.[43] *Godey's* editor and contributors recognized the primary function of the pictures as a way to attract the audience, and were aware of the secondary role that texts played in the magazine.

However, the image had almost a fetishistic character and cult value. Its sensual language represented an open door to idolatry and potential deviance from the moral crusade. The pictorial texts of antebellum women's magazines were a double-edged sword. Therefore most reformers recommended a well-controlled use of visual signs. While some reformers were ardent opponents of periodicals such as *Godey's,* the liberal ministers who competed with the feminine writers of domestic fiction for the emerging literary market shared the cultural tools of secularization. They tended to frame images into typographical constraints and reduced the polyvalence of the message by adding the printed word. They monitored and "illustrated" the images with editorial comments and titles. Figures were disciplined by words, but the efficacy of such a submission remained questionable. As visual representations multiplied in antebellum print, written discourse began to accept a new dependence upon images for conveying messages. Even the conservative Sarah J. Hale overcame her long prejudice against the display of fashion as a symbol of extravagance and luxury. Hale came to advocate the manipulation of images for the service of reformist ideas rather than the total elimination of images. The history of *Godey's,* then, reveals the victory of the commercial strategy and the adaptation of the reformist discourse to the market. Images were framed by an ideological discourse rather than burned; they were ultimately controlled and charged with discursive meaning rather than destroyed.

Fashionable Mothers

By the mid-1840s each issue of *Godey's* included about four "instructive" embellishments—religious or secular—in addition to the monthly fashion plate, miscellaneous patterns in the work department, and models of cottages.[44] However, fashion plates too increasingly depicted domestic and sentimental scenes, when the ideology of domesticity began to infiltrate all pictorial texts. Attractive watercolored engravings appeared to be an appropriate medium for moral messages. They were tableaux vivants staging motionless women in domestic scenes. For instance, the comment on the engraving "A Domestic Scene" in the August 1845 issue (Fig. 4.3) read as follows:

> Our readers will notice a striking improvement in the style of our recent fashion plates. We give, this month, the latest fashions for ladies and children, in the form of a domestic scene, which serves at once to exhibit the last

Fig. 4.3. (August 1845). "A Domestic Scene." Fashion was tailored to the ideology of domesticity and motherhood. (Courtesy of Olin Library, Cornell University.)

fancy in dress, and the most recent improvements in the form of the cradle, easy chair, foot-cushion, etc. Where fine touches of art can be thrown in "after this fashion," we hold it our duty to see that it is done.[45]

The fashionables went home instead of going to the party or the promenade. They were conforming to the cult of true womanhood. Sentimental mothers appeared to substitute for coquettes. Hence the fashion plate appeared similar to other engravings of domestic and sentimental scenes, such as the engraving entitled "Maternal Instruction" and published in the March 1845 issue in support of Sarah J. Hale's female education campaign (Fig. 4.4).[46] Sometimes domestic engravings filled the gap when the magazine had no fashion to offer. One significant case was a delicate engraving titled "Infancy" in the issue of February 1845 that best epitomized the sentimental culture of antebellum America (Fig. 4.5). "In lieu of the fashion this month we have given a coloured steel engraving—a novelty at least, be its success what it may; we can only add that it is doubly as expensive as the fashions." The sleeping infant with the black kitty was a fine illustration of domesticity and motherhood, presented as a luxury in comparison with fashion plates. However, repeated requests brought back the fashions, for the sentimental cult of domesticity with no fashion at all was less popular among subscribers than "sentimentalized" fashion.

One final point bears comment. Convincing evidence of nineteenth-century public taste consists in the many engravings that women—and perhaps men, too—tore from the issues to enhance their homes and apartments. The plates were highly valued by subscribers. For instance, *Godey's* reported a story emphasizing the prominence of its fashions; one man had "cut out the fashions lately and sold them for as much as the whole number cost him, and then had his females improved to the amount of a whole year's subscription by the interesting contents."[47] The demand for paintings and images to post on the walls of private homes was increasing in an era of commercialized goods. The possession of objects, particularly pictures with the power of representing reality and perhaps sameness, was a means of confirming status in an apparently mobile society.[48] Thus, more than Sarah J. Hale's sentimental and moralistic editorials, the steel-engraved ladies of *Godey's* made the emerging feminine press a lucrative business.

In conclusion, *Godey's Lady's Book* created a separate sphere of antebellum print culture. The magazine's visual texts were didactic. They were repetitive and set a pattern, an archetype of ladyhood. Color prints provided women readers with lessons of manners, behavior, and dress as well as entertainment. But more important, *Godey's* engravings made nineteenth-century women "visible" and outlined the female subject and the female distinctiveness in print. To be sure, *Godey's* world was a society of white middle-class Protestant women in private homes—a world that could occasionally be reappropriated by other social groups.[49] The aesthetic specificity of the magazine reflected the specialization of its reading audience and confirmed a historical moment of

Fig. 4.4. (March 1845). "Maternal Instruction." Sara J. Hale advocated female education to prepare mothers for nurturing. (Courtesy of Olin Library, Cornell University.)

social and gendered stratification. In addition, *Godey's* engravings were the publication's best selling point and allied publisher and reading public. The pictorial commodity-text was profitable to the former and pleasing to the latter.

The lessons of *Godey's* visual texts were conformist. They embodied an ideology of domesticity, maternal instruction, and the power of sentiment. Nevertheless, the use of a visible language to translate middle-class women's

Fig. 4.5. (February 1845). "Infancy." Other sentimental images occasionally took the place of fashion engravings, but Godey's *ladies remained the most popular feature of the magazine. (Courtesy of Olin Library, Cornell University.)*

existence represented in itself a resistance to the traditional authority of the printed word. Images designed as messengers of moral reform could simply be contemplated for the pleasure of *Godey's* reader-viewers. Even though the relationship of visual texts to editorials remained tense and unstable, gendered visual representations were successfully incorporated in antebellum print culture.

Ultimately, the feminization of American culture facilitated the introduction of illustrations in a great variety of nineteenth-century books and periodicals, including the Bible. This was perceived by contemporary critics as the popularization and the deprecation of culture. For instance, Emerson noted in his journal that "the Illustrations in modern books mark the decline of art. 'Tis the dramdrinking of the eye, & candy for food; as whales & horses & elephants, produced on the stage, show decline of drama."[50] Both in print and in the theater, the public constituted a major force in the transformation and stratification of American culture. While women's pictorial representations shared in the construction of sentimentality and domestic femininity, they imposed a change on American public print culture. Their contribution to a major text of nineteenth-century culture was important. Moreover, we could not understand the power of sentiment and the emergence of a feminine voice in American nineteenth-century culture if we ignored the sentimentalists' confrontation with and eventual acceptance of visual texts. Originally at odds with the ideology of republican simplicity and sentimentality, visual texts came to serve as medium and midwife for the dissemination of the culture of sentiment.

5

Bodily Bonds: The Intersecting Rhetorics of Feminism and Abolition

Karen Sánchez-Eppler

As Lydia Maria Child tells it in 1836, the story of the woman and the story of the slave are the same story:

> I have been told of a young physician who went into the far Southern states to settle, and there became in love with a very handsome and modest girl who lived in service. He married her; and about a year after the event a gentleman called at the house and announced himself as Mr. J. of Mobile. He said to Dr. W., "Sir, I have a trifling affair of business to settle with you. You have married a slave of mine." The young physician resented the language; for he had not entertained the slightest suspicion that the girl had any other than white ancestors since the flood. But Mr. J. furnished proofs of his claim.[1]

Convinced, and under the threat of having his wife sold at public auction, the doctor bought her for eight hundred dollars. When he informed her of the purchase, "The poor woman burst into tears and said, 'That as Mr. J. *was her own father,* she had hoped that when he heard she had found an honorable protector he would have left her in peace.' " The horror of the story lies in the perversion of an almost fairytale courtship—complete with a suitor who has traveled far, a modest girl, and love—into an economic transaction, and the perversion of the bonds of paternity into the profits of bondage. It is the collapse of the assumed difference between family and slavery that makes this anecdote so disturbing; in this story the institutions of marriage and of slavery are not merely analogous, they are coextensive and indistinguishable. The passage of the woman from father to husband, and of the slave from one master to another, collapse into each other. Not only are the new husband and the new master one man, but he needs only one name, for bourgeois idealizations of marriage and Southern apologies for slavery both consider him an honorable protector.

This merger of slavery and marriage redefines love and protection as terms of ownership, thereby identifying the modest girl, object of this love and honorable protection, as an object of transaction. Significantly, Child places the anecdote within a section of her *Anti-Slavery Catechism* that asserts the difficulty of distinguishing the bodies of slaves from the bodies of free people. Indeed, the story concludes a catalogue of bodily features ("nose prominent," "tibia of the leg straight") that do not protect one from enslavement.[2] In this story the composite of bodily traits that identify a girl as marriageable proves misleading, putting into question the presumption that the body can provide reliable information about the institutional and racial status of the whole person. What matters about the girl for Child's purposes is that a doctor intimately acquainted with her flesh perceives no hint of blackness. If the body is an inescapable sign of identity, it is also an insecure and often illegible sign.

In Child's story the conflation of the figures of woman and slave, and of the institutions of marriage and bondage, results from difficulties in interpreting the human body. I wish to suggest that it is the problems of having, representing, or interpreting a body that structure both feminist and abolitionist discourses, since the rhetorics of the two reforms share the recognition that, for both women and blacks, it is their physical difference from the cultural norms of white masculinity that obstructs their claim to personhood. Thus the social and political goals of both feminism and abolition depend upon an act of representation, the inscription of black and female bodies into the discourses of personhood. Despite this similarity of aims, I find that the alliance attempted by feminist-abolitionist texts is never particularly easy or equitable. Indeed, I will argue that, although the identifications of women and slave, marriage and slavery, that characterize these texts may occasionally prove mutually empowering, such pairings generally tend toward asymmetry and exploitation. This chapter thus interrogates the intersection of antebellum feminist and abolitionist discourses through an analysis of the attitudes toward black and female bodies revealed there.

The composite term that names this intersection, "feminist-abolitionist," has come into currency with the writings of twentieth-century historians.[3] Women involved in both the abolitionist and woman's rights movements also tended to advocate temperance, oppose prostitution, and work to reform schools, prisons, and diets; they referred to themselves as "universal reformers." My use of the term "feminist-abolitionist" is thus an anachronistic convenience, the hyphen neatly articulating the very connections and distinctions that I intend to explore. I will therefore focus on those writings in which the rhetorical crossings of women and slaves predominate: the political speeches and pamphlets that equate the figure of the woman and the figure of the slave; the sentimental novels and gift-book stories in which antislavery women attempt to represent the slave and more obliquely depict their own fears and desires, so that the racial and the sexual come to displace each other; and the more conservative Sunday-school primers that, in trying to domesticate slavery, recast its oppressions in familial terms, demonstrating the complicity of the two institutions and hence the degree to which domestic and sentimental antislavery writings are implicated in the very oppressions they seek to reform.

Feminists and abolitionists were acutely aware of the dependence of personhood on the condition of the human body, since the political and legal subordination of both women and slaves was predicated upon biology. Medical treatises of the period consistently assert that a woman's psyche and intellect are determined by her reproductive organs.[4] Indeed, to the political satirist, the leaders of the woman's rights movement are nothing but wombs in constant danger of parturition:

> How funny it would sound in the newspapers, that Lucy Stone, pleading a cause, took suddenly ill in the pains of parturition, and perhaps gave birth to a fine bouncing boy in court; or that Rev. Antonia Brown was arrested in the middle of her sermon in the pulpit from the same cause, and presented a "pledge" to her husband and the congregation. . . . A similar event might happen on the floor of Congress, in a storm at sea, or in the raging tempest of battle, and then what is to become of the woman legislator?[5]

In this lampoon the reproductive function interrupts and replaces women's attempts to speak; their public delivery of arguments, sermons, and service is superseded by delivery of children. The joke betrays male fear of female fertility while fashioning the woman's womb and its relentless fecundity into a silencing gag.

The body of the black was similarly thought to define his or her role as servant and laborer. Subservience, one Southern doctor explained, was built into the very structure of African bones. The black was made into a "submissive knee-bender" by the decree of the Almighty, for "in the anatomical conformation of his knees, we see 'genu flexit' written in his physical structure, being more flexed or bent than any other kind of man."[6] As God writes "subservience" upon the body of the black—in Latin, of course—the doctor reads it; or, more crudely, as the master inscribes his name with hot irons ("He is *branded on the forehead* with the letters A.M. and *on each cheek* with the letters J.G."), or the fact of slavery with scars ("His back shows *lasting impressions of the whip,* and leaves no doubt of his being a *slave*"), the body of the slave attains the status of a text.[7] Thus the bodies of women and slaves were read against them; for both, the human body was seen to function as the foundation not only of a general subjection but also of a specific exclusion from political discourse. For women and slaves the ability to speak was predicated upon the reinterpretation of their flesh. Feminists and abolitionists shared a strategy: to invert patriarchal readings and so reclaim the body. Transformed from a silent site of oppression into a symbol of that oppression, the body became, within both feminist and abolitionist discourses, a means of gaining rhetorical force.

Though the female body—and particularly female sexual desires, as I hope to demonstrate—are at least covertly inscribed within feminist-abolitionist texts, the paradigmatic body reclaimed in these writings is that of the slave. The slave, so explicitly an object to be sold, provides feminism as well as abolition with its most graphic example of the extent to which the human body may designate identity. "The denial of our duty to act [against slavery] is a denial of our right to act," wrote Angelina Grimké in 1837, "and if we have no right to act then may *we* well be termed the 'white slaves of the North' for like our brethren in bonds, we must seal our lips in silence and despair."[8] As I have already suggested, the alliance between black bodies and female bodies achieved by the rhetorical crossing of feminist-abolitionist texts was not necessarily equitable. By identifying with the slave, and by insisting on the muteness of the slave, Grimké asserts her right to act and speak, thus differentiating herself from her "brethren" in bonds. The bound and silent figure of the slave metaphorically represents woman's oppression and so grants the white woman an access to political discourse denied the slave, exemplifying the way in which slave labor produces—both literally and metaphorically—even the most basic of freedom's privileges.[9]

In feminist writings the metaphoric linking of women and slaves proves ubiquitous: marriage and property laws, the conventional adoption of a husband's name, or even the length of fashionable skirts are explained and decried by reference to women's "slavery." This strategy serves to emphasize the restrictions of woman's sphere, and, despite luxuries and social civilities, to class the bourgeois woman among the oppressed. Sarah Grimké, beginning her survey of the condition of women with ancient history, notes that "the cupidity of man soon led him to regard women as property, and hence we find them sold to those who wished to marry them," while within marriage, as defined by nineteenth-century laws of coverture, "the very being of a woman, like that of a slave, is absorbed in her master."[10] "A woman," Elizabeth Cady Stanton explains to the woman's rights convention of 1856, "has no name! She is Mrs. John or James, Peter or Paul, just as she changes masters; like the Southern slave, she takes the name of her owner."[11] The image of the slave evoked not simply the loss of "liberty" but the loss of all claims to self-possession. At stake in the feminists' likening of women to slaves is the recognition that personhood can be annihilated and a person owned, absorbed, and un-named. The irony inherent in such comparisons is that the enlightening and empowering motions of identification that connect feminism and abolition come inextricably bound to a process of absorption not unlike the one that they expose. Though the metaphoric linking of women and slaves uses their shared position as bodies to be bought, owned, and designated as a grounds of resistance, it nevertheless obliterates the particularity of black and female experience, making their distinct exploitations appear as one. The difficulty of preventing moments of identification from becoming acts of appropriation constitutes the essential dilemma of feminist-abolitionist rhetoric.

The body of the woman and the body of the slave need not, of course, only merge through metaphor, and it is hardly surprising that the figure of the female slave features prominently in both discourses. Yet even in the case of the literally enslaved woman, the combining of feminist and abolitionist concerns supports both reciprocal and appropriative strategies. The difference between the stereotypic cultural conceptions of black and female bodies was such that, in the crossing of feminist and abolitionist rhetoric, the status of the slave and the status of the woman could each be improved by an alliance with the body of the other. Their two sorts of bodies were prisons in different ways, and for each the prison of the other was liberating. So for the female slave, the frail body of the bourgeois lady promised not weakness but the modesty and virtue of a delicacy supposed at once physical and moral. Concern for the roughness and impropriety with which slave women were treated redefined their suffering as feminine, and hence endowed with all the moral value generally attributed to nineteenth-century American womanhood. Conversely, for the nineteenth-century woman there were certain assets to be claimed from the body of the slave. "Those who think the physical circumstances of women would make a part in the affairs of national government unsuitable," Margaret Fuller argues, "are by no means those who think it impossible for Negresses to endure field work even during pregnancy."[12] The strength to plant, and hoe, and pick, and endure is available to the urban middle-class woman insofar as she can be equated with the laboring slave woman, and that equation suggests the possibility of reshaping physical circumstances. Fuller's words provide a perfect example of the chiasmic alignment of abolition and woman's rights, for though embedded within a discussion devoted to feminist concerns, this passage achieves a double efficacy, simultaneously declaring the physical strength of the woman and implying the need to protect the exploited slave.[13]

Just as the figure of the female slave served feminist rhetorical purposes, she also proved useful in abolitionist campaigns and was frequently employed to attract women to abolitionist work. William Lloyd Garrison, for example, headed the "Ladies' Department" of *The Liberator* with the picture of a black woman on her knees and in chains; beneath it ran the plea, "Am I not a woman and a sister?" Such tactics did not attempt to identify woman's status with that of the slave but rather relied upon the ties of sisterly sympathy, presuming that one woman would be particularly sensitive to the sufferings of another. Such a strategy emphasized the difference between the free woman's condition and the bondage of the slave, since it was this difference that enabled the free woman to work for her sister's emancipation.

The particular horror and appeal of the slave woman lay in the magnitude of her sexual vulnerability, and the Ladies' Department admonished its female readers to work for the immediate emancipation of their one million enslaved sisters "exposed to all the violence of lust and passion—and treated with more indelicacy and cruelty than cattle."[14] The sexual exploitation of female slaves served abolitionists as a proof that slave owners laid claim not merely to the slave's time, labor, and obedience—assets purchased, after all, with the wages paid by the Northern industrialist—but to their flesh. The abolitionist comparison of slave and cattle, like the feminist analogy between woman and slave, marks the slip from person to chattel. More startling than the comparison of the slave to a cow, however, is the Ladies' Department's equation of "indelicacy" with "cruelty," for set beside the menace of brandings, whippings, beatings, and starvation, rudeness seems an insignificant care. This concern with indelicacy becomes explicable, however, in terms of the overlap of feminist and abolitionist discourses. To the male abolitionist, the application of those notions of modesty and purity that governed the world of nineteenth-century ladies to the extremely different situation of the slave must have seemed a useful strategy for gaining female support on an economic, political, and hence unfeminine issue. Viewed from this perspective, the language of feminine modesty simply reinforces traditional female roles. Even here, however, the emphasis on sexual exploitation suggests that the abolitionist's easy differentiation between the free woman and the enslaved one may conceal grounds of identification. For in stressing the aspect of slavery that would seem most familiar to a female readership, the abolitionist press implicitly suggests that the Ladies' Department's readers may be bound like the slaves they are urged to free.

As the examples of the Grimkés and Stanton demonstrate, feminist-abolitionists emphasize the similarities in the condition of women and slaves; nevertheless, their treatment of the figure of the sexually exploited female slave betrays an opposing desire to deny any share in this vulnerability. The same metaphoric structure that makes possible the identification of women and slaves can also preclude such identification. Thus in the writings of antislavery women the frequent emphasis on the specifically feminine trial of sexual abuse serves to project the white woman's sexual anxieties onto the sexualized body of the female slave. Concern over the slave woman's sexual victimization displaces the free woman's fear of confronting the sexual elements of her own bodily experience, either as a positive force or as a mechanism of oppression. The prevalence of such fear is illustrated by the caution with which even the most radical feminist thinkers avoid public discussion of "woman's rights in marriage"; it is only in their private correspondence that the leaders of the woman's rights movement allude to sexual rights. "It seems to me that we are not ready" to bring this issue before the 1856 convention, Lucy Stone writes to Susan B. Anthony:

> No two of us think alike about it, and yet it is clear to me that question underlies the whole movement, and all our little skirmishing for better laws and the right to vote, will yet be swallowed up in the real question viz.: Has woman a right to herself? It is very little to me to have the right to vote, to own property, etc., if I may not keep my body, and its uses, in my absolute right. Not one wife in a thousand can do that now.[15]

The figure of the slave woman, whose inability to keep her body and its uses under her own control is widely and openly recognized, becomes a perfect conduit for the largely unarticulated and unacknowledged failure of the free woman to own her own body in marriage. In one sense, then, it is the very indelicacy of the slave woman's position that makes her a useful proxy in such indelicate matters.

Garrison's Ladies' Department attests to the importance of women to the antislavery movement. In 1832 the Boston Female Anti-Slavery Society was founded as an "auxiliary" to the all-male New England Anti-Slavery Society. By 1838 there were forty-one female auxiliary societies in Massachusetts alone.[16] The function of these auxiliaries was to provide support—mostly in the form of fund-raising—for the work of the male organizations. Thus the auxiliaries behaved much like other female philanthropic or benevolence societies, and most of the women who worked in them gave no public speeches, wrote no political pamphlets, and did not see their antislavery activities as challenging the traditions of male authority and female domesticity. Nevertheless, in their work against slavery these female societies transformed conventional womanly activities into tools of political persuasion, "presenting," as Angelina Grimké explains, the slave's "kneeling image constantly before the public eye." Toward this end they stitched the pathetic figure of the manacled slave onto bags, pincushions, and pen wipers ("Even the children of the north are inscribing on their handiwork, 'May the points of our needles prick the slaveholder's conscience' "), and wrote virtually all the sentimental tales that describe the slaves' sufferings.[17]

In many ways, then, the antislavery stories that abolitionist women wrote for Sunday-school primers, juvenile miscellanies, antislavery newspapers, and gift books need to be assessed as a variety of female handiwork refashioned for political, didactic, and pecuniary purposes. The genre is fundamentally feminine: not only were these stories—like virtually all the domestic and sentimental fiction of the period—primarily penned by women, but beyond this, women largely controlled their production, editing the gift books and miscellanies that contained them, and publishing many of these volumes under the auspices of female antislavery societies.[18] The most substantial and longest-lived abolitionist publishing endeavor of this type, the Boston Female Anti-Slavery Society's annual gift book *The Liberty Bell,* provides the most obvious illustration of these practices, and one that subsequent antislavery collections sought to imitate.[19] In their efforts to raise funds the Boston auxiliary organized an antislavery fair, and it was for the sixth fair, as a further educational and fund-raising gesture, that *The Liberty Bell* was published. Under Maria Weston Chapman's skillful editorial hands, it appeared at virtually every fair from 1839 to 1858, to be sold alongside the quilts and jams.[20] The minutes of the committee for the tenth antislavery fair claimed that *The Liberty Bell* "always doubles the money invested in it." Since the cost of producing the volume was three hundred to four hundred dollars (covered by donations drawn largely from among the contributors), the committee's claim would assess *The Liberty Bell* at slightly less than a fifth of the fair's average proceeds of four thousand dollars a year.[21]

One important feature of the tales published in *The Liberty Bell* was that they were considered salable. The depiction of the slave was thought to have its own market value. The reasons the volumes sold, moreover, appear paradoxically at odds both with each other and with abolitionist beliefs. On the one hand the horrific events narrated in these tales attract precisely to the extent that the buyers of these representations of slavery are fascinated by the abuses they ostensibly oppose. For despite their clear abolitionist stance, such stories are fueled by the allure of bondage, an appeal which suggests that the valuation of depictions of slavery may rest upon the same psychic ground as slaveholding itself. On the other hand, the acceptability of these tales depends upon their adherence to a feminine and domestic demeanor that softens the cruelty they describe and makes their political goals more palatable to a less politicized readership. Explaining the success of *The Liberty Bell,* Chapman admits as much, suggestively presenting her gift book as a mother who treats the public "like children, to whom a medicine is made as pleasant as its nature permits. A childish mind receives a small measure of truth in gilt edges where it would reject it in 'whity-brown.' "[22] Though plain by gift-book standards, the embossed leather and gilded edges of *The Liberty Bell* permitted it to fit without apparent incongruity into any household library. Despite their subject matter, the antislavery stories it contained attempt a similar and uneasy compliance with the conventions that governed nineteenth-century domestic fiction. The contradictory nature of antislavery fiction's appeal thus raises more general questions about what it means to depict slavery, and hence about the politics and power of representation.

Critics have frequently argued that sentimental fiction provided an inappropriate vehicle for educating the public to slavery's real terrors.[23] This criticism, however, simply echoes the authors' own anxieties about the realism of the stories they tell. Almost every antislavery story begins by citing its source: a meeting with the hero or heroine, an account of the events in the newspaper, or most often just having been told.[24] "The truth of incidents" claimed in Harriet Beecher Stowe's preface to *Uncle Tom's Cabin* is documented by her subsequently published *Key* to the novel—the genre's most sustained and impressive attempt to demonstrate its veracity. But her very effort to prove that her novel is "a collection and arrangement of real incidents . . . a mosaic of facts" propounds the difference between her narrative and her key to it, since "slavery, in some of its workings, it too dreadful for the purposes of art. A work which should represent it strictly as it is, would be a work which could not be read."[25] The reading of these stories, and therefore both their marketability and their political efficacy, depends upon their success in rearranging the real. The decision to rearrange it into sentimental tales, I will argue, is highly appropriate, not only because of the dominance of the form during the period, or because of its popular appeal and consequent market value, but also because sentimental fiction constitutes an intensely bodily genre. The concern with the human body as site and symbol of the self that links the struggles of feminists and abolitionists, also informs the genre in which nineteenth-century women wrote their antislavery stories.

The tears of the reader are pledged in these sentimental stories as a means of rescuing the bodies of slaves. Emblematic of this process, Child's story of "Mary French and Susan Easton" relates how the white Mary, kidnapped, stained black, and sold into slavery, is quite literally freed by weeping; her true identity is revealed because, "where the tears had run down her cheeks, there was a streak whiter than the rest of her face."[26] Her weeping obliterates the differential of color and makes Mary white, thereby asserting the power of sentiment to change the condition of the human body or at least, read symbolically, to alter how that condition is perceived. The ability of sentimental fiction to liberate the bodies of slaves is, moreover, intimately connected to the bodily nature of the genre itself. Sentiment and feeling refer at once to

emotion and to physical sensation, and in sentimental fiction these two versions of *sentire* blend as the eyes of readers take in the printed word and blur it
with tears. Reading sentimental fiction is thus a bodily act, and the success of
a story is gauged, in part, by its ability to translate words into pulse beats and
sobs. This physicality of the reading experience radically contracts the distance between narrated events and the moment of their reading, as the feelings in the story are made tangibly present in the flesh of the reader. In
particular, tears designate a border realm between the story and its reading,
since the tears shed by characters initiate an answering moistness in the
reader's eye.[27] The assurance in this fiction that emotion can be attested and
measured by physical response makes this conflation possible; the palpability
of the character's emotional experience is precisely what allows it to be
shared. In sentimental fiction bodily signs are adamantly and repeatedly presented as the preferred and most potent mechanisms both for communicating
meaning and for marking the fact of its transmission.[28]

Sentimental narrative functions through stereotypes, so that upon first encountering a character there is no difficulty in ascertaining his or her moral
worth. In sentimental writing the self is externally displayed, and the body
provides a reliable sign of who one is. Nina Gordon, the heroine of *Dred*
(Stowe's other antislavery novel), develops an instinctive goodness more potent than her lover Edward Clayton's principled virtue. In her instantaneous
and unproblematic discrimination of good from evil, Nina provides a para-
digm for reading the novel that contains her:

> Looking back almost fiercely, a moment, she turned and said to Clayton:
> "I hate that man!"
> "Who is it?" said Clayton.
> "I don't know!" said Nina. "I never saw him before. But I hate him! He is a
> bad man! I'd as soon have a serpent come near me as that man!"
> "Well, the poor fellow's face isn't prepossessing," said Clayton. "But I
> should not be prepared for such an anathema. . . . How can you be so posi-
> tive about a person you've only seen once!" . . .
> "Oh," said Nina, resuming her usual gay tones, "don't you know that girls
> and dogs, and other inferior creatures, have the gift of seeing what's in
> people? It doesn't belong to highly cultivated folks like you, but to us poor
> creatures, who have to trust to our instincts. So, beware!"[29]

Skill in reading the body of the stranger belongs not to the highly cultivated
man who talks of what is prepossessing and what an anathema, but to girls
who hate and will call a man bad. To Nina Mr. Jekyl's face is "very repulsive,"
and in feeling herself repelled, pushed away by his visage, she weighs the
evidence of his character in the reaction of her body to his. Jokingly shared
with dogs, the girl's capacity to read signs by instinct is as physical as the traits
it correctly interprets. The succeeding chapters prove the adequacy of Nina's
reaction to Mr. Jekyl, and so endorse her and the sentimental novel's mechanisms of assessment.[30]

Nina Gordon is the ideal reader of all sentimental fiction, not simply of
antislavery tales, but her ability to read bodies correctly is more important for

antislavery fiction, where the physical vocabulary has been suddenly enlarged to include very different looking bodies, making the interpretative task more difficult. The problem, for the antislavery writer, lies in depicting a black body that can be instantly recognized not only as a loyal or rebellious servant but as a hero or heroine. Stowe introduces Dred:

> He was a tall black man, of magnificent stature and proportions. His skin was intensely black, and polished like marble. A loose shirt of red flannel, which opened very wide at the breast, gave a display of a neck and chest of herculean strength. The sleeves of the shirt, rolled up nearly to the shoulders, showed the muscles of a gladiator. The head, which rose with an imperial air from the broad shoulders, was large and massive, and developed with equal force both in the reflective and perceptive department. The perceptive organs jutted like dark ridges over the eyes, while that part of the head which phrenologists attribute to moral and intellectual sentiments rose like an ample dome above them.[31]

A magnificent, herculean, imperial gladiator—with these words Stowe arrays Dred in the vocabulary of classical heroism. That gladiators were also slaves only strengthens the claims Stowe desires to make for this slave. The density of such terms, however, equally evinces her sense of the difficulty of granting and sustaining Dred's heroic status. She therefore supplements her attempt to fashion Dred into a polished black marble icon of classical heroism with the pseudoscientific language of phrenology. The phrenologist, like the reader of sentimental fiction, reads internal characteristics from the external signs offered by the body. By enlisting the phrenologist in her descriptive task, Stowe garners the authority of study for what she has previously presented as instinctual knowledge. Her need for these multiple buttresses attests to the frailty of this structure. The precariousness of Dred's heroic stature is all the more telling because, in Stowe's description, the heroic and the phrenological have combined to present him less as a man than as a monument. A structure of magnificent proportions crowned by an ample dome, this massive figure of polished marble achieves a truly architectural splendor. In this description Stowe has not so much described Dred as built his body.

Stowe's difficulty in creating a slave hero is best demonstrated, however, not by the body she constructs him in but by the features she silently omits. For though Stowe describes Dred as having eyes of that "unfathomable blackness and darkness which is often a striking characteristic of the African eye," she avoids detailing the rest of his visage. In "The Slave-Wife," Frances Green, less sensitive to the racism that underlies this dilemma, gives her hero, Laco Ray, a face that exemplifies Stowe's problem:

> Tall, muscular, and every way well-proportioned, he had the large expansion of chest and shoulders that are seen in the best representations of Hercules. He was quite black, the skin soft and glossy; but the features had none of the revolting characteristics which are supposed by some to be inseparable from the African visage. On the contrary they were remarkably fine—the nose aquiline—the mouth even handsome—the forehead singularly high and broad.[32]

Green's Laco Ray inhabits in 1845 virtually the same body Stowe gives to
Dred in 1856, confirming the genre's reliance on stereotypes: every hero,
even a black one, is simply another in a familiar series of "best representations
of Hercules." In making her black Hercules, however, Green registers her
need to reject "the revolting characteristics" of nose, mouth, and brow that
she criticizes others for supposing to be "inseparable from the African visage." Her desire to separate them is, obviously, as suspect as the assumption
of their inseparability. Her own insecurity about attaining such a separation
betrays itself in adverbs as she constantly modifies her description to emphasize its unexpectedness: "remarkably" fine, "even" handsome, "singularly"
high and broad; what she finds most exceptional about Laco Ray's features is
that they belong to him. Making a black hero involves not only dyeing the
traditional figure of the hero to a darker hue, but also separating blackness
from the configuration of traits that in the bodily grammar of sentimental
fiction signals revulsion. In replacing or omitting revolting features, both
Green and Stowe remake the black body in order to mold the slave into a
hero. These features revolt, moreover, not only because they fail to conform
to white criteria for beauty but, more interestingly, because they threaten to
overturn sentimental fiction's stable matrix of bodily signs.

The project of depicting the body of the sympathetic black thus becomes a
project of racial amalgamation. Child's story of Mary French's transition from
white to black and back to white again begins with an idyllic scene in which
Mary and her free black playmate Susan frolic with a white-and-black spotted
rabbit. In his alternating patches of color the rabbit presents an ideal of
amalgamation that would not blur racial distinctions into mulatto indiffer-
entiation but rather preserve the clarity of difference without the hierarchies
of valuation imposed by prejudice. The problem in Child's story, as in Stowe's
and Green's, is that this sort of equality-in-difference becomes impossible to
maintain. Susan, kidnapped with Mary, cannot prove her right to freedom by
bodily traits; her father—afraid of being kidnapped himself—cannot search
for her; and Mary's father does nothing to pursue this search, once he has
redeemed his own daughter. The racial prejudice implicit in her only half-
happy ending is obviously one of Child's points. Nevertheless, her concluding
remarks instance such racial hierarchization: "The only difference between
Mary French and Susan Easton is that the black color could be rubbed off
from Mary's skin, while from Susan's it could not."[33] Despite her clear desire
for a different answer, the only solution to racial prejudice that Child's story
can offer is rubbing off blackness; though she does not say this, it is impossible
to imagine what one could produce by such a purging except whiteness. If
Mary's liberating tears offer, as I have argued, a perfect emblem for sentimental fiction's power to emancipate, that emblem includes the recognition that
the freedom it offers depends upon the black being washed white.[34] The
problem of antislavery fiction is that the very effort to depict goodness in
black involves the obliteration of blackness.[35]

Child's story challenges the prevalent bodily vocabulary that interprets dark skin as an unvarying sign of slavery: for Susan, being black and being a slave are not the same thing. Yet whatever Susan's "right to be free," even under antebellum law, the blackness of her body is itself described as a form of enslavement, and one that no act of emancipation can rub off. The painful longing for such an emancipation from one's own skin is explored in Eliza Lee Follen's story "A Melancholy Boy." Throughout most of this story Follen relates a series of anecdotes about the good but inexplicably unhappy Harry, without in any way describing his physical appearance, though the publication of this piece in *The Liberty Bell* would prompt readers to expect that some abolitionist issue is at stake. In the last paragraph of her tale, Follen "discover[s] the cause of Harry's melancholy":

> I was returning from a walk, and saw him at a little brook that ran behind my house, washing his face and hands vehemently, and rubbing them very hard. I then remembered that I had often seen him there doing the same thing. "It seems to me, Harry," I said, "that your face and hands are clean now; and why do you rub your face so violently?" "I am trying," he said, "to wash away this color; I can never be happy till I get rid of this color."[36]

Harry does not name his color, though he does distinguish himself from the other boys: "They are all white." Follen too refrains from naming "this color," so that the story centers upon the absence of the word "black." Both Harry and Follen attempt to escape his blackness, not only by violent scrubbings but also by suppressing the word that names it. In Harry's hopeless efforts to attain personhood through the denial of his body, antislavery fiction locates the problems of representation established by the encounter between sentimental narration and abolitionist ideals within the psyche of the very entity it wishes to represent.

With its reliance on the body as the privileged structure for communicating meaning, sentimental fiction thus constantly reinscribes the troubling relation between personhood and corporeality that underlies the projects of both abolition and feminism. The issues I have been exploring are not peripheral to feminist concerns, for by responding to the representational problems posed by the black body with a rhetoric of racial amalgamation, the women who wrote these antislavery stories encode the racial problematic within a sexual one. The "rubbing off" of blackness that characterizes antislavery fiction imitates the whitening produced by miscegenation. Moreover, miscegenation provides an essential motif of virtually all antislavery fiction, for even in those stories in which escape, slave rebellion, or the separation of families dominate the plot, its multiple challenges suffuse the text. My identification of the human body as the site at which feminist and abolitionist discourses intersect can be further particularized in the images of the black woman's rape by the white man; or in their unsanctioned, unprotected, and unequal love; or in the always suppressed possibility of the white woman's desire for the black man; or in the black man's never sufficiently castrated attraction to the white woman; or most of all, in the ubiquitous light-skinned slave whose body attests to the sexual mingling of black and white. Though it marks the intersection of abolitionist and feminist discourses, the body of the light-skinned slave means differently for each of them: the less easily race can be read from his or her flesh, the more clearly the white man's repeated penetrations of the black body are imprinted there. The quadroon's one-fourth blackness represents two generations of miscegenating intercourse, the octoroon's three; their numerical names attest to society's desire to keep track of an ever less visible black ancestry even at the cost of counting the generations of institutionalized sexual exploitation.

Critical discussions of the mulattos, quadroons, and octoroons who figure in these texts have dealt almost exclusively with the obvious racist allegiances that make a light-skinned hero or heroine more attractive to a white audience, and that presume that the feelings of identification so essential for sentimental fiction cannot cross race lines.[37] I am not interested in attempting to defend either authors or audiences from this charge. My discussion of the rhetoric of amalgamation already has suggested that the light-skinned body is valued in this fiction precisely because of its ability to mask the alien African blackness that the fictional mulatto is nevertheless purported to represent. I would contend, however, that an acknowledgement of this racism ought to inaugurate, not foreclose, discussion of antislavery fiction's fascination with miscegenation. For at stake in the obsession with the fictionalized figure of the mulatto is the essential dilemma of both feminist and abolitionist projects: that the recognition of ownership of one's own body as essential to claiming personhood is matched by the fear of being imprisoned, silenced, deprived of personhood by that same body. The fictional mulatto combines this problematics of corporality and identity for both discourses, because miscegenation and the children it produces stand as a bodily challenge to the conventions of reading the body, thus simultaneously insisting that the body is a sign of identity and undermining the assurance with which that sign can be read. Moreover, stories of miscegenation inevitably link the racial and the sexual, demonstrating the asymmetry of abolitionist and feminist concerns—and the by now familiar ways in which, by identifying with her enslaved sister, the free woman comes to betray her.

The form miscegenation usually took in the American South was, of course, the rape and concubinage of slave women by their white masters. Caroline Healey Dall's "Amy," published in *The Liberty Bell* of 1849, tells this story, and records in its telling the interlocking structure of patriarchy's dual systems of racial oppression and sexual exploitation. The story begins with a marriage: "In Southern fashion, Edith was not quite sixteen when she was wooed and won, and borne, a willing captive, to a patriarchal dwelling." Edith's ambiguous role as a willing captive within the patriarchal systems of marriage and slaveholding becomes more sinisterly evident as the story progresses and she eventually proves willing to prostitute her slave and half sister Amy. Dall explains: "The offspring of a lawless and unrequited affection," Amy "had, nevertheless, unconsciously dedicated her whole being to vestal chastity. But nothing availed." Despite prevailing cultural expectations, the problem of

Amy's ancestry is not that as the child of lawless sexuality she has inherited lascivious desires, but rather that as the child of sexual exploitation she has inherited the role of being exploited. Her body displays not only a history of past miscegenation but also a promise of future mixings. A friend of Edith's new husband sees Amy, reads both her desirability and her vulnerability on her "graceful form," and reenacts a parodic version (or is it?) of the wooing and winning with which the story begins. The woman Charles Hartley must woo in order to win Amy is, however, not Amy but her mistress, Edith. In this transaction Amy is prostituted as much by the white woman's reluctance to discuss sex as by the white man's desire to indulge in it. For as Charles keeps pressing Edith to procure Amy for him, she comes to see her slave's sexual modesty as a threat to her own delicacy:

> Not only did the whole subject distress her, but to be so besought on such a subject, by one until lately a stranger, was a perpetual wound to her delicacy. She felt herself losing ground in her own self-respect. Her husband regarded it as a desecration, and repeatedly asked whether her own life was to be worn out in defense of Amy.

In the end, concurring with her husband's insistence on the sanctity of her delicacy, Edith signs the "deed of transfer."

In Dall's story the pairing of feminist and abolitionist concerns proves double-edged: for if Edith's inability to prevent male desire, or to refute male conceptions of feminine purity, allies her to her powerless slaves and names her a captive of patriarchy, she nevertheless remains fully complicitous in Amy's sexual victimization. The role of feminine delicacy that she accepts is paid for not just by her own loss of efficacy but by Amy's destruction. Dall's critique of female delicacy identifies it as an essential prop both for the subordination and demoralization of women and for the exploitation of slaves. The narrative voice in which Dall tells this story, however, conforms to the requirements of the delicacy it condemns. In describing Amy as "dedicated . . . to a vestal chastity," it is the narrator, not Edith's husband, who first equates female purity with the sacred; while in calling the lust that fathered Amy "affection," Dall mitigates the very evil her story was intended to expose. The problem is that traditional notions of female purity attach both to the body— in its vulnerability to rape or enforced concubinage—and to language. The conventions of chastity count speech as a sexual assault; hence Edith can describe Charles's propositions as a "perpetual wound." Dall fears that, if she named explicitly the obscene events that constitute her plot, her readers would experience it as the infliction of wounds. The cultural critique voiced by Dall is leveled at her own prose, for in respecting the sensibilities of her readers she adheres to the dictates of a linguistic delicacy that she has shown to simultaneously protect against and inflict physical indecencies.[38]

The sacrifice of Amy's chastity serves not only to defend Edith's delicacy but also, paradoxically, to provide her with a variety of safely mediated sexual experience. After all, it is to Edith that Charles brings his suit for sexual favors, and—after the requisite protestations of lost self-respect—it is Edith who yields. That she can yield Amy's body rather than her own demonstrates the usefulness of the slave woman as a surrogate for the white woman's sexuality, and particularly the usefulness of the mulatta, who in being part white and part black (and in Amy's case, being more explicitly half sibling and half not) simultaneously embodies self and other. Thus, through the prostitution of Amy, Edith can be perceived as gaining a degree of sexual license normally forbidden to the proper bourgeois woman. Edith's husband and her husband's friend, however, fill virtually interchangeable roles in this narrative, both equally involved in demanding Edith's compliance. Her husband's anger over her desecration is directed at her initial defense of Amy's chastity, not at Charles's presumption in bringing the matter up. Consequently, even Edith's passive and unconscious circumvention of sexual prohibitions ultimately functions as a demonstration that the white woman, like her slave, remains a sexual possession of the white man. In these terms fictional depictions of the slave woman's sexual vulnerability may themselves constitute an act of betrayal not unlike Edith's own, for in such stories antislavery rhetoric disguises, and so permits, the white woman's unacknowledgeable feelings of sexual victimization and desire. The insights and emotions granted by such conflations of the racial and the sexual remain divorced from her body. If, as Lucy Stone insisted, the ability to control the "uses" of one's own body constitutes the most basic condition of freedom, then for the white woman the strongest proof that she is not owned by the white man lies in the inadmissible possibility of using her body elsewhere—a possibility only granted her, within antislavery fiction, through a vicarious reading of the body of the slave.[39]

In antislavery fiction the story of the white woman's desire for the black man is not told, and his desire for her is constantly reduced to the safer dimensions of a loyal slave's nominally asexual adoration of his good and kind mistress.[40] Child comes closest to giving voice to these desires, not in her fiction but in her first abolitionist tract, *An Appeal in Favor of That Class of Americans Called Africans.* While this book established her as an abolitionist leader, it cost both her popular readership (so many subscriptions to the *Juvenile Miscellany* were canceled by horrified parents that the series was forced to fold), and, with her expulsion from the Atheneum, her position in Boston literary society. Perhaps chief among the *Appeal*'s many challenges to societal norms was Child's call for the repeal of antimiscegenation laws. Although her attack on these discriminatory statutes explicitly distinguishes between society's refusal to sanction interracial marriage and its willingness to condone such liaisons out of wedlock, she implies that what is at stake in these contradictory attitudes is not miscegenation per se but rather the patriarchal melding of sexual and racial oppression that assures the supremacy of the white man, granting only him the freedom to choose his sexual partners.

> An unjust law exists in this Commonwealth, by which marriages between persons of different color is pronounced illegal. I am perfectly aware of the gross ridicule to which I may subject myself by alluding to this particular; but I have lived too long, and observed too much, to be disturbed by the world's mockery. . . . Under existing circumstances, none but those whose condition

in life is too low to be much affected by public opinion, will form such alliances; and they, when they choose to do so, *will* make such marriages in spite of the law. I know two or three instances where women of the laboring class have been united to reputable, industrious colored men. These husbands regularly bring home their wages, and are kind to their families. If by some odd chances, which not unfrequently occur in the world, their wives should become heirs to any property, the children may be wronged out of it, because the law pronounces them illegitimate. And while this injustice exists with regard to *honest*, industrious individuals, who are merely guilty of differing from us in a matter of taste, neither the legislation nor customs of slaveholding States exert their influence against *immoral* connexions.

In the next paragraph she discusses the "temporary connexions" made by "[w]hite gentlemen of the first-rank" and New Orleans quadroons.[41] Her examples of illegal miscegenating marriages pointedly make the woman white and the man black, while the case of the quadroon concubine pairs race and sex differently. Child's care in this passage to discriminate her own desires from those she discusses indicates the strength of the taboo against which she writes. For even as she disclaims any concern for the "world mockery," Child admits the impossibility, at least under the prevailing social conditions, of any but the very low so utterly discounting public opinion as to enter into such a union. Child only risks a defense of this most subversive version of miscegenation once she has placed the sturdy barrier of class between herself and the women who enact it. By asserting that the female laborers who choose black mates are "merely guilty of differing from us in a matter of taste," Child insists on the distinction between tastes and morals, and on the comparative insignificance of the former. But by using this moment to forge an identification with her readers based on a shared set of tastes, she backs away from her argument, suggesting the power of social sanctions to limit desires. Thus even here, in perhaps the most daring argument in her most daring text, Child refrains from denouncing society's distaste for a form of miscegenation that would threaten and exclude the white man. Instead, as she names herself part of the social "us," her persuasive strategy of identification collapses into a defensive one.

In light of Child's caveats it is hardly surprising that, at least so far as I am aware, no antislavery fiction admits to the possibility of a white woman loving or wedding a black man.[42] Yet I would like to suggest that this forbidden desire constitutes a repressed but never completely obliterated narrative within even the most conventional of these stories. Recalling Stowe's and Green's portraits of their black heroes, it is now evident that one of the tasks implicit in the amalgamating strategies that constructed these Herculeses is the creation of a black man who can be easily assimilated to the white woman's sexual tastes. Once again it is the figure of the mulatta who permits this desire to be inscribed. The light skin of the mulatta names her white, yet her black ancestry keeps her union with the black hero from being labeled miscegenation. Through this figure the love of a white-skinned woman and a black-skinned man can be designated, and even endorsed, without being scandalous. The polysemous body of the fictional mulatta simultaneously expresses the white woman's desires and protects her from them by marking them safely alien.

Clearly not intended to articulate a feminist position, Frances Green's "The Slave-Wife" tells the familiar abolitionist story of a slave woman's sexual exploitation by her master, despite her (legally null) marriage. But because of her complexion this story encloses another narrative, the tale of a white woman's preference for a black lover. Even hidden under the mask of the mulatta, this story of the inadmissible union of a white woman and a black man is so threatening that it must be dismantled at the very moment it is made, so that the story becomes a sequence of alternating disavowals and contradictions. Laco Ray's description of his wife proffers a double reading of her race: "She was white. At least no one would suspect that she had any African blood in her veins." The modifications that follow cannot erase the clarity of that first adamant assertion of her whiteness. Laco's wife is named Clusy; it is a slave name, unfit for other roles, so that Clusy's name and her body sustain the tension already noted between her African blood and white flesh. Just as Clusy's flesh, ancestry, and name offer conflicting signs to her identity, the story's plot consists of a series of displacements in which Laco Ray and his master alternately claim the trophy that is Clusy. Their competition, like Clusy's ambiguous race, serves to contain the white woman's scandalous desire for the black man; since, as master and husband each attempts to claim exclusive sexual rights, the question of the woman's choice and desire is made moot. Laco Ray's narration of this rivalry makes it clear that he sees the price of loss as the distinctly patriarchal threat of castration: "She was beautiful. She was in her master's power. She was in the power of every white man that chose to possess her, she was no longer mine. She was not my wife." The question of "The Slave-Wife" is whether or not a black man can possess a woman—particularly a white woman—and from its very title, which simultaneously makes Clusy a wife and yet fetters that role with the apparently contradictory one of slave, the answer remains ambiguous. Despite Laco's sense of dispossession, the white man's power never quite manages to control Clusy. Finally, as Laco reports it, Clusy, continuing to reject the master's "wishes," "was bound to the stake; and while cruel and vulgar men mocked her agony, THERE *our babe was born!*" The torture that attempts to make Clusy the white man's sexual property only succeeds in eliciting proof of her sexual intimacy with a black man. Yet once again the message is double, for the child who marks Laco's potency in the face of the master's power is stillborn. Weak from childbirth and beatings, Clusy escapes with Laco Ray, only to die before reaching Canada. The story ends here in a stalemate. The inconclusiveness of both Laco's and his master's attempts to claim Clusy reflects Green's own incapacity to give the white woman to the black man, even as it attests to her desire to do so.

Laco's final request that his auditor "publish it abroad" recasts the story not as one of male possession, whether white or black, but as one of female desires and female virtue: "for if any woman can hear [this story] without a wish, a determination to labor with all her might to abolish THE SLAVERY OF WOMAN, I impeach her virtue—she is *not* TRUE—she is NOT PURE."[43] The passage asserts that sexual virtue consists not of a delicacy that eschews sexual topics but of a purity that opposes sexual exploitation. This definition of sexual virtue as resistance to the slavery of woman makes abolition a question of woman's rights. Laco's phrase "the slavery of woman" carries two meanings, and Clusy's story illustrates the impossibility of separating them. What interests me about this merger of feminist and abolitionist arguments is that, unlike many of the instances discussed above, Green's narrative appears to be oblivious to the connections it nonetheless makes. The rhetoric of "The Slave-Wife" stresses the contradictions inherent in Clusy's double role as chattel and spouse, and disregards the ways in which the two terms might be identical, and Green's title a tautology. Thus the story defines slavery as a woman's issue at the same time that it writes woman's desire out of woman's rights, denying and hiding the sexual body of the white woman. Yet by depicting Laco Ray and his master as rival claimants for the possession of Clusy, the story implicitly presents her positions as wife and slave as analogous: in both cases she is male property; in neither case are her desires, including her subversive preference for her black husband, permitted autonomous expression. From a feminist perspective these implications discredit Laco Ray's desire to have Clusy as his own, and hence to own her, and therefore undermine his sympathetic position in Green's abolitionist argument. That the links between sexual and racial oppression strategically forged by feminist-abolitionists hold, even within narratives whose logic is jeopardized by this coupling, suggests that these links have become so normative as to be unavoidable. Thus the antislavery stories written by women who appear to have no intention of questioning marital or familial relations constantly employ rhetoric or depict scenarios that jar against their benign assumptions about woman's proper domestic place.

Antislavery fiction's focus on miscegenation evades the difficulties of representing blackness by casting the racial problematics of slavery into the terms of sexual oppression. In defining the question of ownership of one's body as a sexual question, the ideal of liberty and the commercial concept of ownership attain not only an intimately corporeal, but also an explicitly marital or domestic, dimension. This presentation of slavery as a sexual, marital, and domestic abuse thematizes the structure of the genre as a whole, since antislavery stories attempt to describe slave experience within the feminine forms of domestic fiction. Sentimental antislavery stories are constructed on the foundation of a presumed alliance between abolitionist goals and domestic values, an alliance that, it should already be obvious, is fraught with asymmetries and contradictions. The domestic realm of women and children occupies, after all, a paradoxical place in both feminist and abolitionist arguments. For feminists, it constitutes not only the source of woman's power but also, antithetically, the "sphere" in which she finds herself incarcerated. For abolitionists, the domestic values that ostensibly offer a positive alternative to the mores of plantation society simultaneously serve to mask slavery's exploitations behind domesticity's gentle features.

Situated outside the specifically abolitionist forums provided by antislavery societies, even further detached from the woman's rights movement, and aimed at the most sentimental figure of the domestic scene—the good child—the antislavery stories written for Sunday-school primers baldly exemplify the narrative disjunctions inherent in attempts to domesticate slavery. Julia Coleman and Matilda Thompson's collection of such stories, *The Child's Anti-Slavery Book,* first published by the evangelical American Tract Society in 1859 and then twice reprinted in the "Books for Sunday School" series of a New York publisher, provides a characteristic and fairly popular sample of the genre. The collection constantly inscribes its own domesticity. The introduction, "A Few Words About American Slave Children," begins by describing the loving, happy homes of the American free children who constitute its readership. Such homes are then replicated within the stories themselves. Thus "Aunt Judy's Story" narrates the life of this elderly ex-slave through a frame in which Mrs. Ford tells her children the tale of their impoverished neighbor, with her daughter Cornelia literally "leaning her little curly head against her mother's knee," while they discuss the likelihood of Judy's children having been torn away from her maternal knee. The virtue of the Ford home marks every exchange. If Cornelia is "getting a little impatient," the narrator turns to remind the child reader, who might mistakenly see this moment as condoning such behavior, that it was "only a little, for Cornelia was remarkable for her sweet and placid disposition." Bountiful meals are consumed in every chapter, and neither parent ever lets an opportunity for a moral lesson go to waste, nor does Mrs. Ford ever fail to revel in "every act of kindness to the poor and needy performed by her children." In these Sunday-school stories, lessons in patience or generosity—the everyday virtues of domestic life—inextricably mingle with the teaching of antislavery. The Fords treat Aunt Judy as a site for the moral education of their children, while the promised story of her life serves as a didactic and desirable form of entertainment: "Dear papa, tell us a story with a poor slave in it, won't you?" Cornelia implores.[44]

The subordination of the poor slave to the family who tells her story bespeaks the dominance inherent in the act of representation: the Ford children "profit" from Aunt Judy in a manner more moralistic than, but not sufficiently distinct from, the material profits reaped by the slave owners her story teaches them to condemn. On the other hand, the family these children inhabit, and the lessons of patience and selflessness they are taught, reproduce, under the benign guise of domesticity, a hierarchy structurally quite similar to that of slavery itself.[45] The sentimental and domestic values engaged in the critique of slavery are compromised by the connection, and implicated in the very patterns they are employed to expose. The values of the loving family embodied in the doting mother and the dutiful child look, despite all disclaimers and despite all differences, much like the values of the plantation. But because the domesticity of women and children is glorified in these stories, the fact of subjugation and the disavowal of freedom implicit in domestic values remain masked.

Thompson and Coleman's defensive insistence on the differences between slavery and family suggests that even the most emphatically domestic writers were aware of the danger that their stories might collapse the very distinctions they were designed to uphold. For example, when in "A Few Words About American Slave Children" they attempt to differentiate between the experiences of slave and free children, the similarities between the two haunt their arguments: "Though born beneath the same sun and on the same soil, with the same natural right to freedom as yourselves, they are nevertheless SLAVES. Alas for them! Their parents cannot train them as they will, for they too have MASTERS." "They too have masters," the passage explains, and whatever is learned about the powerlessness of slave parents, the notion that all children have masters is equally clear—for who, except the child, stands at the other side of that "too"? This conception of all children as unfree slips between the authors' emphatic insistence (so emphatic because so precarious?): "Children, you are free and happy. . . . *You are free children!*" Yet the very description of this freedom reveals it to be, at best, deferred: "When you become men and women you will have full liberty to earn your living, to go, to come, to seek pleasure or profit in any way that you may choose, so long as you do not meddle with the rights of other people."[46] In short, the liberty described is one projected into the future, not one attainable for the child within familial structures.

The male bias of even this deferred freedom is made obvious by a nearly identical passage from another antislavery book for children from the period. This one, *The Child's Book on Slavery; or, Slavery Made Plain,* was published as part of a series "for Sabbath Schools" in Cincinnati. It says: "When the Child grows to be a man or woman he can go and do for himself, is his own ruler, and can act just as he pleases, if he only does right. He can go and come, he can buy and sell; if he has a wife and children, they cannot be taken away, and he is all his life *free.*"[47] The absurdity of the child grown to be a woman ever having a wife makes it clear that the passage's slide into the singular masculine pronoun, and everything logically attributable to *him,* is not only idiomatically conventional but poignantly symptomatic. Indeed, the ability to have "a wife and children," like the ability to "go and come" or "buy and sell," serves to define freedom, so that the juxtaposition of these pairs categorizes women and children not as potential free persons but rather as the sign and condition of another's freedom. The freedom so defined in these antislavery books is available to neither child nor woman. The domestic ideology that informs the genre can no more accommodate an actual, corporeal, and present freedom than can the slave ideology itself.

The homological ideologies of the family and of slave society need not imply, antislavery writers insist, that both structures support the same meanings: thus the patriarchal pattern that would signal exploitation and power in the case of a plantation society could mean benevolent protection and love within a familial setting. "The relation between the child and the parent is first and chiefly for the child's good, but the relation between the slave and his master is for the master's pleasure," the anonymous author of *The Child's Book on Slavery* explains. In both cases the less powerful "must obey" the more powerful, but, the author asserts, the good garnered by such obedience accrues differently.[48] Leveled against proslavery assurances that bondage is beneficial to the weaker African race, this logic also defends against the specter of parental pleasure in the subservience of the child, and by extension, against that of patriarchal pleasure in the conventions of domestic hierarchy. The difference between slavery and domestic order is cast as a conflict between selfish hedonism and benevolence; in this Sunday-school primer the critique of pecuniary motives is displaced by a discussion of moral considerations. By situating antislavery discourse within an idealized domestic setting, these stories purport to offer moral and emotional standards by which to measure, and through which to correct, the evils of slavery. The problem is that these standards are implicated in the values and structures of authority and profit they seek to criticize. The contradictions inherent in the alliance of abolitionist thought with domestic ideals can be identified, in part, as the conflict between a structural or material and an emotional or moral conception of social reality. Failing to discover tangible and stable grounds on which to distinguish idealized domestic values from the abhorred system of slavery, antislavery writers retreat to the realm of the intangible; once they do so, their arguments for the difference between slavery and domesticity reconstruct this opposition in terms of the tension between physical and spiritual ontologies and epistemologies.

Feminist-abolitionist awareness of the need to recognize the links between one's identity and one's body, and of all the difficulties inherent in such a recognition, informs, as I have argued, the problems of representation that characterize antislavery fiction. The domestic and sentimental conventions of this fiction, however, simultaneously subscribe to a moral, emotional, and fundamentally spiritual code that devalues bodily constraints to focus on the soul. As employed in the service of patriarchal authority, the distinction between body and soul traditionally functioned to increase, not decrease, social control over the body. Historically this distinction had buttressed Christian apologies for slavery, as it enabled the pious to simultaneously exploit bodies and save souls.[49] Similarly, an emphasis on the special and discrete nature of the spiritual realm permitted to women's souls a power that was denied to their bodies. It has been frequently demonstrated that, in losing economic and political power with the rise of bourgeois society, the American woman increased her value as the moral and spiritual guardian of the nation: her gain in moral status bolstered her exclusion from the political and commercial arenas.[50] The writers of antislavery fiction seem well aware of the oppressive consequences of locating personhood in the soul. The hypocritical minister who defends slavery as a means of converting the heathens of Africa, and levies docility with the threat of hellfire for those who do not follow the biblical injunction "Servants obey your masters," serves as a stock villain of this fiction. Equally familiar is the ineffectually kind mistress who, like

Stowe's Mrs. Shelby, is prevented by her husband from participating in economic decisions but is expected to provide enough piety and benevolence for the whole family.[51] Despite these depictions of the ways in which evocations of a spiritual reality can be used as a placebo for women's and slaves' lack of social power, antislavery fiction nevertheless endorses the belief in an alternate spiritual realm where power and efficacy are distributed differently. From this perspective the powerlessness of women and slaves would not matter because, whatever the condition of their bodies, their souls could remain blessed and free.

The most famous instance of such recourse to the refuge provided by a separate spiritual reality is, of course, the victory of Tom's faith-filled spiritual power over Simon Legree's physical brutality.

> "Did n't I pay down twelve hundred dollars, cash, for all there is inside yer old cussed black shell? Ain't yer mine, now, body and soul?" he said, giving Tom a violent kick with his heavy boot; "tell me!"
> In the very depth of physical suffering, bowed by brutal oppression, this question shot a gleam of joy and triumph through Tom's soul. . . .
> "No! no! no! my soul ain't yours, Mas'r! You have n't bought it,—ye can't buy it! It's been bought and paid for, by one that is able to keep it."[52]

In this passage Stowe insists on the oppressive presence of physical reality: the constraints of Tom's position can be weighted and measured; the boot is heavy. The triumph of Tom's soul is thus emphatically presented as rebutting material conceptions of personhood. In response to Legree's threats and abuses, Tom insists on the irrelevance of the condition of his body in identifying him not as a thing but as a man.[53] The primacy granted Tom's soul in constituting his identity is the culmination of a process evident throughout the novel, for while Tom's body is explicitly and frequently described by Stowe in the same Herculean terms she would later use in her portrait of Dred, her emphasis on the childlike and feminine character of his soul serves to supplant these physical descriptions, so that in most readers' minds, and in George Cruikshank's 1852 illustrations, Tom appears effeminate and physically weak. Thus her celebration of Tom's soul serves to erase his flesh. Equally telling is Stowe's failure to imagine an America in which blacks could be recognized as persons. Perhaps the most disturbing insight of her novel is that the utopian freedom she constructs is predicated upon the absence of black bodies: Tom's "victory" wins him the freedom of heaven; George, Eliza, and the rest find theirs only in Liberia.

The Christian and sentimental vision of noncorporeal freedom and personhood obfuscates the conception of the corporeality of the self with which I credit feminist-abolitionist discourse. Yet I would argue that antislavery fiction's recourse to the obliteration of black bodies as the only solution to the problem of slavery actually confirms the ways in which feminist-abolitionist projects of liberation forced a recognition of the bodiliness of personhood. Antislavery writers' tendency to do away with bodies stands as a testimony to their terrified sense that the body is inescapable. Thus, graphically extending the ways in which the freedom praised by domestic fiction excludes women and children, the freedom offered by antislavery fiction regularly depends upon killing off black bodies, defining death as a glorious emancipation from plantation slavery. "A Thought upon Emancipation" in the *Liberty Chimes* offers this vision of immediate abolition:

> Even, now, the slave himself need no longer be a slave. He has the heroism to prefer death to slavery and the system is at an end.
>
> Let the terrible determination go forth through all Slavedom, that the slave *will not* work—*will not* eat—*will not* rise up or lie down at the bidding of an owner and will be free or *die,* and it is done. Tomorrow's sun beholds a notion of freedom indeed.[54]

What is done, terminated, in this fantasy is not only slavery but all slaves. The apocalyptic tone of the piece does provide the radical reinterpretation of freedom it promises. Antislavery writing responds to slavery's annihilation of personhood with its own act of annihilation.

The obliteration of the body thus stands as the pain-filled consequence of recognizing the extent to which the body designates identity. Indeed, this glorification of death is but a more extreme example of processes already evident in the domestic, amalgamating, and appropriate strategies that characterize feminist-abolitionist discourse's various attempts to transform the body from a site of oppression into the grounds of resisting that oppression. The discovery that these efforts to liberate the body result in its repression and annihilation attests to the difficulties and resistance inherent in acknowledging the corporeality of personhood. The bodies feminists and abolitionists wish reclaimed, and the bodies they exploit, deny, or obliterate in the attempted rescue, are the same.

6

Vanishing Americans: Gender, Empire, and New Historicism

Lora Romero

The Last of the Mohicans is one of approximately forty novels published in the United States between 1824 and 1834 that, taken together, suggest the existence of a virtual "cult of the Vanishing American" in the antebellum period. Requisite to membership in this cult was a belief that the rapid decrease in the native population noted by many Jacksonian-era observers was both spontaneous and ineluctable.[1] James Fenimore Cooper would seem to betray his indoctrination in the cult of the Vanishing American when he states, in the introduction to the 1831 edition of his novel, that it was "the seemingly inevitable fate of all [native tribes]" to "disappear before the advances . . . of civilisation [just] as the verdure of their native forests falls before the nipping frost."[2] The elegiac mode here performs the historical sleight of hand crucial to the topos of the doomed aboriginal: it represents the disappearance of the native not just as natural but as having already happened.[3]

In the novel itself, of course, Cooper's Indians "vanish" in somewhat more spectacular fashion than the introductory invocation of forest and frost leads us to anticipate. However pacific the introduction's simile, in the narrative proper individual representatives of the doomed race expire in utterly sensational ways. Indeed, the frequency with which Cooper's Indians plunge to their death from great heights is positively astounding.

The most memorable instance of this is the villainous Magua's spectacular demise at the end of the novel. Evading pursuit by Cooper's white hero Hawk-eye, Magua attempts to leap from the brow of a mountain to an adjacent precipice, but he falls "short of his mark" and finds himself dangling from a "giddy height," clinging desperately to a shrub growing from the side of the precipice. Bent on destroying his enemy, Hawk-eye fires. The wounded Magua's hold loosens, and "his dark person [is] seen cutting the air with its head downwards, for a fleeting instant . . . in its rapid flight to destruction" (338).

To claim that Cooper foreshadows Magua's Miltonic fall earlier would grossly understate the case. Indeed, the fall of dark persons from on high is a virtual theme in *The Last of the Mohicans*. Similar rapid flights to destruction abound, for example, in an early confrontation between whites and enemy Indians that takes place in the vertiginous topography of a huge cavern. One Indian plunges "into [a] deep and yawning abyss" (69). A second hurls "headlong among the clefts of [an] island" (70). A third tumbles down an "irrecoverable precipice" (71), while yet another drops "like lead" into the "foaming waters" below (75).

Mere sensationalism does not quite account for Cooper's fascination with the precipitous dark person. The figure sometimes surfaces in relatively banal forms—for example, when the noble savage Uncas at one point darts "through the air" and leaps upon Magua, "driving him many yards . . . headlong and prostrate" (113), or later when, in his fatal attempt to save Cora Munro's life, Uncas leaps between her and Magua in an act of what Cooper calls "headlong precipitation" (336). And perhaps the most banal reiteration of the figure occurs when the novelist describes a Huron, tomahawk in his hand and malice in his heart, rushing at Uncas. A quick-witted white man sticks out his foot to trip the "eager savage" as he passes, and the Huron is "precipitated . . . headlong" to the ground (238). Etymologically considered ("precipitation" is from *praeceps* or "headlong"), the phrase is as peculiarly reiterative as the headlong aboriginal it describes.

I would like to suggest that the redundancy of both phrase and figure in Cooper's novel signals that text's participation in and instantiation of a larger antebellum cultural discourse in which the ethnographic and pedagogic overlap. Cooper at one point refers to an enemy Huron who is about to plunge down a precipice as a "prodigy" (69). An educational treatise written by a doctor and appearing six years after *The Last of the Mohicans* discusses the phenomenon of precocity and provides a compelling if unlikely analogue to Cooper's precipitous native. In his *Remarks on the Influence of Mental Cultivation and Mental Excitement upon Health,* Dr. Amariah Brigham records the case of a white prodigy, one William M., born in Philadelphia on the Fourth of July, 1820. While still a toddler, William M. astonished those around him with his musical talents, his conversational skills, and his lofty moral sentiments.

According to Brigham, "the heads of great thinkers . . . are wonderfully large." At birth William M.'s head "was of ordinary size," but "very soon, after an attack of dropsy of the brain, it began to grow inordinately." Indeed, by the time the child learned to walk, his head had grown so large that "he was apt to fall, especially forwards, from readily losing his equilibrium." This tendency proved to be more than a minor annoyance. At eight years of age he suffered a precipitous demise—a death both untimely and literally headlong. Losing his balance one day, he fell headfirst against a door, bruised his forehead, "became very sick, and died the next evening." William M.'s fatal loss of equilibrium evinces the thesis advanced in this section of Brigham's treatise, namely, that "mental precocity is generally a symptom of disease; and hence those who exhibit it very frequently, die young." A "passion for books" and other mental excitements may, in the doctor's opinion, presage early death.[4]

The ethnographic subtext of Brigham's thesis (and hence the treatise's relevance to Cooper's novel) becomes more legible when William M.'s story is juxtaposed with Margaret Fuller's discussion of equilibrium and race in her account of a journey into Indian territory in *A Summer on the Lakes* (1844). In fact, the case of William M. reads like a curiously materialist interpretation of what Fuller calls "civilized man['s] larger mind." Fuller sees the difference between "civilized" and "savage" as in part a matter of proportions, a difference of relative development of mind and body. Civilized man "is constantly breaking bounds, in proportion as the mental gets the better of the mere instinctive existence." In the process, however, "he loses in harmony of being what he gains in height and extension; the civilized man is a larger mind but a more imperfect nature than the savage." What Fuller calls "civilized man['s] larger *mind*," Brigham translates into civilized man's larger *head*—but even Fuller's analysis has a materialist component: she asserts that Indian tribes subjugated by whites cease to bear physical resemblance to members of their race as yet uncontaminated by civilization. Unlike other natives, members of conquered tribes, she writes, are "no longer strong, tall, or finely proportioned."[5]

Whereas Fuller imagines that physical degeneration in the form of disproportion is desirable because it fosters spiritual development, Brigham believes in "the necessity of giving more attention to the health and growth of the body, and less to the cultivation of the mind . . . than is now given." But Brigham's concern extends beyond individual bodies and their well-being. Educational treatises published in the United States in the antebellum period slide easily from the individual to the race. Brigham's preface declares: "The people of the United States ought to become the most vigorous and powerful race of human beings, both in mind and body, that the world has ever known."[6] William M.'s significant birthplace (Philadelphia) and birth date (July 4) render him the local instance of an alleged racial defiance of Brigham's imperialist imperative.

The same entanglement of child rearing and empire building surfaces in the work of Catherine Beecher, whose popular advice to housewives and whose former position as head of the prestigious Hartford Female Seminary guaranteed her pedagogy both domestic and institutional influence.[7] Like Brigham, Beecher worried that Anglo-American children were "becoming less and less healthful and good-looking" and that they were every year producing children even "more puny and degenerate" than themselves. Beecher contrasts puny Anglo-Americans with the robust ancient Greeks, who, she asserts, were of a stock so vigorous that they "conquered nearly the whole world."[8] This last comment suggests the way in which early nineteenth-century educational treatises—characteristically if not constitutionally—traverse the discursive registers of home and empire. The figure of the prodigy, one may conclude, organizes into a single discursive economy two distinct cultural arenas expressed through binarisms of feminine and masculine, private and public, suburbia and frontier, sentiment and adventure.[9] Expressing these binarisms in somewhat different terms, I would claim that prodigy illuminates the affiliations of the micro- and the macropolitical.

I

In *The History of Sexuality,* Michel Foucault supplies a model for uncovering the connections between micro- and macropolitics. Anticipating one possible objection to his characterization of modern government as "power organized around the management of life rather than the menace of death,"[10] he concedes that the modernity of the genocidal might seem to suggest that the life-destroying power of the sovereign not only survived his decapitation but actually escalated in the nineteenth and twentieth centuries. Yet even if race remains a largely undeveloped category of analysis in the history it traces, *The History of Sexuality* does theorize interracial conflict as an inevitable component of modernity. Foucault asserts that, precisely inasmuch as power legitimates and incarnates itself through "the right of the social body to ensure, maintain, or develop its life," so racial holocaust becomes "vital" to its expression. He suggests the historical simultaneity of *productive* technologies promoting the well-being of the individual, and *deductive* technologies ensuring the survival of the race, when he writes that in eighteenth- and nineteenth-century Europe "precocious sexuality was presented . . . as an epidemic menace that risked compromising not only the future health of adults but the future of the entire society and species."[11] Modifying Foucault's analysis slightly, I will be locating antebellum representations of the prodigy—a less explicitly sexualized relative of the precocious child—on the discursive axis of two distinctive forms of power in modern Western societies.

Foucault's remarks on genocide unsettle the thumbnail literary history proposed earlier in *The History of Sexuality.* There Foucault proposes that the rise of the micropolitical corresponds roughly with the displacement of narratives of adventure by narratives of sentiment. "[W]e have passed from a pleasure to be recounted . . . centering on the heroic . . . narration of 'trials' of bravery," he contends, "to a literature ordered according to the infinite task of extracting [truth] from the depths of oneself."[12] Perhaps one consequence of this statement is that Foucauldian criticism has concentrated on domestic, realist, and sentimental fictions to the neglect of adventure fictions (which, because they so often unfold on borders between "civilized" and "savage," frequently engage questions of the survival of races). Foucauldian New Historicist critics writing about the nineteenth century—particularly Richard Brodhead, Nancy Armstrong, and D. A. Miller—have constructed the home and its narratives as, in Miller's words, the domain of an "extralegal series of 'micro-powers' " and hence the proper sphere for Foucauldian inquiry.[13] But if we take seriously Foucault's comments about the involution of micro- and macropowers around questions of race, then we would expect to uncover not the superannuation of heroism by sentiment but rather their simultaneity and coimplication. The ease with which educational treatises like Beecher's and Brigham's oscillate from the individual to the race suggests the pertinence of Foucauldian analysis to race relations. Similarly, analysis of the figure of the precipitous aboriginal whose precocity signals his inevitable demise in *The*

Last of the Mohicans suggests that this type of analysis is as relevant to imperial fictions as it is to domestic ones.

Such reading of the relation between home and frontier, however, suggests more than the need for simple expansion of the domain of New Historicism. I would like to use this reading as an occasion to interrogate the politics of Foucauldian analysis itself—at least as that analysis has been translated into the discourse of U.S. intellectuals. Uncovering the interaction between micro- and macropolitical concerns raises some questions about the gender and racial politics of the Foucauldian "shift" from which New Historicist criticism on the nineteenth century proceeds. A shift from an economy of punishment to one of discipline is not just passively evidenced but actively deployed in early nineteenth-century U.S. representations of the prodigy. It is not simply that antebellum texts like *The Last of the Mohicans* either prefigure or preempt contemporary theoretical and critical developments (although I would indeed claim that New Historicism of the Foucauldian variety has in its discussion of power recapitulated more than it has analyzed an important component of nineteenth-century discourse). More important, I would argue that a reading of antebellum texts demonstrates that narratives of the shift from punishment to discipline (like the one that Foucauldian New Historicism has given us) perform their cultural work at the expense of both middle-class white women and aboriginal peoples. Whatever its politics within its own cultural setting, Foucauldian knowledge does not encounter a political vacuum when it enters contemporary U.S. critical discourse. Instead it meets with a history extending back to the antebellum period in which intellectuals have deployed narratives of a shift in the nature of power toward politically suspicious ends. For this reason, contemporary intellectuals in the United States whose work has been influenced by Foucault (myself included) need to historicize their own discourse, by reconstructing its genealogy and inquiring into the rhetorical work performed in the U.S. context by the Foucauldian shift that supplies their work with its solid historical foundations.

II

Just as Brigham encodes in William M.'s brief life the ethnographic logic supporting an account of the decline of Anglo-Americans, so, compacted within Cooper's precipitous aboriginal, is a logic ensuring the ideological transformation of Native Americans into Vanishing Americans. Despite the spectacular nature of their individual deaths. Cooper's natives, every bit as much as his introductory reference to the "verdure . . . fall[ing] before the nipping frost," expunge imperialist conflict from the Jacksonian cultural memory. They do so by foregrounding issues of proportion and equilibrium so crucial to antebellum accounts of the disappearance of races.

Cooper incorporates the racial other as an earlier and now irretrievably lost version of the self. Perhaps this is part of the reason why our culture has come to regard *The Last of the Mohicans* and other nineteenth-century Anglo-American frontier fictions as "children's literature." Just as Freud in his essay on "The Sexual Aberrations" collapses the "primitive" or "archaic" and the infantile,[14] Cooper conflates racial difference and temporal distance on an evolutionary continuum of human history. For him, in other words, it is as though aboriginals represent a phase that the human race goes through but must inevitably get over. Regardless of whether the ethnopedagogic text celebrates equilibrium (in the case of Cooper and Brigham) or disequilibrium (in the case of Fuller), in equating the savage and the juvenile it starts by assuming that certain Americans must vanish.

Cooper's concern with proportion registers his debt to ethnopedagogic thinking. The novel's white characters marvel over the "perfection of form which abounds among the uncorrupted natives" (53), and the narrator himself praises what he calls Uncas's "beautiful proportions" (275). Uncas is "an unblemished specimen of the noblest proportions of man" and resembles "some precious relic of the Grecian chisel" (53). In the Western tradition the ancient Greeks had long represented the ideal of physical beauty, but in the antebellum United States their beautiful proportions had become the sine qua non of a call for educational reform. Beecher, for example, launches her critique of the U.S. educational system with the observation that the Greeks "were remarkable, not only for their wisdom and strength, but for their great beauty, so that the statues they made to resemble their own men and women have, ever since, been regarded as the most perfect forms of human beauty." "Perfect forms" here conveys roughly what "beautiful proportions" connotes in Cooper: a balance of intellectual and physcial culture—hence Beecher's interest in the Greek educational system as a model for contemporary times. According to her, the Greeks' perfection of form derived from the fact that "[t]hey had two kinds of schools—the one to train the minds, and the other to train the bodies of their children."[15]

Cooper expresses a similar nostalgia for primitive equilibrium, but he lacks Beecher's confidence in the power of mere institutional reform to restore that equilibrium. He imagines that civilization necessarily spells the end of archaic proportions. Hence Cooper contrasts Uncas's "beautiful proportions" with the white man David Gamut's "rare proportions" (17). Gamut, writes the novelist, possesses "all the bones and joints of other men, without any of their proportions." While Cooper reassures us that Gamut is not actually physically "deformed," his description of Gamut does little to assuage his reader's anxiety on that score:

> His head was large; his shoulders narrow; his arms long and dangling; while his hands were small, if not delicate. His legs and thighs were thin nearly to emaciation, but of extraordinary length; and his knees would have been considered tremendous, had they not been outdone by the broader foundations [i.e., his feet] on which this false superstructure of blended human orders, was so profanely reared. (16)

Gamut's peculiar proportions are just one sign that he is the vehicle by which civilization is carried into the wilderness. Around him also accrue linked images of language, femininity, and power. Referring to Gamut's annoying habit of bursting into song whenever the proximity of enemy Indians demands absolute silence (Gamut is a psalmodist by profession), Hawk-eye laments the fact that, although the "Lord never intended that the man should place all his endeavours in his throat, [Gamut had] fallen into the hands of some silly woman, when he should have been gathering his education under a blue sky, and among the beauties of the forest" (224).

While perhaps Cooper, like Hawk-eye, believes that God "never intended that the *man*" privilege language at the expense of the development of the body, both seem to believe that the Supreme Being intended that *woman* do so. This is suggested by Cooper's habitual association of feminine control over education in the settlements with both the proliferation of words and precipitous behavior. For example, as darkness begins to settle on his party's search for clues to the whereabouts of the captive Munro sisters, Hawk-eye advises his companions to abandon the trail until morning: "[I]n the morning we shall be fresh, and ready to undertake our work like men, and not like babbling women, or eager boys" (189).

Hawk-eye's association of loquacious femininity and headstrong boys has antecedents in Rousseauan notions of noble savagery. In *Emile,* women's control over the education of children threatens the survival of the white race: "[P]uberty and sexual potency always arrive earlier in learned and civilized peoples than in ignorant and barbarous peoples," and this explains why Europeans (unlike noble savages) are "exhausted early, remain small, weak, . . . ill-formed," and die young. "Man's weakness," Rousseau writes, proceeds from "the inequality between his strength and his desires."[16] Only in boyhood and savagery is there an equilibrium of body (what we can get) and mind (what we want), and for Rousseau, equilibrium is synonymous with nobility—a quality whose residual existence boyhood guarantees in civilized societies.

Emile's antifeminism derives from Rousseau's belief that, because their lack of physical strength prevents them from attaining self-sufficiency, women inevitably want more than they can get. The satisfaction of even a woman's most basic wants necessarily requires that she defraud her constitutional destiny by using words to persuade others to do for her what she cannot do for herself. Women, feels Rousseau, must and should rely upon men to get what they want. The problem arises when women are given unsupervised control over the education of boys. Whereas the father can discipline the child through simple physical coercion (which Rousseau heartily recommends), the mother must resort to complex sentimental manipulations expressed in words. Individual pedagogical errors are avenged upon the race as the son discovers that the efficacy of the verbal tool obviates the necessity of bodily vigor. The boy learns how to defraud the body through "feminine" acts of representation, destroys the juvenile balance of needs and strength, and thereby becomes a prodigy. Put in Cooper's terms, in *Emile* babbling women yield eager boys.

Cooper's Rousseauan subtext emerges when one of his noble savages asserts, "Men speak not twice" (314). Real men do not need words because they have physical strength. Women and precocious sons, however, require verbal prosthetics to get what they want. Furthermore, for Cooper as well as for Rousseau, words represent a whole economy of power marked as feminine. Thus, after declaring himself a warrior and not a reader, Hawk-eye asserts that he, unlike Gamut, is no "whimpering boy, at the apron string of one of your old gals" (117). Free of books, Hawk-eye liberates himself from the power that nineteenth-century domesticity gave to women—liberates himself from what Leslie Fiedler calls the "gentle tyranny of home and woman."[17] Hence when Gamut demands that Hawk-eye buttress one of his numerous philosophical speculations with some authoritative textual prop, the enraged scout demands: "[W]hat have such as I, who am a warrior of the wilderness . . . to do with books! I never read but in one [the book of nature], and the words that are written there are too simple and too plain to need much schooling" (117). I would argue that the fiction of the "plainness" of the book of nature in this passage supports another fiction: that of the legibility of paternal power imagined as simple physical force. Cooper attempts to differentiate between knowledge gained from experience on the trail and "bookish knowledge" (189) in order to create the fiction of power relations "plain" as nature itself.

Both the disregard for books and the association of them with the newly empowered antebellum woman are staples of the period. Although *the book* is usually associated with the reign of the father, in the antebellum period *books* seem to be associated with the reign of the mother. The pervasiveness of this association is suggested by Thoreau's chapter on "Reading" in *Walden*. There the author expresses his disgust at not just the quality of popular books but also their quantity. Embedded within Thoreau's anxiety about multiplicity lies an anxiety about the mother's assumption of the educational duties formerly administered by the father—or so Thoreau's confusion of mechanical production and female sexual reproduction leads one to suspect.

Thoreau confuses the printing press with the womb when he derides the "modern cheap and fertile press." Machinelike literary mothers produce not only insubstantial volumes (like the popular series called "Little Reading," which Thoreau had come across one day in his local library), but also insubstantial people. Thoreau characterizes the readers of "Little Reading" as themselves little, like the "modern puny and degenerate race" described by Beecher. They are "pygmies and manikins" and "a race of tit-men." The author distinguishes this modern race from the archaic, athletic, robust race of men nurtured by literary fathers before the age of mechanical reproduction. According to "Reading," in a heroic age long past, it "require[d] a training such as the athletes underwent" to read literature. Whereas the modern press is "fertile," "the heroic writers of antiquity" produced works which were "solitary."[18]

Thoreau's opposition of the feminine, the diminutive, and the multiple against the masculine, the massive, and the singular services a Rousseauan distinction between power conceived of as a physical force and power conceived of as verbal and sentimental manipulation. The solidity of the paternal book in "Reading" symbolizes the visibility of power relations under the patriarch, and the robustness of the (male) reader of the (male) classics denotes his ability both to see and to fight whatever threatens his autonomy. Hence Thoreau writes that, even if read in translation (in what he calls "our *mother* tongue"), the massive "heroic books" are written in a language alien to the modern reader. They "will always be in a language dead to degenerate times," and therefore they require their readers to seek "laboriously . . . the meaning of each word and line." The laboriousness of the reading preserves the autonomy of the subject. The classics speak in a "*father* tongue, a reserved and select expression" that does not compromise volition because, rather than lulling the reader to sleep, it demands that he "devote [his] most alert and wakeful hours" to reading. By contrast, we learn our "mother tongue . . . unconsciously" and hence read popular books like sleepwalkers. In "Reading," the smallness of books written by women suggests not just their trivial contents, but also the microscopic scale of maternal power. Thoreau's comment that readers of little books are "machines" anticipates the Foucauldian anxiety over a power whose invisibility (accomplished through domestication, decentering, and proliferation) only augments its efficiency.[19]

Although Thoreau's chapter reads like an attempt to disempower the domestic woman, the same disparaging association of mass production and female generativity made by Thoreau surfaces even in the texts apparently most instrumental in instituting the reign of the mother. Domestic ideology's demonic double, what Michael Paul Rogin dubs "momism,"[20] is if anything even more evident in the work of Hannah More, the British author generally credited with the founding of domestic ideology. Her influential treatise on female education was reprinted in numerous U.S. editions between 1800 and 1826 and helped determine the shape of domesticity in this country as well as in Britain.

In *Strictures on the Modern System of Female Education,* More, like Thoreau, expresses anxiety about the quantity of "little books" on the market. "Real" knowledge and piety, she writes, have suffered from "that profusion of little, amusing, sentimental books with which the youthful library overflows."[21] After questioning the pedagogical value of multiplying the number of books students read, More is overcome by a proto-Malthusian vision of the uncontrollably generative popular press.

> Who are those ever multiplying authors, that with unparalleled fecundity are overstocking the world with their quick-succeeding progeny? They are the novel-writers; the easiness of whose productions is at once the cause of their own fruitfulness, and of the almost infinitely numerous race of imitators, to whom they give birth.

More's nightmare vision collapses the mechanical production increasingly characterizing the book industry with female sexual reproduction. Mass production of children (the creation of a "race of imitators") is the evil twin of domestic ideology's attempt to standardize child-rearing practices. The hysteria over the abundance of books in the antebellum period both represents and creates an anxiety over the violation of the independence of the subject by disciplinary methods directed at the interior rather than at the body. An anxiety over the decorporealization of power compels the advice offered time and again in educational treatises in the early nineteenth century: more emphasis should be placed upon the cultivation of the juvenile body and less upon that of the juvenile mind. In More's text, the excessively cerebral Anglo-Saxon stands on the verge of disappearing as power disappears. The Anglo-Saxon race is threatened with the same "quick succession of slavery, effeminacy, . . . vice, . . . and degeneracy" that overtook the inhabitants of ancient Rome.[22]

For Cooper, to read in the book of nature is to be educated through the paternal apprenticeship system rather than the maternal representational system. Cooper suggests this when at one point in the narrative Chingachgook and Hawk-eye lose Magua's trail. Uncas, who has long since uncovered the proper path, nevertheless assumes a "calm and dignified demeanour" suggestive of "dependen[ce] on the sagacity and intelligence of the seniors of the party" (213). Savage society, in Cooper as in Rousseau, does not produce prodigies. According to the novelist, when members of Indian tribes convene to confer on matters important to the whole community,

> there is never to be found any impatient aspirant after permature distinction, standing ready to move his auditors to some hasty, and, perhaps, injudicious discussion, in order that his own reputation may be the gainer. An act of so much precipitancy and presumption, would seal the downfall of precocious intellect for ever. It rested solely with the oldest and most experienced of the men to lay the subject of the conference before the people. (292)

Indian society then offers a highly visible version of power. According to the narrator, the power of the Indian leader is the power of physical force: "the authority of an Indian chief [is] so little conventional, that it [is] oftener maintained by physical superiority, than by any moral supremacy he might possess" (92).

If basing power on physical superiority prevents aboriginal precocity, it also makes the patriarch's control over the tribe tenuous. Even Cooper's most noble savages seem barely restrained by the father. Uncas's "dignified and calm demeanor" disappears at a moment's notice. As soon as Chingachgook solicits his help, Uncas bounds "forward like a deer" and directs his elders to the proper trail (213). The young Mohican's sudden shift from rocklike self-restraint to frenetic activity is one that characterizes natives whether represented individually or in groups. Such fluctuations in Indian demeanor suggest what Cooper imagines as the fundamental exteriority to the self of power legitimated by physical superiority. Despite its patriarchal nature, Indian government permits radical independence because, like the authority exercised by Foucault's sovereign, that restraint is imagined to be of a strictly corporeal nature.

Fiedler's "gentle tyranny," on the other hand, would subvert radical native independence and undermine native proportions. This is in fact what happens to Uncas. Aware at some level of Uncas's admiration of her, Cora gains an "intuitive consciousness of her power" over the young Mohican (79). Like the ethnologists of his day, Cooper believed that Indians experienced no romantic passion.[23] Hence he calls Uncas's enamored ministrations to Cora both a "departure from the dignity of his manhood" and an "utter innovation on . . . Indian customs" (56). His love "elevate[s] him far above the intelligence, and advance[s] him . . . centuries before the practices of his nation" (115). Falling under Cora's power, educated without his knowledge, Uncas dies a racial prodigy of the sort Brigham imagined—only in Cooper's text the figure is more explicitly sexualized.

Cora's gentle tyranny appears to "seal the downfall" of Uncas's "precocious intellect." Hawk-eye notes the Mohican's uncharacteristic precipitancy during their search for the captive Munro sisters. He chastises Uncas for suddenly becoming "as impatient as a man in the settlements" (185). The noble savage turned eager savage repeatedly puts himself at risk in pursuing the captive Cora Munro: "In vain Hawk-eye called to him to respect the covers; the young Mohican braved the dangerous fire of his enemies, and soon compelled them to a flight as swift as his own headlong speed" (334).

Significantly, it is this precocious development under woman's invisible tutelage that makes Uncas the *last* of the Mohicans. At the end of the novel, he stands upon a ledge overlooking Magua, who is threatening Cora with a tomahawk. The impassioned Mohican leaps "frantically, from a fearful height" and falls between Magua and his intended victim, but only to himself fall victim to his enemy's tomahawk (337). Cooper reports Magua's headlong death at Hawk-eye's hands on the very next page of the novel; the language of precipitancy, and the reiteration of the image of the headlong Indian, all encourage us to confuse the two red men. Invoking the antebellum figure of the prodigy, Cooper's text replaces Hawk-eye's rifle with the middle-class woman's apron strings.[24] It translates fire power into mother power.

The Last of the Mohicans deflects attention from the macropolitical realm represented in the text by the army (for which Hawk-eye is a scout), and attributes to women the responsibility for the disappearance of the native. But the prodigy's presence does more than deflect. The threat that woman's invisible power poses to the male subject produces the need for some space (the frontier) to elude her miasmic influence and hence makes imperative the macropolitical controls effecting Indian removal from contiguous territories. In other words, Cooper's "discovery" of the discipline deployed against his white men legitimates the technologies of punishment deployed against his red men.

III

Antebellum discourse, I have argued, uses images of the modern proliferation of words as a sign that feminine words have replaced masculine muscle as the basis of authority. Momist imagery of the loss of autonomy resulting from this feminization of power expresses nostalgia for a form of power whose lack of psychic consequences guarantees that it does not compromise the autonomy of the male subject. Yet neither this subject nor this form of power ever existed. Because it is administered and experienced by human agents, even "simple" brute force must have psychic consequences and must produce subjectivities particular to it.

The myth of simple brute force in antebellum discourse generates what Renato Rosaldo calls "imperialist nostalgia." "When the so-called civilizing process destabilizes forms of life, the agents of change experience transformations of other cultures as if they were personal losses."[25] Developing Rosaldo's point, Amy Kaplan suggests that such nostalgia makes aggression against Third World peoples the logical consequence of antifeminism directed against First World women, because in its mythology "the empire figures as the site where you can be all that you can no longer be at home—a 'real live man'—where you can recover the autonomy denied by social forces of modernization, often aligned in this way of thinking with feminization."[26]

Following Rosaldo and Kaplan, I would argue that in our own time scholarship on the alleged feminization of society itself participates in the imperialist nostalgia of the discourse it analyzes. Traditionally, momist texts like Cooper's were seen as evidence of a historical "feminization of American culture" in which expanded female leisure and literacy permitted Hawthorne's "scribbling women" to usurp the cultural offices once occupied by less prolific but more profound male authors.[27] More recently, New Historicist criticism of the Foucauldian variety has encouraged us to regard the feminization of culture as a symptom of a larger feminization of power. Yet the novelty of New Historicism does not reside in its emphasis on power. Earlier cultural analysis also equated feminization with normalization. Richard Brodhead's recent characterization of the modern ideal of maternal love as a power whose "silken threads are harder to burst than the iron chains of authority" employed by "old-style paternal discipline," recalls Fiedler's analysis of the rise of a "gentle tyranny of home and woman" in the nineteenth-century.[28] And D. A. Miller's revelation of a nineteenth-century "field of power relations" masquerading as a "domesticating pedagogy" harks back to Ann Douglas's discussion of the "manifold possibilities" offered by Victorian maternal influence for "devious social control."[29] Finally, Nancy Armstrong's assertion that domestic ideology provided the "logic" that permitted women to enter the world of work through social services, and thereby extended "subtle techniques of domestic surveillance beyond the middle-class home and into the lives of those much lower down on the economic ladder," mirrors Christopher Lasch's claim that the "rise of the 'helping professions' " allowed "society in the guise of a 'nurturing mother' [to invade] the family, the stronghold of . . . private rights."[30]

Neither the poststructuralist upheaval that divides the cultural analysis of the 1960s and 1970s from that of the 1980s, nor the feminist critiques to which these analyses have been subjected, have altered the basic narrative: normalization is still women's work. What is even more startling is that this narrative appears to date back to antebellum times. Yet the failure of New Historicists to articulate a genuinely novel reading of the nineteenth century troubles me far less than their apparent obliviousness to the rhetorical content of what they present as historical facts.[31] Even if exposing the rhetorical work of Foucauldian history does not in and of itself undermine the facticity of New Historicist claims (all facts require human interpreters and so all truth is necessarily rhetorical), its practitioners cannot possibly hope to direct their own rhetoric toward progressive ends without first inquiring into the gender and race politics perpetuated by their use of Foucauldian knowledge.[32]

New Historicists' dependence upon Foucault's narrative of modernization would seem to account for their apparent obliviousness to the way in which they have been retelling a politically suspect nineteenth-century narrative of modernization. Despite the emphasis I have put on it, Foucault's assertion that the West's commitment to managing the life of its own population also entails a commitment to massive destruction of populations designated as "other" is parenthetical to the history outlined in the first volume of *The History of Sexuality*. Whereas his brief comments on modern racial holocausts suggest the simultaneity of deductive and productive manifestations of power, Foucault's larger historical narrative (as represented by both *The History of Sexuality* and *Discipline and Punish*) is founded upon a temporal distinction between them such that the deductive (punishment) represents the premodern, and the productive (discipline) the modern, form of power. Hence Foucault's own narrative is subject to the same critique to which I have subjected antebellum narratives of modernization. Inasmuch as he defines modernity as the decorporealization of power, he participates in the construction of an utterly mythic time in which authority represented physical superiority (an era personified in *Emile* by the father who governs by means of the lash rather than through maternal entreaty). Foucault's temporalization of the difference between discipline and punishment suggests that even contemporay images of modernity collaborate in the production of the imperialist nostalgia I have been describing.

7

Class and the Strategies of Sympathy

Amy Schrager Lang

In 1851 the *North American Review* published a series of articles on political economy written by Francis Bowen, editor of the *Review* from 1843 until 1854 and, later, Alvord Professor of Natural Religion, Moral Philosophy, and Civil Polity at Harvard University. "There is a danger," Bowen wrote, "from which no civilized community is entirely free, lest the several classes of its society should nourish mutual jealousy and hatred, which may finally break out into open hostilities, under the mistaken opinion that their interests are opposite, and that one or more of them possess an undue advantage, which they are always ready to exercise by oppressing the others."[1] In the particular case of the United States, Bowen insisted, this mistaken opinion could only be held by those who failed to appreciate the "peculiar mobility" of American society. Today's pauper was, after all, tomorrow's merchant—"the man who labored for another last year," Abraham Lincoln declared, "this year labors for himself, and next year he will hire others to labor for him."[2]

This continuous displacement of master by man tended, in Bowen's view, to blur, if not altogether obliterate, the boundary between capital and labor. In fact, it was this very fluidity of boundaries that the term "class" was meant to capture; unlike "caste" or "rank," "class" identified the groupings into which all societies naturally divided, the way stations en route from pauperism to wealth. Properly considered—that is, considered not historically but teleologically—class antagonism would thus necessarily dissolve in a perfect harmony of interests.

While not everyone agreed with Bowen's analysis of class in America, he was hardly alone in his attention to social taxonomy and the operation of class. Throughout the 1840s and 1850s, scholars, legislators, journalists, reformers, and writers of every political stripe ventured their opinions about the nature and ramifications of class in America. *Harper's Monthly* ran sketches of "The Factory Boy"; *Democratic Review* printed titles like "Poverty and Misery, versus Reform and Progress"; *Merchant's Magazine and Commercial Review, Southern Quarterly Review,* and *North American Review* devoted their pages to articles on "Abuses of Classification," "The Distribution of Wealth," and "The True Theory of Labor and Capital." Likewise, from the

"Knights and Squires" of the *Pequod* to the fading aristocrats of the house of the seven gables, from the protagonists of domestic fiction, oppressed by the vicious poor and the dissolute rich alike, to Whitman's spectral "shape" rising from "[t]he ashes and the rags—its hands tight to the throats of kings," antebellum literature records the anxiety that accompanied the recognition and naming of class divisions in the United States in the years surrounding the European revolutions of 1848.

Not everyone, as I have suggested, shared Bowen's views. Nonetheless, while Europeans took to the streets, Americans increasingly promulgated and embraced images of harmony. Even as the extremes of wealth and poverty grew, as the women's rights movement gathered strength, and conflict over slavery intensified, the doctrine of the harmony of interests was expounded not only as economic theory but as spiritual principle. The consummate emblem of that harmony, bridging the economic and the spiritual, was the idealized middle-class home. If social mobility seemed to the likes of Bowen to assure a harmony of interests in the marketplace, the champions of domesticity saw in the stability of gender—that is, in the naturalizing and fixing of gender distinctions—the prospect of an even more perfect harmony. Like the vast, undifferentiated expanse of empire,[3] the narrow and highly ordered space of the middle-class home operated to contain the danger of class antagonism by providing an image of social harmony founded not on political principles or economic behavior but on the "natural" differentiation of the sexes. Nowhere is this image more clearly drawn than in domestic fiction, where the problem of class is neither resolved nor repressed but rather displaced, and where harmony—spiritual, familial, and social—is the highest good.

The displacement of class by gender is peculiarly apparent in a novel like Maria Cummins's 1854 best-seller *The Lamplighter,* a novel that conforms in every respect to our assumptions about domestic fiction. Cummins follows her young protagonist, Gerty Flint, from a childhood of poverty and abuse into middle-class comfort, piety, and marriage. An orphan of mysterious parentage, Gerty has been left, more or less accidentally, in the charge of her vicious landlady. Filled with a sense of the injustice of her lot, Gerty is befriended early in the story by a sympathetic local lamplighter who promises to "bring her something." Gerty, who needs everything, speculates about what the "something" might be: "Would it be something to eat? O, if it were only some shoes! But he wouldn't think of *that.*"[4]

And indeed, he doesn't. The "something" turns out not to be shoes but a kitten, a gift which leaves Gerty in a quandary. In the slum in which Gerty lives, the narrator mildly observes, "there were a great many cats" and, appealing though Gerty finds them, she knows "that food and shelter were most grudgingly accorded to herself and would not certainly be extended to her pets."[5] Gerty understands all too well that pets are a luxury of the middle class; to the poor they are a burden, and so is the kitten to Gerty.

Nonetheless, the function of the gift is clear. The kitten elicits a maternal and self-sacrificing "tenderness" from the otherwise belligerent Gerty. It reveals her specifically feminine fitness to move out of her deprived and depraved surroundings. In fact, Gerty's affection for the kitten provokes the conflict with her slatternly and unfeeling guardian that leaves Gerty homeless—whereupon she is adopted by the lamplighter. The kitten, then, establishes Gerty's right to a home. Gerty joins the ranks of the worthy poor, where her schooling in self-control and the domestic arts commences immediately. Thus prepared, she rises eventually into the middle class.

In this brief episode, class is both superseded and made visible by gender. In lieu of the contingencies of history, Cummins offers the unchanging nature of women, incorporating maternal self-sacrifice, Christian forbearance, and innate gentility. No abstract or literary issue, the problem of class in *The Lamplighter* is a problem of material inequity; it is, literally, the problem of who does and who does not have shoes. But that problem is immediately tied to the matter of gender, which, on the one hand, serves as the lens through which substantial inequality becomes visible, and on the other hand, obscures its origin in class. The kitten and the shoes both imply and answer each other; to think about the kitten is to remember the shoes, but it is also to find a solution in kittens to the problems of bare feet.

The Lamplighter depends, in other words, on a strategy of displacement in which the language of class yields to the language of gender. The problem of poverty is not repressed but translated into a vocabulary that makes its redress inevitable: the distortions of poverty are answered by the natural-ness of gender. Gerty stops breaking windows in retaliation for injuries done her, she exchanges rage for patience, the terms of her identity shift from poor to female, and she is awarded a home. Once gender is established as the source of social mobility and the guarantor of social harmony, the narra-tive focus shifts from social justice to individual reform, from deprivation to self-control.

Here, as elsewhere, what makes the erasure of class possible is not simply the fact that gender, like race, is deeply implicated in class status. Rather, gender and race are structurally able to substitute for class because the con-junction of attributes that define class position are rendered so intrinsic or else so transcendent that they pass either below or above history. As the contin-gency of social status is acknowledged, the potential for conflict becomes visible; conversely, that potential vanishes as the space between the attributes that are taken to constitute class and in which an explanation of their conjunc-tion might be undertaken collapses. The doctrine of harmony, of which I would propose this is the literary analogue, subsumes difference into one harmonious whole by means of a kaleidoscopic substitution of terms, terms which compose the social vocabularies in which writers and critics alike gov-ern and recover meaning.

For the most part, nineteenth-century public discourse about class has been elided in discussions of the social reality in which antebellum literature takes its place. Moreover, class itself—the experience of differentials of wealth, power, and prestige—has gone largely unaddressed as subject or structure in that literature. Instead, heightened critical interest in the constructed nature of race and gender has tended, paradoxically, to direct attention away from class, itself a wholly contingent category. Gender and race are imbued with the determinants of class which becomes, then, the silent term in the class-race-gender triad. Or, alternatively, the broadly economic terminology employed by many New Historicist critics in an effort to demonstrate the complicity of texts in the culture of their production has subordinated the problem of difference to the structural identity of the text with hegemonic culture. In both cases, the recognition and the erasure of class are virtually simultaneous; recent scholarship is, in this sense, oddly consonant with the literature it describes.

My intent in this chapter is to demonstrate that vocabularies of class, race, and gender continually displace one another in midnineteenth-century sentimental fiction, and to investigate the impact of those displacements on the success of sentimental representation. *The Lamplighter* serves as a kind of normative model, intended to suggest the social and novelistic benefits of this pattern of displacement for the propagation of a doctrine of harmony. The two texts on which this chapter focuses—Harriet Beecher Stowe's *Uncle Tom's Cabin* (1852) and Rebecca Harding Davis's *Life in the Iron Mills* (1861)—diverge from this model not only in their structure but in their overt intent. In them, the commitment to social justice abandoned in *The Lamplighter* dramatically complicates the scheme I have described. In contrast to *The Lamplighter,* with its attention to the spiritual and social redemption of the individual, each of these texts treats the plight of a group of people— chattel slaves in one case and wage slaves in the other—for whom the prospect of mobility is closed, and each focuses on a protagonist whose gender identification is highly unstable.

In distinguishing her "primitive" method of storytelling from that of the novelist, one of the most popular sentimental writers of the midnineteenth century described herself as entering "unceremoniously and unannounced, into people's houses."[6] Just so do we enter Uncle Tom's cabin in chapter 4 of Harriet Beecher Stowe's famous antislavery narrative. We are invited inside not by the occupants of the cabin but by the narrator, who has already taken us on a tour of the plantation house. "Let us enter the dwelling," she suggests, and in we go. While Aunt Chloe tends to the baking, the eye of the narrator pans the cottage, noting its various domestic arrangements and arriving finally at "the hero of our story," Uncle Tom himself, whom we are offered in "daguerreotype."

> He was a large, broad-chested, powerfully-made man, of a full glossy black, and a face whose truly African features were characterized by an expression of grave and steady good sense, united with much kindliness and benevolence. There was something about his whole air self-respecting and dignified, yet united with a confiding and humble simplicity.[7]

The very fact that Tom is the subject of a portrait, albeit a photographic one, suggests, of course, that this is no "thing" but a man. Moreover, the identification of the portrait as a daguerreotype assures us of its fidelity not merely to the outward man but to the inner one—aspects of the self understood by sentimental culture to be inextricably connected. Like other features of Tom's representation, the daguerreotype operates to assure us of Tom's humanity.[8]

Equally striking, however, is the sureness of the artist's hand, her unhesitating ability to read Tom's character in his face. However exotic he may be— with his "truly African features"—Tom is no enigma. His blackness, the outward sign of his enslavement, is not opaque but, like a daguerreotype, a transparency through which his essential nature shines. Tom's condition as slave is, after all, only an accident of history; it neither obstructs our view of him nor does it, apparently, shape his character. He is as confidently drawn as any of the white planters, traders, mothers, or children in *Uncle Tom's Cabin.*

By contrast, when Rebecca Harding Davis introduces us to Hugh Wolfe, the working class "hero" of *Life in the Iron Mills,* the problem of literary representation and its adequacy arises immediately. The story of *Life in the Iron Mills* is a "simple" one. The hunchbacked Deborah, a picker in the cotton mills, is in love with her cousin Hugh Wolfe, a Welsh ironworker who does not reciprocate her feelings. Ignorant and inarticulate, Wolfe spends his idle moments at the foundry carving figures out of korl, a waste product of iron refining. One rainy night when she brings Wolfe his supper in the mill, Deborah witnesses a tour of inspection by the mill owner's son and several of his friends. Quite by accident, the visitors discover one of Wolfe's figures, "a woman, white, of giant proportions, crouching on the ground, her arms flung out in some wild gesture of warning."[9] One of the men—an aristocratic figure named Mitchell—comments on Wolfe's talent and on the impossibility of its development without money. Overhearing this, Deborah steals Mitchell's wallet containing a check for an enormous sum and gives it to Wolfe. Wolfe's first impulse is to return the wallet, but he is overcome by temptation. Arrested and sentenced to nineteen years in prison for the theft, Wolfe commits suicide. Deborah, after serving a much briefer prison term, is rescued by the Quakers and lives out her days in a neighboring community of Friends.

In sharp contrast to *Uncle Tom's Cabin,* when the narrator of *Life in the Iron Mills* sets out to introduce us to her protagonist, she is beset by difficulty. The narrator's view of the protagonist is obstructed, first, by a failure of vision itself. It is difficult, she observes, to see anything through the stifling smoke of the mills on a rainy day. But she is not only blinded by rain and smoke; her vision is impaired as well by the indistinctness of the object at which she is looking. Wolfe is one of "masses of men, with dull, besotted faces" (*IM,* 12), "myriads of . . . furnace-tenders" (*IM,* 14) any of whom might serve equally well as the object of her contemplation. In fact, the narrator herself does not know and thus cannot tell why she has chosen his story from all the others. The lives of the Wolfes are not individual but "like those of their class." Their "duplicates" are "swarming the streets to-day" (*IM,* 15). Davis has no trouble locating Wolfe in history—his own or the town's—or claiming him as a legitimate subject for her narrative. Rather, the problem is the portrait itself. While Uncle Tom can be rendered with all the fidelity of the daguerreotype, Hugh Wolfe apparently cannot be drawn at all.

Both *Uncle Tom's Cabin* and *Life in the Iron Mills,* published just nine years later, sketch "life among the lowly." Each was written by a white, middle-class, Christian woman in an effort to arouse compassion for the victims of an unjust economic system to which neither had direct access. The comparison of these systems—chattel slavery and wage slavery—was, moreover, a staple of the slavery debate. Predictably, apologists for Southern slavery insisted that the plight of the wage slave was far worse than that of the chattel slave, who at the very least was clothed and fed. In lieu of the "false, antagonistic . . . relations" of the market, George Fitzhugh argued, slavery interposed the natural relations of the family. Abolitionists like Stowe likewise expounded the relationship between these forms of enslavement, contending that chattel slavery was only "the more bold and palpable infringement of human rights" (*UTC,* 231).

Stowe's famous indictment of chattel slavery stands, arguably, as the apotheosis of sentimental narrative. *Uncle Tom's Cabin* successfully normalizes the chattel slave—that is, it offers the grounds for the slaves' prospective membership in the middle class—thereby providing the theological, political and, most crucially, emotional basis for emancipation as well as the promise of "another and better day" of Christian brotherhood. Of course *Life in the Iron Mills* also invokes "the promise of the Dawn," but, unable even to represent its subject, it is unable to move beyond it into the golden future. The chattel slave not only can be daguerreotyped; he can be, as Uncle Tom is, transfigured. By attending to his story, we can move beyond history to the fulfillment of the kingdom of Christ in America. The wage slave, on the contrary, remains enmired almost to the point of invisibility in the mud of a present, sinful world. One is forced to ask why Davis's figure of the wage slave resists so thoroughly the sentimental treatment to which the chattel slave all too readily lends himself.

We can begin to answer that question by looking at the ways in which *Life in the Iron Mills* violates our expectations. Hugh Wolfe, "stooping all night over boiling cauldrons of metal, laired by day in dens of drunkenness and infamy" (*IM,* 12), is, by all rights, industry's victim, a martyr of the laboring classes—a Stephen Blackpool or perhaps a John Barton. We not only recognize his story, we anticipate the manner of its telling: the middle-class narrator who invites us to see "the romance" in the daily rounds of the Manchester mill hand or the American slave; the guide who, so to speak, familiarizes the lives of the lowly to the moral benefit of an all-comprehending reader and the social benefit of the oppressed. The tacit understanding is that the narrator's "lifelike" picture of how the other half lives, a picture both true and immediately apprehensible, will inspire our compassion as it did hers.

In *Life in the Iron Mills,* however, this sympathetic understanding is set aside from the outset. Accustomed to being invited into the story—"Let us enter the dwelling"—by a friendly narrator who resembles no one so much as ourselves, we are instead flatly shut out. "A cloudy day: do you know what that is in a town of iron-works?" (*IM,* 11). The question is not rhetorical but accusatory; clearly, we do *not* know what such a day in such a town is.

"Dilettantes" in clean clothes who think "it an altogether serious thing to be alive" (*IM,* 12–13), we are repeatedly reminded by the narrator that we cannot possibly grasp the drunken jest, the horrible joke, that is the life of the ironworker. We are "another order of being" (*IM,* 27); between us and Wolfe lies "a great gulf never to be passed" (*IM,* 30). Egotists, Pantheists, Arminians all, we would rather busy ourselves "making straight paths for [our] feet on the hills" (*IM,* 14) than contemplate the "massed, vile, slimy lives" of people like the Wolfes.

Whereas the optimistic sentimental narrative ordinarily projects a sincere and highly impressionable reader from whose eyes the scales will fall upon being confronted with the truth, Davis's hostile narrator doubts even the willingness of her reader to come down into the "nightmare fog" where the mill workers live. This assault on the reader is, presumably, meant to dislodge us from our position of complacent indifference to the plight of the industrial worker. Self-regard, if nothing else, will lead us to disprove the narrator's charges against us by attending to her protagonist. But ultimately the story offers us no alternative position in which to locate ourselves. So blinded are we by middle-class privilege that we are, it would seem, incapable of useful intervention on behalf of the ironworker. And so brutalized is he by the conditions of industrial life that he too is unable to act. Chided into allying ourselves emotionally with the victims of industry, we nonetheless remain trapped in our own world.

No sooner, in fact, have we acknowledged both our reluctance and our ignorance and agreed to be instructed by the narrator, than we discover that she too is barred from the town. Standing at a window above the street, she can "scarcely see" the "crowd of drunken Irishmen" (*IM,* 11) idling away their time outside the grocery opposite. From the back window overlooking the river, her view is no better. But here the impediment is not the smoggy day but her own imagination, which associates the "dumb appeal upon the face of the negro-like river slavishly bearing its burden" with the "slow stream of human life creeping past" on the street. This "fancy" the narrator quickly dismisses as "an idle one." The river, figured as a chattel slave, is no "type" of the life of the wage slave, for its future "liberation" is assured: it flows eventually beyond the town into "odorous sunlight . . . air, fields and mountains." The "future of the Welsh puddler," by contrast, is "to be stowed away, after his grimy work is done, in a hole in the muddy graveyard" (*IM,* 13).

Brief—even casual—as it is, the association of chattel and wage slave in the figure of the river and the narrator's repudiation of that figure is instructive. What is most immediately striking, in this context, is its implication that the black, bowed though he is under the burden of slavery, is moving inexorably toward liberation—toward the sunshine. This is not, as I hope to show, just wishful thinking on Davis's part but consonant with a broader view of the nature of slavery among Northern whites. As important as the allusion to chattel slavery is, however, something less conspicuous but of equal importance happens in this passage: the association of the stream of life with the literal stream of the river is rejected as pathetic fallacy. Fancy, the artist's stock in trade, is shown, despite the narrator, to be not merely "idle" but actively misleading. In fact, the tendency of literary language throughout *Life in the Iron Mills* is to falsify.

The mills, for example, in which "crowds of half-clad men, looking like revengeful ghosts in the red light, hurried, throwing masses of glittering fire" (*IM*, 20), are early likened to a "street in Hell." And indeed, insofar as the mills are demonic places in which men are held in thrall to the "unsleeping engines" of industry, the comparison is evocative. Later in the story, however, one of the visitors to the ironworks reverts to this analogy, now casting it in the erudite language of the highly educated. "Your works look like Dante's Inferno," the aristocratic Mitchell comments to Kirby, the mill owner's son; "Yonder is Farinata himself in the burning tomb" (*IM*, 27). The allusion seems at first to have a salutory effect: it prompts Kirby to look "curiously around, as if seeing the faces of his hands for the first time." But if the point of the allusion is to intensify the real, to make us—or Kirby—feel more acutely the plight of the ironworkers, the reference to Dante fails, for Kirby replies, "They're bad enough, that's true" (*IM*, 27). This response, needless to say, misses the point—as does the association of the ironworker with the sinful Italian nobleman. But what, after all, is the point? The appropriation of the real to the literary is, as Davis's narrator presents it, precisely a way *not* to see. By first rewriting the mill worker as Farinata, and then by dismissing him as "bad" and thus deserving of such an inferno, the visitors render the hands invisible. The allusion solves the moral problem that might otherwise be posed by the condition of labor in the mills, and allows the visitors to turn their attention to what really matters, the hard facts of industry—"net profits," "coal facilities," "hands employed."

The repudiation, if not the unmasking, of the literary is perfectly in keeping with the dictates of sentimental storytelling of the kind *Uncle Tom's Cabin* represents, with its commitment to the artless, lifelike tale. In a letter to her editor just prior to the publication of the first installment of *Uncle Tom's Cabin,* Stowe outlined her intentions: "My vocation is simply that of a painter, and my object will be to hold up in the most lifelike and graphic manner possible Slavery." "There is," she continued, "no arguing with *pictures,* and everybody is impressed by them, whether they mean to be or not."[10] Stowe's account of her vocation strikes the keynote of sentimental fiction. "Unpretending" stories written to move and instruct the middle-class family cozily gathered around the hearth, these stories were not, their authors insisted, properly "literature"—that deathlike form with "stony eyes, fleshless joints, and ossified heart" fit only for the library shelf.[11]

This is not to say that the sentimentalist denied her invention. Despite her portrayal of herself as a painter who does not paint but only "holds up" the picture of slavery, Stowe explains in the preface to *The Key to Uncle Tom's Cabin* that "[i]n fictitious writing, it is possible to find refuge from the hard and the terrible, by inventing scenes and characters of a more pleasing nature."[12] *Uncle Tom's Cabin* may be "lifelike," but it is not a "work of fact." Quite the contrary, if her critics "call the fiction dreadful," she exclaims in an

1853 letter to the Earl of Shaftesbury, "what will they say of the fact, where I cannot deny, suppress, or color?"[13]

Stowe's two accounts of her role as artist are less contradictory than they at first appear. The lifelike tale told by the sentimental storyteller was no invention of a dissembling literary art. It was at once a story waiting to be told and a story everyone already knew—a kind of "found" art. And its claim to sincerity depended on its repudiation of the "literary." The novel, with its intricate plot and startling developments, substituted artifice for substance, erudition for feeling, author for subject. Sentimental writers embraced instead an ideal of self-effacing simplicity, of "naturalness." What allows Stowe simultaneously to claim artlessness and artistry, then, is a tacit agreement between the sentimental writer and reader that certain artifices will be accepted as "natural," and further that the "natural" will be understood to point toward the ideal.

In *Life in the Iron Mills,* however, the "simple" sentimental picture is rendered impossible by the inaccessibility of the mills to the middle-class narrator, "idly tapping on the window-pane" as if to draw our attention to the barrier that stands between her and the lives of those on the street below. But equally impossible is the self-consciously literary sketch of the kind Melville, for example, offers in "The Tartarus of Maids."[14] If the first possibility is foreclosed by the narrator's inability to "enter the dwelling" of the iron-worker, the second is precluded by her inchoate recognition of the resemblance between economic and literary appropriation. She is no more willing to allegorize the mill worker than she is able to daguerreotype him.

In *Life in the Iron Mills* we are, in fact, in epistemological difficulty from the start. The narrator who demands that we "hide [our] disgust, take no heeds of [our] clean clothes, and come right down . . . into the thickest of the fog and mud and foul effluvia" (*IM,* 13) remains herself shut in the house. *If* we could "go into this mill," the narrator observes, we would surely discover there the "terrible tragedy" (*IM,* 23) of the mill worker, but this neither she nor we can do. The requirement that we enter the mill gives way to a far less strenuous request that we "hear this story." But of course we can only hear what the narrator can tell. And just as our narrator cannot enter the mills, so, she claims, she "can paint nothing" of the "reality of soul-starvation" that lurks behind the "besotted faces on the street" (*IM,* 23). Unable actually to enter or imaginatively to project herself into Wolfe's "dwelling," she can paint no "lifelike" picture.

Part of the problem is the ambiguity surrounding that "dwelling" itself. For Davis's mill workers, the central distinctions of middle-class culture are of no consequence. Home is no refuge, and labor is not productive but wasting. The cellar in which Wolfe lives is neither preferable to the mill where he spends most of his time nor, in a broad sense, any less its product than pig iron. Wolfe's "real" life—as worker and as artist—is led in the ironworks where, after laboring to transform ore into metal, he struggles in vain to transform industrial waste into art, to render the dregs of industry "beautiful and pure."

But if Wolfe's home is "unnatural" by middle-class standards, so are all the other aspects of his life. For Wolfe, who labors at night and takes such rest as he can during the day, even time is inverted. And so too is gender: Wolfe's thin muscles, weak nerves, and "meek woman's face" belie his employment as an iron puddler and earn him the "sobriquet" Molly Wolfe.

Like Uncle Tom, then, Hugh Wolfe is a highly feminized figure—a figure, some have argued, for the female artist[15]—but the resemblance ends there. The feminization of Tom is part of a systematic attempt to invest slaves with piety, innocence, affection, and nobility of purpose—traits meant to assure white middle-class readers of the fundamental ethical and emotional identity of blacks and whites. Like Bowen's account of the false antagonism of labor and capital, *Uncle Tom's Cabin* presents the differing interests of slave and slaveholder as illusory, a chimera of history. Tom's feminine qualities are central to his role as harbinger of the social and spiritual millennium to come. By contrast, the feminization of Hugh Wolfe is utterly debilitating; rather than providing grounds for his future success, Wolfe's feminine qualities ensure his demise. They make him physically and emotionally unfit for the only life he is likely to know. Like the disconcerting strength of the korl woman, the weakness of the feminized Wolfe heightens rather than diminishes our sense of the unnaturalness of his life.

But whereas Davis continually draws our attention to the distortions of industrial life—from the comfortless cellar to Deborah's hunched back—the logic of *Uncle Tom's Cabin* directs us to see lives of the slaves as versions of our own. The slave quarters, for example, are as much the outgrowth of a particular system of economic exploitation as the tenements of the mill workers, but Tom's cabin is nonetheless presented to us not as a hovel but as a veritable bastion of domesticity. Only the easy intrusion of whites—slaveholders, traders, and narrators—into the cabin reminds us that, for the slave, there is no private life. In both *Uncle Tom's Cabin* and *Life in the Iron Mills*, then, the separate spheres of men and women, work and family, are compromised, but in one we witness the doomed but insistent efforts of the chattel slave to restore the boundary between these, while in the other, normalcy— the social arrangements of the middle class—are beyond the imagination as well as the capacity of the characters. Unlike Chloe and Tom, neither Deborah nor Wolfe, for all their discontent, sees the middle class as imitable.

Having located her characters in a wholly alien world, it is not surprising that the narrator of *Life in the Iron Mills* can offer only the "fragments" of a story, the "outside outlines of a night" (*IM*, 23). By contrast, the narrator who so unceremoniously enters Uncle Tom's cabin is, so to speak, in full possession of her subject. Uncle Tom, after all, belongs quite literally to middle-class whites like herself—and her reader. This is not to suggest that Stowe did not mean to extend a full humanity to her slave characters; nevertheless, the central concern of *Uncle Tom's Cabin*—the transformation of a "thing" into a "man"—implies a plasticity that lends itself to Stowe's literary as well as her political purposes even as the form of representation she invokes—the daguerreotype—paradoxically hints at a deathlike fixing of its subject. The literal appropriation of the labor of slaves, in other words, facilitates their literary appropriation by the white artist.

Without rehearsing the arguments of the slavery debate, it is fair to say that, in that debate, the issue of slavery was as often as not subordinated to the question of the nature of blackness. For proponents of slavery, race served to naturalize the subordinate status of blacks. For others like Stowe who argued that racial difference was not sufficient to justify slavery, blackness nonetheless stood as a paradox. On the one hand, the black, dispossessed of himself, could be "owned," both actually and symbolically, by others. On the other hand, the black was taken to be profoundly unknowable, altogether unlike his white owner. Inscrutably black, essentially Other, and powerless to represent himself—legally or literarily—the American slave could, for these very reasons, be freely represented by the free white writer whose possession he was.

My point is not simply that, as Other, the slave was a blank screen on which the white writer could project any image she pleased. It is rather that blackness is widely understood in the midnineteenth century as a state of becoming. Even among the defenders of slavery, who insisted on the natural and therefore permanent "semi-civilization" of blacks, the question arose of what blacks would become over time, living among whites.[16] For romantic racialists like Stowe, the untapped potential of blacks was one of the most pressing arguments against slavery. Like the children (all of them girls) with whom he is continually associated, Uncle Tom is in the process of becoming—in Tom's case, becoming a Christian and ultimately a martyr, but in the case of other black characters, becoming independent, industrious, educated, prosperous, or pious. Like Alexander Kinmont, who claimed that blacks were destined to develop "a later but far nobler civilization" than that of whites, or William Ellery Channing, who saw in blacks "the germs of a meek, long-suffering, loving virtue,"[17] Stowe's narrative projects a rosy future in which the enslaved black emerges as free, Christian, and altogether respectable. Leaving aside Stowe's patronizing tone, that future is intimated from the outset by Uncle Tom's cabin, which—from its neat garden patch to the carpeted corner that serves as "drawing room" and the "brilliant scriptural prints" that decorate its walls—resembles nothing so much as a playhouse in which the life of middle-class adulthood is being rehearsed.

The prophetic mode of Stowe's narrative depends on the plasticity of its object, the black slave, and that plasticity, in turn, is a central feature of the developmental schemes used by whites to understand both the present and the future of the victims of chattel slavery. As yet unmade, the black could be molded to the artist's liking. In fact, he could be cast, as he is in *Uncle Tom's Cabin,* more or less in the image of his white creator. What is reflected here is not the sentimentalist's "ability to confuse the natural and the ideal"[18] so much as her willingness to reimagine the real as a type of the ideal. The success of *Uncle Tom's Cabin* depends on the narrator's capacity to project in fully realized form the man who lurks in the "thing" and, on the basis of this projection, to call for his emancipation. Insofar as it draws out the human potential, defined as the potential for middle-class respectability, in those whose full humanity is in doubt—the black or, more commonly, the poor and unruly orphan girl—sentimental narrative is oriented always toward the future[19] and, I would suggest, toward the home where differentials of class are most conspicuously inscribed.

Unlike the infinitely malleable Uncle Tom, however, Hugh Wolfe must be "hewed and hacked" out of the recalcitrant korl—the industrial waste that is both his sculptural medium and his matter—by a narrator who questions the capacity of literary language to make his story "a real thing" to her resisting reader. The object of the narrator's regard in *Life in the Iron Mills* is not the man *in posse* but the man the industrial world has already produced, the man with no future. Fixed in an interminable present, inarticulate, uneduated, born "in vice," "starved" in infancy, stained in body and soul, Wolfe is, so to speak, already completed—or rather, finished.

The irony is obvious, for Wolfe, unlike Uncle Tom, is free, white, and male. He is not legally bound to the mills; he is, as we say, master of his own destiny. As Doctor May, one of the visitors to the mill, complacently remarks, "you have it in you to be a great sculptor. . . . A man may make himself anything he chooses. . . . Make yourself what you will. It is your right" (*IM,* 37). A free agent by right, Wolfe is nonetheless represented as entirely the product of his circumstances, a figure not of human potential but of human waste.

But he is also, of course, a figure of the artist. The argument for Wolfe's humanity lies not in the man, dumb and brutelike, but in the korl woman, whose "wild, eager face, like that of a starving wolf's" (*IM,* 32) is, like the starving Hugh Wolfe, incomprehensible to the jeering Kirby and the complacent Doctor May. Nor can Wolfe explain it. Only the aristocratic Mitchell sees "the soul of the thing," but he sees it with an eye "bright and deep and cold as Arctic air," the eye of an "amused spectator at a play" (*IM,* 36). The korl sculpture, the tragedy of the furnace tender, the "rare mosaic" he examined that morning, and, we must assume, the peculiar institution of the South that he has come to the border state to "study"—these are to him as one. The narrator of *Life in the Iron Mills* must defend her subject not only against the Kirbys who would deny his soul and the genial Mays who would deny his plight but also, most crucially, against the tranquil gaze, the reified consciousness, of the Mitchells who see in Wolfe an "amusing study"—all of these, it must be added, versions of both narrator and reader.

Needless to say, the vehemence of the narrator, her inversion of the usual narrative stance, her insistence on the failure of narrative and her own inadequacy, are all calculated for effect. She does, after all, tell her story and more. As she herself admits, the "tiresome" story of Hugh Wolfe hides a "secret" that she "dare not put . . . into words," a "terrible dumb question" that is, paradoxically, "from the very extremity of its darkness, the most solemn prophecy . . . the world has known of the Hope to come" (*IM,* 14). The question—"Is this the End?"—is articulated only twice: once in the poetic epigraph that opens the story and again, at it close, by the korl woman.

Complicit though art may be in the system of capitalist exploitation, only art, it turns out, can speak the terrible question and reveal the prophecy. Wolfe is mute, but his sculpture is invested with the power of speech. The "pale, vague lips" of the korl woman "tremble" with the terrible question (*IM*, 64). Wolfe cannot be figured, much less transfigured, but the korl woman is touched by the "blessing hand" of the "Dawn" (*IM*, 65), just as Deborah, named after the Biblical prophetess, is later touched by the Quaker woman.

Prophecy, both social and religious, fails in *Life in the Iron Mills* because in the end art has been made to substitute for life after all. That is to say, prophecy fails because the narrator has made us acutely aware not only of the distance between the artifice, the story or the sculpture, and the Truth, the "reality" of Hugh Wolfe's "soul-starvation," but also of the inevitable tendency of art to appropriate the life of its subject, the mill hand, just as the mill owner appropriates his labor. Thus when we learn of Deborah's transformation at the hands of the Quakers in a "homely pine house, on one of these hills" overlooking "broad, wooded slopes and clover-crimsoned meadows" (*IM*, 63), we realize that we are being asked to accept the pathetic fallacy of the river after all. Likewise when the narrator attempts, at the close of the story, to re-present the truth of Hugh Wolfe's futile life as a higher one, the transcendent truth of "the day that shall surely come," we resist; the narrator has, in effect, taught us too well. Fully persuaded that the ironworker lives and dies in the mills only to be replaced by his duplicate, that his aspirations will always be thwarted by the conditions of industrial life, we believe that he is America's future, that he will no more disappear than the wheels of industry grind to a halt; he prefigures not the millennium but, we suspect, the apocalypse.

Insofar as wage slavery is taken to be a necessary concomitant of industry, it is irremediable and, like the mills themselves, inescapable. But chattel slavery, by contrast, could be abolished, and that without endangering the nation. For Stowe's narrator, slavery is not just a sin but an anachronism and an aberration. The remnant of an altogether un-American seignorialism, it belongs to the feudal past, not to the democratic future. As George Harris's invocation of the American Revolution implies, slavery constitutes a falling away from the very ideals on which the nation was founded. Emancipation, in *Uncle Tom's Cabin,* does not threaten but guarantee the future of America; in fact, emancipation alone will avert the wrath of God and secure America for the millennium. Moreover, emancipation not only must but can be accomplished. Although the narrator goes to some lengths in *Uncle Tom's Cabin* to demonstrate the complicity of the North in Southern slavery, she understands the effects of emancipation as local and short-term. Once possessed of "property, reputation, and education" and all the advantages of "Christian republican society," the emancipated slaves can be returned to Africa to put into practice "the lessons they have learned in America" (*UTC*, 449).

If one were to credit their titles alone, to go from *Uncle Tom's Cabin* to *Life in the Iron Mills* is simply to go from home to work. At the imaginative center of Stowe's narrative is the family home: its affectionate ties are the story's ideal, its disruption a sin, its absence the sign of an unredeemable evil. Uncle Tom's "real" life is led in his cabin, surrounded by his wife and children. An ideal site, the cabin thus can serve, at the end of the narrative, as a "memorial," pointing back to slavery, a death in life, and forward to emancipation, a life after death.

In establishing the emotional grounds for the identification of her middle-class reader with the slave, Stowe's narrator invests her black characters with the virtues they will, she assures us, come to have once free. In this sense, Uncle Tom fuses hope and destiny. Like their middle-class counterparts in antebellum America, the slaves in *Uncle Tom's Cabin* live "suspended between the facts of [their] present social condition and the promise of [their] future."[20] And just as the middle-class American was thus plagued with anxiety concerning his own social identity, so too was he plagued with anxiety over the "true" nature of the black. Arguably, in that anxiety we can read the demise of slavery. The sentimentalist's "monumental effort to reorganize culture from the woman's point of view"[21] is not, that is, without its class bias; in fact, the achievements of sentimentalism depend on its reorganization of culture from the point of view of the parlor, the "cultural podium" of the white middle-class woman.

The drive to impose the forms of the future on the present, so apparent in *Uncle Tom's Cabin*, is stymied in *Life in the Iron Mills*, where all forward movement is blocked by the combination of inadequate narrator, unwilling reader, and mute subject. As the English industrial novel suggests, even where home is a cellar with a pile of rotting straw for a bed, where "real" life is stooping over a cauldron of boiling metal all night, it is possible to project a future millennium in which masters and men, Christians all, unite. But it is possible only by an act of appropriation. With an irony that eludes its unself-conscious narrator, *Uncle Tom's Cabin* appropriates the black slave—an embodied object, a "thing" waiting to be claimed—in the interest of ending his appropriation by others. This irony is the stumbling block for the narrator of *Life in the Iron Mills*. Rejecting all modes of representation as forms of appropriation, refusing to pretend to know her subject just as she refuses to let her reader pretend to know what a cloudy day in an iron mill town is, she exposes the artless "scribbling women" and the erudite literary men—Stowe and Melville alike—in their truest character, as members of the possessing class.

Yet like them, she must find a way to tell her story. Freeing her eyes to see the promise of the dawn in the nearly impenetrable darkness of her story, she falls victim to the common fate of the reforming artist. Having refused to take possession of her human subject, she is, in the end, the uneasy possessor of the korl woman, the only remaining evidence of Wolfe's existence. *Uncle Tom's Cabin* ends with the inevitable transfiguration of Tom's homely dwelling into the symbolic site of liberation; *Life in the Iron Mills* ends, inevitably, as it began. Just as Hugh Wolfe is rendered invisible by the smoke of the mills at the beginning of the story, so at the end the visible, tangible figure of the korl woman, "a rough, ungainly thing," painful to look at, is kept hidden behind a curtain in the narrator's library.

The representational quandary posed by class is answered by recourse to gender as surely in *Life in the Iron Mills* as it is in *Uncle Tom's Cabin* (or, for that matter, in *The Lamplighter*), but the literary and political consequences for the story are altogether different. For Stowe, slavery is the testing ground of middle-class culture. The success of *Uncle Tom's Cabin* depends on the placement of the chattel slave in a developmental scheme which makes immanent his middle-class character and thus brings him, provisionally at least, into the world of the reader. The virtues of that world are measured, in turn, by its capacity to assimilate to itself both slave and slaveholder. The developmental scheme that governs the representation of slaves in *Uncle Tom's Cabin*, in other words, not only lends itself to the millennial hopes of the narrator, but also implies an absolute standard of value against which everyone and everything can be measured.

In Davis's grim account of industrial life, on the contrary, the shifting vocabularies of class and gender expose the limits of middle-class sentimental culture. At the end of *Life in the Iron Mills,* we are returned to the domestic world of the middle-class narrator which, unlike the satanic mills, "belongs to the open sunlight." But that world—a world in which vision is ostensibly restored—is one in which mill workers become once again invisible, a world from which darkness is banished, and in which epistemological problems are solved by faith. Having placed the wage slave out of sight of that world and beyond the ameliorative influence of genteel reform, Davis is left with only a morally equivocal art to mediate between the sunlit world of her middle-class reader and the gloom of the mills. Class cannot be dismissed as obscuring a deeper "human" reality, nor can it be dissolved into race or gender. Rather, class stands as irreducible to the end, and art—suspect from the first— emerges as the real subject of *Life in the Iron Mills.*

8

Unseemly Sentiments: The Cultural Problem of Gambling

Ann Fabian

Writing in 1842, Lydia Maria Child admitted that she had "often anathematized the spirit of Trade, which reigns triumphant, not only on the 'Change, but in our halls of legislation, and even in our churches." She saw the money changers returned to the temple; she saw thought, sentiment, love, and philanthropy turned from higher spiritual ends to the vicious designs of profit. "Thought is sold under the hammer, and sentiment in its holiest forms stands labelled for the market. Love is offered to the highest bidder, and sixpences are given to purchase religion for starving souls."

Child hoped that this victory of Trade was only temporary, and called upon a congeries of priceless virtues for the germ of a sentimental critique of all that was selfish and self-serving in the expanding capitalist marketplace of the mid-nineteenth-century North. She reminded an audience schooled in the basic sentimental tenet that a region of heart lay beyond the corruptions of the market, that money was "not wealth." "I know the universal opinion of mankind is to the contrary; but it is nevertheless a mistake. Our real losses are those in which the *heart* is concerned."[1]

Yet even for Child, the relations between the selfless sentiments of home and hearth and the selfish strivings of the market were never those of simple opposition. The white middle-class Northerners who, in the middle decades of the last century, shaped so much of the country to their own ends, did so by employing, by appropriating, by deploying an aresenal of sentimental tools. Their intricate alliance of market and sentiment followed delicate negotiations always involving gender, class, and race. Mothers raised little boys to become manly clerks; Northern abolitionists denounced the monstrosity of the Southern markets in human flesh, markets which made their own wage system seem to them all the more free and just. White women, who found sources of personal power in the language of sentiment, managed to use that power to reshape not only their own recalcitrant children, but also the young African Americans and Indians whom they so often took under their charge.[2] The glorious sentiments that Child extolled, in other words, were set to work in the uneven and unequal social worlds where people made their lives. What seemed to her the tragic triumph of commerce, may have seemed to others the equally tragic triumph of sentiment.

But the middle class was by no means in total accord on the precise nature of the relations between the commercial and the sentimental. Nor were they in exact accord over who might use the language of sentiment and to what ends.[3] Sometimes antebellum audiences accepted and followed the language and logic of sentiment, sometimes they did not. One eccentric, unpleasant, and perhaps even dishonest character named Jonathan Harrington Green tried to use the tools of sentimental reformers to help fallen gamblers and to keep young clerks from gamblers' clutches. Despite the great antebellum appetite for reforms and reformers, his crusade never took off. His connections to the languages and projects of various reformers, including temperance advocates, abolitionists, and antionanists, were constantly vexed by the problem of gambling itself. When he talked about gambling, he twisted the concerns about vice, salvation, and addiction that shaped far more successful crusades. The gamblers he described and pitted against society in their never-ending addiction to gain simply did not possess selves capable of salvation and transformation. Green stumbled over the contradictions at the heart of sentimental market culture, and his difficulties offer us an occasion to investigate how sentimental commerce balanced what might be called commerce in sentiment. Like other antebellum reformers who employed a language of sentiment and salvation, he offers us serious contemplation about the connections among human beings in a social world where each and every man was bent on gain.[4]

Jonathan Harrington Green was a gambler, a reformer, a businessman, and a writer. In each enterprise he ran into trouble, each time because he had violated the precise terms of the alliance between the commercial and the sentimental that was so basic to middle-class culture. He talked about money and its dangers in sentimental terms, but he also trafficked in sentiment, trying to turn a profit by calling on the priceless virtues Child so cherished. He wrote books in which he witnessed the tragic seduction of innocent clerks, but sentimental tragedy was always undercut by adventure, and cautions not to gamble were contradicted by careful elaborations of rules for the card games of gamblers. He offered sentimental portraits of gamblers' victims, but his victims always turned into victimizers, stealing money from innocent loved ones. He started an antigambling society in New York, offering, for a fee, to supervise the recreations of employees entrusted with company cash. Thus he turned against the working-class audience who would have relished his adventures in the underworld of crime and vice and enjoyed his revelations of greed and corruption among the rich, and set himself up instead as spy and informer. He tried to turn himself into a figure of authority, parading his deep acquaintance with vice, but his authority was constantly undermined by his past as a petty criminal and crooked card player.

But if gambling provided little satisfaction as a base for sentimental reform, it did provide fertile ground for speculation on the delicate combinations of the commercial and sentimental that characterized middle-class individuals in the early years of the nineteenth century. In what follows I will turn to Green's many books and also to a number of incidents in his life, for it was as much his biography as what he wrote that made him both nightmare and clown to the audiences he tried to woo. Green's vision of gamblers' exaggerated lust for gain, his descriptions of their callous rejection of all sentimental ties in a constant search for wealth, and his portraits of their characters distorted by the endless transfer of cash, all helped tame the struggle for money that was becoming characteristic of middle-class men.

I

Green was born in Lawrenceburg, Indiana, around 1812, the son of a pious mother and a drunken father. His mother died when he was seven, but not before eliciting from her son a deathbed promise that he would never drink. It never occurred to the mother that her sober son might turn sobriety to his advantage at the card table and make a career of gambling. His father bound him out to an "unkind master" and set out for Cincinnati. Green went through a series of apprenticeships, mainly with carpenters, but finding all training unsatisfactory, he never "finished his trade." He ran off instead to find his dissipated father. In the sort of mismanagement of interests and passions that was to emerge as thematic in his portraits of gamblers and their victims, Green confessed that "the deep and abiding anxiety which I felt to see my father, and to enjoy his society once more, made my lose all control over myself, and sacrifice my interest to my passion."[5]

The passion, here briefly directed to family, was soon to turn in another direction. In Cincinnati Green found work as a joiner and tried to save enough money to continue his search for his "aged and greyheaded father." But before he could find his father, he fell in with a "bad set of boys" who took him to visit a ten-pin alley. The proprietor of the bowling alley turned out to be a man who lived by the old ruse of thimbles, and Green and his newfound friends were drawn into a plot to fleece a well-dressed gentleman. The conspirators were caught. Green was arrested, and in jail began his apprenticeship as a card sharp, the one trade he might be said to have finished.[6]

Out of jail, he embarked on his new career, apparently using his skills to skim profits from the heady economic development of the Mississippi Valley during the late 1820s and early 1830s. Green profited during these "Flush Times," but always from their more marginal, slightly criminal manifestations. He tended bar in hotels and on steamboats; ran errands, so he said, for a gang of counterfeiters; and gambled. He worked on steamboats and on flatboards, as a carpenter and as a card salesman. Green's sort of physical mobility was just what made the economic development of this section of the American West possible, but physical mobility hardly translated into social mobility. He also spent some time in jail in New Orleans and in New York, and managed to acquire a wife who served in his stories as one of the many targets his gambling enemies used to discredit his eforts at reform.[7]

He began each of his many books on gambling with brief autobiographies, using various versions of his life to highlight aspects of his arguments about the dangers of gambling in a society devised to find the positive in the search for money. Green's life testified to his expertise in crime, but it also provided him with the adventurous tales that spiced his pious pleas for parents and children to avoid gamblers and gambling.

Green gave up gambling in 1841 or 1842, persuaded, so he claimed, by an itinerant Baptist preacher named George Light, and tried to make money by writing books and peddling them, and by lecturing on and demonstrating gamblers' card tricks. His first book, *An Exposure of the Arts and Miseries of Gambling Designed Especially as a Warning to the Youthful and Inexperienced Against the Evils of That Odious and Destructive Vice,* appeared in 1843. In 1844 and 1845 he traveled through the Northeast and Middle West, adding antigambling societies to a landscape already covered with reform and voluntary associations. In each town he called on an editor or on a Baptist or Methodist minister, and with their endorsement in hand rented a hall for an evening's performance. Green won initial support by demonstrating gamblers' card tricks in the privacy of ministerial studies, and in public tried to win wide followings by combining sleight of hand with emotional appeals to those who had been gulled by gamblers. He also tried to cultivate temperance organizations, hoping to develop an alliance of reform organizations. In the tales Green told, unfortunately, victims fell into gamblers' snares trapped by their own greed; his stories offered little satisfaction to those bent on pious endeavor.[8]

Critics varied in their views on the evenings spent with the "reformed gambler." To some he conducted his meetings with "utmost solemnity"; to others he delivered "heart rending and blood chilling narrations"; and to still others he "was truly amusing." He ended each evening with an announcement that all playing cards were marked, and challenged the audience to present him with a deck he could not read. He brought to mind traveling magicians as often as he did itinerant ministers, and those who watched him deemed him more often a fraud than a contrite reformer. By Green's own reckoning, there were never many who embraced the reform of gamblers as the height of sentimental endeavor. When he passed the hat, few subscribed to his crusades.[9]

But it was not theatricality that got Green into trouble; temperance reformers, in particular, had long eased audiences toward moral resolve with liberal doses of entertainment.[10] Something was wrong with his construction of gamblers as victims, with his descriptions of gambling as a vice, and with the world perverted by gamblers that he described. Green's crusade proved to be worth neither sentimental nor monetary investment. He offered no saved souls, no vision of a world perfected or made ready for the millennium. What Green promised at the end of his crusade was a world made more ready for economic expansion, not for the ties and sacrifices of sentiment.

After he abandoned his life of vice, Green found himself in a very ambiguous class position. Like many of his working-class cohorts, he found no place in an artisan world that was changing around him; at first, failure as an artisan seems to have launched him into his life of small-time vice. But the gambler's world offered him ample opportunity to exercise imagination, and like the new generation of middle-class clerks who were learning to make money by handling it, Green saw himself as a sort of speculator. He offered economic and moral counsel to the middle class, but he offered it as an ex-thief and scoundrel who had no experience of the proper equation of money and character, and therefore no cultural authority for advising his fellow men.[11]

He also saw opportunity in the expanding world of popular fiction. None of this made his life easy, for he seemed to be torn by the contradictions in the evolving class structure of the culture of the antebellum North. He was a relatively successful author; his books went through numerous editions, appearing in the popular libraries of G. B. Zieber and Dick and Fitzgerald. Still, he complained constantly of poverty, suggesting a gambler's inability to accumulate money, while at the same time acknowledging that reform-minded audiences might question funds in an ex-gambler's hands.

But money was not the only problem. He aimed his books at a strangely mixed audience, at those who might share an interest in sensational revelations of crime and vice and in sentimental descriptions of victimized youths and their grieving parents. But Green was not content with description, and used his experience as an ex-gambler and his skills as a storyteller to launch a crusade. He addressed youths who would have delighted in what Mark Twain dubbed "robber books," but to cover himself, he laced them with a moral message aimed at those who would confiscate them. Like those of many reformers, his books carried contradictory messages, and audiences read them in different ways.

With a gambler's patience, Green built his books around repeating structures, some as trite as *Pilgrim's Progress,* some as old as all rogue's tales. Sad young men and grieving parents approached him and told stories of loss and destruction at the hands of plotting thieves posing as gamblers. Money entrusted to youths—money inherited, money sent by an employer from one part of the country to another, money confided in trust for a relative or friend, but never money earned—drew gamblers with irresistible force. Green had an acute sense of how his audiences imagined the dangers of unearned wealth, and of just how a belief in the irrational forces of luck made one vulnerable to those who posed as gamblers. He was careful to show that only the very naive still gambled, and he placed himself outside the gangs of gambling crooks, presenting himself as confessor hero, interpreter, and expert witness.[12]

He opened his first book with a typical story: "An Affecting Account of a Young Man Brought to Ruin and Untimely Death by Gambling." The affect Green hoped to achieve drew force from sentimental assumptions about the interconnected economic and emotional ties between parents and children, and from Green's intimate acquaintance with the facts of the tale. While traveling, he met the parents of a young man who had fallen victim to a plot designed by deceiving gamblers. The boy's Philadelphia education had not prepared him to defend himself from the snares of the smooth-talking Virginians who took from the boy all he had, including the mortgage on the poor parents' farm. The victorious gamblers had turned the parents out to wander in search of their child and his story. The boy, Green revealed, had "committed suicide by blowing his brains out with a pistol." He had died in New Orleans, the last stop of many a doomed gambler, and the "old parents . . . removed to some small village not far from the city of New York, to spend their remaining days, bowed down with decrepitude, indigence, and sorrow, yea, untold sorrow."[13]

Green always arrived too late, encountering victims like these long after gamblers had vanished with the money. His late arrival positioned him well as a sentimental witness, and he claimed to suffer along with his grieving acquaintances. As Philip Fisher put it: "Only a witness who cannot effect action will experience suffering as deeply as the victim."[14] But if Green experienced suffering as an innocent, his interpretations depended on his revelations as an expert, revelations that implicated him in the very plots he described.

And here Green's stories differed from the other gamblers' tales that appeared among the popular fictions of the 1840s and 1850s. Because he had distinct aspirations as a reformer—aspirations that depended on a literal, factual descripton of the world—Green tried to straddle a divide between fact and fiction. Although Green's wily gamblers shared some of their fictional counterparts' characteristics, the fictional gamblers who seduced young clerks were drawn to the New World from a corrupted and vice-ridden European aristocracy. "Roués," "unprincipled libertines," they inhabited a Gothic world where they took advantage of the monied innocents of the young republic.[15]

Those who wrote of gamblers were careful to keep their distance from gamblers' plots. Charles Burdett first published *The Gambler; or the Policeman's Story* in 1848, and Green may well have read Burdett's story before he set himself up in New York. Like Green, Burdett drew on sentimental structures of seduction and betrayal, mixing them with more sensational elements of mystery and revelation, but he was very careful to distance himself from all knowledge of the plots gamblers used to fleece their victims. Burdett framed his story as a third-person account, sharing authorship with the policeman who brought him the tale. He confessed that he "deprived himself of much of the credit which might be accorded to him had he permitted the work" to appear without acknowledging its source, but he also protected himself from implication in criminal schemes.[16]

As might be expected, Poe understood better than most how a gambler's ability to fleece trusting victims might stand for an author's need to play off the trust of an audience. Poe read Green's books and defended him against those who accused him of trying to make money from pain and suffering. "We have nothing to do with his private object," Poe wrote, "nor will the public object be one iota the less attained because in attaining it, the public puts money in the pocket of Mr. Green." Poe decided Green's books also had virtues. "They bear within them distinct internal evidence of their truth. The volumes have often, too, a less painful interest, and are sometimes exceedingly amusing."[17]

Poe's darker portrait of the cursed solitude and dark anonymity that Green found among gamblers appeared in his story "William Wilson," about a haunted and murderous gamester. Green had announced that gamblers were "without sympathy," and Poe elaborated on the defect to explore how gambling, especially dishonest gambling, confused human exchange, both verbal and monetary.[18] William Wilson, the murderous gambling narrator, describes how far he has wandered from human sympathy. He confesses to an "unpardonable crime," to years of "unspeakable misery," to telling a tale hard to believe, and to having offended "all manly and honorable sentiment."

> It could hardly be credited, however, that I had even here, so utterly fallen from the gentlemanly estate, as to seek acquaintance with the vilest arts of the gambler by profession, and, having become an adept in his despicable science, to practice it habitually as a means of increasing my already enormous income at the expense of the weak-minded among my fellow-collegians. Such, nevertheless, was the fact.

Weak-minded collegians, fodder for the gambler, and weak-minded readers, fodder for the writer, shared a common sense of the credible. Neither readers nor college card players could read "William Wilson" with assurance that their interpretations were correct. In these two sentences, one very long, one very short, the narrator reveals to readers what Wilson's good and noble double revealed to those he had cheated. A complicated sequence of feints and asides, a revelation rendered complex like a crooked game, is answered with the assurance: "Such, nevertheless, was the fact." But within the story fact and fiction, like the conventions for card games and their violation, are both inventions. For the corrupted William Wilson there is no realm of exchange free from human manipulations and distortions. Poe's story elaborates Green's clumsy attempts to describe a society in which the real basis of all human relations was competitive search for gain, not selfless love; in which the powers of fate and luck that had defined the human condition had been eclipsed by the conviction that men made and remade themselves and their worlds following only the most selfish of dictates. The conviction of human responsibility for the shape of the world, which contained the germ of a post-Calvinist hope for salvation also contained the seeds of a worldly damnation. For neither Poe nor Green was there, as William Wilson put it, an "oasis of fatality" where people met as equals. All had been corrupted by the designs of human will. For Green the revelation was reduced to a repeated and perhaps trivial assertion that all those who seemed to gamble in fact employed a mere sham of luck to lure the hapless into their carefully constructed schemes.

II

Most contemporaries read Green more as a practical guide to virtuous commerce than as a metaphysician. One declared his stories "eminently useful in counteracting one of the most pernicious and demoralizing vices of the age";

another deemed him "highly useful to young men, especially to those who design to travel south or west."[19] But Green deemed himself useful, not to his young readers, but to their employers. And here he betrayed one half of his audience to serve the other. Betrayal is clearest in New York where, in the late 1840s, Green tried to rationalize his sentimental crusade and to sell the services of a sort of credit agency designed to wipe out gambling. Green's biggest moment on the economic and cultural stage of the antebellum United States began in a jail cell.

In the mid-1840s Green settled in New Haven and began lecturing Yale students on the dangers lurking in billiard parlors and ten-pin alleys. He also worked as a bookseller, a stationer, and a bounty hunter. He followed a murder suspect into Canada, but was himself arrested when he tried to return to the States. A U.S. custom's inspector found he was carrying canceled treasury notes, refused to believe he was an agent of the Treasury Department, and sent him off to the Tombs in New York City as a possible counterfeiter. Green spent twelve days in the famous jail, one for each of the years he had spent gambling. When Horace Greeley heard of the plight of the well-known "reformed gambler," he invited him to save New York from the gamblers who stole "not less than five millions of dollars . . . annually" and destroyed "one thousand young men."[20]

To combat this frightening vice, Green devised the New York Association for the Suppression of Gambling. The A.S.G. is interesting on a number of levels. Recalling all he had learned of a boom economy in the Mississippi Valley, Green saw the same dangers of unearned wealth on the edges of Wall Street, where young clerks lost at night all they had "earned" during the day. They had not learned the difference between speculation on the exchange and speculation; nor, Green argued, had they learned to hold on to money that hardly seemed the fruit of their own labors. Green also took all he had learned from sentimental crusades and tried to make reform of lost souls a pure business proposition. He invited Greeley, along with an elderly merchant, two educators, and a phrenologist, to sit on the board of his association. Respectability, however, still eluded him, for in the hands of businessmen the moral judgments of disinterested reformers turned easily to blackmail, and Green found his Association the Object of suspicion, scorn, and laughter.

In the spring of 1850 Green began "collecting facts and statistics regarding the matter of gambling in New York." Green found thirty times Greeley's one thousand victims of gambling, and counted among New York's gambling hells all manner of public and private establishments where money was wagered on cards, dice, dogs, and numbers.[21] But Green turned his association away from sentimental benevolence and individual salvation and launched it at merchants who had to employ young clerks they did not know. In doing so, he turned away from his initial reform efforts of the 1840s, when he used his tales to draw on sentimental ties to gamblers' victims and presented gambling as a moral problem.

In New York in the early 1850s he turned instead to his repeated cautions about the dangers of unearned wealth, and presented gambling as a commercial and financial problem. So much speculative wealth in stocks and real estate had become akin to gambling that it seemed more profitable to Green to draw financial, rather than moral, distinctions. And like crusades against drink and prostitution, the crusade against gambling was about something more than the simple spread of vice. If temperance reformers worried about the discipline of a work force off the job, and moral reformers worried about changing class and gender relations in urban settings, Green tried to make gambling reform address the problems created both by money no longer earned in slow, productive endeavor, and by the anonymous commercial relations of the urban North.[22]

In the 1830s the minister William Alcott pointed out those most vulnerable to the vice of gambling: "Man is so constituted as to be unable to bear, with safety, a rapid accumulation of property. As in knowledge, so in the present case, what is gained by hard digging is usually retained and what is gained *easily* usually goes quickly." Green recognized that a decade of demographic change had only made matters worse: "The population of our larger villages is rapidly increasing; and the influx consists largely of young men, unsettled in character, inexperienced, and in far too many cases—wanting alike in just parental instruction and a deep-toned sense of obligation."[23]

Green's attack on the efficacy of parental instruction suggested that he no longer looked to the middle-class hearth as the source of support for his crusade. He no longer addressed women; he no longer described weeping wives, mothers, and sisters. And he went further, claiming that the silly idea of a domestic realm untouched by market relations actually made it easier for gamblers to trap innocent victims. Like Child and her colleagues, Green cast a critical eye on children's amusements, arguing that inappropriate reading in the parlor meant certain risk to family finances, for it was folly to pretend that any middle-class household had escaped the fall into capitalism.[24]

Green also criticized the ministers and reformers who concentrated on temperance alone, reminding them that dishonest clerks could do far more harm than drunken workers. He aimed at an audience of employers and tried once more to make a market for his distinctive kind of knowledge. He had already located all the gambling houses in New York, he said, and he now offered to watch them, for a fee, and report the presence of any wayward clerks. He also announced that the Association would lobby for antigambling laws and fight for the abolition of lotteries in states where they were still legal.[25]

These practical aspirations, designed to serve the banal ends of commerce, moved gambling reform far from its lofty sentimental origins. Sentiment had produced little revenue for Green, but in New York he turned again to the language of disinterested sentiment to protect credit relations and apprehend gambling clerks. When he did so, he created a dilemma for the middle-class employers who had turned to reform as a benevolent enterprise free from the direct profits of the market. He stripped self-interest free of kind disinterest. He offered Association subscribers the services of "The Intelligence Office, J. H. Green, Chief Agent," a sort of private police force designed to patrol the dangerous border between work and recreation. Subscription fees were determined by the number of employees and by the amount of trust Green figured was necessary to run a given business. Banking associations, insurance companies, and railroads thus paid far more than smaller companies.[26]

Green was not the only man of his generation to sense the need for professional substitutes for the kind of knowledge of character that had been generated easily in a village of familiars, and to look for economic opportunity in the expanding credit relations of the antebellum Northern economy. And he was not the only man who tried to build a business on a benevolent foundation. Like the abolitionist silk merchant Lewis Tappan, Green knew that markets expanding socially and geographically made participants vulnerable to the venality, bad judgments, and bad luck of their customers, associates, and employees. When Tappan began his Mercantile Agency, a credit agency designed to keep tabs for subscribers on the fiscal histories of inland merchants, he built on both his knowledge of business and his knowledge of the benevolent networks of abolitionists. He used his friends in the movement to sketch portraits of merchants who needed credit from their urban suppliers. Tappan's biographer has argued that the agency's significance lay in the way Tappan used older assumptions about character and a belief that character could be discerned by personal observation, in combination with newer methods of communication and finance, and faith in the power of information to solve problems of credit in an expanding economy.[27]

Green built his Intelligence Office on the need for trust within large companies. Through a combination of undercover work and blackmail, Green promised to find out the names of every individual who gambled in New York and to note them all down in a "private book." Subscribers would have the right to scan the book for the names of any trusted employees whose addiction to vice was sure to lead to fraud and defalcation. Green offered first to warn those commencing a career of gambling, but when admonition failed, he promised to inform employers of the presence of gamblers on their payrolls.[28]

Both Green and Tappan were accused of spying—Tappan by the Southern press, and Green by the Northern audience he tried to press into service. Although Tappan's credit agency ran into financial difficulties, few within the Evangelical community of the North questioned his authority to investigate the connections between character and financial probity and to market his investigations to those with direct interest in the fiscal health of their fellow men. In contrast, when Green began his surveillance of employees at their leisure, he found he had little of Tappan's cultural authority to draw upon.

When Rensselaer N. Havens, the elderly insurance executive Green had recruited as president of the Association for the Suppression of Gambling, rose to address its first and only anniversary meeting in May 1851, he began by defending the Association against unnamed attackers. Rather than detailing the accomplishments of the Association's first year, he used his address to denounce accusers who had gone beyond mere "comment" and settled into "abuse." The abuse was aimed directly at Green's Intelligence Office. No one commented on Green's lectures on gambling, on his attempts to lobby for stricter laws and enforcement, or on his tracts on gambling. "But," Havens confessed, "the moment that we place the finger on the sore spot of personal deportment, there is an extraordinary nervousness awakened or stimulated lest we tred [*sic*] on individual rights." He saw no problem with "scrutiny and observation of character," and no difference between scrutiny and observation as a disinterested moral task and as a commercial service.[29]

But few in his audience were gifted with Poe's ironic indifference to those who reformed gambling for a fee. A reporter for the *New York Daily Tribune* described an audience more raucous than indignant, moved more to laughter than to moral outrage. He noted that "[s]everal ladies were present in the galleries and in the area of the Building, who seemed to take a lively interest in the proceedings." The lively interest reappeared throughout the report in parenthetical asides: members of the crowd applauded the speakers and shouted an occasional "Hear, hear!"; they gasped with "sensation" whenever statistics on gambling were read aloud, and interrupted sermons and speeches with "laughter," with "roars of laughter," and with "immoderate roars of laughter." One retelling of a gambling joke produced "[i]mmense laughter, in which the ladies heartily joined!"[30]

While Green had begun his career in earnest sentimental endeavor, by the early 1850s his audiences responded with gasps of sensation rather than sighs of sentiment, with laughter rather than tears. As Karen Halttunen has suggested, the raw concerns with sincerity and sentiment that characterized Northern middle-class culture in the 1830s had lost their edge by the 1850s. Green offered a sort of postsentimental mockery of sentiment. He evoked the sentimental world of suffering victims, but by charging a fee for his vision and offering it as commercial service, he painted a sentimental world no longer worthy of pious endeavor.[31]

The market Green sought for his reformer's skills was one shaped not by moral resolve but by the very commercialized leisure he liked to rail against. By midcentury the redoubtable "reformed gambler" had so diminished in stature that the popular publisher Dick and Fitzgerald reissued his books as part of a series on parlor amusements. When *One Hundred Tricks with Cards: Gamblers' Tricks with Cards Exposed and Explained* appeared in 1850, card tricks had already lost their sting.[32]

Still, Green's work was torn by attempts to maintain contradictory positions, to ignore the logical divisions shaping the commerical culture of the midnineteenth-century United States. Green had a sense of the class divisions of the Northern marketplace. To carry out business transactions, those who controlled capital frequently depended on those without. Instead of appealing to the poor by criticizing men of wealth as selfish gamblers who lived off the toil of others, Green addressed men of property who were looking for ways to protect their purses. And instead of flattering his wealthy backers with paeans to their benevolence, he offered his gamblers to Northern middle-class audiences as ugly reflections of their own constant search for gain, of their own newfound capacity to make money by its simple transfer from hand to hand, and of their own increasing tendency to live off wealth produced for them by others. The world of home, hearth, and sentiment that many like Child viewed as a sanctuary from the sullied world of the market was but an empty myth—and a myth, moreover, that ill prepared men for life in a commercial world of strangers.[33]

III

There is one more incident in the reformed gambler's life that suggests the distinct place of gambling in a society where some men made fortunes by lucky speculations, while most had to settle for delayed gratification and slight gain. In February 1845 Green had the bumps on his head analyzed by the famous New York phrenologist Orson Squire Fowler. Fowler reported that Green had a skull "calculated to make money very fast, yet illy calculated to keep it, because he had the *back* portion of Acquisitiveness, which *gets* money, yet not the fore part which keeps it."[34]

When Fowler bisected Green's Acquisitive Bump (the site, if ever there was one, of economic man's "propensity to truck, barter, and exchange"), he not only found economic man inscribed in the human bone structure, but described precisely how gambling perverted the getting and spending that the middle class held to be the natural state of human kind. Gamblers stood for all those who had eluded the magic of the "invisible hand," for all those who had escaped the touch that turned the selfish relations of the market into the social relations of a commercial society. Gamblers kepy money in a kind of constant flux, neither producing, nor consuming, nor offering anything in exchange for the money that passed through their hands. As Fowler noticed, they even rejected the great project of accumulation that transformed voracious men on the make into upstanding and stable citizens. They did not feel the pull Max Weber was later to label a "man's duty to his possessions."[35]

Nor did they feel a need to offer something in exchange for the cash they took. In the late twentieth century the risks of the gaming table, the fantasies of great, glorious, and sudden wealth, have themselves been offered as products to be consumed, but in the early decades of the last century it was simply impossible to imagine consumption of products so abstract. Green and his few allies among ministers and moral philosophers designated gamblers as those who neither produced nor consumed. Gamblers brought no product to market and, to make matters worse, they took from those who did, "without rendering an equivalent."[36]

Green reminded his readers often that since gamblers themselves produced no wealth, they depended on a never-ending supply of victims to provide them with cash. They attracted prey by disguising their own work as part of the play of others, and by disguising their own rational schemes as the irrational blessings of fortune. They then destroyed those they had trapped by disguising their own dispassionate self-interest as the same passion for gaming that kept victims at the table, and by seducing young men away from proper and productive connections with the female sex.

The gamblers' mixture of work and play was particularly grating to employers who worried about the recreations of those obliged to labor for a living. Gambling was doubly odious for it not only induced its victims to defy injunctions to save, but also made them lose all sense of the carefully measured time necessary for wage labor.[37] It also drew men into a homosocial world where women figured only incidentally either as bait for seduction or as victims of loss. Gambling stories described a system of exchanges among men, depicting a world of money and finance far more open to middle-class men than to women, but these exchanges became pathological when male victims failed to escape the gambling seducers and return to women and home.[38]

Gambling also worked a more insidious destruction, undermining the carefully made individuals who carried out the capitalist projects of the early nineteenth century. Green tried to get readers to recognize the animosity of gamblers and the dangers of the infection they spread. "A man never, never can promote his own present enjoyment by becoming a pirate upon all the best interests of society: and such is the gambler. His hand is against every man, and every good man's hand ought to be against him, not to injure him as an individual but to keep him from destroying others."[39]

Green's phrase here echoed that of an earlier opponent of gambling. In 1814 the Reverend Eliphalet Nott addressed the graduates of Union College on the dangers of the gaming table, where "[e]very man's interest clashes with every man's interest, and every man's hand is literally against every man."[40] Nott isolated the social pathology of gambling perhaps to better make clear the salubrious social relations of the market, but he also touched on the interplay of passions and interests that Green used to shape stories of his own life and those of young men carrying money entrusted to them.

The political scientist Albert O. Hirschman has argued that by the late eighteenth century one set of deadly passions—those associated with greed and money-making—had been intellectually transformed from dangerous and destabilizing forces into innocent "interests and "given the task of holding back those passions that had long been thought to be much less reprehensible." Because of its "constancy and persistence," he writes, the "passion of accumulation" was deemed the basis of social and political stability.[41]

Hirschman has more serious subjects in mind, but gambling plays a small role in a popular version of the drama he describes. For Green and his audience, it served as one means to think about passion for gain run amok and to isolate as vicious and evil some forms of the search for gain in which all men were said to be engaged. In 1854 the Reverend E. H. Chapin repeated Green's warnings on the ways gamblers played with emotion in the culture of commerce. "In other men," he wrote, "the indulgence of vice blends with the play of the emotional nature; passion swamps the brain. But this man trains himself to restrain passion with all the solicitude of a stoic."[42] The emotions still so crucial to sentimental connections served gamblers as a convenient route of infection. Green finally had the peculiar role of using popular sentimental figures to address audiences in the urban North on the dangers of sentiment itself. Although Green's efforts assured him a place on the margins of nineteenth-century popular culture, his message did not fall on fertile soil. His misbegotten, oddly mishapen figures of sentiment could never be made to serve the interests of the antebellum middle class.

9

The Identity of Slavery

Shirley Samuels

I

The uncertain status of the body in slavery discourse may be evoked by two images from the cultural history of slavery. The first is the female "topsy-turvy doll" popular in the nineteenth-century American South (and still produced). Held one way, the doll appears as a white woman with long skirts. Flipping over her skirts does not reveal her legs, but rather exposes another racial identity: the head of a black woman, whose long skirts now cover the head of the white woman.[1] This visual and physical change from white to black and black to white appears also in a second form of popular representation, Lydia Maria Child's 1831 children's story "Mary French and Susan Easton," in which two little girls, one white and one black, are kidnaped and sold into slavery. The white girl has been disguised; she appears black, but her tears gradually dissolve this surface identity, revealing the white body beneath the black surface, and she is restored to her family. Her friend's tears cannot accomplish a similar miracle: because they do not change her surface identity, she is left in slavery.[2]

The tears that mark the formation of a sentimental subject here crucially reveal that subject as white, and such an identification of sentimental subjects and white bodies, or more exactly, white interiors, appears in both pro- and antislavery literature in the early republic.[3] And the double gesture of at once presenting and refusing a reversibility of identity—the topsy-turvy doll can be only one color at a time, and Mary French can appear black, but Susan Easton cannot appear white—shows up repeatedly as white and black are paired and set in opposition. Such an opposition of white and black, an opposition that keeps them together but insists that they cannot mix, is insistently mapped onto national oppositions by nineteenth-century American writers, whose opposition of North and South correlates individual and national bodies.

Representing slavery in nineteenth-century America involved either fixing the slave's identity in the body as a matter of "blood" or "skin," or unfixing the identity of slavery by understanding identity as transcending the body.[4] I want to focus here on how such uncertain locations of identity function across rival accounts of slavery, both the justification of it and the opposition to it, and to examine as well how these configurations of the body and identity, of exteriors and interiors, bring together an apparently incongruous range of concerns, including abolition, the "science" of phrenology, and the "woman question." These diverse concerns raise the problem of the families that produce and reproduce bodies and identities. Hence I will explore appeals to families as "nurseries of the state" in slavery discourse, and will further investigate how the intense concentration on the family as the locus or warrant of identity makes visible matters of miscegenation and incest that threaten to undo that very identity.[5]

Racial, gender, and national problems of identity appear provocatively in the following different yet representative texts: *The Devil in America,* a proslavery epic, written just before the Civil War by a Southern minister; *The Slave's Friend,* an abolition journal for children published in the 1830s; and *The Romance of the Republic,* an abolitionist novel written just after the Civil War by Lydia Maria Child. I will look at how such texts constitute their readers and their characters as subjects, in what is by now the understood double sense, both as agents of and as subjects to power. These problems of subjects and bodies involve, as the sociologist of science Bruno Latour has suggested, "acts of differentiation and identification, not differences and identities. The words 'same' and 'other' are the consequences of trials of strength, defeats and victories. They cannot themselves describe these links."[6] The problem of identity that I want to explore here, a problem that slavery at once poses and exacerbates, is a problem of such trials of recognition.

II

Although the primary aim of *The Devil in America* (1859) is to argue in favor of slavery, its subtitle gives a breathtakingly indiscriminate indication of its proposed scope and of the topics the text correlates:

Spirit-Rapping—Mormonism;

Woman's Rights Conventions and Speeches;

Abolitionism;

Harper's Ferry Raid & Black Republicanism;

Defeat of Satan,

And Final Triumph of the Gospel.

Attributed to a Reverend Gladney, president of the Aberdeen Female College in Mississippi, the work ranges from nasty satires about abolition and woman's rights agitation to attacks on any other mode of reform that entangles the question of rights and the problem of the body, including the natural rights proposed by Thomas Paine and the biological origins that had recently been advanced by Charles Darwin. In each case, the reform activity is exposed as part of a plot by Satan, who has sent demons on specific missions to destroy the United States of America. The Demon of Atheism, for instance, has been sent to use "Philosophers" and "sons of science" to "prove that men and monkeys are the same."[7] The faith that maintains the difference between men and monkeys will be assailed by an atheism that asserts a frightening sameness among species, that indeed erodes differences as such. Everywhere heightening anxieties about inheritance and embodiment, property and identity, the work thus relays both a counterhistory of abolition as a strategy by the devil to destroy the union, and a deep anxiety about maintaining a series of differences, each one imagined to entail the next, between men and monkeys, men and women, white and black, North and South, master and slave. Such differences might almost be considered constitutive of antebellum American culture.[8]

The mission of the Demon of Fanaticism, for example, is to destroy American women: "Teach her to hate the sphere for her design'd, / And prove that she is treated as a slave / While from the rights of man she is debarr'd."[9] Staging the unnaturalness of natural or equal rights, the poem argues that a woman barred from "the rights of man" is saved from the clutches of the demonic atheist Thomas Paine. Not unexpectedly, the narrator cites the proper alternative, the sentimental ideal of domestic life: " 'Tis hers to crown with joy the quiet home, / The infant mind with her own image stamp. . . . / In short, to act on earth an angel's part" (*D*, 72). The angelic mission of the white woman is to stamp an image of herself on the tabula rasa of the infant mind, or, to shift the metaphor, to become the coin of the realm she rules by reproducing her own image. That is, this passage presents reproduction not as a biological process, but as a mechanical stamping; the mother's task becomes the reproduction of identity, a reproduction that does not allow for difference or deviation or, as we will see in a moment, for the accident or mixture of biology or blood.

Satan purposes a perversely similar stamping of identity onto the interiors of bodies, as he instructs his demons on how to arouse dissension in the North by producing abolitionists. But Satan's proposal mixes bodies and identities in just the way that "angelic" reproduction avoids. The demons are first to "work upon the mind," and "there an idol-image firmly fix":

> A negro image let that idol be,
> Whose shadow dark cast on the souls of men,
> Shall give a kindred hue to all within . . .
> And all whose surface white [shall] have hearts within
> Tinged with the hue of Ethiopian's skin.
>
> (*D*, 77)

Fixing an "idol-image" on the mind involves not merely the internalizing of that image, but also an internal mixing of images and bodies. The exterior "hue" of the "Ethiopian" thus becomes "kindred" to the interior of the superficially white abolitionist, as if enacting an extraordinary version of miscegenation. That first the mind, then the soul, then the heart will be "tinged" with the color of the skin also intimates a link between the logic of miscegenation and the logic of sentimentality: both involve the impression of, and mixing of, external and physical states in the interior state of the heart. But the incongruity of stamping or fixing identity on the heart as a tingeing of the skin suggests an anxious mixing of images and bodies, and raises again the question that *The Devil in America* works to disavow in its "stamping" or "fixing" of identities in bodies: where does identity get located, in the heart or on the skin, in the interior or on the exterior? Responding to this question evokes, in the first instance, a translation of biological reproduction into replication (images replicating themselves), and in the second, a sort of internal miscegenation (images and skins mixing with hearts and generating monstrous kindred).

Addressing, for a different purpose, the disjunctive relation between interiors and bodies, the abolitionist journal *The Slave's Friend* tells young readers that "the chestnut has a dark skin. . . . But its *kernel* is all white and sweet. The apple, though it looks so pretty, has many little black grains at the heart. . . . Now little boys and girls can't be abolitionists until they get rid of all these black grains in their hearts."[10] In this garden account of bodies, the chestnut's black skin gets overlooked because of a "sweet" white interior, but the apple's white interior is flawed by a black heart. Acquiring abolitionist citizenship apparently is accomplished through expelling the heart's black grains of slavery. But what marks this contrast of pro- and antislavery discourses is the *lack* of contrast: at heart, they argue the same perspective; at heart, they call for a white interior. Both pro- and antislavery writings exhibit, from different sides, the tension between attempts to locate and to inscribe the black/white identity of and in the body, and attempts to escape such a biologized essentialism or biological design or destiny.

Such biologized destinies have been used to link the identities of white women and slaves, linked because their bodies mark their identities as subjected rather than as subjects. The problem raised in both instances, it has recently been suggested, is that "the extent to which the body designates identity" in feminist-abolitionist discourse makes for the "difficulties and resistance inherent in acknowledging the corporeality of personhood. The bodies feminists and abolitionists wish reclaimed, and the bodies they exploit, deny, or obliterate in the attempted rescue, are the same."[11] Yet if this account of reclaiming and denying the body points to an essential tension in both pro- and antislavery work, the identification of corporeality and personhood, rather than not being acknowledged, is placed squarely at issue in these works. Whether the struggle is over the identity of the body or the identity that the body represents—"body" and "identity," again, appearing as objects of struggle, not fixed terms—such a struggle both unites and opposes pro- and antislavery arguments, and beyond that, foregrounds the complex problem of the body and embodiment. Further, the corporealizing and transcendentalizing double impulse of sentimental discourse at once installs identity in bodies and makes bodies the signs of an identity that transcends them.

Similar attention to the transmission of identity through the body appears, of course, in other popular discussions of the problem of embodiment in midcentury America. For example, Orson Squire Fowler, the popularizer of phrenology and family reformation, promoted the belief that what mothers looked at during pregnancy could shape the characters of their unborn children. He preached a mode of identity at once fixed by the contours of the skull and malleable, after a phrenological diagnosis of the skull's characteristics.[12] This paradox resembles the paradox of antislavery battles in which identity is an essentialist matter of natural bodies (for men, women, slaves, or children), even as the identity located in these bodies must be reformed or transcended.

An extraordinary range of cultural issues involving the question of how the body conveys or contains identity is communicated in this paradox. Yoking several of them, *The Devil in America* expands its scope of operation to rail against: "Infidelity, Woman's Rights, Abolitionism, and Spiritualism! . . . Why is it that these monstrous errors are so often united, and that the adoption of one seems necessarily to lead to the embrace of the other?" (*D*, 183). Rather than offering anything like an explicit answer to this question, the narrator merely suggests that slavery, because it provides the antidote to promiscuous uniting, adopting, or embracing across these different kinds, must be what protects the South: "The prevalence of these isms at the North, and their absence here, cannot be accidents." The North

> must hide its head in shame over the blasphemies of its infidel conventions, the indecencies of its free-love doctrines, the wickedness and inhumanity of its spiritualism and the treason of its abolitionists. The South can boast of "freedom" from all these isms; and the price which it pays for this freedom is the institution of slavery. The South accepts the terms, and thinks it has made, for once, a great "bargain." (*D*, 185)

What links these "isms"? If each involves a propping of spiritual or erotic or political meanings on the body, each also and more significantly moves to "transcend" the confines of biology/body. In each case, biology does not equal destiny: infidelity, feminism, spiritualism, abolition—all involve what might be called a politics of transcendence, a way of attaching significance to identities, meanings, and values beyond the bodily and the physical just where the body and the physical seem most at issue. Combatting the concept that biology equals destiny brings together the wide diversity of "monstrous errors" that include abolition and woman's rights along with phrenology, spiritualism, mesmerism, and "free love."[13] And the blasphemy, the indecency, and the treason of these "united errors" is crucially the "embrace" of their uncertain mixture.

The Demon of Discord, sent to foment Civil War, again asserts just this matter of ineradicably separate identities: " 'twixt the North and South the question is / Shall black be turned to white and white to black?" Such a topsy-turvy suggestion involves not simply reversing skin color, but inverting the order of the universe:

> Since serve some must, which shall the other serve, . . .
> The question here of right is very plain;
> The right of each to slaves is just the same,
> With equal right of color and of form.
>
> (*D*, 77–78)

Equal rights here means that each has the right to "color" and "form," even as one color means slavery and the other ownership. Equal rights, in other words, means separate but equal rights, since an equal "right" to a distinct color or form merely establishes one's place as served or serving. Following this perverse logic, abolishing slavery appears not only as the abolition of an "equal right" to servitude, but also as the eradication of natural hierarchical differences between male and female spheres and, indeed, the abolition of the difference between male and female.

In calling attention to the "bargain" that the South has made in trading monstrous errors for the "equal" rights of slavery, the narrator parodically adapts a "Yankee" term to differentiate the institution of slavery from the nominally "free" labor and "free" trade of Northern capitalism. The narrator further proposes what the North has overlooked in its capitalistic formulations. It has just begun to "learn that *capital* is *kinky heads,*—/ Of which the South has all, the North has none!" (*D*, 141), and this may account for the North's desire to intervene in the Southern economy. What at first appears an unsurprising exposure of the North's motives—that the concern for liberty and liberation is a cover for economic jealousy—turns out to be somewhat more surprising. If "capital" is indeed "kinky heads," this is because the proslavery argument works to return capital to its physical root—"capital," after all, derives from *caput* or "head." That is, the proslavery argument here insists on an identity between the body and the economy, just the identification that the disembodying and impersonal working of capitalism seems to complicate.[14] In such a move of embodiment, it may become possible to see how these errors intersect: "Where Atheism and Pantheism, . . . Fourierism and Tribunism, Materialism and Mesmerism have leavened the public mind, and free thinking, free love, and free license are almost as much in vogue as 'free soil, free niggers, and Fremont,' we may well expect a monstrum horrendum" (*D*, 187).[15] Restoring a monstrous body to such disembodied and disembodying practices, the narrator anticipates a monstrous birth out of convulsions at once political and bodily, in what appears as a birth announcement of the Civil War.

III

The question of how bodies are reproduced in slavery discourse is raised again in *The Devil in America,* as the Demon of Discord condemns abolitionists for exploiting images of slavery's bodies. He describes how "overcharged pedagogues" have

> Frightful pictures to the children showed
> Of monsters holding lashes in their hands . . .
> Till infant tears were trickling down their cheeks;
> And pictures on the mind engraved for life.
>
> (*D*, 135)

Such permanent engraving of monstrous images on the infant mind appears as another version of *The Devil in America*'s earlier account of how incorporating images into bodies produces abolitionists. In this production of infant abolitionists, "trickling" tears correspond to the internal engraving of pictures of the lash. We can begin to uncover what is at stake here in a sentimental pedagogy linked to picturing, the body and the lash, and the stark physicality of seeing conceived of as engraving impressions on the mind, by considering in more detail the program of showing "frightful pictures" to children.[16]

While a pedagogical concern about molding the minds of children might have appeared as a reason for not telling them about slavery, early abolitionists saw the matter differently: young readers of *The Slave's Friend,* which indeed showed monsters with whips, were told to "read it through very carefully and *think* while you *read.* Fix the stories so in your memory that you will never forget them. And may God so stamp them upon your heart that you will always *feel* them."[17] *The Slave's Friend* presents reading as a physical act of inscribing stories onto the mind and having them stamped onto the heart. The sentimental progress from seeing to thinking to feeling is accomplished through a process of internalization that again recalls the transformed identity of abolitionists who internalized the image of the "Ethiopian." Reading operates here not merely as a means to correct thinking but also as the mode of correct thinking: namely, the refusal to reduce meanings to bodies or to merely physical surfaces (skin color, for instance), and the insistence on thinking and feeling as antidotes to identifying identity with nothing more than the body.[18]

Crucially, whipping and reading get perversely connected as external disciplines made internal, or interiorized. *The Slave's Friend* counterposes pictures of the lash to pictures of whites teaching black children to read. The sentimental lesson juxtaposes these two modes of training—the whip as the external model and reading as the internalized one—and in so doing, contrasts the Northern model of managing heads and hearts with the Southern model of disciplining bodies. An antislavery version of the *New England Primer,* for instance, the *Anti-Slavery Alphabet,* begins, of course, with "A is for Abolitionist," and later states, "W is for the Whipping Post / To which the slave is bound, / While on his naked back the lash / Makes many a bleeding wound."[19] Abolitionist education thus appears as a process of learning to read or to recognize letters of the alphabet through looking at the lash. Internalizing the image of the lash, that is, works as a means of memorizing letters, while letters function as a disciplinary process that at once wards off the lash and keeps it perpetually in view.

Hence these documents about reading uneasily stand in for the body of the slave, even as they represent and reproduce that body. Vexed relations between reading, freeing, and selling recur throughout. Children in *The Slave's Friend* say, for instance, "I long to see all slaves free; to have children attend Sabbath schools; to have them taught to read, write, and cipher. What a joyful time that will be, Ann! Then . . . all can sing, 'Hail Columbia, happy land' " (*SF,* 36). This juxtaposition of a liberationist strategy of reading and the potentially coercive effects of reform is indicated by the juxtaposition of freedom *from* slavery and the freedom *to* attend Sunday school, to learn to read, and to sing patriotic songs. In other words, freedom gets bound up here with a lesson about the allegiance owed to religious and national duty and identity. (Translating the lash into text and icon also meant that national symbols could be read less patriotically: in another issue of *The Slave's Friend* a child's comments conflate the blood raised by the whip with the symbol of the nation that allowed such violence: "The *stripes* in the national flag make me think of the stripes the poor slaves suffer.")[20] And of course, reading *is* a liberationist strategy—a connection perhaps most explicit in the autobiographical writings of Frederick Douglass and salient in other slave narratives.[21] Here, however, it at once subsumes and emphasizes the difference between illiterate slave children and the assumed reader of the text, the slave's friend.

The reading lesson thus appears as part of a crucial antislavery lesson in capitalism, precisely the link between abolition and capitalism that *The Devil in America* indicts. The children imagined as readers of *The Slave's Friend* ask, "What can we do?" They are told that to fight slavery means to read, and to earn money to buy books: "By putting the money you earn into the Anti-Slavery treasury, books can be printed" (*SF*, 37). By the fifth issue of volume 2, they are told that "about 250,000 copies of the Slave's Friend have been published"; the response of the publishers is to promote juvenile antislavery societies. Lewis Tappan, the financier-abolitionist, asked rhetorically in 1836, "Does any one doubt the propriety of children associating to form anti-slavery societies? There are already Juvenile Temperance, Missionary, and I believe Peace Societies. . . . Is not slavery as bad as intemperance?" (*SF*, 66, 68).[22] For children to associate in reform societies is not new—just as linking reading to reform is not a new strategy. Both enterprises join the nineteenth-century American project to incorporate nationalism and religion in reading lessons. And I do not, of course, want to expose reform strategies as based upon merely economic motives, nor do I want to suggest that economic strategies "explain" the reform impulse.[23] Rather, I want to point out some implications of their interdependence: the lesson in reading (a necessary lesson in abstraction from merely physical pictures or signs on paper, or from merely corporeal identities) and the lesson in capitalism (the abstraction from physical heads to systems of exchange) are in fact related lessons—what might even be called twin lessons in abolitionist bookkeeping.

To aid in forming the juvenile antislavery society, a constitution was prepared: "The object of this Society shall be to collect money for the anti-Slavery cause, to read and circulate The Slave's Friend, to do all in our power to have the free colored people respected and well-treated, and the enslaved set at liberty" (*SF*, 71–72). The ordering of priorities here marks both the limits of what children might be expected to perform and the function of *The Slave's Friend*: to educate children to raise money as a response to moral trouble. Hence an equivalence is established between the circulation of texts and the circulation of money, as if reading and capitalism indicated each other. In fact, a competition is set up among the societies to raise money and distribute more literature. The Juvenile Anti-Slavery Society of Rhode Island, for example, is reported to have given $100 to the cause, which translates immediately into 15,000 copies of *The Slave's Friend*. This translation of antislavery sentiment into reading *The Slave's Friend* leads to fund-raising to buy more copies of *The Slave's Friend,* so more can read it and raise more funds to buy more copies of it.

The grown-up version, the New England Anti-Slavery Society, concentrates on similar questions of freedom and identity, reading and economy. The system of ownership that they seek to overturn in slavery will be reinscribed in the ordering of marriages and families. For them, "Immediate Abolition" means that "every husband shall have his own wife and every wife her own husband," that "parents shall have the control and government of their own children, and that children shall belong to their parents."[24] But this proposed system of family government and control is not exactly compatible with their interest in controlling what amounts to the circulation of children. The reformers explain that abolition "will enable us to take 100,000 infants, who are annually born to slave parents, and doomed to a life of ignorance and servitude—place them in infant schools, and transfer them into primary and sabbath schools; from these into high schools and Bible classes; and . . . from Bible classes into the Christian church. Thus they will become ornaments to society . . . instead of mere animals."[25] What happens to the parents of these 100,000 infants while such a "transfer" takes place? Presumably they will give up their babies to be "ornaments" for Northern reformers, whereas they would not want to give them up to be "animals" in Southern slavery. Which returns us to the twin concerns of the body and capital we have been sketching throughout. The state-controlled nursery of 100,000 infants accords with the worst imaginings of the proslavery faction: capitalist reproduction—the baby factory—has replaced the ideal of the family reiterated in the proslavery critique of the monstrous errors of abolition and capital both.

IV

Not only the reform of families, but also the reform of marriage was seen by some as the natural extension of abolishing slavery. Of course the destruction of marriages and families through slavery, at a time when the family had become the focus of attention as an instrument of both civilization and character formation, provided further ammunition for abolitionists. As *The Family and Slavery* explained, "The Family is the head, the heart, the fountain of society, and it has not a privilege that slavery does not nullify, a right that it does not violate." In attacking the destruction of families in slavery, the American Tract Society not atypically claimed, "The family is appointed for the *discipline* of the race." The abolitionist Henry Wright even declared that no one who wanted to "save the world, will overlook the family institution."[26]

The apocalyptic rhetoric which marshaled the family institution in a battle over the "world" was countered by a grimmer view of the confining effects of that institution. As another reformer asserted, *"There are today in our midst ten times as many fugitives from Matrimony as there are fugitives from Slavery."*[27] This fugitive view of marriage was connected to the abolitionist views on slavery in the pamphlet "Slavery and Marriage: A Dialogue" (1850), attributed to John Humphrey Noyes, founder of the experimental Oneida colony. The characters in this stylized dramatic dialogue, Major South and Judge North, first rehearse the familiar terms of the national debate over slavery. They are interrupted by the proselytizing Mr. Free Church, who adapts arguments common to both pro- and antislavery forces as he attempts to enlist abolitionists in the cause of free love or "perfectionism," an attempt that also mocks them by applying antislavery arguments to the abolition of marriage.

Mr Free Church "holds the same opinion about Marriage that [Judge North does] of Slavery, that it is an arbitrary institution and contrary to natural liberty. . . . The catalogue of women's abuses under the tyranny of matrimony, compare very well with the cruel lot of the slaves." The proposed "natural" alternative of "liberty" for women confined by marriage creates as much anxiety for Judge North as his arguments for freedom from slavery have for Major South. Yet to defend the institution of marriage, he unself-consciously adapts the terms that Major South has previously used to defend slavery: "The *law* protects women," and besides, "Woman is devotedly attached to marriage"; it is wrong to be "advocating its abolition." As he points out the faulty assumption that legality and rights indicate each other, Mr. Free Church argues that "Marriage separates and breaks up families [so] union at the *altar,* as it is justly called, (considering the cruelty of the sacrifice) mutilates two family circles."

But "the abolition of Marriage," an anxious Judge North contends, still echoing a Southern reaction to the proposed abolition of slavery, "would lead to unbridled licentiousness and social ruin." Such anxiety about freedom and lawlessness links the world views of North and South; more important, it grounds the stability of the national social order in the family. Mr. Free Church replies that families would "fare better under a system of free-labor and free-love in Association, than they do under the Marriage system where each family is at the mercy of one man."[28] Through this call for free love and free labor—a call, in effect, for a free market economy in family relations—the tract suggests that the practices of the marriage system must be repudiated in order to develop a new social order that would include the abolition of slavery. A civil war fought for this new order would be fought for the freedom of families.

In linking marriage to slavery, however, the tract invokes the catalogue of women's abuses under the tyranny of matrimony without explicitly addressing how they might be subsumed by the catalogue of women's abuses, abuses of both labor and love, under the tyranny of slavery. That is, as it presents the arbitrary tyranny of matrimony, this tract proclaims the family comparable to slavery, being "at the mercy of one man," but refrains from exploring how the family in literal slavery is at the mercy of one man. As other writers show, for the families held in slavery to be at the mercy of one man creates the Southern version of the baby factory.[29] The slave system's production of children, for example—a system that crucially generates miscegenation and often incest— is the subject of Richard Hildreth's antislavery novel *The Slave* (1836). Here the family at the mercy of one man is the plantation at the mercy of Colonel Moore, the "faultless pattern of a true *Virginian* gentleman . . . of liberty, indeed he was always a warm and energetic admirer." Although Colonel Moore "used to vindicate the cause of the French Revolution" and "*the rights of man,*" these are the rights of white men: the "gentleman" leaves the rights of his male slaves to an overseer, and appropriates the rights as well as the bodies of the female ones. The French Revolution supplies the model of rebellion with which his son and slave, the young Archy Moore, identifies. Hearing from his father about the "abstract beauty of liberty and equality [it was] the French republicans with whom I sympathized.[30]

As a slave, Archy has difficulty translating these abstractions into the American scene. He learns to sympathize with himself, and to desire liberty and equality, from learning about his family. Southern slave codes decreed that the child follow the condition of the mother, that is, that the racial identity of the mother determine the identity of the child. Such practices suggest that slave children have invisible fathers, as though mothers were alone responsible for reproduction.[31] Archy undergoes a "revolution of feel- ing" when his dying mother tells him of his paternity. Shocked that he is the "slave of my own father"—and this conflation of relations makes visible the relations implicit in the slave system—Archy explains that "as his slave, his apparent kindness had gained my affection . . . as his son, I soon began to feel that I might claim . . . an equal birth-right with my brethren." The discovery of his father's identity does not change Archy's legal status, but it relocates the abstract question of rights in family identity and introduces the issues of incest and miscegenation that threaten that identity.

To claim an "equal birthright" with his brethren appears, in the peculiar institution of the plantation, as an assertion of sexual desire toward women on the plantation, regardless of birth or relation. Following this logic, Archy falls in love with his half-sister, like him the child of a slave mother:

> Cassy knew herself to be Colonel Moore's daughter; but . . . I had discov- ered that she had no idea, that I was his son. [His wife] Mrs. Moore was perfectly well informed [but] she discovered in it no impediment to my marriage with Cassy. Nor did I; for how could that same regard for the *decencies of life* . . . that refused to acknowledge our paternity, or to recog- nize any relationship between us, pretend at the same time . . . to forbid our union?[32]

A refusal to acknowledge the paternity of Cassy and Archy is thus a refusal to acknowledge any biological relationship between them. They cannot legally be related because they have no legal father; their identity can be derived only through the mother. Such disregard for the *"decencies of life"* disavows the "facts" of life involving biological reproduction and translates into miscegenation and incest.

The family boundaries that both miscegenation and incest foreground were well recognized by nineteenth-century legislation. "State criminal codes," as the legal theorist Eva Saks presents it, "usually listed miscegenation next to incest as two crimes of 'blood.' " This problematic association of interracial and intrafamilial crimes of blood was elaborated on by an antebellum Mississippi statesman who declared: "The same law which forbids consanguinous amalgamation forbids ethnical amalgamation. Both are incestuous. Amalgamation is incest."[33] What at once links and produces these crimes of blood is the invisible father. Such generation without a father is perhaps epitomized by Topsy's famous remark in *Uncle Tom's Cabin* that she "never was born," since she was "raised by a speculator." Her remark joins the Southern logic of fatherlessness and the Northern logic of capitalism—she has been born and raised in a system of speculation and exchange.[34] Similarly, in a later version, *The White Slave* (1852), Archy is told: "As slaves could not be married, there could be . . . no widows among them; and as to the children, not being born in lawful wedlock, they could not become fatherless,—for they had no fathers,—being in the eye of the law, as he had heard the learned Judge Hallett observe from the bench, the children of nobody."[35]

But such denying of natural reproduction creates another dilemma for Archy and Cassy. Their father intervenes to prevent their marriage, not out of moral outrage but because his refusal to recognize familial relations, and the miscegenation-incest linkage, allows him to express a competing sexual desire for his daughter. She resists him and finally forestalls an attempted rape by calling him "father," a name that still has the power to inhibit his sexual performance, although it does not prevent him from threatening future attempts. The family thus becomes almost indiscriminately sexualized when at the mercy of one man, since neither miscegenation nor incest taboos prohibit sexual relations. Familial relations collapse into indiscriminate incestuous/ miscegenated relations. Even Archy's mother acquires sexual significance: "I describe her more like a lover than a son." Archy resembles his father perhaps most in this matter of desire for both his mother and his sister.[36] Like his father, Archy keeps both desire and reproduction in the family.

V

One register of the desire to keep repdocution within families is the replication of names that number rather than rename generations of sons. In Lydia Maria Child's novel *The Romance of the Republic* (1867), Gerald Fitzgerald's name already identifies him as his own son. His two sons (by different mothers) both receive this name. Their resemblance to their father is surpassed only by their resemblance to each other. In such a family, one "could see no difference" between identical sons. This reproduction with no difference, or the identical appearance they have as sons of the same father, bypasses the racial identity each has inherited from his mother, although, until the Civil War, that racial identity codes one as slave and the other as free. The novel repeatedly interrogates such problems of antebellum national identity, while presenting the struggle for family identity in a republic at once incestuous and miscegenous.

Both mothers of Gerald Fitzgerald's sons—the Northern Lily Bell and the Southern Rosa Royal—grow up believing they are white. Only one will have her juridical status redetermined. Since her father never freed her mother, Rosa Royal follows her mother's condition as a slave. She discovers her status after her father's death, when she is put up for sale as part of the movable goods of the estate she thought to have inherited. Still ignorant that the Louisiana codes of slavery invalidate a marriage contract with a slave, Rosa believes she has escaped her condition by marrying Gerald Fitzgerald. When she finds out that her marriage is a fraud—he has purchased her rather than married her—and that he has not only married the Northern Lily Bell and fathered a legitimate heir, but also sold her to the aptly named Mr. Bruteman, Rosa finds herself "in a terrible tempest of hatred and revenge." The children of the two "wives" of Gerald Fitzgerald are lying together: "I looked at the two babies, and thought how one was born to be indulged and honored, while the other was born a slave, liable to be sold by his unfeeling father. . . . Mine was only a week the oldest, and was no larger than his brother. They were so exactly alike that I could distinguish them only by their dress. I exchanged the dresses."[37] The babies are so alike that even their mothers need their "dress" to determine their identity. Not even skin deep, racial difference becomes as superficial as a different garment.

Even the photographs that had just been perfected as a mark of fixed identities are inadequate: because of their similarity, the photograph of the illegitimate son identifies the legitimate one. Locating or fixing identity, as we have seen, was a midnineteenth-century preoccupation. The midnineteenth-century inventions of photography and fingerprinting emerge from attempts to fix identity at the surface of the skin, or, as Oliver Wendell Holmes proclaimed of photography, to skin the surface of the visible world.[38] *The Romance of the Republic,* too early for fingerprints, has photographs and tattoos to mark the skins of its characters. The only visible difference between these brothers is the "G.F." tattooed on one son's arm as a register of his identity which he cannot read: he calls himself George Falkner rather than Gerald Fitzgerald; although he later learns to read the mark of his name on his skin, he still can't read his skin for the sign of whether he is slave or free. The surface does not indicate—for either son—what status they have as subjects of the republic. These competing imperatives of reading the bodily and the extrabodily foreground the problem of identity and its relation to the problem of the body.

The major conflicts in the novel involve attempts to locate, identify, and claim the lost members of families, most of them lost because of slavery or attempts to escape slavery. In the middle of the novel, for example, two runaway slaves try to leave a ship from New Orleans, significantly called *The King Cotton,* as it arrives in Boston. One of the slaves, "passing" as white, is in fact legally "white"; the other masquerades as his slave, but is instead his wife.[39] Detained when they try to land, the stowaways run, and the captain calls after them, "Stop, thief!" The theft they commit, of course, is to steal their own bodies.

"There's no safety for property now-a-days," complains the New England shipowner, Mr. Bell. Sending his grandson out to return the runaways, he is unaware that the escaped slave has been substituted for the grandson before him: although both are his grandsons, the one he sends after the runaways could be claimed as a slave, while the runaway could legally inherit Mr. Bell's property, as well as his own brother. As he sends Gerald Fitzgerald to return his brother to slavery, Mr. Bell lectures him: "It is every way for my interest to make sure of returning those negroes; and your interest is somewhat connected with mine" (*R,* 311). The connections of interest and property more crucially involve what it means to claim a body and to make claims about what the surface of the skin indicates, or in short, how property and identity are embodied in the novel.

When he later discovers that "the Gerald he had been educating as his grandson was in fact . . . born a slave" (*R,* 390), Mr. Bell is confronted with an insupportable dilemma: "My property . . . must either go to Gerald, who you say has negro blood in his veins, or to this other fellow, who is a slave with a negro wife" (*R,* 394). He dies in an apoplectic fit, confronting "the vulgar phantom of a slave son" (*R,* 396). Leaving his grandson to his grandson (a common means, under slavery, of keeping property and identity in the family—Archy Moore, for instance, "belongs" to his brother) has been turned, by their switched identities, into leaving him to himself. His property cannot *go* to Gerald; his property *is* Gerald. The peculiarity of the "peculiar institution"—a peculiarity which involves the conversion of people into property (*pecu* is the root both of "peculiar" and "pecuniary")—could not be more disturbingly enacted. The issue of property has become the at once peculiar and pecuniary issue of knowing which of your offspring you should leave to which, which is a proper subject and which an object of subjection. Gerald has discovered himself to be not the heir to property, but the property of the heir.[40]

The Civil War brings these mirroring doubles face to face, as brothers of the North and South confront each other. When the first Gerald Fitzgerald goes off to fight, he writes home: "whether I had seen a vision or a reality . . . I saw such a likeness of myself as I never saw excepting in the mirror" (*R,* 405). This mirrored likeness frightens him: "I thought I had seen myself; and that, you know, is said to be a warning of approaching death" (*R,* 404–5). The vision of an oncoming doppleganger does prove to be a warning: he dies after battle in the arms of his brother. When, after his death, this brother/double is discovered, Rosa's husband comments, "I could see no difference . . . his transformation into a gentleman would be an easy process" (*R,* 413).[41] The paradox here is both that you can *see* no difference (identity is only skin deep), and that he must be *transformed* (seeing no difference is not enough).

In its insistent attempts both to tell and to remove such differences, *A Romance of the Republic* asks what romance can be had in a republic in which identity is so easily dislocated. As the novel imaginatively traces the consequences of Southern amalgamation, not knowing the difference becomes both a familial and a national issue. The "fraternal" Civil War most violently engages such differences at the level of the national family.

Child's romance of the republic is a romance that combines miscegenation and incest. Like Archy Moore, the young Gerald Fitzgerald falls in love with his own sister. Rather than having the same father, he and his sister have the same mother, Rosa, who intervenes to protect them from committing incest. Rosa has first to explain to her suspicious husband that she loves Gerald Fitzgerald because he is her son and not because she wants him as a lover. (His father, Gerald Fitzgerald, was indeed her lover.) Rosa's son, Gerald Fitzgerald, dies with her daughter's picture on his breast. And her daughter then falls in love with a cousin—we are told improbably that "the dangers of too close relationship are safely diminished," because "nations and races have been pretty thoroughly mixed up in the ancestry of our children" (*R*, 432). Lydia Maria Child's family romance, in other words, promotes mixture rather than sameness, though its mixture appears as a dizzying proliferation of deviance in a miscegenous family.

The brothers of the *Romance* are not, as in Twain's narrative, simply traded back: instead of being sold down the river, the son of the slave mother is killed in the Civil War; instead of remaining in the still-prejudiced United States, the other goes off to Europe, where color might matter less. Neither stays at "home"—neither has a republic to have a romance in. The scandals of the literature we have been examining—its scenarios of incest and miscegenation—bring home to the reader (who has brought this literature home to read) how much this romance is a matter of what happens at home. As a part of the post–Civil War attempt to resolve the trauma of families in a miscegenous republic, the novel tries to recover postbellum national identity in the wake of national disintegration. The major struggle, over who can be a subject in this republic, still centers on the problem of embodiment. And too often, to be identified as white and to be identified as a subject appear the same, even in a novel that proposes to open up the republic for all.

The question remains: what happens to identity when to look at another is to look in the mirror? If seeing yourself leads to death, the violence of this recognition suggests the violence of civil war. And it also suggests the images with which I began: although the identity of slavery can sometimes be turned upside down or washed away, when the doll is reversed, we discover that the slave woman and the white woman are the same.[42] Both identities are within its body, and the identities are not only exchangeable, but related. Although these narratives reject the reversibility the doll proposes—where black can become white, and white black—beneath the complications and rationalizations of their tales of miscegenation, concealment, and babies switched at birth, lies this obsessional figure of the ambiguity and instability of bodily identity.

10

Narratives of the Female Body:
The Greek Slave

Joy S. Kasson

Viewers of art objects in midnineteenth-century America brought to their encounter with painting or sculpture a set of expectations very foreign to twentieth-century aesthetic values. The gulf had already opened in 1903, when Henry James looked back on the career of sculptor William Wetmore Story a half century earlier and commented that works of art in Story's generation did not appeal to what he considered the aesthetic sense, but rather to "the sense of the romantic, the anecdotic, the supposedly historic, the explicitly pathetic. It was still the age in which an image had, before anything else, to tell a story."[1] The stories that art objects told their audiences sometimes affirmed and sometimes subverted their ostensible meaning. Some were poorly articulated and may be recovered only in indirect ways, while others were recorded in letters between artists and patrons, in descriptions of art objects that were published in newspapers and magazines, and in printed catalogues of art exhibitions. Imagining a past, present, and future as well as an emotional context for a fictional subject, audiences participated in the production of meaning and revealed many of their own assumptions. Fervent believers in the equivalence between words and images, they saw in art objects representations of the world as they understood it.

In the 1840s and 1850s a particular work of sculpture caught the imagination of American viewers; artists, writers, and newspaper readers recorded their reactions to it in great detail. Hiram Powers's *The Greek Slave* depicted a nude woman in chains; but the artist carefully established a narrative context that allowed audiences to subdue the discomfort that the subject might otherwise have provoked. In the narratives they constructed to explain to themselves the enormous appeal it exercised upon them, Powers and his contemporaries defined for themselves the symbolic significance of the female body. And since, as anthropologist Mary Douglas has pointed out, images of the human body often reveal shared assumptions about the body politic, a careful examination of the reception of *The Greek Slave* also suggests some insights into the complex dynamic of nineteenth-century American culture.[2]

Fig. 10.1. Hiram Powers, The Greek Slave. *No work of art tells us more about the construction of gender in sentimental culture than this sculpture, viewed by more than 100,000 Americans in the 1840s. (Yale University Art Gallery, Olive Louise Dann Fund.)*

The Greek Slave (Fig. 10.1) was the first American sculpture to receive national and international acclaim. Between 1844 and 1869, Powers sculpted six full-length versions of the statue, as well as numerous three-quarter-size replicas and as many as sixty-seven busts.[3] Traveling exhibitions brought the sculpture to more than a dozen American cities, where it was viewed by more than a hundred thousand people. Sketches and engravings of *The Greek Slave* appeared in guidebooks, art journals, and popular magazines. Magazine articles, pamphlets, travel literature, and popular sketches contained accounts of the sculpture, its audience, and the experience of viewing it.

When he began work on *The Greek Slave* in 1842, Powers was still a newcomer to the art world. The son of a Vermont farmer who emigrated to Ohio, Powers had worked for a clockmaker and built automated figures for a wax museum in Cincinnati, before beginning to receive recognition for his portrait busts. With the help of a patron, Nicholas Longworth, Powers moved to Florence in 1837. There he joined a growing community of Anglo-American artists, selling portrait and ideal busts to visiting countrymen and hoping for commissions for public sculpture at home. But Powers, like the other sculptors of his generation, also aspired to success in "ideal" sculpture, the portrayal of literary, historical, and biblical subjects. Before beginning *The Greek Slave,* Powers had modeled another ideal subject, *Eve Tempted.* The response generated by this sculpture suggested to Powers both the rewards and the pitfalls of his aspirations toward a "higher" form of art. *Eve* had received praise from the distinguished Danish sculptor Bertel Thorwaldsen, and was much admired by visitors to Powers's studio in Florence.[4] But a prospective buyer later canceled his order, accused by his own brother of "indiscretion" in seeking to bring a nude sculpture home to "a quiet, old fashioned, utilitarian place" like Albany.[5] While finishing *Eve* and waiting for a buyer for it, Powers began a second nude female subject, mindful of both the importance of narrative content and the demand for modesty among his American audience. To a benefactor, Col. John Preston, Powers described his new work:

> [It] is of a young girl—nude, with her hands bound and in such a position as to conceal a portion of the figure, thereby rendering the exposure of the nakedness less exceptionable to our American fastidiousness. The feet also will be bound to a fixture and the face turned to one side, and downwards with an expression of modesty and Christian resignation. That she is a Christian will be inferred by a cross, suspended by a chain around her neck and hanging or resting on her bosom. I said a young girl, but the form will express puberty.[6]

Although Powers was later to change some of the details, this earliest description contains the crucial elements that made *The Greek Slave* a success: nudity, modesty, constraint, and Christian resignation.

In choosing a subject that had a strong narrative component but did not refer to a specific literary source, Powers made a bold decision. European neoclassicists such as Canova and Thorwaldsen had produced numerous Venuses, Psyches, and other mythological figures, and Horatio Greenough had chosen a character from a Byron poem for his first ideal sculpture, *Medora,* in 1832. But with *Eve,* a biblical figure carrying the sanction of an authoritative and morally irreproachable text, the frank nudity of the sculpture had still made Powers's audience uneasy. So for *The Greek Slave,* Powers invented his own story, the tale of a contemporary Greek woman captured by the Turks, abducted from her own country, and sold into slavery. Although the narrative had literary echoes—Byron had died supporting the cause of Greek independence, and Shelley wrote compassionately of Greek slave women[7]—it did not refer to a specific literary text. Rather, it took its drama from the Western interest in the Greek wars and in its fascination with the forbidden realm of the Turkish harem.

As Malek Alloula has recently pointed out, the Western interest in the concealed women of the harem combined titillation, voyeurism, and an illusion of power in the face of the mysterious Other.[8] Literary treatments of the Orient abounded in the nineteenth century, as seen in poetry such as Byron's *Bride of Abydos* (1813) and Thomas Moore's *Lalla Rookh* (1817); operas like *The Caliph of Bagdad,* which played in New York in 1827; and Mozart's *Abduction from the Seraglio.*[9] A classic work of English pornography, *The Lustful Turk* (1828), portrayed the sexual awakening of English girls captured by a Turkish dey; among the women of his harem is a Greek girl pining for her homeland.[10] The French painter Ingres had been painting scenes from the Turkish baths since the beginning of the century, and in 1820–22 had worked in Florence in the same studio as sculptor Lorenzo Bartolini, who later became Powers's friend.[11] In 1839 Ingres painted a composition, *Odalisque with Slave* (Fig. 10.2), that made explicit the sensuality that Westerners associated with the Turkish harem; the painting was engraved by Reveil, and Ingres produced another copy in 1842.[12] In the same year that Powers began *The Greek Slave,* French sculptor James Pradier exhibited an *Odalisque* at the Salon of 1841: a nude, seated figure wearing a turban and looking back over her shoulder with a seductive glance.[13] For nineteenth-century Western observers, the Turkish harem represented an alluring and alarming phenomenon, a place of enslavement and sensual gratification, a forbidden realm in which viewers confronted their own erotic desires.

Powers, of course, did not depict a woman of the harem. He chose instead a subject that played upon his audience's assumptions about the harem without actually portraying it. His *Greek Slave* stands exposed in the slave market, her clothes removed, her wrists chained. The combination of nudity and restraint signaled to the viewers what would be her fate, and her future in the harem is the great unstated drama that gave the sculpture its poignancy. Powers presented a woman in a chaste and tranquil pose, but the narrative suggested by the sculpture implied violence and sensuality.

Twenty years later a Czech artist would paint a picture that made explicit the violence and sensuality that were implicit in *The Greek Slave.* Jaroslav Čermák's *Episode in the Massacre of Syria* (1861) depicts a woman struggling with her captors (Fig. 10.3). As with the Greek slave, her clothes are torn away, and a cross lies at her feet; in this ferocious painting she is surrounded

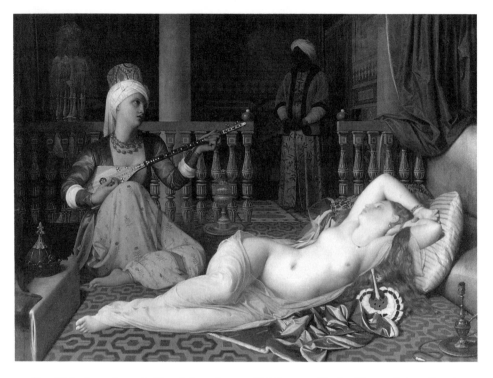

Fig. 10.2. Jean-Auguste-Dominique Ingres, Odalisque with the Slave. *Orientalism in art and literature suggested that the harem was a realm of forbidden sensuality in which the female body existed only for men's pleasure. (Fogg Art Museum, Harvard University, bequest of Grenville L. Winthrop.)*

by the corpses of her husband and child. The painter contrasts the whiteness of her skin with the swarthiness of her captors, who grasp her thighs and bind her arms. By 1879, when the painting was reproduced in *The Art Treasures of America*, it had found its way into the respectable collection of T. A. Havemeyer of New York.[14] Whereas Powers felt it necessary to muffle the drama that gave *The Greek Slave* its poignancy, later artists and patrons were willing to confront more directly what one commentator called the "hot energy" of the scene.[15] Perhaps the popularity of Powers's sculpture inspired Cermak's painting; at any rate, the later painting brings to the surface the violence, the fear of the swarthy captors, and the erotic energy to which viewers responded in *The Greek Slave*.

Painfully aware of what he called "American fastidiousness" about nudity in art, Powers in *The Greek Slave* attempted to present an attractive female subject encased in a narrative that would simultaneously invite and repel erotic associations. *The Greek Slave* owes its pose to a well-known ancient sculpture, the Venus of Cnidus, a Roman copy of which was at the Vatican museum.[16] The early London reviews praised its classicism, declaring that "it

Fig. 10.3. Jaroslav Čermák, Episode in the Massacre of Syria *(engraving). This turbu-
lent painting makes explicit the violence and fear of the barbarian "other" that were
taken for granted in so many of the narratives inspired by* The Greek Slave. *(Strahan,
Art Treasures of America, vol. 1.)*

competes successfully with the best remnants of Greek art," but they also
commented on its texture, softness, and modeling, resulting from Powers's
use of special files he had invented to give the skin a lifelike finish.[17] The
sculptor admitted to using a live model, a practice viewed with suspicion by

American audiences; but he told an interviewer that the young girl who posed for him was virtuous, innocent, and forced to work as a model only by financial want.[18] Powers took care to surround his modern-day Venus with a thick web of explanation in order to counteract the sensuous appeal of the image itself.

About the time *The Greek Slave* was delivered to its first owner, who put it on display in London, a book was published by C. Edwards Lester, the American consul in Genoa, containing lengthy accounts of Powers's life, works, and conversations. Lester quoted Powers's outspoken defense of his nude sculptures: "It was not my object for interest's sake to set before my countrymen demoralizing subjects, and thus get even my bread at the expense of public chastity." Powers insisted that "a pure abstract human form tempered with chaste expression and attitude" was "calculated to awaken the highest emotions of the soul for the pure and beautiful." He even tried to argue that, since the "society of chaste and well educated women has a tendency to exalt the mind," redeeming feminine influence is not "limited to the face alone"—a suggestion whose humor was undoubtedly unintentional. Turning to *The Greek Slave* in particular, Powers insisted on the importance of the narrative framework, which provided what he called the circumstances that could justify depiction of a nude subject.

> The Slave has been taken from one of the Greek Islands by the Turks, in the time of the Greek Revolution; the history of which is familiar to all. Her father and mother, and perhaps all her kindred, have been destroyed by her foes, and she alone preserved as a treasure too valuable to be thrown away. She is now among barbarian strangers, under the pressure of a full recollection of the calamitous events which have brought her to her present state; and she stands exposed to the gaze of the people she abhors, and awaits her fate with intense anxiety, tempered indeed by the support of her reliance upon the goodness of God. Gather all these afflictions together, and add to them the fortitude and resignation of a Christian, and no room will be left for shame.[19]

In his description, Powers interpreted the meaning of nudity in his sculpture; he redirected the viewer's gaze from the female subject's body to her face, stressing her emotions: anxiety, fortitude, and resignation. His reference to "barbarian strangers" evoked all the associations of the harem. But, interestingly, he used his reference to these exotic foreigners to define an unacceptable way of viewing the subject, treating her as an object "too valuable to be thrown away," displaying her "exposed to the gaze of the people she abhors." If the viewer did not wish to be associated with the "barbarian" enemy, he would not gaze at her in the way they do. There is no shame in her pose, because the viewers to whom the sculpture was addressed, the men and women of the nineteenth-century West, accepted the distinction between themselves and her captors and agreed to view her in a different way. By objectifying improper viewing, the device of the imaginary Turkish captors enabled Powers to invite his audience to view *The Greek Slave,* while leaving intact the suggestion that the female nude would under other circumstances by synonymous with "shame."

Powers's suggestion that *The Greek Slave* could be truly seen only through a certain kind of looking was elaborated upon by one of his most important commentators. In 1847, Reverend Orville Dewey published an article on "Powers' Statues" in *The Union Magazine of Literature and Art*. Eleven years earlier, in a travel book called *The Old World and the New*, Dewey had made some awkward and thoroughly conventional comments about art, but in 1847 he spoke out firmly about the value of Powers's sculpture.[20] Comparing *Eve* and *The Greek Slave* to the standard examples of excellence in ancient sculpture, the Apollo Belvedere and the Venus de Medici, Dewey pronounced Powers' works superior. "There is *no* sentiment in the Venus, but modesty. She is not in a situation to express any sentiment, or any *other* sentiment. She has neither done anything nor is going to do anything, nor is she in a situation, to awaken any moral emotion. . . . There ought to be some reason for exposure *besides* beauty." Insisting that Powers's sculpture expressed more than "the beauty of mere form, of the moulding of limbs and muscles," Dewey emphasized the centrality of narrative to the interpretation of the art works. The story, he insisted, was more important than the appearance of the sculpture itself. Indeed, Dewey suggested that the "sentiment" evoked by the sculpture could change the very way the viewer looked at it. In looking at *The Greek Slave,* Dewey asserted, the receptive viewer—the Christian, he might have added, rather than the "barbarian"—ceased to see a nude sculpture at all. "The Greek Slave is clothed all over with sentiment; sheltered, protected by it from every profane eye. Brocade, cloth of gold, could not be a more complete protection than the vesture of the holiness in which she stands." Whereas Powers had suggested that the viewer's gaze could avoid the subject's body and focus on her face, Dewey went one step further, suggesting that the viewer could see *The Greek Slave* without seeing her body at all. The artist is able "to make the spiritual reign over the corporeal; to sink form in ideality; in this particular case, to make the appeal to the soul entirely control the appeal to sense."[21]

Powers and his friends had found a way to reassure American audiences suspicious of nudity in art. Earlier in the century Adolph Ulrich Wertmuller's *Danae and the Shower of Gold* (1787) had caused a scandal when it was exhibited in New York and Philadelphia, as did other painted nudes in the first quarter of the century.[22] A pair of French paintings depicting the temptation of Adam and Eve and the expulsion from the Garden of Eden were criticized for their nudity during an American tour in 1832–35.[23] Horatio Greenough's *Chanting Cherubs* (1831) had been attacked as immodest when displayed in New York.[24] When Powers sent *The Greek Slave* on a tour of American cities in 1847, he made sure the sculpture was accompanied by texts that would instruct and direct the viewers' gaze. By 1848, enough had been written about the sculpture for Powers and his agent, Miner Kellogg, to compile a booklet that could be republished for every city where *The Greek Slave* was displayed.[25] Press notices, poems, and tributes by American diplomats and travelers, with Dewey's article prominently featured, stressed the propriety, even the nobility, of Powers's undertaking. The American tour, which earned

$23,000 in receipts, thus introduced a large audience not only to a work of art but to a series of narratives, ostensibly describing the sculpture, but also defining a shared concept of woman's body and woman's nature.

The Greek Slave served its viewers as a focus for curiosity about the human body. Despite the disclaimers of Powers and others that it could be seen without noticing its nudity, *The Greek Slave* offered a morally sanctioned occasion for viewing the female body.[26] As Peter Gay has argued, nineteenth-century reticence about sexuality does not necessarily mean that sexuality was not an important force in people's lives. "It is a mistake to think that nineteenth-century bourgeois did not know what they did not discuss, did not practice what they did not confess, or did not enjoy what they did not publish."[27] In his multivolume work *The Bourgeois Experience, Victoria to Freud*, Gay traces a history of sexual expressiveness in European and American bourgeois culture, arguing that works of nude sculpture like *The Greek Slave* played an important role in providing morally sanctioned visual pleasure.[28]

Many of the contemporary printed comments on *The Greek Slave* stressed the writer's own response to the female subject's beauty. "Why hauntest thou my dreams," asked one poet, describing the "maiden shape . . . Severe in vestal grace, yet warm / And flexible with the delicate glow of youth."[29] While one observer commented that she could now for the first time understand the story of Pygmalion, another writer imagined the statue coming to life if offered true love: "Ah, then I know should gush the woman's tears! . . . / The marble eyelids lift—the pale lips should / Quick pant, as Love his flashing pinion bent."[30] By imagining a different scene, the nude subject in the arms of "holy love," the poet made explicit the suppressed eroticism of the sculpture. In this narrative the speaker allowed himself to experience the feelings of desire that other commentators had associated with the "barbarian" masters of the harem. Despite the disclaimers of Powers and his supporters, the statue's success at least partially depended on its ability to provide erotic pleasure.

Modern critics have commented on the importance of *The Greek Slave* as a focus for sexual fantasy among its viewers, male and female. Like the popular literature that could be read in gift books and annuals and in the journals that reviewed *The Greek Slave,* the narrative suggested by the statue offered viewers an opportunity to identify with the desired-love-object-as-victim as well as with her pursuer.[31] Suzanne Kappeler has argued that pornography is defined by conventions of representation in which the author and the spectator share an illusion of power over the victim.[32] Without suggesting that *The Greek Slave* was actually pornographic, we may speculate that the subject of a woman in bondage provided a similar kind of excitement for male spectators. Women spectators may have responded to the sculpture as a fantasy of domination. Numerous women wrote about their reactions to *The Greek Slave,* including E. Anna Lewis, who reported sinking into a trance for five hours, and Clara Cushman, who declared, "I could have wept with a perfect agony of tears," and added that the sculpture put her into "a train of dreamy delicious revery, in which hours might have passed unnoticed."[33] Both these observers reported an experience that paralleled that of the slave herself: enthrallment, which they experienced as satisfying and pleasurable.

Exhibitors seemed to recognize at least tacitly the erotic potential of the statue, for it was sometimes displayed with special viewing times for women and children. However, most commentators took special pains to deny the sculpture's sensual appeal. Hence the importance in poems and descriptions of *The Greek Slave* of the words "chaste" and "chastity." "O chastity of Art!" proclaimed the writer of a prize ode to the statue, winner of a contest in the *New York Evening Mirror.* "Beneath her soul's immeasurable woe, / All sensuous vision lies subdued." The writer goes on to celebrate "[h]er pure thoughts clustering around her form, / Like seraph garments, whiter than the snows."[34] Dewey's insistence that the nude sculpture was clothed in morality was echoed by numerous other commentators. "Unclothed, yet clothed upon," began a poem by James Freeman Clark, who continued, "She stands not bare—/ Another robe, of purity, is there."[35] A poet writing in *The Knicker-bocker Magazine* amplified the image: "Naked yet clothed with chastity, She stands / And as a shield throws back the sun's hot rays, / Her modest mien repels each vulgar gaze."[36]

This insistence that the nude sculpture is really clothed, and that a woman who is about to be sexually violated is chaste, seems paradoxical. A Freudian critic might see in this insistence on purity a repressed eroticism, with viewers denying their own sense of the danger and appeal of the nude as a physical force by focusing on the opposite qualities of spirituality and ideality.

To many observers, the Greek slave's spirituality was essential to her appeal. Although an occasional critic wished she showed more anger and defiance (like the subject of Čermák's later painting), most observers praised her for her tranquillity and found it appealing.[37] As one poet put it:

> Though all Earth's ties were snapt by that sharp pain,
> Though hope nor fear within her breast remain,
> Life's wrongs are over; neither shame nor harm
> Can reach that inner realm of perfect calm.[38]

Similarly, art critic and poet Henry Tuckerman described the Greek slave as almost superhuman in her transcendence of her painful situation:

> Do no human pulses quiver in those wrists that bear the gyves
> With a noble, sweet endurance, such as moulds heroic lives . . .
> Half unconscious of thy bondage, on the wings of Faith elate
> Thou art gifted with a being high above thy seeming fate!—
> . . . .
> Words of triumph, not of wailing, for the cheer of Hope is thine,
> And, immortal in thy beauty, sorrow grows with thee divine.[39]

Both these poems stress the subject's aloofness, her isolation in a spiritual state that puts her beyond the reach of her worldly woes. In these narratives, like some of the others that reveal the writer's attraction to the female subject, her remoteness and self-possession are seen as part of her appeal. In this sense she seems to embody the aspect of female sexuality that Freud described in his essay "On Narcissism: An Introduction":

> Women, especially if they grow up with good looks, develop a certain self-containment which compensates them for the social restrictions that are imposed upon them in their choice of object. Strictly speaking, it is only themselves that such women love with an intensity comparable to that of the man's love for them. . . . Such women have the greatest fascination for men . . . for it seems very evident that another person's narcissism has a great attraction for those who have renounced part of their own narcissism and are in search of object-love.[40]

Freud suggested that female "self-containment" might originate as a response to "social restrictions"; certainly the Greek slave could be seen as symbolizing in her dire extremity the restraints placed upon all women in society. If female narcissism is especially attractive, as Freud suggests, to men who have renounced a measure of their own narcissistic impulses, then *The Greek Slave* may have spoken particularly strongly to the bustling culture of nineteenth-century America which, as numerous commentators lamented, allowed so little time for aesthetic cultivation or reflection.[41]

In their ambivalent attitude toward the female body—beautiful but dangerous, to be admired but not seen—Powers and his supporters reflected the complex and contradictory attitudes toward human sexuality that characterized antebellum America. As Stephen Nissenbaum has pointed out, American anxiety about the integrity of the body, and in particular about the dangers of sexuality, sprang into full force in the 1830s.[42] Medical literature of the same period stressed female vulnerability, woman's delicate nervous system, and the way in which modern life posed a threat to her role as a wife and mother.[43]

The Greek Slave addressed this anxiety about the body and this sense of female vulnerability. Literally imperiled by a dangerous sexuality, the female subject represents woman's body at risk. The first published engraving of the sculpture made it seem leaner, less robust, and more conventionally pretty than it was, suggesting that the engraver responded to a sense of the subject's vulnerability and portrayed her more like a pale, wan heroine than a Venus-like figure (Fig. 10.4).[44] By the 1830s, as Nancy Cott has suggested, the doctrine of female passionlessness had begun to gain widespread popularity, giving women moral authority at the cost of a repression their sexuality.[45] Of course sexuality did bring risks for nineteenth-century women, ranging from death in childbirth to venereal disease.[46] The figure of *The Greek Slave,* chained and acquiescent in the face of imminent sexual violation, served as an epitome of female sexuality as many understood it at the time: resigned, aloof, passionless, and endangered.

The slave has also been deprived of her ability to serve as wife and mother. Several of the written narratives focused on this aspect of the story: torn from her family and home, the Greek slave represented the fragility of woman's domestic life as well as of her physical integrity. One writer, E. Anna Lewis,

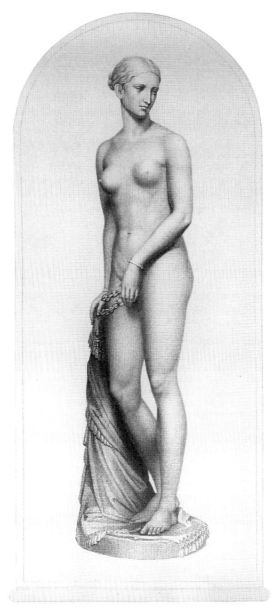

Fig. 10.4. This engraving of The Greek Slave *helped Powers to reach an even wider audience; at the same time, the author's representation of the statue interpreted the image by heightening the subject's frailty and vulnerability. (*Art-Journal *12 [1850].)*

reported the train of thoughts that rushed through her mind as she gazed at the statue: "The history of her fallen country, her Greek home, her Greek lover, her Greek friends, her capture, her exposure in the public market place; the freezing of every drop of her young blood beneath the libidinous gaze of shameless traffickers in beauty; the breaking up of the deep waters of her heart; then, their calm settling down over its hopeless ruins."[47] Similarly, some of the poetry inspired by *The Greek Slave* stressed her separation from home and family. According to one poet, her

> . . . expressive, drooping,
> Tender, melancholy eyes, are vainly
> Looking for that far-off one, she fondly
> Loves in her deep sorrow, and her weary
> Heart is throbbing, with dear memories of
> Her distant, happy cottage-home in Greece.
> Alas! The spoiler came, and ruthless, tore
> The lily from its pearly stem, to bloom
> In base Constantinople's foul Bazaar![48]

Here the language of ravishment is applied to the removal of the young woman from her home, and the reader's emotions are carefully focused on past domesticity rather than future sensuality. Similarly, another poem uses loss of home as a metaphor—or euphemism—for physical violation:

> Dim through veiling lids she ever sees
> Those sweeping mountain lines, those clustered trees,
> The low home clinging to the hillside, where
> Glitters each point and line amid the purple air.
> Her happy home! She sees it as it stood—
> Before the wave of war swept over it in blood.
> Now all is gone! No more for her, no more—
> Or Love, Trust, Hope and Joy on Life's dull shore
> All cruel wrongs, all bitter anguish borne
> Her virgin soul is crushed, her heart is torn.
> Debased, defiled and trampled in the dust.[49]

Construction of a sentimentalized, domestic past could place the Greek slave more securely in the realm of respectability; but it also reminded viewers of their own fears of domestic disarray. If, as Stephen Nissenbaum has argued, heightened anxiety about illness and sexuality corresponded to enormous changes in the everyday life of most Americans—namely, the shift from a household economy to a market economy, and the creation of "woman's sphere" apart from the world of work—the image of the slave's disrupted domestic idyll might resonate with the concerns of its audience as much as the suggestion that she faced physical danger. The note of nostalgia and regret for a lost past, barely suggested by Powers himself, appears so frequently in popular responses to the sculpture as to suggest that Powers had tapped a deeper vein than he knew.

Many of the narratives about *The Greek Slave* comment specifically on the fact that she is about to be sold in the slave market. One art historian has argued that the sculpture evoked the issue of American slavery and reflected Powers's abolitionist views.[50] The connection was evident to some observers: when *The Greek Slave* was displayed at the Crystal Palace exhibition in 1851, the British magazine *Punch* published an engraving showing a black woman chained to a pedestal, with the caption, "The Virginian Slave. Intended as a companion to Powers' 'Greek Slave' " (Fig. 10.5).[51] However, *The Greek Slave* was as popular in New Orleans, home of one of its purchasers, as in Boston, and much of its audience was apparently oblivious to the ironies of driving past American slave marts to shed tears over the fate of the white marble captive.

In 1857, when the Cosmopolitan Art Association publicized the sale of one of the copies of *The Greek Slave* (which the association subsequently purchased and gave away to a subscriber selected by lottery), it played humorously with the notion that the sale recapitulated the plight of the sculpture's subject. "THE GREEK SLAVE TO BE SOLD," proclaimed the headline in the *Cosmopolitan Art Journal;* the article added that the "renowned statute" was about "to be brought to the ignominious block."[52] Indeed, a few years before the Civil War, the journal reprinted a facetious advertisement from the *New-York Evening Express* that commented on the sale of

> not only a slave, but a woman; not only a woman, but a young and exquisitely beautiful one—white as driven snow, with a most faultless form and most perfect features! Was ever such a thing heard of! . . . And still more awful, for a week before the sale this slave will be exposed, perfectly nude, in the most public places in the city . . . that all the rich nabobs may feast their eyes upon her beauties, and calculate how much she would be worth to ornament their palatial residences up town.[53]

The humor here seems to dismiss the idea of a serious antislavery interpretation of *The Greek Slave,* but it also suggests discomfort with the idea of sale at auction and with the display that accompanied it. Feminist film critics have argued that the gaze of the viewer necessarily suggests power over the viewed subject.[54] Sale of the statue, in this sense, is not so different from sale of the slave, and in both cases viewing is as much an act of appropriation as owning.

To extend the argument further, the position of *The Greek Slave* as a market commodity suggests the contention by Claude Lévi-Strauss that women function in the social structure both as signs and as objects of value, owing to their role as signifying exchange between men.[55] The viewers' fascination with an image of a woman displayed for gaze and sale may thus reflect the position of women in culture generally, subject to observation and commodification. The special understanding claimed by female viewers such as Clara Cushman may suggest a broader sense in which the Greek slave, exposed and vulnerable, seemed an appropriate symbol for women in American culture.[56]

Finally, the recurrent comments on the "mart" in which the Greek slave stands for sale recall the fears of critics such as Henry Tuckerman and James Jackson Jarves that the commercial spirit was overwhelming American culture

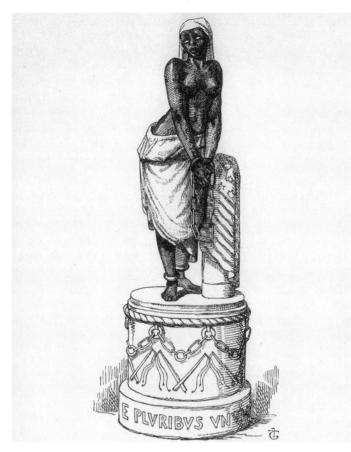

*Fig. 10.5. "The Virginian Slave. Intended as a Companion to Powers' 'Greek Slave' "
(engraving). The irony of the statue's popularity in the South as well as in the North was
not lost on this artist, who emphasized the parallel between the enslavement of Africans
and that of Powers's white marble heroine. (*Punch 20 [1851].)

in the 1840s and 1850s. In the *Book of the Artists,* Tuckerman asked, "Reader,
did you ever spring into an omnibus at the head of Wall street, with a resolution to seek a more humanizing element of life than the hard struggle for
pecuniary triumphs?"[57] Art, he suggested in his book, might provide an escape from the inhuman world of commerce. In his poem on *The Greek Slave,*
Tuckerman had characterized her as standing among "a herd of gazers, . . . a
noisy mart," in imagery that recalled his description of Wall Street.[58] The rise
of commercial culture brought about many changes in American life, and the
images of a victim sacrificed to commerce struck a responsive chord on many
different levels.
    Much of the energy behind the narratives generated by *The Greek Slave* —
narratives constructed by the artist, his defenders, viewers, and critics of all

sorts—centers on the subject's relationship to the exercise of power. On one hand, the sculpture seemed to depict the epitome of powerlessness: a woman completely at the mercy of others, stripped of her clothing as well as her culture (represented by the locket, the cross, and the Greek liberty cap laid aside with her clothing on the post beside her). On the other hand, Powers and his supporters all insisted that the female subject transcended her suffering to become an example of spiritual power.

The chain, of course, is the clearest expression of her powerlessness. Although some reviewers criticized Powers's use of the chain, arguing that it was historically inaccurate and improbable (had her captors unchained her to undress her, then chained her again?), others recognized immediately its symbolic importance.[59] As sculptor John Rogers observes: "Look at Powers' Greek Slave—there is nothing in the world that has made that so popular but that *chain*. . . . There are plenty of figures as graceful as that and it is only the effect of the chain that has made it so popular."[60] The chain suggested hopeless constraint, overwhelming odds. It helped to hide the statute's genitals even while explaining why they were exposed.

Interestingly enough, however, many of those who commented on *The Greek Slave* during the height of its popularity saw this enslaved female subject as an epitome of spiritual power. For many observers the narrative became one of the triumph of faith over adversity. "It represents a being superior to suffering, and raised above degradation by inward purity and force of character," declared the introduction to the pamphlet that accompanied the sculpture on its American tour. "The Greek Slave is an emblem of all trial to which humanity is subject, and may be regarded as a type of resignation, uncompromising virtue, or sublime patience."[61] For most observers, this spirituality gave the Greek slave a measure of superiority over her captors. The readers of these pamphlets apparently accepted the notion that the seeming powerlessness of this victimized woman could, from another point of view, be seen as a position of spiritual superiority, ascendence, even triumph.

Even the chain, the symbol of her powerlessness, to some commentators represented also her power. "What is the chain to thee, who has the power / To bind in admiration all who gaze upon thine eloquent brow and matchless form?" asked Lydia Sigourney. "We are ourselves thy slaves, most Beautiful!"[62] For Elizabeth Barrett Browning, the slave's moral power had revolutionary implications:

> Appeal, fair stone,
> From God's pure heights of beauty against man's wrong!
> Catch up in thy divine face, not alone
> East griefs but west, and strike and shame the strong,
> By thunders of white silence, overthrown.[63]

Browning's poem suggested the possibility of a violent reversal of roles: the strong could be overthrown. Other observers elaborated upon *The Greek Slave*'s potential for working a transformation. A reviewer in the *New York Courier and Enquirer* reported that the statue's beauty "subdues the whole man. . . . Loud talking men are hushed . . . and groups of women hover together as if to seek protection from their own sex's beauty."[64] In this passage the language of conquest applied to the slave in the narrative version of her situation is directed toward the viewer, who is in turn conquered by her: the audience is subdued, held, they yield, they are hushed, they seek protection. A poet in the *Detroit Advertiser* made the analogy explicit:

> In mute idolatry, spell-bound I stood
> MYSELF THE SLAVE, of her, the ideal of
> The Sculptor's inspiration! For I felt
> I was indeed a captive.[65]

Visual depictions of the experience of viewing *The Greek Slave* stress the dignity and authority, and by extension the power, of the image. An engraving of the sculpture as displayed at the 1851 Crystal Palace exhibition in London exaggerates the size of the sculpture. Although only the size of a small woman ($65\frac{1}{2}''$ high), the statue appears to tower over the figures of the spectators.[66] The sculpture also appears enlarged in an engraving published in 1857, showing the *The Greek Slave* on display in the Dusseldorf Gallery in New York (Fig. 10.6). In the engraving, spectators stand respectfully around the sculpture. Although men elsewhere in the gallery are wearing hats, the men closest to *The Greek Slave* have removed theirs. Two groups are conversing quietly; a young girl walking past in the foreground has stopped in her tracks and looks back, fascinated. The catalogue of the Cosmopolitan Art Association, which sponsored the exhibition depicted in this engraving, emphasized the atmosphere of decorum, even reverence, that surrounded the sculpture. "Its presence is a magic circle, within whose precincts all are held spell-bound and almost speechless," one review read.[67] "It is most curious to observe the effect produced upon visitors," wrote another visitor.

> They enter gaily, or with an air of curiosity; they look at the beauteous figure, and the whole manner undergoes a change. Men take off their hats, ladies seat themselves silently, and almost unconsciously; and usually it is minutes before a word is uttered. All conversation is carried on in a hushed tone, and everybody looks serious on departing.[68]

Such descriptions, of course, served a prescriptive function, informing readers of the attitude and decorum expected of them in the art gallery. However, the descriptions, like the engraving, stressed the weight and solemnity of the occasion. Furthermore, the engraving emphasized the relationship between the women in the audience and the sculpture. Unlike other depictions of art spectatorship published at about the same time, this engraving shows women actively looking at the sculpture, appearing to explain and interpret it to their

Fig. 10.6. This engraving of The Greek Slave *served as an advice manual to prospective viewers, illustrating the reverence with which the statue was to be viewed, as well as suggesting interesting parallels between the marble subject and its female viewers. (Cosmopolitan Art Journal 2 [December 1857].)*

Hiram Powers   Eng.d by R. Thew

The Greek Slave.

FROM THE ORIGINAL STATUE IN THE DUSSELDORF GALLERY, TO BE AWARDED AS A PREMIUM TO SUBSCRIBERS, IN JANUARY 1858
BY THE COSMOPOLITAN ART ASSOCIATION

male companions, who look not at the sculpture but at them. The sculpture appears larger than life, and its proximity enlivens the women who surround it.

Although overtly an image of submission and resignation, *The Greek Slave* thus suggested to its viewers a suppressed possibility of resistence, of overthrow, of empowerment. It is for this reason that the sculpture, judged vapid and bland, static and derivative by the standards of twentieth-century taste, seemed so vivid and moving to its contemporaries. *The Greek Slave* seethed with meanings for nineteenth-century viewers, who articulated many of their interpretations in the form of narratives: stories of loss and danger, faith and triumph. These narratives, furthermore, told the story of the female body as these commentators understood it: vulnerable, dangerous, and endangered, representing beauty and shame, attractive in its self-absorption, but threatening to overwhelm the viewer. The contradictory meanings embodied in *The Greek Slave*—eroticism indulged and denied, passion and passionlessness, power and powerlessness—were the meanings with which its viewers themselves struggled in a rapidly changing culture.

11

Sympathy as Strategy in Sedgwick's *Hope Leslie*

Dana Nelson

The Politics of Sentiment

In her 1860 article "How Should Women Write?" Mary Bryan traces women's growing involvement in literary fields. It is in response to men's demand "for intellectual food through the length and breadth of the land; . . . they want books for every year, for every month—mirrors to 'catch the manners living as they rise,' lenses to concentrate the rays of the new stars that dawn upon them."[1] Woman, responding as always to man's call, "steps forward to take her part in the intellectual labor," but then is strangely hindered by the qualms of the male establishment. Bryan incisively chronicles the dilemma of women writers in nineteenth-century America:

> Thus is apparent what has gradually been admitted, that it is woman's duty to write—but how and what? This is yet a mooted question. Men, after much demur and hesitation, have given women liberty to write; but they cannot yet consent to allow them full freedom. . . . With metaphysics [women] have nothing to do; it is too deep a sea for their lead to sound; nor must they grapple with those great social and moral problems with which every strong soul is now wrestling. . . . Having prescribed these bounds to the female pen, men are the first to condemn her efforts as tame and commonplace, because they lack earnestness and strength.[2]

Bryan herein argues forcefully in behalf of women writers who have begun to confront the "earnest age we live in." These women recognize that "there are active influences at work, all tending to one grand object—moral, social and physical advancement." These are women, Bryan asserts, who have come to understand that "the pen is the compass-needle that points to this pole" of social change.[3]

Bryan presents an admittedly utopian hope that women writers will become "God's chosen instrument in this work of gradual reformation, this reconciling of the harsh contrasts in society that jar so upon our sense of harmony, this righting of the grievous wrongs and evils over which we weep and pray, this final uniting of men into one common brotherhood by the bonds of sympathy and affection."[4] She perceives literature as a powerful agent of "gradual reform" that might resolve the awful contradictions of antebellum America. Her essay at once acknowledges and projects the social mission of nineteenth-century women's fiction.

A little more than thirty years before Bryan's complaints, Catherine Maria Sedgwick was mounting her own effort against the male-dominated publishing and cultural industry through her historical frontier novel *Hope Leslie* (1827). As Lucy Freibert and Barbara White observe, Sedgwick, among several other women authors, "played an important role in the development of the [frontier novel] . . . and authored one-quarter of the examples published before 1828, when the frontier romance had become a clearly recognizable genre."[5] Frontier novels explicitly took as their subject one of the "awful contradictions" in America, in both a historical and a contemporary sense—the Anglo-American conquest of the Native Americans and the assimilation of their lands. Some of the women who wrote early frontier novels, Sedgwick and Lydia Maria Child in particular, presented a clear challenge to Anglo-American policy toward the Native Americans, dealing explicitly with issues of miscegenation and presenting more generally favorable and sympathetic versions of Indianness than male colleagues such as James Fenimore Cooper, Robert Montgomery Bird, and William Gilmore Simms. Labeled pejoratively and dismissed as "sentimental" in the past, these novels are now being reconsidered. We might, then, reexamine the so-called "sympathetic" frame of reference employed by writers like Sedgwick, and ask how it provided a more positive cultural vision, proposing likenesses between cultures, and developing affinities and relationships between characters, of different "racial" groups.

Despite the evidence of sympathy toward Native Americans in such texts, we should not, as Annette Kolodny cautions, simply conclude that these women writers were in fact advocating radical social change. Kolodny's insight is important: sentimental portrayals which manipulated the emotions of a reader "represented a genuine political tool for writers otherwise disenfranchised." Through the sentimental development of a scene, these women writers did hope to influence their male compatriots and family to an increased awareness and responsiveness. Yet, Kolodny argues, women writers of domestic fictions tended more toward amelioration of social contradictions rather than toward the solutions that Mary Bryan envisioned taking place through women's powerful visions.[6] The situation, we can see, is a delicate one, for women's authorial position was a crucial component of their social vision. Without some kind of credibility, they had no voice with which to advocate alternative social models. The question, then, more properly should address *how* Catherine Maria Sedgwick uses sentiment in *Hope Leslie*. Does she simply utilize it as an effective strategy to gain authorial advantage, or does she also employ it to proffer an alternative social vision?

Lady Writer, Lady Historian

Hope Leslie, or, Early Times in the Massachusetts was published in two volumes in 1827. The work was well received, and was compared favorably by critics to Cooper's *Last of the Mohicans*.[7] Sedgwick herself claimed to be somewhat abashed by the overwhelmingly favorable reviews published in women's magazines and in the *North Atlantic Review*.[8] She was apparently not disconcerted, though, at the controversy which arose over her depiction of Indians, the defense for which she had already prepared in her original preface:

> In our histories, it was perhaps natural that [the Indians] should be repre-
> sented as "surly dogs," who preferred to die rather than live, from no other
> motive than a stupid or malignant obstinacy. Their own historians or poets, if
> they had such, would as naturally, and with more justice, have extolled their
> high-souled courage and patriotism. The writer is aware that it may be
> thought that the character of Magawisca has no prototype . . . it may be
> sufficient to remark, that . . . we are confined not to the actual, but to the
> possible. (6)

Nor was she surprised by criticism of her less than hagiographic view of the Puritans, which she carefully qualified but refused to back down from in a private letter. Insisting that she bore only "filial reverence" to the Puritans, Sedgwick yet avers that "their bigotry, their superstition, and above all their intolerance, were too apparent on the pages of history to be forgotten."[9]

Clearly, and despite the numerous textual apologies regarding her humble inadequacies as historian and author, Sedgwick had set out to redefine opinion about both race *and* gender. Sedgwick's refusal to accord Puritan historians de facto authority over her subject is basic to her fictional design, and her critique of Puritan racism is inextricable from her insistent attention to the debilitating effects of patriarchy in early America. Sedgwick was not alone here: as numerous critics have now documented at length, the frontier vision of Sedgwick and other female frontier novelists and diarists specifically counters the "Adamic myth" and its valorization of white male conquest— conquest over nonwhite males and women of any color.[10] Rather, *Hope Leslie* is remarkable for its valorization and foregrounding of feminine heroics: a woman who actively resists her male superiors in order to act on the good impulses of her heart.

Indeed, the enterprise of racial re-visioning is inseparable from a confrontation with patriarchal authority in *Hope Leslie,* as the narrator's asides attest. Nor is her critique merely historical, as her narrator's repeated disclaimers of authority begin to suggest. For instance, while offering her readers a "formal introduction to the government-mansion" (143), the narrator pauses to clarify her unpretentious, lackeylike relation to the "mighty master of fiction." Rather than attempting to "imitate the miracles wrought by the rod of the prophet," the narrator promises to rely for her description on quotations from "an authentic record of the times" (143).[11] Here, as in her preface, Sedgwick has her narrator assure male authorities (and those who are invested in upholding them) that she does not presume upon their rank. Her preface confirms this in the first and final sentences: "The following volumes are not offered to the public as being in any degree an historical narrative, or a relation of real events. . . . These volumes are . . . far from being intended as a substitute for genuine history" (5–6). Her repeated insistence, however, combined with comments sandwiched between these apologies, might suggest that the apologies themselves are less sincere than calculatingly rhetorical, designed to assuage those who, as Mary Bryan insists, refuse to grant women writers any "metaphysical" or political authority. Furthermore, as we can see in her flattering reference to James Fenimore Cooper's *The Last of the Mohicans* (81), such deferral actually highlights Sedgwick's own authority (via her good judgment) at the same time that it calls attention to her *alternative* (and differently authoritative) account.

A closer examination in this vein illuminates Sedgwick's subversive political commentary on the patriarchal assumptions of both the Puritans and her contemporary male audience. Sedgwick promises the same kind of deference and submission to male authority that she models in her novel through Mrs. Fletcher, Esther Downing, and Mrs. Winthrop. But *Hope Leslie* cagily qualifies the value of their meek subservience, suggesting that such behavior breeds an unthinking temper and frank servility. The novel presents a paragon of Puritan girlhood in Esther Downing, who, the narrator at one point reflects, "could not have disputed the nice points of faith, sanctification and justification, with certain celebrated contemporary female theologians" (135). And sandwiched within her honorific depiction of Mrs. Winthrop is a comparison of the Puritan first lady to a horse on a bit, "guided by the slightest intimation from him who held the rein" (145).

These narrative asides make clear that, for the narrator, the more admirable course is the more independent one, and we see that Sedgwick's performance as author of *Hope Leslie* is more in the spirit of the title character. Hope, following her own heart and genius, often defies patriarchal authority, secretly moving to assert a humane justice toward people whom the Puritans would trample, like the unfairly harassed Nelema.[12] "It may be seen that Hope Leslie," the narrator notes, "was superior to some of the prejudices of the age" (123). Similarly, while Sedgwick protests her reverent distance from any actually historical enterprise, she in fact broadly tackles it, beginning in her prefatory comments on the (ad)vantage of historical perspective.

From the beginning of chapter 4—a central one to this analysis—Sedgwick indicates her willingness to confront authorized history. She takes as her epigraph a modified version of one of the most censorial comments of early Anglo-American historical legacy: "It would have been happy if they had converted some before they had killed any."[13] In the chapter that follows, Sedgwick delivers two versions of the Pequot (or Pequod) war, one based on actual Puritan accounts, and the other fictionalized from a sympathetic stance and wary rereading of the same Puritan accounts. While Natty Bumppo can acknowledge that "every story has its two sides" (*The Last of the Mohicans,* 23), Cooper refuses to follow through on his implied challenge to Anglo historical authority. Instead, Chingachgook's side of the story supports the Anglo-American version in its refusal to confront it, since Chingachgook tells only of the good days before white contact, and how his tribe is coming to an elegiac end—carefully avoiding any attribution of direct blame for this to the European invaders.[14] *Hope Leslie*'s two-sided history is decidedly more confrontational.

The Wand of Feeling

One of the methods Sedgwick uses to explore racial configurations is to stage debates between various characters on precisely this subject. For example, Digby, a veteran of the Pequot "war," is thoroughly suspicious of any Indian: "They are a treacherous race . . . a kind of beast we don't comprehend" (41–42). He maintains a staunch party line represented in the historical accounts of the Pequot massacre by Hubbard, Trumbull, and Winthrop. In contrast, Everell (who is decidedly attracted to Magawisca) is skeptical, and he doggedly questions Digby's defensive assertions. When Digby insists that "we know these Pequods were famed above all the Indian tribes for their cunning," Everell counters: "And what is superior cunning among savages but superior sense?" (43). Their exchange points toward the power of representation, the way the same incident can be interpreted differently, depending on the prejudices or sympathies the interpreter brings to it. This point is underscored by the narrator's comment on the authority of the combined accounts. When Everell bests Digby, the narrator observes that Digby felt "the impatience that a man feels when he is sure he is right, without being able to make it appear" (43).

By a similar process of narrative intervention, Magawisca's account of the Pequot "war" is lent important authority. Her side of the story focuses on the cruelty of the Puritans' planned attack on sleeping women, old people, and children, by sneaking up and setting fire to the village—fire "taken from our hearth-stone, where the English had been so often warmed and cherished" (49). Magawisca's story, supported by the narrator's consequent expansion, thoroughly subverts the command of the male Puritans' versions. First, it insistently historicizes and contextualizes the situation, emphasizing the causal, reactive quality of "Pequod treachery" and subtly revealing colonial treachery. Further, it recognizes the Indian foe as human, not "beast," emphasizing Pequot families, hearths, and homes. Magawisca's account challenges the unexamined politics of historical representation embedded in authorized histories, focusing particularly upon the persuasive power of the narrator. We see this especially when Magawisca exploits that power: the tale she tells to Everell serves to defer an explanation of her recent actions, which would confirm Digby's suspicions of imminent danger.[15]

Magawisca prefaces her story with a warning for Everell, which doubles as a metahistorical commentary for the reader: "Then listen to me: and when the hour of vengeance comes, if it should come, remember it was provoked" (47).

Like Fredric Jameson's caveat, "always historicize," Magawisca's words reply to Digby's dehistoricized observations on Indian "nature." The Indians are not by "nature" vengeful, but are so in this situation because of wrongs received at the hands of the Puritans.

Magawisca recounts the burning of Mystic and the ensuing massacre of surviving women and children: "All about sat women and children in family clusters, awaiting unmoved their fate. The English had penetrated . . . Death was dealt freely. None resisted" (53). Everell is so moved by this account that he weeps, highlighting the power the narrator accrues simply by being able to *tell* the story. Magawisca's alternative version of the Pequot war transforms Everell's imagination, which,

> touched by the wand of feeling, presented a very different picture of those defenseless families of savages, pent in the recesses of their native forests, and there exterminated, not by superior natural force, but by the adventitious circumstances of arms, skill and knowledge; from that offered by those who "then living and worthy of credit did affirm, that in the morning entering into the swamp, they saw several heaps of them [the Pequods (Sedgwick)] sitting close together, upon whom they discharged their pieces, laden with ten or twelve pistol bullets at a time, putting the muzzles of their pieces under the boughs, within a few yards of them." (54)

Everell is sympathetic to Magawisca initially through what seems to be an adolescent crush. In this scene, however, we see his sympathy raised to a more intellectual level. While he had earlier accepted that "our people had all the honour of the fight" (48), Everell's historical understanding is complicated by Magawisca's story. This happens precisely through his emotional openness toward Magawisca. Sedgwick's point here is unmistakable, offering as it does both a new historical method and a radical vision of cross-cultural relations.

When Magawisca finishes, the narrator smoothly picks up the threads of the story to fill in the "factual" and most gruesome background from Puritan records, quoting Winthrop and Hubbard. While the narrator has protested before that she merely follows the histories of the Puritan fathers, here she does not hesitate to direct the intentions of those accounts to a different purpose:

> In the relations of their enemies, the courage of the Pequods was distorted into ferocity, and their fortitude, in their last extremity, thus set forth: "many were killed in the swamp, like sullen dogs, that would rather in their self-willed madness, sit still to be shot or cut in pieces than receive their lives for asking, at the hands of those into whose power they had now fallen." (54)

The narrator highlights the unfeelingly prejudiced nature of the histories available, and the apparent contradictions between the Puritan mission and Christian humaneness. Her comments point up that, once one is conscious of the political aspect of historical representation, quite different versions can be constructed—versions more balanced and hence more accurate. And it is precisely the sympathetic frame of reference which can provide this perspective.

The text thereby underscores what Susanne Kappeler has insightfully analysed, the dominative structure of representation.[16] Magawisca's story not only affirms the possibility of sympathetic history, but insists on the inherent necessity of it, as the narrator recounts Everell's thoughts: "Here it was not merely changing sculptors to give the advantage to one or the other of the artist's subjects; but it was putting the chisel into the hands of truth, and giving it to whom it belonged" (53).[17] The Father of Puritan History, who in his story represents his own political ends and thereby dominates the Pequots not once (materially) but triply (materially, textually, historically), is not possessed of the "hands of truth." Rather, the narrator suggests, it is the silenced object of Puritan representation—the Indians, and by inference white women—whose story speaks both emotively and truly.

Having issued a challenge to the authorized white versions of the Pequot war, the narrator combines forces with Magawisca through an acute analysis of the Pequot dilemma. Importantly, the focus is here on the more dangerous and less pitiable Pequot chief, Mononotto. Magawisca's tale, sentimental though its tone may be, has paved the way for the narrator's radical and unsentimentalized commentary on Mononotto's dilemma. The narrator notes that "Magawisca had said truly to Everell, that her father's nature had been changed by the wrongs he had received" (56), hereby historicizing Mononotto's behavior and refuting the received Puritan version of Indians as "naturally" savage. While Sassacus manifested "a jealousy of [the English] encroachments" and "employed all his art and influence and authority, to unite the tribes for the extirpation of the dangerous invaders," Mononotto, "foreseeing no danger from them, was the advocate of a hospitable reception, and pacific conduct" (56). It was ironically Saccacus, as the narrator is at pains to indicate, who was right about the "dangerous invaders" (and "invaders" is doubly emphasized when repeated as the last word of the chapter.

Mononotto is betrayed by his own generous impulses: "He had seen his people slaughtered, or driven from their homes and hunting-grounds, into shameful exile; his wife had died in captivity, and his children lived in servile dependency in the house of his enemies" (51). Only "in this extremity"—and not at all unreasonably, the narrator implies—is Mononotto driven to revenge. Apart from establishing sympathy for Mononotto at a personal level, the narrator also uses his story as a trenchant comment on the broader predicament of the various Indian nations which, divided between those who counseled war and those who advocated hospitality, were finally unable to forestall English treachery. Thus through a sympathetic frame of reference, Sedgwick is able to establish a historical dialogue that had been suppressed from the Puritan accounts.

The Sweet Sacrifice of History

Sedgwick's sympathetic construction of the racial Other has important implications at a semiotic level. In his study of the Spanish conquest of America,

Tzvetan Todorov develops a useful semiotic model of analysis for both "positive" and "negative" colonial depictions of the racial Other. Examining the underlying characteristics of colonial discourse, Todorov differentiates between two "touchstones of alterity," one of which is structured around "a present and immediate second person" (i.e., *me* vs. *you*), and one which revolves on "the absent or distant third person" (i.e., *me* or *us* vs. *them*). He argues that it is at this point (where the Other is designated as either present or absent) "that we can see how the theme of perception of the other and that of symbolic (or semiotic) behavior intersect."[18] Whether one regards the racial Other as a second person and immediate presence, or as a third person, absence can profoundly affect the possible actions conceptually available toward that Other.

This frame is illuminating in a careful analysis of Sedgwick's radically conceived chapter 4, which by enacting dialogue between English and Pequot characters, places the relationship in a *me/you* semiotic frame. Within this second-person symbolic relation, the narrator speaks to the cruelty of Puritan policy toward the Pequots, acted out in the semiotic perspective of a third-person frame. From the *us/them* vantage, the Puritans can act viciously and record with no sense of irony the very passage the narrator quotes from Bradford: "It was a fearful sight to see them thus frying in the fire, and the streams of blood quenching the same, and the horrible scent thereof; but the victory seemed a sweet sacrifice, and they gave the praise thereof to God" (54). Such a perspective is impossible when one recognizes the Other as an immediate presence, indeed, talks and listens to the Other as Everell does.

Todorov's frame is also helpful to explain a curious passage that follows only two chapters later. The passage is a patriotic paean to "the noble pilgrims" which also serves to counter the powerfully dialogic version of history constructed earlier. After the scene in which the Fletcher family is ruthlessly slaughtered by Mononotto and his accomplices, the narrator pauses to address the reader directly. "We hope our readers will not think we have wantonly sported with their feelings." The narrator continues to explain that such events, "feebly related," were common in early Puritan life: "Not only families, but villages, were cut off by the most dreaded of all foes—the ruthless, vengeful savage" (72). The semiotic structure here—the "touchstone of alterity"—is suddenly not second but third person. In the passage that ensues, we witness the representational implications of this switch, the violence now permitted, easily effaced, and rationalized.

"In the quiet possession of blessings transmitted," the narrator elaborates, "we are, perhaps, in danger of forgetting, or undervaluing the sufferings by which they were obtained. We forget that the noble pilgrims lived and endured for us" (72). Chronicling the sacrifices made, the narrator then outlines their mission: "to open the forests to the sun-beam, and to the light of the Sun of Righteousness." In reward, the Puritans "saw, with sublime joy, a multitude of people where the solitary savage roamed the forest—the forest vanished, and the pleasant villages and busy cities appeared—the tangled footpath expanded to the thronged high-way—the consecrated church planted on the rock of heathen sacrifice" (73). The implications of this passage's semiotic structure are a stunning contrast to those of chapter 4. Here the women, children, families of Indians are transmuted (via the third-person frame of reference) into a "single, solitary savage." The historical context of the colonial conquest is effaced—the Puritans are "rewarded" for sacrificing "the land of their birth . . . their homes . . . all delights of the sense" (72). And the historical struggle, textually elided, is sanctioned by the merit of the Puritans' religion, their metaphorically and literally "enlightening" influence on the land itself. The narrator continues to make an oblique reference to the colonists' actions against America's original population:

> And that we might realize this vision—enter into this promised land of faith—they endured hardship, and braved death—deeming, as said one of their company, that "he is not worthy to live at all, who, for fear or danger of death, shunneth his country's service, or his own honour—since death is inevitable and the fame of virtue is immortal."
> If these were the fervors of enthusiasm, it was an enthusiasm kindled and fed by the holy flame that glows on the altar of God. (73)

Here we have a holy mission, not colonial treachery. We see the traces of deleted historical content when we begin to ask questions about this passage. What magnitude of service could "the country" require against that "single, solitary savage"? How much work can it be to build a church on a rock—unless the expression is a metaphor that represses a less pleasant meaning? Rather this passage, in sharp contrast to chapter 4, uncritically highlights how the representatives of that "consecrated church," built on the "rock of sacrifice," can also choose the terms by which their history will be written. Todorov's ironic observation on Spanish narratives of conquest is equally appropriate here: societies that employ writing may be considered more advanced than oral cultures, "but we may hesitate to choose between sacrifice societies and massacre societies."[19]

It is, perhaps, impossible to explain the juxtaposition of these two exceedingly divergent passages. Which one did Sedgwick intend? Maybe both. Cultural hegemony is pervasive, and enlightenment not always foolproof. Albert Memmi emphasizes the imaginative difficulties of "the colonizer who refuses": "It is not easy to escape mentally from a concrete situation, to refuse its ideology while continuing to live with its actual relationships."[20] Certainly Sedgwick does not abandon her attempt to deal fairly with her Indian characters at this point. As will be discussed, Sedgwick establishes a modicum of cross-racial understanding, indicating that the most serious racial difficulties arose at the hands of the whites. Further, she offers an alternative behavior model to the received frontier wisdom of her day. But finally, she does not see clearly to a resolution of racial misunderstanding, and instead establishes a metaphor which allows the Indians to peacefully fade from the vision of her text.

Rent by a Divided Duty

Tension and ambivalence mark the remainder of *Hope Leslie*. Sedgwick is at
many points more successful than other frontier novelists in establishing cultural relativity between whites and Indians. That is, Sedgwick allows her
Indians dignity in their difference; while she highlights similarities between
the two groups, she does not try to make Indians human by showing them to
be identical to Anglo-Americans. She reveals the Indians to be governed by
cultural and moral principles different from those of the Puritans. Magawisca
is the most frequent spokesperson here. For instance, in defending her
brother against one of Hope's few racist outbursts, Magawisca affirms the
moral integrity of her culture: "Yes, an Indian, in whose veins runs the blood
of the strongest . . . who never turned their backs on friends or enemies, and
whose souls have returned to the Great Spirit, stainless as they came from
him" (188). Magawisca also defends the legitimacy of the Indian life-style.
When Hope pleads with her to stay in Boston, insisting that her "noble mind
must not be wasted in those hideous solitudes," Magawisca makes it completely clear that such a life—though different from Hope's—is equally valuable to her. Notably, Hope accepts Magawisca's answer.

As Mary Kelley discusses in her valuable introduction to the Rutgers edition of *Hope Leslie,* Sedgwick goes a long way toward suggesting cross-racial
equality through her "parallel" portrayals of Hope and Magawisca. Magawisca is, Kelley notes, "the only Indian woman in early American fiction
invested with substance and strength" (xxvi). Her character in many ways
corresponds to Hope's, and in some ways exceeds it. The respect her character accrues during the narrative is not merely token. As Kelley observes,
both Hope and Magawisca challenge their culture's patriarchal order. It is
Magawisca who commits the "ultimate act of resistance" when she prevents
Everell's execution, sacrificing her arm: "hers is the most heroic act in the
entire novel" (xxvii).[21]

Sedgwick also demonstrates an awareness that, as Todorov puts it, "each of
us is the other's barbarian."[22] When Magawisca informs Hope of Faith's
marriage to Oneco, Hope shudders, exclaiming, "God forbid! . . . My sister
married to an Indian!" (188). The narrator then relates how Magawisca recoiled "with a look of proud contempt, that showed she reciprocated in full
measure, the scorn expressed for her race" (188). Significantly, Magawisca's
reciprocal scorn is fully authorized by her version of the massacre at Mystic.
Such a reciprocal awareness serves Sedgwick's enterprise here by complicating received history, suggesting an alternative story that is ever present in the
authorized text.

Finally, Sedgwick uses Magawisca to comment on the historical construction of racial difference. At her trial, affirming her enmity toward white
colonists, Magawisca asks, "[C]an we grasp in friendship the hand raised to
strike us?" In this argument the colonists' relations with the Native Americans
are again contextualized. Although Magawisca holds Anglo and Indian differences presently to be ineradicable, those differences arose historically because

of colonial hostility and double-dealing. And through this narrative tack, which serves always to contextualize Indian violence, Sedgwick suggests an alternative to "Indian-hating." In their later summaries of this cultural phenomenon, Robert Montgomery Bird and James Hall would insist that white "Indian-haters" responded "naturally" to the treachery and violence of the Indian foes. Everell in particular, and also his father, are witness to the violent murder of the rest of their family. Yet unlike Nathan Slaughter in Robert Montgomery Bird's novel *Nick of the Woods,* the two men in *Hope Leslie* do *not* swear "eternal vengeance."[23] Instead, by relying on their religious faith, their sensibility, and their recognition of the humanity of their enemies, the two men continue in life without becoming embittered toward the Indian race. Everell applauds Hope's rescue of Nelema, and himself engineers Magawisca's escape from Puritan punishment.

Flowers Wild and Cultivated

In the end, however, while Sedgwick goes far toward suggesting a relative cultural standard and an alternative model for cross-racial relations, she is not able to fully resolve the implications of her critique for her contemporay audience. Instead, she adopts a Manichean allegory aesthetized by a garden metaphor to dispense with the Indians at the end of her narrative. Having earlier associated the Puritans with enlightenment (they "open the forests to the sun-beam, and to the light of the Sun of Righteousness,") Sedgwick has Magawisca herself adopt those abstract and naturalized terms in her own defense: "Take my own word, I am your enemy; the sun-beam and the shadow cannot mingle" (292). Magawisca, however, more frequently emphasizes the incompatibility of the two peoples with a flower metaphor. On two occasions she elaborates in relation to Mary's embrace of Indian life-ways. Through Mary, Magawisca is able to emphasize that the differences are not inherent or racial, but cultural. This qualification, though revolutionary in its own right and starkly opposed to Cooper's formulation of white and red "gifts," ultimately finds no constructive resolution. "The lily of Maqua's valley, will never again make the English garden sweet," Magawisca says, preparing Hope for their meeting (188). Pleasant though this figure may be, Magawisca later reveals its full implications, this time as she warns Hope of Mary's inevitable return to Oneco: "When she flies from you, as she will, mourn not over her, Hope Leslie—the wild flower would perish in your gardens—the forest is like a native home to her—and she will sing as gaily again as the bird that hath found its mate" (331–32).

The Indian's destiny in *Hope Leslie* is here made clear, for the Puritan's mission, as the narrator has indicated, is to *cultivate* the forest. Sedgwick's reference to the principle of *vacuum domicilium* (126) is neither gratuitous nor obsequious.[24] Rather it is the unspoken ideological principle which structures Sedgwick's own vision—a fiction which ignores the evidence of agricultural technology among the Indians and predicates its proprietary right both upon an imagined lack in the Indians, and an imagined superiority in the

Europeans. The guilt latent in this formulation creeps into the narrator's passing reference to the Native American inhabitants of the Housatonick valley. These people were an "agricultural tribe," the narrator admits, pointedly elaborating "as far as that epithet could ever be applied to our savages" (85). We must note the stance of authority over the Indians which the narrator assumes at this point, a proprietary authority which underscores Indian Otherness: "our savages." The text elsewhere declines to speak to Indian husbandry in any significant detail, and, like Winthrop's arguments about *vacuum domicilium* in "Reasons to be Considered . . . ," focuses only on the domestication of the wilderness performed by the Europeans, metaphorically contrasting domestic flowers (hardy, enduring) to the wild lily (fading toward extinction).[25] The "garden" in *Hope Leslie* is not simply a domestic space, but a political and moral space which provides proof of the superiority of, and justification for, the dominance of the Anglo-Americans. Thus we see how women's visions of gardens in the wilderness may yet have oppressive political implications, tacitly depending as they do upon space cleared in violent conquest by their husbands and sons.[26]

Indian destiny will, according to the text, be "lost in the deep, voiceless obscurity of those unknown regions" (339). The narrator here refers by "regions" to "far western forests," but in Sedgwick's own lifetime, even those forests were being cultivated. Thus *Hope Leslie* never successfully challenges the euphemistic Anglo construction of the ultimate "fate" of the Indians. Rather, the text succumbs to the same processes of historical representation that it condemns in the Puritan accounts of the Pequot massacre, in which Indian genocide is something that happens outside the agency of whites and is left to the "deep, voiceless obscurity" of Anglo-American history.

Hope Leslie is finally equivocal. While Sedgwick clearly sees the necessity of reenvisioning racial constructs, she is so clearly invested in Anglo-America's historical inheritance that she cannot resolve the "Indian problem" in any meaningful way for her contemporay readers. Her "sentimental" metaphor of wild and domestic flowers allows her to gloss over the horrible results of Anglo policy toward Native Americans which she had earlier confronted. Yet we must not overlook how *Hope Leslie* provides a powerful reading that challenged and revised contemporary historical, racial, and gender formulations precisely through its "sentimental" dimensions. *Hope Leslie* confronts directly the brutal effects of Anglo-American policy toward the Native Americans by sympathetically deploying Magawisca's alternative history. This "very different picture" provides a model for a dialogic history which realizes practical implications (through the recognition and subsequent actions of Everell) as well as theoretical ones (metahistorical and textual). The novel thus establishes a space of authority for Sedgwick as woman author, through its challenges to male cultural authority emblematized in the title character of the story and through her own revisioning of Puritan history. The legacy of sentiment in *Hope Leslie* is mixed, and is important precisely because it allows us to analyze the powerful hegemony of racism, as well as the redoubled vision of resistance to it by a woman writer in nineteenth-century America.

12

Relic, Fetish, Femmage: The Aesthetics of Sentiment in the Work of Stowe

Lynn Wardley

I

When, in the middle of *Uncle Tom's Cabin,* Ophelia steps into Dinah's kitchen, she enters the "Chaos and Old Night" of the plantation household, evidenced in the famous catalogue of Dinah's accumulations.[1] "The more drawers and closets there were" in the St. Clare pantry, "the more hiding-holes Dinah could make for the accommodation of old rags, hair combs, ribbons, cast-off artificial flowers, and other articles of *vertu* wherein her soul delighted" (I. 298–299). The revelation of the cook's pomade stored in a gilded china dish further alarms the guest from Vermont, for whom such an unpalatable mix as Dinah's "har *grease*" in her "mistress's best saucers" be-speaks only the jumble of the savage mind (I. 300). Ophelia determines that Old Dinah is hopelessly "shif'less" and that Dinah's mistress, the indolent aristocrat Marie St. Clare, is criminally helpless, and here the New England spinster's "reformatory tour" begins in earnest (I. 298).

Critics of *Uncle Tom's Cabin* have aligned the novel's depiction of disorderly domesticity with its anti-slavery appeal. Seen this way, Dinah's drawers are one symptom of slavery's violation of the "systematic order" Catharine Beecher, in her popular *Treatise on Domestic Economy* (1843), judged essential to the harmonious operation of the home. Slavery's abuse of the family wrecks domesticity's soteriological mission to "renovate degraded man" and to serve as the base of the "glorious temple" of a Christian polity.[2] But Dinah's system lacks "logic and reason" and her collection coherence only to the uninitiated: the "fine damask tablecloth" in which "some raw meat" is wrapped graphically expresses the brutality enveloped by an only superficially civilized domesticity (I. 298, 299). Dinah's arrangements threaten to move beyond a symbolics of critique and into the realm of intervention, as Ophelia's discovery of Methodist hymn-book, bloody cloth, and "sundry sweet herbs" in another cupboard, implicitly raises the suspicion of occult practices in the slave's domain (I. 209). To treat Dinah's kitchen as a symptom risks overlooking another cultural order in the Louisiana interior, represented by what are arguably fetishes concealed in Dinah's drawers, and by Dinah's phenomenal success in "ignoring or opposing" unwelcome interference "without any actual or observable contest" (I. 298). What happens to Dinah in *Uncle Tom's Cabin*? The cook is conspicuously absent when "Tom, Adolph, and about half a dozen others of the St. Clare estate" are sold at auction (II. 154).

This essay returns to the scene of Dinah's labors in order to argue that critics of Stowe's sentimental bestseller have too quickly dismissed the fact of its curious success in "ignoring or opposing" business as usual, "without any actual or observable contest." In what follows, I suggest that Stowe's sentimental practice is linked to Dinah's rituals and articles of dissent, that is, to the fetishism intimated in Dinah's unseen opposition and in her hidden accumulation of hymnal, bloody cloth and sundry herbs. To us, Stowe's is a portrait of an orientalized Dinah, described "seated on the kitchen floor, smoking a short, stumpy pipe, to which she was much addicted, and which she always kindled up, as a sort of censer, whenever she felt the need of inspiration in her arrangements" (I. 297). But although this description can be read within Stowe's colonizing frame of primitivism and progress, it does not mean that Dinah's gifts can be disregarded. As John Blassingame points out, witches, sorcerers, and conjurers of African extraction practiced among the slave populations, where they were, according to W. E. B. Du Bois, the "chief remaining institution" of "former group life."[3] Ongoing historical debate regarding the retention of African cultural practices among the African Americans of the antebellum South has prepared the ground for speculation that the sentimentalist's representation of the canny woman in her "high, brilliant, Madras turban" was informed by the active presence of African survivals (I. 302). Such survivals may have left more traces on the aesthetics of sentiment in the United States than we have yet imagined.

For example, Mechal Sobel's examination of black and white values in eighteenth-century Virginia demonstrates that it is a surviving West African perception of death as a homecoming and heaven as a home, that by the end of the century becomes "an American expectation." Students of American sentimental culture, accustomed to associating its domestication of death with the declining faith in Calvinist doctrine, the mysticism of Swedenborg, and the rise of American Spiritualism from within the Protestant middle classes, should also take into consideration both Sobel's thesis and Ann Braude's recent account of the strong affiliation between the belief in mediumship and spirit possession among white American spiritualists in the nineteenth century, and similar beliefs introduced by the cultures of the West African populations predating modern Spiritualism's ascent.[4]

Seen with this cross-cultural influence in mind, the "anthropomorphising instinct" Ann Douglas identifies in the sentimental writer and disparagingly links to the sentimentalists' interest in a nascent consumer society might also (or might instead) be read in connection to the West African understanding of the afterlife and to the practice of fetishism. "The primitive religion of Africa," writes Du Bois, "as developed by the African village underlies the religions of the world." "Fetish" is a "spiritual explanation of physical evil and it explains by making all things spirit, both the good and the bad, and by seeking a spiritual cure for physical ill."[5] Harriet Beecher Stowe's recurrent representation of the uncanny power of Victorian material culture to elicit emotion, provoke somatic response, bewitch, heal, or avenge wrong, resonates not only with the Catholic faith in the power of relics, but also with the Pan-African religions of the antebellum South. Bourgeois sentimentalism empowers such ordinary possessions as old shoes, worn clothing, portraits, and cut hair; but these are objects whose "close contact with the body" also made them "dangerous instruments for conjure."[6]

Stowe reveals a brief awareness of "fetish and obi" in *The Key to Uncle Tom's Cabin* (1853).[7] The word fetish is notoriously imprecise, and many scholars dismiss it as the product of a colonial or an ethnographic mentality, preferring to translate the term fetish back into the native terminology of the religion or society being described. In tracing the idea of the fetish to the cross-cultural spaces of the coast of West Africa during the sixteenth century, anthropologist William Pietz notes that the origin of the word derives from the Latin for "manufacture" and the Portuguese for "witchcraft" or "magical practice." While the fetish is familiar to us from a variety of popular and social scientific discourses of the nineteenth century (Comte, Marx, and Freud), Pietz argues that a study of its conceptual genealogy must include William Bosman's eighteenth-century text *Accurate Description of the Coast of Guinea,* which provided the "image and conception on which Enlightenment intellectuals based their elaboration of the notion [of fetishism] into a general theory of primitive religion."[8] It is probably through such a lens that fetishism came down to Harriet Stowe; the Vermont Sinclairs betray, even as their suspicions exaggerate, the Northerner's impression of the Southerner's primitive folkways when Ophelia plans her trip to Louisiana. Ophelia's "old gray-headed father" dips into his "Morse's Atlas . . . and looked out the exact latitude and longitude" of "Orleans," and reads "Flint's Travels in the South and West" in order to prepare his eldest daughter for her adventure. Ophelia's good mother wonders if " 'Orleans wasn't an awful wicked place, 'most equal to going to the Sandwich Islands' " (I. 227). One glance at the "mystic old aloe," poised "like some hoary old enchanter" on the lawn of her cousin's Moorish mansion, leads Ophelia to judge the admittedly " 'pretty place' " " 'rather old and heathenish' " (I. 235).

But Stowe's belief that some spirit inhabits all things is not only an exoticized import from the Roman Catholic and African American religions of New Orleans and beyond. It is by 1852 one familiar element of the nineteenth-century domestic ideology the tenets of which Stowe's writing reflected and helped to shape. Emphasizing the formative nature of both the mother and the interior, theologians (like Horace Bushnell) and domesticians (like Catharine Beecher) described the "spirit of the house" that passes "by transmission" into the "little plastic nature of the child." Historian David Handlin explains that when the popular evangelical minister Bushnell refers to the "spirit of the house," he means not only the influence of the "parents but also the impact of inanimate objects on the developing child."[9] The irresistible, even supernatural, transmission associated with maternal nurture and with the impressions left by the immediate environment is also ascribed to the sentimental novel, for the novel, as Richard Brodhead argues, shares some of the domestician's labor of "invisible persuasion" in the nineteenth century in the United States. Like Eva's lock of hair, Rachel Halliday's rocking chair, or Dinah's accumulations, the sentimental novel itself goes to work "without any actual or observable contest." In the case of *Uncle Tom's Cabin,* the text's production, as well as its reception, betrays its close contact with the body. "The book insisted on getting itself into being," Stowe explains, "and would take no denial."[10]

Stowe's account of the "birth" of her bestseller anticipates critical evaluations of the bodily nature of the sentimental genre and the genre's connection to women. Associated with the physical labor of reproduction, sickness, and death, a feminized sentimentalism is also linked to the "sivilizing" work of socialization from which men and boys "light out." But it might prove more accurate to remark that the anti-sentimentalist rebels less against the dominion of white women's civilizing influence than he recoils from the fantasy of femininity, or, more precisely, of maternity, decivilized. To chronicle the reception of the aesthetics of sentiment is to record its transformation from a medium of sympathy to one of vicariousness; from health to morbidity; and from transparency to duplicity.[11] "The wet eye of the sentimentalist," writes James Baldwin in his seminal essay on Stowe, "betrays his . . . arid heart; and . . . secret and violent inhumanity." Baldwin's indictment of "everybody's protest novel" uncloaks the racist assumptions within the abolitionist *Uncle Tom's Cabin.* Yet Baldwin's charges of shape-shifting and of violent effects are also leveled by others to implicate, not a bourgeois-identified Harriet Stowe, but the female reformer affiliated with the unorthodox or subaltern. Thus critic Helen Waite Papashvily calls sentimental fiction "witches' broth," adding that V. L. Parrington was mistaken to find it " 'weak as cambric tea.' Like the rest of his sex, he did not detect the faint bitter taste of poison in the cup."[12]

Recent readings of *Uncle Tom's Cabin* rehearse this apparent fascination for the author's hidden hand. Judgments of the sentimental novel's potential to subvert dominant patriarchal operations—a potential remarked by Papashvily, but celebrated since by others—have given ground to speculation about the conservative and hegemonic character of the genre. Despite its phenomenal success in the arsenal of abolitionist rhetoric, *Uncle Tom's Cabin* has also been assessed as a document in the service of bourgeois imperialist and racist ends. Unable to settle the question of the bestseller's political effects, I mean instead to insist that the scope of sentimental writing cannot fully be realized without reconsidering its multiple roots in what historian Jon Butler vividly describes as the "antebellum spiritual hothouse."[13] Stowe's belief in the force of inspired possessions cannot be read simply as an interested embrace of the mystical nature of commodities, as a medium for the cathartic expression of an oppressed female population, or as the bourgeois' gesture to primitive culture. It must also be reassessed within the context of the numerous sub-cultural practices in the ninteenth-century United States, such as the ongoing art of conjure. In the following two sections, I examine the depiction of domestic animism first in *Uncle Tom's Cabin,* and then in Stowe's non-fictional *Household Papers and Stories,* sketching its connection to contemporary evangelical, ethnographic, commercial, and evolutionary accounts of maternal, spiritual, and cultural transmission. A final section turns to Charlotte Perkins Gilman's reformation of her great-aunt's model domesticity, a re-modelling motivated by Gilman's uneasy recognition of the simultaneously somatic and necromatic nature of the "spirit of the house."

II

[T]o be really great in little things . . . noble and heroic in the insipid details of everyday life.

Stowe, "The Cathedral"

What's near is dear.

African American saying

Displaying what cultural historian Dolf Sternberger describes as the "precious mementos" of the nineteenth century, mementos which play "such a crucial part not only in novels, but also in daily circumstances of the period," a midcentury American novel announces itself as sentimental. Sternberger's catalogue of all the "curls, yellowed letters, preserved childhood garments, dried clovers, withered roses that formed an ever-accumulating, nostalgically redolent mass of memory stimuli" recalls the cults and the cultural debris of motherhood, of childhood, and of mourning we associate with sentimental fiction in general and *Uncle Tom's Cabin* (1852) in particular. Staging Little Eva's death, Stowe makes Eva's "doling out of mementos to the spectators the substance of the scene." Detailing the "little coats of many a form and pattern, piles of aprons and rows of small stockings"—"even a pair of little shoes, worn and rubbed at the toes," once the property of Mrs. Bird's late son Henry—Stowe is said to have drawn on her personal collection of preserved childhood garments once belonging to her dead baby Charley (I. 132).[14]

Linked to the mortal bodies of their original owners, Stowe's sentimental things display the properties of sacred relics, here justified as the Protestant mother's spiritual props. But although the collection performs the conservative work of consolation, it can also serve more subversive ends. As Gillian Brown points out, the garments of the dead child Henry help Eliza's small son Harry in his escape[15]; this links the cherished baby clothes to Dinah's potent objects. Augustine St. Clare has always appreciated the volatile power of Dinah's things, and when he cautions that to pry into the details of slavery is like looking "too close into the details of Dinah's kitchen" (II. 8), we might assume he means that the devil is in the details of each. The devil, as his cousin Ophelia insists, inhabits the slave economy. But other spirits are apparently conjured not only when the cook needs culinary inspiration, but also when she plots to resist Miss Ophelia's instructions as wordlessly as she has circumvented the interference of the St. Clares.

Whether Miss Ophelia mistakes them (for the detritus of the shiftless) or St. Clare shuns them (as dangerous to know), Dinah's fetishes are categorized and contained as the effects of an orientalized African difference. Stowe reinforces this impression when, with what Hortense Spillers calls a "fatal binarity," Stowe constructs in *The Key to Uncle Tom's Cabin* (1853) a key to the African's psychology. In the African, "sensations and impressions are very vivid and their fancy and imagination lively," while the Anglo-Saxon race is "cool, logical, practical." Like the "Hebrews of old and the Orientals of the present," Africans are endowed with "supposing peculiarities of nervous construction quite different from those of the whites," and this contributes to the fact that in "their own climate" they are "believers in spells, in 'fetish and obi,' in the 'evil eye,' and other singular influences."[16]

But whites and blacks are not as morphologically distinct as the *Key* would have readers believe, either in Stowe's personal experience or in her fiction. "Some peculiarity in the nervous system, in the connecting link between soul and body," notes Calvin Stowe, speaking of himself, "may bring some, more than others, into an almost abnormal contact with the spirit world." If Calvin Stowe was rather regularly visited by ghosts, his wife Harriet joined the ranks of amateur American spiritualists when she called on mediums, participated in seances, and experimented with planchette, a ouija-board-like instrument designed for extraworldy communication. Pursuing contact with her late son Henry in what biographers interpret as an attempt to challenge the Calvinist's account of the fate of the unconverted, Stowe also communicated with the spirit of Charlotte Brontë, who reassured her that the living are always surrounded by spirits, some of whom serve as sympathetic guides.[17]

The mesmerism and spiritualism practiced by Stowe and others in her middle-class milieu resonated with West African religious beliefs introduced in the slave populations. In her *Key to Uncle Tom's Cabin,* Stowe identifies the epitome of otherworldy contact in the slaves' accounts "of visions, of heavenly voices, of mysterious transmissions of knowledge from heart to heart without the intervention of the senses, or what the Quakers call being 'baptized into the spirit' of those who are distant."[18] Specific possessions facilitate such extrasensory transmissions, and in *Uncle Tom's Cabin* blacks and whites are bound equally by the spell of stories or charms that conjure a spectral presence or compel an involuntary response. This is so much the case that precious memento, sacred relic, and African fetish may be indistinguishable, as in the example of Little Eva's lock of hair, given to Uncle Tom on her deathbed to be worn close to his heart. Simon Legree, who eventually recognizes in this token the memento sent him by his own Christian mother, also understands it to be the protective *mojo* or *gris gris* of African custom, the "devilish" "witch thing" that Sambo now folds into a paper and that threatens to work a fix on Legree. " 'What's that, you dog?' said

Legree." Sambo answers that it is " 'something that niggers get from witches. Keeps 'em from feeling when they's flogged. [Tom] had it tied around his neck with a black string' " (II. 216).[19] While the reader might have anticipated some occult action on the "superstitious" Legree's gothic plantation, Stowe demonstrates that even within the most orderly of domestic environments—the Indiana Quaker settlement—things are not what they seem. While there is "certainly nothing very startling about such everyday animism" as that exhibited in Quaker Rachel Halliday's "creechy-crawchy" and "persuasive old chair" (II. 196), the comfortable rocker's very appeal to familiar associations deflects the fact of the Quakers' historical persecution as witches, and the fact that a rocker's rocking, like a Quaker's quaking, might denote possession.[20]

Witness the transformation of Tom Loker in Quaker hands. If the slave catcher boasts that after three weeks among the Quakers he has not been converted, he cannot deny that he has been cured, literally and figuratively, of a bad heart: although he has come to Indiana to catch the enslaved Eliza, he helps her plot an escape while he recovers from rheumatic fever and mends his broken leg. A regenerated man, Loker "arose from his bed" to develop his talents "more happily" by "trapping bears, wolves, and other inhabitants of the forest" (II. 233). What determines his metamorphosis seems not to be Quaker prayer or discipline but a more insidious maternal force: the Quaker healer Aunt Dorcas swaddles the immobilized slave catcher in a "chrysalis" of white sheets (" 'The devil!' says Tom Loker, giving a great throw to the bedclothes") and feeds him vaguely mysterious nostrums (II. 232). The Quakers "do fix up a sick fellow first rate," Tom must confess. "[N]o mistake. Make jist the tallest kind o' broth and knickknacks" (II. 233).

The image of a maternal influence at once homely and arcane, far from being unorthodox, constituted one of the strongest messages of antebellum domestic ideology. This image assumed a special force in redressing the Calvinist's circumscription of feminine agency and in countering the Protestant suspicion of image, art, and sacred maternity, associated with Catholic idolatry. While critics argue that in the nineteenth century a vigorous masculine Calvinism informing elite New England culture succumbed to an enfeebling feminization, in fact it was in Calvinism that liberal Protestants like Stowe discerned an enervating and "slow poison, producing life-thoughts of morbid action."[21] To associate sin and vice with corrigible habits, and not with innate depravity, emphasized the importance of nurture and education in the deliberate development of human character, a development overseen by middle-class women in the context of what Ruth H. Bloch and Kathryn Kish Sklar call the ideology of the "moral mother" and of "qualitative motherhood" respectively. Crucial to the spread of this new historical formation was the work of domestic reformer Catharine Beecher. Believing that the growth and equilibrium of the social organism at large required the self-regulation of its individual members, Beecher saw it as the mother's responsibility to train children "whose plastic nature will receive and retain every impression you make; who will transmit what they receive from you to their children, to pass again to the next generation, and then the next, until a *whole nation* may possibly receive its character and destiny from your hands!"[22]

Here in *Miss Beecher's Housekeeper and Healthkeeper* (1876), cultural and biological transmission are crucially, if also rather casually, equated. In this, Catharine Beecher's account of maternal influence resembles that of her sister Harriet, whose Quakers rehabilitate the infantilized Tom Loker body and soul, and also that of the Beechers' influential contemporary, the minister Horace Bushnell. In Bushnell's popular *Christian Nurture* (1847, 1861) the apparent biologization of cultural traits found an ardent spokesperson. Although historians date the vogue for neo-Lamarckian thought in the United States sometime near the end of the nineteenth century, Bushnell's agenda for a meliorating and naturalized Christian training relied on the Lamarckian belief in the heritability of acquired traits. "Good principles and habits, intellectual culture, domestic virtue, industry, order, faith, law," pass bodily into the next generation.[23]

> Consider a very important fact in human physiology, which goes far to explain, or take away the seeming extravagance of the truth I am endeavoring to establish, viz., that qualities of education, habit, feeling and character, have a tendency to always grow in, by long continuance, and become thoroughly inbred in the stock. (*CN*, 171)

Identifying the progress of Western civilization with the Christian mission, Bushnell explains the mechanism by which Christianity itself, "by a habit or fixed process of culture, tends by a fixed law of nature to become a propagated quality" functional in the "stock" (*CN*, 172). Bushnell's account of a Christian stock in *Christian Nurture,* introduces the topic of race into the discussion of the transmission, across generations, of "civilization." More explicit is his text of 1860, *The Census and Slavery,* in which Bushnell describes the situation of the African American, a stock now "thousands of years behind, in the scale of culture."[24] The minister here raises the familiar specter of amalgamation, only to dismiss the threat it poses to the hegemony of the "civilized type," by which he means the Anglo-Saxon. Even should the "inferior and far less cultivated stock" "intermix with the superior, it will always be seen that the superior lives the other down, and finally quite lives it away" (*Census,* 12).

Uncle Tom's Cabin also addresses American race relations as a problem of transmission, turning the scandal of slavery into the scandal of bad mothering. For instance, the abolitionist sentiments of Augustine St. Clare seem motivated not by a desire to manumit blacks for their own sake, but by an apprehension that a brutalized slave population will pass its characteristics on to white children like his own Eva: "They are in our houses; they are the associates of our children, and they form their minds faster than we can; for they are a race that children always will cling to and assimilate with" (II. 24). St. Clare expresses what John Blassingame records as the antebellum Southerner's frequent observation of the Africanization of his offspring. "[Blacks] are of necessity the constant attendants upon [white] children in their early years," one southerner writes in 1820.

> From them they learn mostly to talk; from them their minds receive their first impressions; and from them a taint is often acquired which remains through the whole of their succeeding lives. Superstition takes complete possession of a benighted mind, and hence the ready credit which is given to tales of witchcraft, of departed spirits and of supernatural appearances, with which servants terrify the young committed to their care, and impressions are made, which no after efforts of the understanding are able entirely to eradicate.[25]

St. Clare is unconcerned over the acquisition of benighted superstitions; on his deathbed he will know the supernatural presence of his dead mother, and his Catholicism will prove syncretic with some African religions in this regard. This master concentrates instead on the perverse "education in barbarism and brutality" of the black under slavery, and hence on the effects of New World slavery on children like his own unruly nephew Henrique (II. 74). "We might as well allow the small-pox to run among [the slaves], and think our children will not take it, as to let them be uninstructed and vicious, and think that our children will not be affected by that" (II. 25). St. Clare maintains that only because Eva is "more angel than ordinary" (II. 24) can she move untainted through the slaves' quarters. But Eva proves to be touched by the slave environment in the form of the horror story of Prue's brutalization. The sad and sensational histories of Prue "sink into [Eva's] heart" (II. 5), while the final drama of Prue's fatal beating drives "every drop of blood" from Eva's cheeks and lips (II. 6).[26] Significantly, Prue's story begins with the death of her infant daughter, deprived of her mother's milk, while Eva's life apparently ends as a consequence of a lethal transmission from poor Prue.

Slavery engenders noxious mothering, and in so suggesting, Stowe implicates her abolitionist novel in the childrearing discourse of midcentury, as exemplified by Bushnell. Contrasting a wholesome Christian nurture to "vicious feeding," Bushnell resurrects the Puritan trope of the minister-patriarch, or of the Word, as God's maternal breast. But he also alludes to the more recent assertion of the influential Jean-Jacques Rousseau that mother's milk is the "first education"; maternal neglect is the first depravity, from which "all degeneracy" follows. In his discussion of maternity in *Emile, or, On Education,* Rousseau focuses on the midwife or wet nurse alien to the family she enters, as Stowe will focus on Prue, whose instincts are thwarted under slavery, but whose influences are absorbed by all the members of a house. But if slavery makes mothers like Cassy, who nurses her daughter to death with laudanum in order to save her from a life enslaved, it also produces women like Marie St. Clare. Little Eva perishes not only after having assimilated Prue's brutalization, but also after having imbibed the negligent maternal practices of the ever suffering Marie, too depraved to have properly nursed, nurtured, and fortified her own daughter. Like Rousseau, who shifts in *Emile* from the condemnation of nurses to the suspicion of a mother so unnatural that she will put out her child to nurse (eventually, warns Rousseau, she will cease wanting to bear children altogether), Stowe shifts from showing the danger posed by the slave culture that white children cling to and assimilate with, to representing the scandalous white mother produced in the patriarchal South. Marie is reminiscent of Rousseau's unfeeling and fashionable French aristocrat, who disdains maternity in order to preserve her beauty.[27]

Stowe's investment, then, in the overtly biological, but potentially super-natural, power of maternal transmissions combines the vocabulary of the nineteenth-century domestic science of child rearing, a romanticized account of maternity, and the appropriation of occult survivals to define the coercive, and possibly radical, powers of women. Yet even as she invests in African survivals, Stowe posits Africanization itself as a problem to be solved by repatriation. Nowhere is her ambivalence stronger than in her ambiguously accented description of the antebellum South. Portraying the slave belt as "another Orient," Stowe paints it as a foreign, decadent, and dangerous place. As shocking to Miss Ophelia's sensibility as initially it is delightful to Uncle Tom's, even the flora in St. Clare's garden is suspect: the grass seems artificial, cultivated into "green velvet" lawns (I. 235). And if the temperate South seems at first blush a viable environment for sustaining the "exotic race, born under the tropical sun" (I. 1), Stowe suggests that the very introduction of the African "exotic" (I. 235) into an insupportable North American climate produces an aberrant African American, and conse-quently, pace Bushnell, an aberrant white population. Signs of the South's pathogenic effects are in evidence in the nineteenth-century New Orleans aptly selected as a site of apparently untenable combinations and infusions. Stowe figures slavery itself as an Eastern import into Louisiana; her depic-tion of Southern folkways parallels the crude ethnological accounts of the Ophelia-like Protestant missionaries on foreign tours, who supplied their supporters back home with the descriptions of such social phenomena as the polygamy of the Indian rajah, child marriage, female infanticide, concubi-nage, eunuchs, bride sale, the bagnio and harem, opium dens, and slave markets. Dinah with her addiction to the pipe, the drunken Prue, the dandi-fied house slave Adolph, the precious Little Eva, Legree and his mistresses, the murderous Cassy, and the odalisque-like Marie, "undulating in all her motions" (I. 260)—all are among the South's orientalized and symptomatic victims.[28]

What emerges in Stowe's Southern environment with its unwholesome in-habitants is a sketch of the "heathenish" Far East; yet the picture also strategi-cally functions as a displaced image of conditions in the urban North. Re-flected in her description of Southern pathology is an allusion to the miasmic theories of earlier cholera epidemics in Northern cities and towns; a popular interest in mesmeric influence; and a perception of the "unnatural" habits formed and exacerbated in "artificial" urban environments.[29] In the figure of the African, "sympathetic and assimilative," who acquires in a "refined fam-ily" the "tastes and feelings" which form the "atmosphere" of the house, but who is no less "liable to become the bond-slave of the coarsest and most brutal" of masters (II. 168), Stowe also gestures to the pliable white child born in a Northern metropolis in which the poor rise suddenly to wealth, and the comfortable just as precipitously fall. Karen Halttunen detects in Stowe's Gothicized South the author's debt to the eighteenth-century Oriental tale, to argue that Stowe uses the portraits of decadent Southern habitations (the Moorish New Orleans mansion; the East-Indian villa on Lake Pontchartrain; and Legree's denlike plantation) to allude to the resurgence of Calvinism's hereditary taint, experienced by the Beecher women as a kind of haunting.[30]

Thus the primitivism evident in Stowe's Orientalization, or Africanization, of the South expresses the author's sense of a spiritually and physically bankrupt North, of "[n]orthern men, northern mothers, northern Christians" whose abolitionism requires them first to "look to the evil among themselves" (II. 317). Yet the antidote to a degenerating middle class is, paradoxically, a charismatic primitivism: intimations of the eighteenth-century Oriental tale within *Uncle Tom's Cabin* might also enlist the tale's impact as a visionary genre, previously employed in the early republic to voice liberal, anti-Calvinist, or anti-patriarchal opinion without engaging in polemical debate. As in a successful sentimental narrative, so in the Oriental tale, writes Emerson, "man passes out of the torpid into the perceiving state" to see "things in their causes, all facts in their connections."[31]

The now pernicious, now restorative influence of Africanization is suggested when Eva and Tom read the Bible together beside Lake Pontchartrain, and Eva sees the language of the New Testament come to life (II. 63–64). Here, Tom's Christianization is arguably matched by Eva's Africanization, as what seems a Protestant act—the private reading and revelation of the Word—is staged on highly charged ground. Lake Pontchartrain served as the site of annual voodoo celebrations led by such priestesses as the two Marie Laveaus, mother and daughter, influential among blacks and whites between 1830 and 1890 in New Orleans, where voodoo seems to have been a matriarchy. Open to the public and, on occasion, to the press, the Pontchartrain meetings attracted Northern as well as Southern attention, and white as well as black participants. Incorporating a notorious landscape into the novel's eschatological tableau, Stowe possibly hints that the dying Eva St. Clare assimilates the occult power of the New Orleans priestess Marie—the power to hoodoo Legree—even as she also identifies with the Virgin Mary.[32]

The cross-cultural infusions suggested in the scene at the lake and involving the iconic Little Eva, link occult and domestic practices. Taken together, Stowe's allusions to the heterodox powers at the heart of the home suggest the increasingly demarcated capacities of mother and house to impress the "sympathetic and assimilative" human being. *Uncle Tom's Cabin* not only mirrored the middle-class preoccupation with the civilizing mother and the spirit of the house; it also gave that preoccupation form, and made that form irresistible. It is clearer than ever that even as Stowe's novel fostered abolition, it empowered the white women of the middle classes and excluded others from the feminine sphere of social and cultural influence. If this were the whole story, there would be no small irony in realizing that Stowe appropriates an African fetishism for a novel that advocates the elimination (through repatriation) as well as the emancipation (through civil disobedience) of African Americans. We may, however, take from Stowe what Stowe takes from fetishism—a consciousness of the dynamic flow of power. Sentimentalism, if the master's tool, can still dismantle the master's house. Retaining within it the remnants of a primitivistic, as well as a Lamarckian, conception of maternal transmission—namely, the notion that an "image placed before [a pregnant woman's] eyes and strongly impressed upon her imagination will be reproduced upon the body of her child"—; and joining the spirit work of the precious memento to the resistance of an African fetishism, the aesthetics of sentiment survives in Stowe's fiction as a stratagem for redressing the assymetries in cultural power.[33] Whether that stratagem could survive the challenge of the growing commodity culture of the postbellum decades remained to be tested in Stowe's *Household Papers and Stories*.

III

The chapter at Lake Pontchartrain prepares for Little Eva's deathbed tableau, long identified as a stock piece in sentimental fiction. But to grant that Eva's beautiful death is "essentially decorative" is not to assume that it is ineffective "in any practical sense," since the scenic or the scopic character of a sentimental aesthetic paradoxically secures its powers of invisible persuasion.[34] Just as "even the dullest and most literal were impressed" by Eva's "singular and dreamy earnestness of expression . . . without exactly knowing why" (I. 211), so is the reader of *Uncle Tom's Cabin* enthralled by a protest novel conceived as a series of pictures: "[For] there is no arguing with *pictures*," Stowe explains; "and everybody is impressed by them, whether they mean to be or not."[35]

First published in installments in the antislavery journal *National Era*, *Uncle Tom's Cabin* might have functioned like a series of genre scenes of slavery, enabling readers slowly to pass "out of the torpid into the perceiving state" and to see what Stowe repeatedly referred to as the facts of slavery. If the "object of these sketches is to awaken sympathy and feeling" (vi), such awakenings are structured by "theatrical dynamics that . . . depend on peoples' ability to represent themselves as tableaux, spectacles, and texts before others."[36] Like Emerson's "actors" who employ the "power of Sympathy . . . to chain the affections of the populace," Little Eva's powers derive partly from her melodramatic gestures, speech, and death, and partly from the theatrical backdrops against which she stars.[37] It is the sentimental's regime of the visible that works rapidly on Eva's immature cousin Henrique, for Eva's dazzling appearance breaks him of his habit of striking slaves. He confesses: "I could love anything for your sake, dear Cousin; for I really think you are the loveliest creature I ever saw" (II. 80, 81).

Readers of *Uncle Tom's Cabin* arguably came to it especially prepared to appreciate, and, like Henrique, to absorb its spectacular appeal. For they came to it with some expectation that the visible environment in general, and the house in particular, left their marks on human behavior. Within the advice literature collected in *Household Papers and Stories,* Stowe explores the "influence of dwelling houses for good and for evil, their influence on the brain, the nerves, and through these on the heart and mind."[38] In this she echoes the nineteenth-century architect Oliver Smith, who opined that our minds and morals are "subject to constant influence and modification, gradual yet lasting, by the inanimate walls with which we are surrounded."[39] If in *Christian Nurture* influence was as "subtly pervasive as the atmosphere [we] breathe" (83), even the subtlest changes in the built environment left impressions on vulnerable subjects. Phrenologist-architect Orson Fowler supported Bushnell's belief in antenatal modification when he commented that an "unhandy house" that "irritated mothers" would "sour the tempers of their children even before birth," whereas a "convenient" house would render all the inmates "amiable and good."[40]

Establishing contiguity between the formative labors of the mother and the determining details of the house, architects and advice givers represented the interior as a medium for extending the maternal body's persuasive powers. Historian David Handlin notes that midcentury domestic manuals often offered pointers on how mother and house might appear coextensive: a woman might wear a kerchief made of the same stuff out of which she had sewn a tablecloth, or weave cuttings of her own hair into picture frames.[41] This particular stress on the visual represented a shift in thinking about houses. Catharine Beecher's *Treatise on Domestic Economy* (1843) emphasized a dynamic interior by focusing not on the still and gentrified parlor but on the kitchen, in which work takes place. But while Beecher's emphasis on an "economy of labor" and the incorporation of technology into even modest homes was a reaction against the influential Andrew Jackson Downing's interest in "the beautiful in architecture," Harriet Beecher Stowe recombined Beecher's and Downing's investments to describe an "economy of the beautiful" that middle-class women should labor to achieve.[42] In effect, Stowe redefined the beautiful as that which functions in the service of a meliorative training, and functions as efficiently as it does (witness the submission and transformation of Henrique) precisely because of its material charm.

We may read Stowe's *Household Papers and Stories* as her effort to preserve and extend the mystic, organic connections between women and objects set forth in *Uncle Tom's Cabin.* This effort is more complicated than critics have assumed. Ann Douglas's important interpretations of the growth of commodity culture as one open, if suspect, avenue of feminine entitlement does not hold up well for Stowe. Her matrifocal domesticity often appears threatened by a milieu in which, as one manufacturer put it, the "business of this age is to make the products of civilization cheap."[43] The "products of civilization" were not always civilizing props. Although one debate raged regarding the cheap diffusion and the questionable impact of chromolithographs in particular, an argument about the proper decoration of houses coincided generally with a long-standing suspicion of the ornamental. Although the eighteenth century had already witnessed attempts to theorize a relation between an obsession with ornament and disease—a relation articulated in terms of paganism and primitivism—nineteenth-century writers recast these attempts in light of the conclusions provided by evolutionary studies.[44] The association of the love of ornament with savagery and degeneracy came down to Stowe in the Protestant polemic against painted and graven luxuries. It would culminate in Adolph Loos's 1908 aesthetic manifesto *Ornament and Crime,* but by then it was almost a commonplace that "cultural evolution is equivalent to the removal of ornament from articles in daily use."[45] Stowe intervenes in a critique of ornament to recuperate the decorative as an instrument of feminine influence. But precisely because of the decorative's potent effects, the homemaker requires instruction in the science of its application.

Turning to interior decoration in the collected *Household Papers and Stories,* Stowe alerts her audience not to the pernicious effects of the primitive within the ornamental, but to the erosion of ritual power in the mass production of domestic ornament. Yet instead of eschewing market commodities in favor of articles produced at home, Stowe offers in essays such as "The Economy of the Beautiful" a modern parable of proper shopping. Here narrator Christopher Crowfield details the extravagant tastes of homeowner Philip, whose purchases include wallpapers of the "heaviest French velvet, with gildings and traceries"; Axminster carpets, designed with "flowery convolutions and medallion-centres, as if the flowers of the tropic were whirling in waltzes"; curtains of "damask, cord, tassels, shades, laces" and "sofas, lounges, screens, etageres, and chairs of every pattern and device" (58–60). Philip's parlor appears as a venue for mock aristocratic display, a kind of stereotypical primitivism, and the conspicuous Victorian consumption that mass production encourages.

Stowe's reaction to Philip's enervating aesthetic is to clean house, not by boycotting mechanically produced goods, but by selecting among them commodities of "artistic culture," made available, thanks to plaster casts and chromolithographs, even to democratic citizens of modest means.

> Pictures . . . and statuary . . . speak constantly to the childish eye, but are out of reach of childish fingers. . . . The beauty once there is always there; though the mother be ill and in her chamber, she has no fears that she shall find it wrecked and shattered. And this style of beauty, inexpensive as it is, is a means of cultivation. No child is ever stimulated to draw or read by an Axminster carpet or a carved centre-table; but a room surrounded with photographs and pictures and fine casts suggests a thousand inquiries, stimulates the little eye and hand. The child is found with its pencil, drawing; or he asks for a book on Venice; or he wants to hear the history of the Roman Forum. (67–68)

Part museum, part schoolroom, Stowe's efficient shelter is fashioned to induce specific desires, habits, and character in subjects. Her attempt to make the private home the normative carrier of the signs of a homogeneous ethnic and class identity responds to Bushnell's preoccupation with the conscious cultivation of the "civilized type." But however familiar this blueprint is to us as the guide to the formation of an American middle class, Stowe also attempts to install within it a map of feminine opposition to bourgeois separate spheres. Just as the uncanny lock of hair gains purchase in its viewer long after its owner's death, so too does the interior impress its occupants long after the mother has left home for extra-domestic engagements. Installed within such reproductions ("photographs and pictures and fine casts") as a help to preserve the "enchantment that was once about [the mother's] person alone" and that has come to "interfuse and penetrate the home which she has created," maternal charisma resurges not in relics from beyond the grave but from inside the commercial market, from which members of the domestic sphere have been cordoned off. Enlightened consumption finds the ideal sentimental purchase in a copy of the "San Sisto 'Madonna and Child,' " for "such a picture, hung against the wall of a child's room, would train a child's eye from infancy" (67–68)—uncannily, even in the absence of the mother from the home. And if we are prone to question the effects of a materialist politics with an occult component, we are well reminded that the careers of mediums and trancers who agitated for abolition did not end with the Civil War. Nor was the meaning of their message inevitably vitiated by its (sometimes spectacular) commercial dissemination.[46]

Stowe's suggestion that even manufactured articles exert the necromantic force that the Victorian ascribed to curls, yellowed letters, and preserved childhood garments is perhaps best demonstrated in her approval of an especially modern kind of object, the photograph, for use in the decoration of houses. Exemplary of the work of art in the age of mechanical reproduction, daguerreotypes and photographs were also seen as "opening onto a larger, preternatural world." Alan Trachtenberg writes that the initial "suspicion of occult practices" never entirely faded from considerations of photography, while "spirit photographers" did a robust trade in capturing not only the likenesses of portrait sitters and of the deceased, but also of their paranormal friends and relatives whose otherwise invisible appearances were caught by the camera. After Walter Benjamin, then, we could say that the photograph entertained residual ritual powers in its use in the (chiefly maternal) work of memorial and mourning.[47]

But like the sentimental relics in *Uncle Tom's Cabin,* the photograph is also recruited to serve more subversive ends than the quietus of consolation. In entirely different hands, the photograph might even further the interests of those social groups excluded from the bourgeois norm, even though this norm is in part constructed, as "The Economy of the Beautiful" suggests, through the culturally homogenizing effects of photography. The photograph's oppositional potential is only suggested in Charles W. Chesnutt's "The Wife of his Youth" (1899), but the suggestion is instructive.[48] In Chesnutt's story, a woman who has never ceased searching for her runaway slave husband knocks unexpectedly on his door. He has altered his identity in order to pass as a member of the light-skinned caste of the Northern city now his home. She requests his assistance in locating the man whose portrait she carries in the form of an "old fashioned daguerreotype in a black case fastened to a string that went around her neck" (16). Although it means the sacrifice of his place in the bourgeois Society of the Blue Veins, this husband acknowledges his wife and, simultaneously, his race—impressed, it seems, both by the hard fact of the daguerreotype and the sympathetic story she tells of her tireless journey toward reunion. But perhaps the motherly old woman's persuasive powers come not only from the material likeness of the picture, which could expose him, or the melodramatics of the story, which move him, but also from the spirit work of conjure. The wife's "blue gums" inform us that she is a conjure woman (10).[49] Perhaps she makes use of the image tied around her neck by a string as both African American fetish (Uncle Tom's "witch thing") and "precious memento" (Little Eva's curls): only two of the faces of "sentimental power."

IV

> There is higher work for Art than the arts. They are the abortive births of
> an imperfect or vitiated instinct.
>
>   Emerson, "Art"

At the end of the nineteenth century, Harriet Beecher Stowe's grand-niece Charlotte Perkins Gilman mounted an indirect attack on her great-aunt's matrifocal domesticity by recognizing the symbiotic presence within domestic life of primitive survivals. The "bodily nature" of Stowe's aesthetics of sentiment symptomized its dysfunctional and decadent character. That domestic women possessed only the "habits of a dark untutored past," Gilman saw evidenced in domestic art, and she expressed dismay that women were at home within "a continuous accumulation of waste," that they decorated the interior with "of all the awful things!—the hair of the dead."[50] Gilman's extended analysis of the socioeconomic relations between the sexes was heavily influenced by the neo-Lamarckian sociologist Lester Ward.[51] Ward's work helped Gilman to her conclusion that the bourgeois woman kept by patriarchy in her separate sphere is "confined to a primitive, a savage plane of occupation," from which she manifests an "equally savage plane of aesthetic taste," visible in outré furnishings, ornamental details, and personal dress tantamount to self-mutilation. "With no evolutionary check on ensuing mutilation," a woman puts her offspring at risk (*Home,* 153). Unspecialized in art, as in industry, the bourgeois woman's arrested or atavistic traits surface in her inability to transcend the body to produce an aesthetics advanced beyond "the arts," beyond the "first-hand industries of savage times" (*WE,* 67).

Yet even as Gilman rejects her great-aunt's understanding of the influence immanent in such sentimental articles as "the hair of the dead," she never questions Stowe's assumption that the immediate environment left an impression on (even unborn) human subjects. Gilman's now notorious tale *The Yellow Wallpaper* (1892) reveals her belief that the impressions made on minds and bodies of mothers reappear in offspring; the maternal power of cultural and biological transmission is on trial in Gilman's Gothic short story, as the "pointless pattern" on the four walls exerts a "vicious" and "sickly" influence on the maternal narrator confined inside them.[52] While Gilman argues that the "race reared under the laws of Beauty" will be "nobler" (*Home,* 158), the yellow wallpaper's commission of "every artistic sin" threatens the race with deculturation and extinction (*YW,* 20). The "love of beauty at home," Gilman elsewhere explains, has been "cruelly aborted" in women consigned to a home that is but a "little ganglion of aborted economic processes" (*Home,* 151). To look closely at the imagery in the yellow wallpaper is to detect a scene of aesthetics, and of obstetrics, gone awry.

Reversing as she does the midcentury axiom of the separate-spheres ideology that the world of commerce and industry is poison, and its only antidote the home, Gilman also plays on her contemporaries' suspicion that the Victorian interior is literally lethal.[53] In 1870, Drs. Brinton and Napheys "accepted moderate arsenic eating" as an aid to the complexion, but "believed that the popularity of wallpaper in homes, which were covered in arsenical dyes . . . had threatened the woman beyond her tolerance level." But while arguing that the middle-class mother long modified by patriarchal culture is herself too unfit to ensure the sound production of the Anglo-Saxon race, Gilman never abandons Stowe's suggestion that domestic women have recourse to antipatriarchal strategies, strategies intimately tied to the feminine/subaltern body Gilman produces in order to transcend. The hysterical, atavistic narrator of *The Yellow Wallpaper* enjoys a perverse mastery over her dominant doctor-husband, whom we last see swooning at her feet. The feasibility of the woman's successful, if costly, resistance is indirectly sounded in the warning issued by Brinton and Napheys as well: "although long use of arsenic had rendered many women immune to the mineral, their husbands occasionally came to untimely deaths as a result of a romantic embrace."[54] We could say that the male physicians' fantasy rehearses the thematics of a duplicitous, even poisonous, femininity we have already remarked. But history suggests that the persistence of the fantasy is motivated, at least in part, by the actual practices of such heterodox figures as midwives, healers, conjurers, and even voodoo matriarchs, at the end of the nineteenth century in the United States.

If in the antebellum United States the aesthetics of sentiment is indebted to African American cultures, the sentimental is also already historically placed within the long tradition of a Western aesthetics in which, as Naomi Schor explains, the primitive, the masses, the detail, "brute Matter," and the feminine are aligned.[55] Recent critical attempts to counter the devaluation of the feminized nineteenth-century genre point to its stylistic legacy of what has been dubbed "femmage"; Modern Art's techniques of collage and assemblage, and arguably, the irrational arrangements of the Surrealists, indicate homage to the salvage aesthetics of scrapbooks, photograph albums, quilts, and valentines practiced by sentimental artists. The legacy of the culture of sentiment bears implications for the subjects of culture as well. Emily Apter, commenting on the incorporation in artist Mary Kelly's *Post-Partum Document* (1982) of the sentimental paraphernalia of "first shoes, photographs, and locks of hair," takes Kelly's postmodern *Document* as an occasion for articulating a "postpartum sentimentality." Apter speculates that postpartum sentimentalism offers a model of a counter-Freudian female fetishism, wherein the breach between mothers and infants is healed in the mnemonic traces of saved and reassembled objects.[56]

I have argued that Stowe's investment in inspirited inanimate things owes something to the viability of the fetish in the heterogeneous cultures of antebellum America, which transmitted to Stowe, as she transmitted to others, prescient strategies for disrupting dominant operations, as witches apparently will. Stowe's sentimental practice is partly motivated by her belief in a Western conception of progress, and this means that her writing never inhibits the colonizing agenda of her imperialist contemporaries. *Uncle Tom's Cabin* ends in a vision of a Christianized Africa, after the model provided by the romantic racialist (and Swedenborgian) Alexander Kinmont. But this vision does not inevitably mark the ends of the sentimental, only the limits of this abolitionist's application. I have also suggested that Stowe's dialogue with domestic ideology, antebellum popular science, and cultural survivals in her sentimental fiction makes sentimentalism itself an especially labile genre for reappropriations. If in her sensational story of the potent "expression" of the "inanimate thing" on the walls (*YW,* 16), Charlotte Gilman takes advantage of the bodily nature of the genre precisely in order to effect a critique of sentimental culture, we might look to her contemporaries, the masculine naturalists, whose literary experiments also represent an official revolt against the aesthetics of sentiment. And if Raymond Williams is correct in saying that in naturalism physical details and entire environments become "actors and agencies" in their own right, we might acknowledge even here the persistence of the sentimental writer and of the Africanisms animating her.[57]

13

The Mulatto, Tragic or Triumphant?
The Nineteenth-Century American
Race Melodrama

Susan Gillman

"White Americans," W. E. B. Du Bois wrote in 1927, "are willing to read about Negroes, but they prefer to read about Negroes who are fools, clowns, prostitutes, or at any rate, in despair and contemplating suicide." Complicating this classic statement of the problematic appeal to a white readership of black stereotypes, Du Bois concludes, "Other sorts of Negroes do not interest them because, as they say, 'they are just like white folks.' " For Du Bois, the most complicated figure of all might be the so-called "tragic mulatto," who, both despairing and appearing just like white folk, is a hybrid not only of both races but also of both Du Boisean sorts of Negroes, those acceptable and those (avowedly) uninteresting to white readers. No wonder, then, that the literary figure of the tragic mulatto has exerted such ambiguous fascination for so many readers, black and white, both those who embrace an assimilationist vision and those who reject the notion of a "white Negro" as tacitly subscribing to the racist ideology of the color line.[1]

Given this ambiguity, it is also no wonder that the late nineteenth-century literature by both black and white writers in which such "white Negroes" predominate has proved a difficult critical nut to crack. How do we approach "racialist" texts replete with all of Du Bois's stereotypical Negroes and more, ranging from the notorious racist Thomas Dixon's *The Clansman: An Historical Romance of the Ku Klux Klan* (1905) to Mark Twain's *The Tragedy of Pudd'nhead Wilson* (1894), to Pauline Hopkins's *Contending Forces: A Romance Illustrative of Negro Life North and South* (1900)? One answer is that, as a coherent body of work, the racially oriented fiction of the turn of the century has simply not been acknowledged by literary historians, at least not in the way, for example, they have acknowledged and named the related body of modern writing known as "Southern Gothic." Another answer is that the wide-ranging literature of the "racial 1890s" has been read one-dimensionally, contained within studies of the mulatto in American fiction. And the mulatto is, as Du Bois suggests, an especially vexed figure to be an icon of "race writing" of any period.

We thus give particularly short shrift to the racialist writing of this period— whether by black or white writers—without the detailed consideration of its historical and narrative function that Hazel Carby has recently called for.[2] What precisely is "this period"? Labeled "The Nadir" of black American history by historian and pioneer Pan-Africanist Rayford W. Logan, it was a time of extended global crisis in race relations, when ideological struggles over black nationalism within the African American community shaped the polarized arguments over separatism versus integration, political activism versus economic self-development, and the positive or negative role (not to mention the very existence) of the "matriarchal" black family. These debates were themselves engendered by the context of turn-of-the-century racism: legal and scientific discourse on issues of blood, race, and sex; miscegenation; Negrophobic mob violence; and the ideologies of imperialism and racial Darwinism. During the American racial hysteria of the 1890s and early 1900s, antiblack repression took multiple forms, legal and extralegal; the political and social gains made by blacks under Reconstruction were gradually eroded; and the ideology of white supremacy ultimately institutionalized itself in a series of Jim Crow laws defining the "Negro's place" in a segregated society.

Simultaneous with this solidification of institutionalized racism, and certainly not coincidentally, there was a flowering of a kind of writing I call the American race melodrama. Encompassing literary, sociological, and scientific texts by both black and white writers, the race melodrama focuses broadly on the situation of the black family—almost always of an interracial genealogy— and specifically on the issue of "race mixture," as a means of negotiating the social tensions surrounding the formation of racial, national, and sexual identity in the post-Reconstruction years. The basic plot of the fictional texts centers on the reconstitution of the black family separated under slavery, culminating in the revelation of secret identities, of hidden race mixture, and finally of separated and reunited parents and children. In making the state of the postslavery black family an index of American race relations, the fictional race melodrama advances the same familial project as does the newly institutionalized study of the black family at the turn of the century, best known through the early work done by W. E. B. Du Bois (*The Philadelphia Negro,* 1899; *The Negro American Family,* 1908), and a later work by E. Franklin Frazier (*The Negro Family in the United States,* 1939). Both the fictional and the sociological texts make the kinship structure of the black family the focal point for both races in their differing confrontations with the American racial system. Although these texts have been categorized and treated quite separately, confined largely to their separate disciplines of literature and sociology, they overlap most notably, as we will see, in their varying representations of the figure of the black mother, who provides a space in which competing claims for racial self-definition—especially the national versus the sexual— may be projected and imaginatively resolved.

The question of the black family and the different genres in which it was represented raises the other major issue I want to address: that of the genre of race melodrama itself. Romance, the generic category the novels most frequently invoke for themselves—as we have seen, for example, in the titles of both the Dixon and the Hopkins novels—problematizes their undeniable relationship to social reality. Rather than romance, however, I use the term "melodrama" instead, in part to frame the texts within the colloquial, popular cultural world that produced them and that they helped to shape. These works exemplify what Peter Brooks calls "the melodramatic imagination": characterized by polarized words, gestures, and moral absolutes, the world of the melodrama is subsumed by "an underlying manichaeism . . . putting us in touch with the conflict of good and evil played out under the surface of things."[3] Both the polarization and the revelation of hidden conflict are essential to the fundamentally unresolved conclusion of the race melodrama, a genre that grapples with still-unresolved racial issues.

I use the term "melodrama" as well to allude to another source of dissatisfaction today with the late nineteenth century's "racial books"—yet another defining phrase, this one from Frances Harper's novel *Iola Leroy; or Shadows Uplifted* (1892).[4] That is, these works combine what we mean today colloquially, and usually pejoratively, by the melodramatic and the didactic. Drawing on a language of love and romance, they are inevitably stories of hidden identity, of kinship disrupted and restored, with parents, children, and lovers representing particular races, regions, or class interests which must come together in the service of racial and national unity.[5] Their authors thus assume an indivisibility of politics from fiction in writing the history of American race relations.

Far, then, from providing simply the sense of order associated with the formulaic conclusion of the melodrama, the race melodrama acknowledges, even embraces, everything that is most unsettling about this period and its cultural expression. In race melodrama virtually all of what Pauline Hopkins in her 1900 novel title calls "contending forces" tangle in complex fashion: the interaction in nineteenth-century "race" discourse of "low" popular cultural forms with legal and scientific discourse; the appeal to the emotions associated with theatrical melodrama as well as the incitement to hysteria characteristic of racial debates, which present themselves simultaneously as appeals to the intellect; the related phenomenon, characteristic of the slave narrative as well, in which outrageous, virtually unbelievable fact sits in uneasy relationship with fictive form (how to represent the horrors of rape and lynching?); the schematic, binary world view of melodrama with its moral categories of absolute virtue and vice; and finally, the way a new U.S. history was being rewritten, by Woodrow Wilson, D. W. Griffith and others, *as race melodrama,* in order to "heal sectional rivalries" and "unite the divided nation."

In addition, and perhaps more important, the race melodrama, defined broadly enough to include the fiction of Mark Twain, Pauline Hopkins, Thomas Dixon, and Sutton Griggs as well as the sociology of W. E. B. Du Bois and Franklin Frazier, not only replicates these most problematic aspects of the cultural context, but also interrogates and, in the process, momentarily

transcends them. Itself a polarized mode of representation, the race melodrama calls into question those polarities that have historically characterized
both the reality and the study of late nineteenth-century American race relations. Fundamentally a literature of *race relations,* the race melodrama forces
us to see in relationship to one another a number of elements that are often—
and misleadingly—treated as separate and opposed: not only blacks and
whites, but also racist writers (like Dixon) and those who see themselves as
racial radicals or liberals, as well as different kinds of "race" writing com-
prised by fiction, sociology, and science.

For us, however, melodrama is generally flattened as a genre, either split
off aesthetically from "literature" and "literary merit" because of its "flat,"
"stereotyped" characters, or else separated from "serious social criticism." To
see melodrama so pejoratively has been a particularly crippling problem for
readers of racial books. It has been said, for example, that the early black
novelist was so "caught between anti-Negro stereotypes and his own counter
stereotypes . . . [that] . . . in the end he avoided the problem by seeking
refuge in the flat static characters of conventional melodrama." Or another
example: George Washington Cable, a white Southern contemporary of
Twain's known for his liberal stance on race, was "unusual" as a novelist in
"presenting the tragic mulatto not only as a figure of romance and melodrama
but also as a political and social being." Even those contemporary critics most
sympathetic to these racial books exhibit serious unease about their reliance
on melodramatic or sensational conventions. Hazel Carby, for example, who
has recently argued in *Reconstructing Womanhood: The Emergence of the
Afro-American Woman Novelist* that black women writers continued throughout the nineteenth century "to adopt and adapt dominant literary conventions . . . as a form of cultural and political intervention," tacitly assumes a
parallel rather than causal relationship between these activities. Similarly,
Richard Yarborough's sympathetic introduction to the Schomburg Library
edition of Hopkins's *Contending Forces* struggles with the "discordances"
resulting from "Hopkins's attempt to incorporate political commentary and
debate into her otherwise relatively conventional sentimental novel," concluding reluctantly that only her focus on African American women allows her "to
relax the stifling restraints of the sentimental literary conventions to which she
is otherwise committed" and to "undermine a bit . . . the melodramatic excess of her depiction elsewhere."[6]

These views share the mistaken assumption that melodrama, as an aesthetic
form, has a trivial or simplistic relation to social context; unlike the kind of
revisionist work that has been done by feminist critics on the once equally
despised midnineteenth-century mode of sentimentality, this dismissive approach refuses the possibility of melodrama's doing cultural work, of the
melodramatic narrative's being itself, as Fredric Jameson says, "a socially
symbolic act, as the ideological—but formal and immanent—response to a
historical dilemma." Indeed, I want to argue, as he does in another context,
that these late nineteenth-century texts announce "a whole renewal of melodrama as a narrative instrument for managing social tensions and conflicts."[7]

This cultural approach circumvents entirely the whole issue of abstract literary value that so preoccupied an earlier generation of critics. For them a plot-oriented catalogue of the "novel of passing" or "mulatto fiction"—the terms themselves betray the inadequacy of the approach—was an appropriate critical method of reading a body of fiction deemed not to have lasting literary merit. I want instead to explore how melodrama as a form has some very different uses, literary and cultural, from those assigned to it. The race melodrama responds formally with varying imaginary resolutions to an array of social contradictions generated in the post-Reconstruction era by the conflicting demands of racial, sexual, and national identities. The resolutions differ as dramatically, and significantly, as do the formulations of the problems facing the black race in white America. But the fundamental cultural contradiction animating these fictions has been given its best-known summation in the famous Du Boisean formulation of "his twoness—an American, a Negro . . . two warring ideals in one dark body."[8]

Du Bois conceives of race in this 1903 formula and throughout his career not as a singular, determining social formation but rather as something seen through nationalist and ultimately global lenses. Responding to American race problems, his Pan-Africanism promotes the resolution of a racially based, global nation-family. Such a project of nation building works by creating what Benedict Anderson calls "imagined communities": "the nation is always conceived as a deep, horizontal comradeship," regardless or in defiance of the actual inequalities of class, caste, race, and gender that may exist. In *amor patriae* as in other affections, there is always "an element of fond imagining," making the novel a form peculiarly adapted to the figuring of nationalism.[9] What does Anderson's inextricable link between fiction and the *amor patriae* of national building offer us for an understanding of the American race melodrama? It suggests, first, an erotics of politics that fuses the melodrama of familial love disrupted and restored with the political project of imagining a viable biracial community. Second, the notion of imagined communities allows us to draw crucial distinctions among the kinds of imaginary resolutions offered in the individual race melodramas, whose social ideals and strategies vary so—ranging from racism to Pan-Africanism, from separatism to assimilation, and from self-help to self-destruction—that it sometimes seems difficult to see them as a coherent group.

I have chosen, therefore, to focus on three different case studies: works by Mark Twain, Pauline Hopkins, and W. E. B. Du Bois. The choice itself bears the burden of my argument that while these are of course not the only kinds of racial books in the nineteenth century, they are indeed representative variations, explicitly giving a sense of the tremendously protean race melodrama. As case studies they should testify to both the range and the ubiquity of the American race melodrama, and at once offer convincing evidence that we cannot afford to dismiss such a major form of cultural expression.

Mark Twain's little-known and unfinished "avenging mulatto" stories consist of three sketches, written from the 1880s to the early 1900s, for racial tragedies in which the son of a white master-father and slave mother takes revenge on the father, culminating in patricide. I offer these partial texts, perhaps perversely, as a parodic mirror image of the conventional tragic mulatto tale, as figured in works both by white "romantic racialists" such as Harriet Beecher Stowe, George Washington Cable, and Kate Chopin, and by black writers such as William Wells Brown, Charles Chesnutt, and Nella Larsen.[10] Twain's sketches seem simply to reverse the terms of their plots while staying firmly within their mapped edges. Rather than the mulatto himself—and the gender is part of the reversal—coming to a tragic end (typically death, separation from a love revealed to be incestuous, or deportation to Europe), Twain's mulatto responds aggressively to his biracial heritage by inflicting the tragic fate on his own white father. But Twain's avenging mulatto (the term, of course, is a deliberate inversion) does more than simply reverse the classic tragic mulatto—more often, in fact, a mulatta. In this racial world of tangled kinship, he also ironically bears a family resemblance to the monstrous mulatto imagined in the racist work of Thomas Dixon, D. W. Griffith, and Charles Carroll. Carroll's quasi-scientific study, *The Negro a Beast, or In the Image of God* (1900), participated in creating perhaps the most common race melodrama of the late nineteenth century, that of black degeneracy and criminality. His work harks back even further to the etymology of the word "mulatto," borrowed from the Spanish and derived from the Latin *mulus,* and spawning the "science of muleology" linking the mulatto to the mule, a hybrid animal, the sterile product of an unnatural mating.[11] Twain's mulatto issues from this tortured genealogy.

My second case study is Pauline E. Hopkins's novel *Of One Blood. Or, the Hidden Self,* published serially in the *Colored American Magazine* (November 1902–November 1903). Drawing on the formulas and strategies of nineteenth-century dime novels and sensation fiction, the novel was characterized in the opening editorial of a magazine in which it appeared as offering "the colored people of the United States, a medium through which they can demonstrate their ability and tastes, in fiction, poetry and art, as well as in the arena of historical, social and economic literature." It pledged to introduce "a monthly magazine of merit into every Negro family" and, further, "to develop and intensify the bonds of that racial brotherhood, which alone can enable a people, to assert their racial rights as men, and demand their privileges as citizens."[12] The conjunction here of familial, cultural, and political projects with Hopkins's own strategic use of popular American narrative forms makes her work representative of the race melodrama, according to Frances Harper: "good racial books . . . of lasting service to the race." These are female-authored and female-centered race narratives dedicated to the black middle-class project of uplift and consolidation of the black community. Like Harper's, Pauline Hopkins's writing offers us a female melodrama, even a maternal race melodrama; but *Of One Blood* is especially important in refiguring the black community as a nation, and the source of civilization as African rather than European. The conventional search for kinship is thus refigured globally as a metaphor for the history of the black diaspora and a Pan-African future.[13]

Finally, I will use as my third case study a selection of Du Bois's sociological writings, ranging from the earliest, most "scientific" work (*The Philadelphia*

Negro, 1899; *The Negro American Family,* 1908) to later, better-known, more "autobiographical" works on the concept of race (*Darkwater: Voices from Within the Veil,* 1921; *Dusk of Dawn: An Essay Toward an Autobiography of a Race Concept,* 1940). Rather than Du Bois's two novels, I take as an exemplary form of the race melodrama his sociology, in order to show the ways in which the genre, while not including all its details, replicates itself in different forms. Du Bois's early sociological studies list among their primary bibliographical sources not only the publications of the U.S. Census and the Department of Labor, as one would expect, but also contemporary novels, poems, and travel narratives (by, for example, Harriet Beecher Stowe and Charles Chesnutt), suggesting that, for one social scientist at least, both fiction and nonfiction were significant sources of information on the black family. Indeed, Du Bois's sociology itself constitutes a kind of race melodrama with the study of the black family, its kinship structure, and especially the role of the black mother, at the center of the project. Finally, his lifelong devotion to the Africanism of the American Negro—to what, in the opening of *The Negro American Family,* he calls "a distinct nexus between Africa and America, . . . broken and perverted, . . . [but] . . . not to be neglected"—forges a crucial link between race and the nation-family.

Together, these three case studies will demonstrate how the American race melodrama bases its different conceptions of race on different conceptions of gender, the latter being controlled through the representation or absence of the black woman. Some of the key texts define a myth of black matriarchy, portraying maternal authority as simultaneously powerful and disruptive—a loaded representation that eventuated in the now-notorious 1965 Moynihan Report, which opened its analysis of the "tangle of pathology" of the black family with a section entitled "Matriarchy." Notwithstanding Moynihan's notoriety, his report stands near the end of a long tradition of writing on "matriarchal black culture," much of it as celebratory as Moynihan's (and that of E. Franklin Frazier before him) is condemnatory.[14] Thus in the historically specific manifestations of the race melodrama, we may also witness some of the form's long-term political implications for how the matrifocal novel works differently in the post-Reconstruction and welfare states. Historically speaking, we might say there is a color line, so to speak, within the race melodrama: the female-centered race narratives, for example, that from the slave narrative onward were read as feminist utopian projects opening up a female space in the midst of the plantation, backfire or encounter new pitfalls in the political context of the new post–civil rights racism. Tracing the formal trajectory of the race melodrama allows us to trace the historically specific formations of "American"—global—racism.

"A Nigger with a Grievance"

Despite Twain's current politically correct reputation and his career-long commitment to the exploration of race questions, trying to locate him in the context of late nineteenth-century good racial books is a frustrating task. In contrast, he places himself quite deliberately within the parameters of the institutional, medico-juridical discourse on race (as I have shown elsewhere).[15] Based on the evidence provided by his own reading, writing, and correspondence, however, he does not seem to have been particularly aware, or else did not record his awareness, of literary and cultural developments either within the black community or on a broader interracial front. His silence accounts for the celebrated discovery in 1985 (the centenary of the publication of *Huckleberry Finn*) of a letter written the year *Huckleberry Finn* was published, pledging Twain's support to a black Yale law student.[16] And hence my reliance on such slim pickings as three unfinished pieces on race, two of them only in note form.

However, the problem of Twain's apparently constitutional inability to complete his race narratives is one issue that the context of his contemporaries' good racial books can speak to. It has always been something of a critical puzzle that *Pudd'nhead Wilson*—after *Huckleberry Finn*, Twain's best-known work on race—originally contained in manuscript form much racial material that never appeared in the published version.[17] Indeed, of the pieces I am discussing here, the "best"-known is a series of passages written in the manuscript of *Pudd'nhead Wilson* but deleted by Twain from the published version, which outline a vestigial patricide plot hatched by the vengeful "white" Tom Driscoll, following his slave mother Roxana's revelation that he is a black slave, son of an aristocratic white man. These canceled passages confirm what several readers and critics have always asserted: the novel culminates with Tom's murder of his supposed white uncle and benefactor, Judge Driscoll, but from "the standpoint of imaginative coherence," Judge Driscoll is the father of Tom just as clearly as Roxana is his mother. And the suppressed patricide plot thus remains in the novel, barely disguised, despite Twain's double stratagem, recognized by Henry Nash Smith and others, of making Roxana the slave of a shadowy brother of Judge Driscoll at the time of Tom's birth, and then creating an even more shadowy figure, Col. Cecil Burleigh Essex, to be Tom's biological father.[18] In fact, in the working notes for the novel, to return once again to the repressed genealogy, Twain made Judge Driscoll himself the father of Tom.

What are we to make of this almost impossibly thin disguise? Consulting a range of contemporary good racial books may help here, by telling us what people could say in the late-nineteenth century about race relations, and how they could say it. Put another way, Twain's personal difficulties with saying what he wanted to say reveal as much about the limits and possibilities of the American race melodrama as they do about him. Most readers have read Twain's well-recorded self-censorship biographically and psychologically rather than culturally, seeing in it either his squeamishness about the fact of miscegenation between white master and female slave, or his ambivalence toward his own father, John Marshall Clemens, whom he clearly identified with the gentlemanly Driscolls, Essexes, and other "F.F.V.'s" (First Families of Virginia) humorously and lovingly satirized in the novel. If we look more closely at Twain's suppressed patricide plot, however, in the context of other possible plots offered by the contemporary race melodrama, it emerges strikingly as a telling variant of the tragic mulatto plot.

In this plot blackness is conceived as taint; the conventions of the search for origins and the revelation of kinship result in fearful exposure, with identity destroyed rather than affirmed. *Pudd'nhead Wilson* draws on but truncates this process, representing only briefly the volcanic "irruption" in Tom Driscoll's psyche upon becoming aware of "the 'nigger' in him." But the manuscript plays with extended moments of realization in passages such as these:

> I must begin a new life to-day—but not outside; no, only inside. I must be the same slangy, useless youth as before, outside, but inside I shall be a nigger with a grievance— . . . I wish I knew my father . . . I will wheedle it out of her some day; and if he is alive, then let him not go out at night. (MMS, 234–35)

> After this he searched the mysteries of human nature and human ways no more . . .; his mind centered itself upon a single problem—how to find his father, in case he was alive—and upon a single purpose: to kill him when he should find him. He said he would make this the whole mission of his life, and allow nothing to stay him or divert him until it was accomplished. (MMS, 243–244AAA)

> He loathed the "nigger" in him, but got pleasure out of bringing this secret "filth," as he called it, into familiar and constant contact with the sacred whites. . . . [And there was one thought that sang always in his heart. He called that his father's death-song.] (MMS, 246–47)

Even in the manuscript the bracketed last sentences are crossed out, emphasizing that the repeated references to the son's killing the father are both the object and the threat.

Race is conceived of (if such an analytical word is appropriate here) almost entirely as a structure of domination and subordination, as relations of power between familial power brokers, father and son. The mother is essentially absent, acknowledged only in one manuscript passage: "that poor lowly and ignorant creature is my mother! Well, she has my respect for one thing—she has never owned a slave." Similarly, almost entirely suppressed are racial-sexual relations—not merely, however, owing to Twain's prudery, but also because the whole focus of the narrative is on the filial relation, figured as filial taboo. Even the published version of *Pudd'nhead Wilson,* mother-centered as it is, bears traces of this paternal shadow plot, both in the displaced murder of the uncle-father and in the oft-noted, disjointed characterization, alternately powerful and flat, of Roxana. The slave mother became a partial but inadequate substitute for the white father, the source and object of the primary emotion.

In Twain's vision, race, represented as a site of unequal filial power relations, is the sole determinant of identity, with little or no attention paid to allied sex-gender relations. Gender division is present, certainly, but submerged in parent-child dynamics. The why of the centrality of the father is no more explicitly acknowledged than is the subordinate role of the mother. This is the vision Twain pursued in the other two race narratives, one a four-page outline, dated in the 1880s, for a story about a mulatto ("$\frac{1}{16}$ negro"), "his father his master & mean," who after the war, "at last, seeing even the best educated negro is at a disadvantage, . . . clips his wiry hair close, wears gloves always (to conceal his telltale nails,) & passes for a white man." He falls in love with his cousin—"he used to 'miss' her on the plantation"—and then the notes break off at the climactic moment of revelation.

> At the time of the climax he is telling the stirring story of the heroic devotion of a poor negro mother to her son—of course not mentioning that he was the son & that *his* is the mother who bears the scar which he has described. Then she steps forward and shows the scar she got in saving him from his own father's brutality. So this gassy man is *his* father, & it is his niece whom XX loves, & who with (perhaps) his daughter, supports him.[19]

Though the genealogical ramifications of the plot are confusing, they seem to include the implication that other people under the illusion that they are white are also exposed.

The latest and longest race narrative comes, significantly, at the end of an unfinished novel, "Which Was It?," that has been published in a collection of Twain's late fantasy and dream writings.[20] The culminating fantasy of this dream tale is a nightmare of total racial role reversal, black over white. The basic plot resembles that of several of Twain's dream writings: a most re-spected and successful family man has a momentary dream of disaster, seem-ing to last for many years, in which he exposes the family to debt, disgrace, and in this case murder. All the stories break off before the dreamer finally awakens, but only this one concludes with an escalating racial nightmare. George Louisiana Purchase Harrison ("It is a curious name, but in its way patriotic. He was born on the date of the signing of the Purchase-treaty") commits a murder, evidence of which is obtained by the free mulatto Jasper, who then blackmails Harrison throughout the rest of the story (179). The payment exacted: Jasper, sired and swindled out of his freedom by his white master, George Harrison's uncle, takes revenge on the nephew by "enslaving" him. "You b'longs to me, now. You's my proppity, same as a nigger," says the ostensible servant Jasper to the ostensible master, who is forced to wait upon him in private. "By God, I kin hang you any minute I wanter! Git up en fetch yo' marster a dram!" (413).

To get a sense of how deeply and repetitively the fantasy of black over white is engaged in this narrative, we need only a few extended passages.

> "En you's a slave!—. . . en I lay I'll learn you the paces! I been one, en I *know* 'em; slave to de meanest white man dat ever walked—en he 'uz *my father*; en I bought my freedom fum him en paid him for it, en he took 'vantage of me en stole it back; en he sold my mother down de river, po' young thing . . ., God damn his soul!—but it's my turn, now; dey's a long bill agin de low-down ornery white race, en you's a-gwyneter *settle* it. . . . You's white, en I's gwyneter take it outer *you*. You en de res'. Ev'ry time I gits a chance." (415, 417)

Harrison's response—"Slave of an ex-slave! it is the final degradation"—underlines the extent to which Twain's central insight into race relations involves the desire for, and certainly the threat of, the absolute exchange of power from white to black. As early as the 1880s, in a notebook entry Twain had predicted "Negro supremacy—the whites underfoot in a hundred years."[21] "Which Was It?" imagines on a personal level the fulfillment of that prediction.

> The meek slouch of the slave was gone from him, . . .; and not even his rags and tatters could rob his great figure of a certain . . . pride of mastership and command. . . . He *looked* the master; but that which had gone from him was not lost, for his discarded droop and humble mien had passed to his white serf, and already they seemed not out of place there, but fit, and . . . at home. (413, 415)

At this point of completed racial role reversal, of "Negro supremacy," when the nightmare of master-become-victim—it is indeed the master's nightmare—is about to begin, the narrative breaks off. It is as if there was simply no more that could be said on race, as if in the early 1900s Twain had reached the limits of either his imagination or the available forms, or both. In fact, despite the numerous gestures made in these three pieces toward writing a stereotypical race melodrama—the cruel white master-father, the heroic slave mother, the tortured mulatto offspring—Twain's racial vision could not ultimately be accommodated by that popular narrative form. His institutionally based conception of race relations—in *Pudd'nhead Wilson,* race as a product of social institutions such as the law and science, race as a fiction of law and custom—differs fundamentally from the familial, kinship-based model of race that we get in the race melodrama. This is why the whole question of male-female sexuality and paternal-maternal relations under slavery is not central to Twain's work, despite the misleading fact that he so often tried to write in the popular form that treats race as a family romance. For Twain the racial body is not a body at all, it is not at all gender-related or gender-specific; rather, in the words of Hortense Spillers on the New World, diasporic plight, it is "a territory of cultural and political maneuver."[22]

Blood Brothers

Of One Blood. Or, the Hidden Self—Pauline Hopkins's last novel, serialized in the *Colored American Magazine*—bends the American race melodrama so that it fulfills all the requirements of the form—revelation of hidden or unknown identities, and the resolution of conflict in marriage—yet it leaves distinctly open-ended the troubling racial and political questions raised by the narrative. I use the term "bend," rather than "transcend" or "transform," to underscore how Hopkins's conclusion requires for its essential tension both the schematic resolution of the form and the more indeterminate conclusion of the race plot. Hopkins bends her melodrama so that a form conventionally devoted to moral polarities accommodates unresolved racial conflict. That is, though narrative order is restored, once we learn all about the characters' mysterious and intertwined pasts under slavery, this knowledge offers no possibility of restoring the American social and moral order.

Instead, *Of One Blood* offers an even more visionary resolution, that of an imagined Pan-African community. Explorers on an archaeological expedition to Africa discover the ancient Ethiopian city of Meroe and argue, long before the writing of Martin Bernal's *Black Athena*, that they have established "the primal existence of the Negro as the most ancient source of all that you value in modern life, even antedating Egypt." Advocating identification with an African heritage, Hopkins also asks, "How can the Anglo-Saxon world bear the establishment of such a theory?"[23] In doing so, *Of One Blood* moves away from the domestic American setting and politics of her three earlier novels, and yet extends their reliance on the formulas of popular melodrama—disguised, false, and multiple identities, babies exchanged in the cradle, magical signs and birthmarks as proof of identity, even mysticism and the occult—in order to refigure the African American as descendant of the ancient Ethiopian and thus to refigure interracial relations on the model of a global family. The biblical refrain runs throughout the novel: "Of one blood have I made all nations of men to dwell upon the whole face of the earth." In Hopkins's biblical riff, "nations" often reads as "races."

Simultaneously, the novel pushes against this utopian and formal resolution. The climactic revelation at the book's end exposes its central romantic triangle as consisting of two brothers and a sister, born and separated under the tangled interracial web of slavery, and doomed because literally "of one blood" and therefore incestuous. Far from invoking an imagined racial-nationalist global community of deep horizontal comradeship, in which all participants address each other as if they were loving brothers and sisters, this impossible love points instead to the horror of a national situation in which siblinghood is rooted in the past sexual brutality and oppression of American slavery. The conventional search for kinship, part of the formal apparatus of the race melodrama, is both fulfilled and exploded. Hearing the conventionally clarifying history that in this case reveals his wife to be his sister, the novel's hero "cursed with a mighty curse the bond that bound him to the white race of his native land" (594).

Hopkins finally thus also exposes the tangled erotics of national imagining. The erotic relations between Dianthe Lusk, a fair-skinned ex-slave and Fisk Jubilee singer, and Reuel Briggs, an olive-complected Harvard medical student of mysterious and apparently lower-class origins, are necessary to imagine the community, but also function to conceal that community's actual inequities and exploitations. Nowhere were these exploitations themselves of so systematically sexual a character, Benedict Anderson reminds us, than in the Creole nation-states of the Americas—as evidenced by their large mulatto and mestizo populations.[24] And so the novel leaves us with a visionary, Pan-African *amor patriae,* a promise of the restoration of the descendants of

Ethiopia to the former glory of the race. It is a national love that substitutes for the love of man and woman.

The novel's two parts, one American, one African, mirror this dichotomous resolution. The American half narrates the relations among Reuel Briggs, medical student and expert in magnetism; his only friend Aubrey Livingstone, a Southern aristocrat; and Dianthe Lusk, the beautiful ex-slave whom they both love. When she temporarily loses her memory after a train accident (in which she is taken for dead but revived by Reuel's magnetizing powers), both men conspire to hide her identity as a Negress by disguising her as a white woman, Felice Adams. In this guise Reuel marries her, but the machinations of Aubrey (who uses his knowledge of Reuel's black heritage to undermine his applications for medical positions) force Reuel to take the post of medical adviser on the archaeological expedition and to entrust Dianthe to the care of his "false friend," as, he says with unknowing accuracy, "I would entrust her to my brother, had I one" (504, 497). This section of the novel closes with the seduction of Dianthe, who inevitably succumbs to the superior "will power" and "invisible influences" of Aubrey, who then dupes her into a bigamous marriage (504–5).

The rest of the novel details the working out both of the tangled American past of the three main characters, and the future history of African Americans as "Ethiopians of the Twentieth Century."[25] This Pan-African future is at once the heritage of all blacks in the diaspora, for the ancient peoples of Ethiopia represented the range of African nations. Reuel Briggs is acknowledged by the inhabitants of the hidden city of Telassar, the remnant of the once-magnificent Ethiopian state, as their long-awaited king Ergamenes, who will restore the race to its ancient glory. They recognize him, despite (as one of the more skeptical expedition members notes) centuries of amalgamation with other races, by the birthmark on his breast, a lotus-lily that marks every descendant of the royal line. This conventional birthmark also marks the site at which Hopkins bends the melodrama to her own conflicting political purposes. For it is "God's mark to prove . . . race and descent," enabling the transformation of Dr. Reuel Briggs into King Ergamenes, and his union with the Ethiopian Queen (a reincarnation of Dianthe, but a bronze rather than white Venus) "that should give to the world a dynasty of dark-skinned rulers, whose destiny should be to restore the prestige of an ancient people" (555, 570). But it is also the fatal mark that proves Reuel and Aubrey to be "blood brothers," and Dianthe their sister. Asked whether each of the children of her slave daughter had this mark, Dianthe's long-lost grandmother says, "Yes, honey; all of one blood!" (607) The end result of this doubly incestuous relationship is that Dianthe is forced to take the poison she intended for Aubrey, who then becomes his own executioner, in the tradition of the kings of Ethiopia. Reuel returns to Africa to rule with Queen Candace over an imagined community that is already under threat: "He views, with serious apprehension, the advance of mighty nations penetrating the dark, mysterious forests of his native land" (621).

The language of blood, especially the concepts of "pure blood" and "pure race" so deeply associated with the nineteenth-century quasi-scientific study of race, was a language in which Hopkins had already deliberately entangled herself in her first novel, *Contending Forces*—as Du Bois, too, was doing in his sociological work.[26] *Of One Blood* makes blood speak conflicting languages. The bloodlines linking Reuel Briggs, Aubrey Livingstone, and Dianthe Lusk connect them first to a common slave-owning father and slave mother, and then ultimately to a glorious ancient Ethiopian dynasty. Similarly, the novel uses the formula "of one blood" both to forge Pan-African unity and to interrogate the white oppressors of blacks. Countering what he is told of "the history of the wrongs endured by the modern Ethiopian," Ai, the ancient Ethiopian prime minister, responds:

> And yet, ye are all of one blood; descended from one common father. Is there ever a flock or herd without its black member? What more beautiful than the satin gloss of the raven's wing, the soft glitter of eyes of blackest tint or the rich black fur of your own native animals? Fair-haired worshippers of Mammon, do you not know that you have been weighed in the balance and found wanting? that your course is done? that Ethiopia's bondage is about over, her travail passed? (560, 585)

We are all of one blood, the novel insists, yet God decrees that some races should rule others. This is the disturbing state of affairs the novel wants at once to repudiate in its present form (white oppression of black) and yet to claim for its utopian vision (the black race returned to its former glory). So it should not be at all surprising that Hopkins's novel imagines a racial-national community based not on horizontal relations between brothers and sisters, but rather a community rooted in profoundly vertical, dynastic relations.

Hopkins's imagined Pan-African community is conceived as a matriarchy, though one destined to await the coming of Ergamenes to inaugurate a dynasty of kings. Ethiopia, Reuel learns, was historically governed by a series of female monarchs, virgin queens, all bearing the name Candace. Moreover, the mother provides the crucial link back to his American heritage. Reuel, having "played the coward's part in hiding his origin," is freed from the bondage of passing by knowledge of his Ethiopian destiny, a hint of which he had always had from his mother (560).

> It was a tradition among those who had known him in childhood that he was descended from a race of African kings. He remembered his mother well. From her he had inherited his mysticism and his occult powers. The nature of the mystic within him was . . . the shadow of Ethiopia's power. The lotus upon his breast he knew to be a birthmark. Many a night he had been aroused from childhood's slumbers, to find his mother bending above him, . . . muttering broken sentences of prayer . . . as she examined his bosom by the candle's rays. (558)

The mother, present throughout the novel as the spirit figure "Mira" who appears to warn her children of danger, usually from one another, is represented by her own mother, old Aunt Hannah, found at the end on Aubrey's plantation, and the source of the culminating revelations about the "one blood" shared by Reuel, Aubrey, and Dianthe. Described as a noted voodoo doctor fitting the description of an African princess, the grandmother tells Dianthe the story of her family history under slavery, a story that includes the revelation of (that popular convention) the switching of babies at birth. After such a history of the destructive social relations of slavery, the novel tells us, there is no possibility for an American happy ending.

This race melodrama ends not in the tidy resolution promised by the form, but back in the same racial tangle that initiated the plot. Rather than transcending or breaking the form, the novel stretches it to accommodate new versions of the racial contradictions it seeks to manage. That is, the new Pan-African social order prefigured in Reuel's identification with all black people must be seen as originating in black womanhood; both his mother and, later, Dianthe as sister enable him to identify with the plight of African American women. "In Reuel's wrongs lay something beyond the reach of punishment by the law's arm; in it was the accumulation of years of foulest wrongs heaped upon the innocent and defenseless women of a race" (594).

Thus Hopkins's last race melodrama offers the fictional resolution of a Pan-African utopia, itself based on one of the most powerful manifestations of American racial tensions: the ideology of black motherhood and, more broadly, of black womanhood. The black mother was inadvertently granted a decisive, potentially disruptive power in forming racial identity by the very slave system that sanctioned her rape by her master and then condemned her offspring legally to follow her condition. Hopkins had initially explored this maternal territory in a specifically American political context in *Contending Forces*, where she showed that, for the black community, the "Woman Question" often conflicted with the "Negro Question"; where the ideal of purity often nullified the "true womanhood" of the black female; and where the identity of the African American woman was inextricably linked to her own painful acknowledgment of her sexual history. Like *Contending Forces*, *Of One Blood* establishes a narrative of origins traced through the maternal line—in profound mockery of slavery's law that the condition of the child follow that of the mother.

But equally important, Hopkins's work is so saturated in late-nineteenth-century popular culture that it maps virtually the full range of forms of cultural expression devoted to the representation of race relations. Some of those are expressive forms we would not expect. To the themes of the occult and mesmerism, long associated in the popular mind with suspicions of perverse sexuality, for example, she gives the historical resonance of sexual relations under slavery. In addition, the studies in occult phenomena that formed part of a newly emerging science of the mind—Hopkins's "hidden self"—offer her a quasi-scientific framework for exploring racial identity. Another emerging discipline, that of archaeology, informs part of Hopkins's analysis of the global Western imperialism well underway in 1900: Reuel's African expedition discovers treasure in the pyramids of Meroe that, we are told, "was collected finally, after indemnifying the government, and carefully exported to England, where it rests today in the care of the Society of Geographical Research" (540). Hopkins draws, too, on the debates of the black women's club movement as well as on the traditions of black nationalism and Pan-Africanism. Despite its masculinist reputation, black nationalist discourse at this time generated some striking views of race-gender relations, as we will see in the case of Du Bois. Culturally speaking, then, *Of One Blood* enacts its own project, summed up in the title, of affirming unity beneath the apparent diversity among social formations and groups. Differences proliferate on the surface of both text and context, but they point to the interdependence of races and nations.

> The slogan of the hour is "Keep the Negro down!" but who is clear enough in vision to decide who hath black blood and who hath it not? Can any one tell? No, not one; for in His own mysterious way He has united the white race and the black race in this new continent. By the transgression of the law He proves His own infallibility: "Of one blood have I made all nations of men to dwell upon the whole face of the earth," is as true today as when given to the inspired writers to be recorded. No man can draw the dividing line between the two races, for they are both of one blood! (607)

Toward a Sociological Melodrama of a Race Concept

Throughout his career, W. E. B. Du Bois addressed the "Negro problem" or, as he insisted, the Negro problems, "for it is not *one* problem, but rather a plexus of social problems . . . [with] . . . their one bond of unity in the fact that they group themselves about those Africans whom two centuries of slave-trading brought into the land."[27] Refuting the stereotype that *the* Negro problem is his genetic inferiority, Du Bois here in 1898 also alludes in part to two particular social issues that would always concern him. The questions of the Africanism of the American black and of his family life intersect repeatedly in the different views of nationalism and sexuality that Du Bois promulgated in a variety of expressive forms throughout his career. As early as 1898, then, Du Bois was already leaning toward one of his major, lifelong approaches to the problems of race in America, that of Pan-Africanism, a philosophy sometimes said to have lain dormant until revived through his organization of the first Pan-African Congress at the Versailles Peace Conference after World War II. Pan-Africanism, with its goal of a world community of blacks, of an African family that had never existed before, implicitly raises the other major issue through which Du Bois continued to analyze race throughout his career: the family, and particularly the role of the mother within the structure of the black family.

Methodologically, Du Bois carried out this analysis through a variety of disciplinary forms, using both science and art—particularly, we will see, the race melodrama—as sources for his study of the familial and global black communities. He himself, however, was not so sanguine about the multidisciplinary approach. "My career as a scientist was to be swallowed up in my role as master of propaganda," wrote Du Bois in *Dusk of Dawn: An Essay Toward an Autobiography of a Race Concept* (1940). And yet the dividing line in his work between science and politics—or between science and art, since Du Bois had insisted elsewhere that "all Art is propaganda"—is not always so apparent, nor is it necessarily useful.[28] Tracing the trajectory of that intersection, from the categorically sociological writing of his early years to the more visionary, prophetic, or poetic work of cultural interpretation for which he became better known, will give us access to the particularly Du Boisean variant on the race melodrama. Though kinship always remains at the center, the early scientific, factual conception of the family, based on statistics and tables of figures, gives way to kinship as an extended metaphor for global race relations. Or, to quote Du Bois's own formulation, in *Dusk of Dawn,* of the trajectory of the race concept which dominated his life:

> It was for me as I have written first a matter of dawning realization, then of study and science; then a matter of inquiry into the diverse strands of my own family; and finally consideration of my connection, physical and spiritual, with Africa and the Negro race in its homeland. (133)

Du Bois did most of his research in sociology after his graduate work at Harvard, where, since sociology did not yet exist as a separate discipline, he studied in the history and political science departments and was significantly influenced by Jamesian pragmatism. He completed his graduate studies at the University of Berlin, where he studied economics and history under the Prussian nationalist Heinrich von Treitschke, and sociology under Gustav von Schmoller's empirically and inductively oriented approach to social policy. This kind of multidisciplinary training was typical for the social scientist of the 1890s, when sociology was just emerging as an academic discipline from the more generalized field of "social science," which included political economy, government, social problems, history, and even social ethics. Despite this intensely classical education, as an American black he could not expect a position at a major university. Following a constricting two-year stint teaching Greek and Latin at Wilberforce, a black parochial school, in 1896 Du Bois was offered a nominal temporary appointment at the University of Pennsylvania and the opportunity to study the black community of Philadelphia, then the largest such in the North. The resulting pioneering study, *The Philadelphia Negro* (1899), led to the ambitious *Atlanta University Publications* (1896–1914), directed by Du Bois during his thirteen years as professor of economics at Atlanta University.

The epic aims of the Atlanta series, partially visible in the Philadelphia study's "final design" to provide information "toward the solution of the many Negro problems of a great American city," suggest how deeply Du Bois, like so many of his contemporaries, believed in the use of scientific investigation as a means of cultural suasion and social change. He conceived of the Atlanta studies as a kind of sociological epic, "a comprehensive plan for studying a human group" in the form of a hundred-year program, consisting of ten-year cycles of volumes on the ten "great subjects" of black life, which would provide "a body of sociological material unsurpassed in human annals." The object of these studies was "primarily scientific . . . a careful search for truth . . . but this is not our sole object; we wish not only to make the Truth clear but to present it in such shape as will encourage and help social reform." In fact, Du Bois was here already joining the scientist to the master of propaganda, maintaining a scientific orientation in the belief, common within the emerging discipline of sociology at this time, that social reform could be built on the foundation of empirically based data.[29]

The Philadelphia Negro relied on intensive door-to-door interviewing to study the geographic distribution of blacks in Philadelphia, "their occupations and daily life, their homes, their organizations, and, above all, their relation to their million white fellow citizens." On the other hand *The Negro American Family* (published in 1908 as one of the Atlanta series) relied on printed sources and a supplemental study of thirteen families for its study of the black family—"its formation, its home, its economic organization and its daily life."[30] In making environmental rather than racial explanations of their subject, both works, however, ignore the current genetic approach to social theory. Instead, they often deplore certain black social patterns, particularly patterns of sexual promiscuity, lack of respect for womanhood and motherhood, and the absence of a real home life. But without a genetic basis, Du Bois's descriptions of his race are, as Arnold Rampersad argues and we shall see, descriptions of a nation. These sociological studies are therefore "historic documents in the representation of black American cultural nationalism."[31]

Du Bois's studies of black family life thus begin in the place of common African ancestry, though they always attribute to slavery's malign influence the far greater power. "Slavery gave the monogamic family ideal to slaves," he wrote in *The Negro American Family*, "but it compelled and desired only the most imperfect practice of its most ordinary morals" (21–22). As to the problem of documenting this situation, he warns at the opening of the study about the unreliability of the literature of slavery: "It is difficult to get a clear picture of the family relations of slaves, between the Southern apologist and his picture of cabin life, with idyllic devotion and careless toil, and that of the abolitionist with his tale of family disruption and cruelty, adultery and illegitimate mulattoes." Despite these misgivings, however, the evidence he cites documents the sexual irregularities under slavery, the separation of parents and children, and the proliferation of the mulatto population—all elements we are familiar with from the race melodrama (1, 18–26). How are we to square his skepticism about the slave literature with his reliance in both the bibliography and the text on such sources as Mrs. Elizabeth D. Livermore's *Zoe; or the Quadroon Triumph*—again, clearly a work of the race melodrama genre? To answer this question, we must first return to the African beginnings that open each major section of the study: "Marriage," "The Home," "The Economics of the Family," "The Family Group."

The connection of the African past to the American present is for Du Bois the starting place, despite the fact that it is "exceedingly difficult and puzzling to know just where to find the broken thread of African and American social history" (9). In *The Negro American Family* he finds the beginnings of that thread in the older matrilineal kinship structure of the African family, which only gradually changed toward "the fuller patriarchal type." Quoting from studies of the Yoruba-speaking peoples and of the Gold Coast, Du Bois addresses "the extraordinary vitality the system of descent through mothers possesses," and theorizes that "the acknowledgment of a father's blood-relationship to his children was brought about . . . [only] . . . by foreign influence." Moreover,

> in spite of legal succession from father to son, children by different mothers, but by the same father, are by many natives still scarcely considered true blood relations. It is no doubt in consequence of the change from kinship in the female line to kinship on both sides of the house that the family has become, to a certain extent, disintegrated. (13–15)

Even, however, the headman of a Gold Coast family—"and by 'family,' " explains the native source, "you must understand the entire lineal descendants of a head *materfamilias,* if I may coin a convenient phrase"—has "all-powerful helpers in the female members of the family." The headman's rule in the family thus becomes "a simple and an easy matter. 'The hand that rocks the cradle rules the world' " (16).

Tracing the female thread to America, however, Du Bois finds that the economic condition of the Negro is affecting the "sex morals" of the race. Economic demand brings black women to the city (where they are hired exclusively in domestic service or sewing, according to *The Philadelphia Negro*) and keeps the men in the country, causing "a dangerous disproportion of the sexes." On this problem, he quotes from Kelly Miller's *Race Adjustment:*

> The enormous preponderance of . . . the female element . . . , especially in our large cities, is a persistent and aggravating factor. . . . The census of 1900 gives 4,447,568 Negro females against 4,393,221 Negro males, leaving an excess of 54,347 of the gentler sex in the United States. This gives a residue of thirteen leftover women to each thousand of the male population . . . , hopeless females for whom there are neither present nor prospective husbands. (36)

This is the nineteenth-century situation of black American womanhood, the vision of the excess gentler sex, those hopeless female breadwinners, sharply contrasting to the "numerous Negro queens, . . . medicine-women, and . . . the participation in public meetings permitted to women by many Negro peoples in Africa" (18).

Du Bois cites allied problems in "sexual mores," most of which have to do with the alleged "impurity" and "immorality" of the black woman, the heritage of debased sexual and social relations under slavery. He devotes equal attention, though, to refuting the resulting charges of impurity among black women, as did the black women's club movement at this time, quoting testimony from social workers and educators in North and South to support his argument that, if the great but unacknowledged class differentiation among American blacks were to be accepted, it would become clear that sexual irregularity is a problem only of the "masses." Hence the conclusions offered in both *The Philadelphia Negro* and *The Negro American Family* that "the better classes of the Negroes should recognize their duty toward the masses" and, indeed, that the "better classes have their chief excuse for being in the work they may do toward lifting the rabble" (*PN*, 392–93). This paternalism fits well with Du Bois's early doctrine of the talented tenth—his belief that it would be the exceptional, well-educated black men who would lead and elevate the masses—as do his specific recommendations for the transition of the masses "from . . . moral darkness to enlightenment," all of which rest on increasing reverence for womanhood, marriage, and motherhood (153).

Writing from the perspective of the 1920s and 1940s, Du Bois came much closer to locating the broken thread of African and American social history in the concept—the imaginary resolution, so to speak—of Africa the motherland. Simultaneously he identified the black race as a whole with black womanhood. "To no modern race do its women mean so much as to the Negro," he wrote in *Darkwater* in a chapter entitled "The Damnation of Women,"

> nor [do they] come so near to the fulfillment of its meaning. As one of our women writes: "Only the black woman can say 'when and where I enter, in the quiet, undisputed dignity of my womanhood, without violence and without suing or special patronage, then and there the whole Negro race enters with me.' "[32]

Du Bois invokes a mythic belief in the "mother-idea" as an innately African concept, one of the great cultural gifts given to the world by the black race. Moreover, he goes even further in his gendering of global relations: "The father and his worship is Asia; Europe is the precocious, self-centered, forward-striving child; but the land of the mother is and was Africa" (513). Creating his own kinship-based narrative locating the origins of human development in Africa, Du Bois also traces his own lineage back to the African motherland, explicitly through a matrilineal descent line: "As I remember . . . backward among my own family, it is the mother I ever recall— . . . All the way back in these dim distances it is mothers and mothers of mothers who seem to count, while fathers are shadowy memories" (514). Historically, this maternal romance is sharply juxtaposed to "the traffic in men" of American slavery, which "struck like doom . . . upon this African mother-idea." Though we know only too well the outcome of this encounter, Du Bois reframes, again in gender-specific terms, how "the crushing weight of slavery fell on black women. Under it there was no legal marriage, no legal family, no legal control over children" (516).

At this point he draws, practically verbatim, on the same sources from the slavery literature that he had both critiqued and used earlier in *The Negro American Family,* but here, to their weight as sociological evidence, he adds the power of race melodrama, latent in the earlier study, "to see the hell beneath the system." On the separation of parents and children, for example, he quotes the Presbyterian synod of Kentucky to its churches in 1835: Families "are torn asunder and permitted to see each other no more."

The shrieks and agony witnessed on such occasions proclaim, with a trumpet tongue, the iniquity of our system. . . . There is not a village or road that does not behold the sad procession of manacled outcasts whose mournful countenances tell that they are exiled by force from all that their hearts hold dear. (516)

Or another example, this one from an unnamed "sister of a president of the United States": "We Southern ladies are complimented with the names of wives, but we are only the mistresses of seraglios" (516). Fusing the documentary evidence he had gathered twenty-three years earlier with his new concept of "woman and color," Du Bois retells the African American "history of insult and degradation" as a maternal melodrama, "both fearful and glorious," that "has birthed the haunting prostitute . . . ,"

but has also given the world an efficient womanhood, whose strength lies in freedom and whose chastity was won in the teeth of temptation and not in prison and swaddling clothes. . . . No other women on earth could have emerged from the hell of force and temptation which once engulfed and still surrounds black women in America. (517, 523, 526)

The ultimate resolution to the Du Boisean race melodrama is, like Pauline Hopkins's, the imagined Pan-African community. It is a community marked racially through color and hair, but, Du Bois says in *Dusk of Dawn,* "the badge of color . . . [is] . . . relatively unimportant save as a badge; the real essence of this kinship is its social heritage of slavery; . . . and this heritage binds together not simply the children of Africa, but extends through yellow Asia and into the South Seas. It is this unity that draws me to Africa" (117). African unity is thus dialectical, both a conjuring of the pre-Oedipal, precapitalist mythic past in the motherland and a product of the slave trade in the American fatherland. As imaginary resolution it not only acknowledges Du Bois's own interracial family history, but also the contradictory history of a race concept. "Perhaps," Du Bois concludes in *Dusk of Dawn,* "it is wrong to speak of it at all as 'a concept' rather than as a group of contradictory forces, facts, and tendencies" (133). Such a multiple and contradictory set of forces as "race" requires precisely the multiple, and to his mind contradictory, methodologies—those of science, propaganda, even the art of the race melodrama—that Du Bois used throughout his career.

The Content of the Form/The Form in History

Even the sketchy evidence offered here demonstrates the remarkable range of topics accommodated by the American race melodrama. From Twain's tragedies of mulatto patricide to Hopkins's well-researched tale of American incest and the African origins of civilization, to Du Bois's unfolding narrative of a Pan-African race concept, this popular form was responsive to the finest distinctions in late-nineteenth-century philosophies and ideologies of race.

Far from an inert, formulaic genre, it responded with different resolutions to different conceptions of racial tensions and conflict. It has—as Du Bois said in *Dusk of Dawn* of the race concept itself—"all sorts of illogical trends and irreconcilable tendencies." Form follows function, we might say.

Certain important trends emerge, however, from among the three case studies represented by Twain, Hopkins, and Du Bois. The genre divides formally into what might be conventionally defined as tragedy and romance, depending on the particular conception of race assumed or promulgated by an individual work. As Twain's inverted tragic mulattoes demonstrate, when race is represented as a sole, determining social formation, the one determinant of individual identity, then tragedy is inevitably the result both formally and socially. Kinship is an issue insofar as it can establish individual racial identity, and establishment of that identity ends in its renunciation along with rejection of kinship. The individual, not the community, is the fundamental social unit of the race melodrama in its tragic mode. The national and, indeed, global scope of racial conflict at the turn of the century is thus contained in the tragic race melodrama, which defines race as a problem primarily limited to the individual.

And yet Twain, well-known as a vocal anti-imperialist, also believed in what Du Bois called in *The Philadelphia Negro* "the duty of whites" to cooperate with blacks in their self-help efforts. In that now celebrated letter written the year *Huckleberry Finn* was published, Twain explained to the dean of the Yale Law School why he wanted to pay the expenses of a black law student whom he had met briefly on one occasion: "I do not believe I would very cheerfully help a white student who would ask a benevolence of a stranger, but I do not feel so about the other color. We have ground the manhood out of them, & the shame is ours, not theirs; and we should pay for it."[33] Perhaps the contradictory impulses exhibited in Twain's life and art—the desire for interracial, communal benevolence vying with both the will to self-punishment ("we should pay for it") and the individualistic, tragic mode of his race melodramas—account for their unfinished state. Twain's version of the contradictory forces of Du Bois's race concept: race as the tragic fate of the individual versus race as the responsibility of a biracial community.

However, in its romance mode the race melodrama accommodates communal rather than individualistic conceptions of race. Both Hopkins and Du Bois may be said to write romances of community that invert the relationship between identity and kinship in Twain's narratives: individual identity becomes significant as a means to establish patterns of kinship and community. This community may be the autonomous urban black culture of the boarding house and church in Hopkins's *Contending Forces,* or the rural world of the Southern black folk (and their middle-class uplifters) in Frances Harper's *Iola Leroy,* or the domestic, woman-centered sphere of Mrs. A. E. Johnson's novel *The Hazeley Family* (1894), or the Pan-African community envisioned by both Hopkins and Du Bois.[34] As an imaginary resolution of racial tensions, the community is oriented as much to the future as to the past, constructing a visionary, prospective history as well as reconstructing the past. Thus Du Bois concludes even his most empirically oriented studies with words of general advice about social reform and social change. Moreover, race is represented not as a single, determining category but as something mediated explicitly through other social categories, primarily gender and nationalism. In the romance mode the race melodrama offers a complex social analysis where racial forces are understood either as generally sexualized (Hopkins) or specifically maternal or paternal (Du Bois). Both of these variants confirm that, as Hortense Spillers argues, American genders are always racially inflected.[35]

Despite the sometimes overwhelmingly structural, formal properties of the race melodrama, it is finally a form in history. The concept of an imagined racial community, for example, leads both Hopkins and Du Bois to a global refiguring of the national, so that black nationalism may become Pan-Africanism. At the very moment of the historical consolidation of world imperialism, we might say, these visionaries summon up the future postcolonial world. If these are limits and possibilities of the American race melodrama at the turn of the century, what, we might conclude by asking, became of it later?

On the one hand, there is the institutionalization of the race melodrama in the arena of social policy. The 1965 *Moynihan Report* sometimes sounds as though it might have been written by Du Bois in 1898. "It was by destroying the Negro family under slavery," the report asserts, "that white America broke the will of the Negro people" (30). Du Bois made the same assessment of slavery's destruction of the black family, but he came, of course, to radically different conclusions about its effect on "black will." The plot is the same, we might say, but the resolution differs, because the nature of the context in which the form speaks is different. Du Bois wrote at the turn of the century in the midst of a full-scale national effort to reinterpret slavery, the Civil War, and its aftermath, usually with the goal of healing sectionalism and fostering national reconciliation, which meant a glossing over or active denial of the slave's experience. Nevertheless, such a revisionary project also meant that slavery was an issue of recent memory to be discussed and debated, rather than, as in the 1960s urban conflict that defines *The Moynihan Report*, a stereotypical touchstone or cliché that few would question. This is the process of the form in history, with *The Moynihan Report* as a new form of the race melodrama.

On the other hand, the race melodrama has also entered new popular cultural spheres in the form, for example, of the musical (*Showboat*) and the maternal melodrama in film (*Imitation of Life*). The protean quality of this highly adaptable nineteenth-century American form could hardly be better demonstrated than by this range of twentieth-century examples. Indeed, we might say of the race melodrama what Du Bois said of the Negro problem itself: "though we ordinarily speak of the Negro problem as though it were one unchanged question, students must recognize the obvious facts that this problem, like others, has had a long historical development, has changed with the growth and evolution of the nation."[36]

14

Runaway Tongue: Resistant Orality in *Uncle Tom's Cabin, Our Nig, Incidents in the Life of a Slave Girl,* and *Beloved*

Harryette Mullen

The mainstream appeal of Harriet Beecher Stowe's *Uncle Tom's Cabin* cata-lyzed literary as well as political activity in the nineteenth century. Leaving aside the numerous attacks, defenses, adaptations, imitations, and parodies the book inspired among white writers, let us note that Stowe, through the unprecedented popularity of her sympathetic black characters, had an impact on black writers so immediate that *Uncle Tom's Cabin* can be regarded as an important precursor of the African American novel. Through the broad influ-ence of this fictional work, Stowe almost single-handedly turned the interests of black readers and writers to the political, cultural, and economic possibili-ties of the novel. Recognizing the value of their personal and collective experi-ence, black writers of both fictional and nonfictional works were influenced by Stowe's exploitation of subliterary genres, her provocative combination of sentimental and slave narrative conventions, and her successful production of a text at once popular and ideological.[1]

Certainly Stowe provided an enabling textual model, especially for fledg-ling writers struggling to represent the subjectivity of black women; yet an-other way of looking at the response of black women writers in the nineteenth century to *Uncle Tom's Cabin* is to notice the different ways their texts "talk back" to Stowe's novel. Stowe's grafting of the sentimental novel, a literary genre associated with white women and the ideology of female domestication, onto the slave narrative, a genre associated with the literary production of black men and linking literacy with freedom and manhood, is countered by black women writers who produced texts that ask where the black woman finds herself, caught between these two literary models. Stowe uses the slave narrative as a reservoir of fact, experience, and realism, while constructing black characters as objects of sentimentality in order to augment the emotive power and political significance of her text.

Harriet Jacobs, the only black woman author to publish a book-length fugitive slave narrative, and Harriet Wilson, the first published black woman novelist, place the slave narrative and the sentimental genre in dialogue, and often in conflict, in order to suggest the ideological limits of "true womanhood" or bourgeois femininity, while they also call into question Frederick Douglass's paradigmatic equation of literacy, freedom, and manhood in his 1845 *Narrative*. As Harriet Jacob's text *Incidents in the Life of a Slave Girl* (1861) and numerous dictated narratives of ex-slaves also suggest, slaves countered institutionalized illiteracy with a resistant orality. Not everyone found opportunities to steal literacy or successfully escape slavery as a fugitive, but oral transmission passed on the verbal skills of runaway tongues: the sass, spunk, and infuriating impudence of slaves who individually and collectively refused to know their place.

Nineteenth-century black women writers struggled in their texts to reconcile an oral tradition of resistance with a literary tradition of submission. Jane Tompkins, while arguing in favor of reading sentimental novels for the "cultural work" they accomplished, nevertheless reads them as texts that instruct women to accept their culturally defined roles in order to exercise the power available to bourgeois white women operating within the ideological limits of "true womanhood."[2]

Slave narratives, on the other hand, do not advise submission to a higher authority imagined as benign; they celebrate flight from overt oppression. Having neither the incentive of cultural rewards available to some white women nor the mobility available to some male fugitives, slave women in particular and black women more generally would have found both the slave narrative and the sentimental novel deficient representations of their experience as black women. For this reason the texts of nineteenth-century black women writers concentrate not only on reconciling the contradictions of disparate literary conventions, but also on grafting literacy onto orality. Their texts, by focusing on a continuum of resistance to oppression available to the illiterate as well as the literate, tend to stress orality as a presence over illiteracy as an absence. The oral tradition often permitted a directness of expression (particularly within family networks in less Europeanized slave communities) about matters of sex, violence, and sexual violence that literary convention—particularly the indirection and euphemistic language of sentimental fiction in its concern with modesty and decorum—rendered "unspeakable." It is in the oral tradition (itself preserved through transcription), rather than either the sentimental novel or the male-dominated slave narrative genre, that we find the most insistent representations of strong black women resisting oppression and also passing on, through their oral expression to their daughters, a tradition of resistance to physical and sexual abuse from white women and men.

Illiterate slave women operated within a tradition of resistant orality, or verbal self-defense, which included speech acts variously labeled sassy or saucy, impudent, impertinent, or insolent: the speech of slaves who refused to know their place, who contested their assigned social and legal inferiority as slaves and as black women.[3] "Impudence" has a sexual connotation: the impudent woman is an outspoken "shameless hussy" whose sexual materiality (pudenda) is exposed. The impudent woman refuses to be modestly silent. Rather, she speaks the violation and exposure, the sexual, reproductive, and economic exploitation of her body, revealing the implicit contradictions of the sex-gender system which render her paradoxically both vulnerable and threatening. Her speech as well as her sexuality threaten patriarchal order, so that her immodest verbal expression and sexual behavior are continually monitored, controlled, and suppressed. The exposure of the slave woman's body—in the field where she worked, on the auction block, at the public whipping post, along with her sexual vulnerability within the master's household—is at odds with the hidden sexuality and corresponding modesty of the respectable bourgeois white woman, whose body is covered, confined, and sheltered within the patriarchal household designated as her domestic sphere.

The literary tradition that produces the sentimental novel is concerned with the white woman's assumption of her proper place, upon her internalization of the values of propriety and decorum, while the African American oral tradition represents the exposed black woman who uses impudent speech in order to defend her own body against abuse. In some instances the stark materiality of their embodied existence gave black women a clarity of vision about their position as slaves and as women that could occasionally produce the riveting eloquence of an Isabella Baumfree, the former slave woman whose chosen name, Sojourner Truth, encapsulates both her determination to move beyond the static confinement of female existence, and the bold self-authorization of an illiterate black woman to enter a discourse from which she had automatically been excluded.

If institutionalized illiteracy was intended to exempt African Americans from access to or participation in the discursive formations of bourgeois society, then to the extent that it succeeded, it also left them outside conventional ideological constructions that played a part in determining white identities. To the degree that undisguised coercion permeated their lives and invaded the interior of their bodies, the self-awareness of such black women was unobscured by ideological constructions of the dominant race and class that shielded the majority of bourgeois white women from sustained consciousness of their own genteel subjugation. Sojourner Truth, memorialized as a body with a voice, packs into a concise "immodest" gesture the ability to shame those who attempt to shame her as a woman. Her power is built upon the paradox of the black woman's possession of a public voice. Because she has endured much worse in slavery, the fear of public humiliation cannot threaten her into silence. She holds up under the gaze of the heckler intent on shaming her off the lecture platform, calmly enduring the scrutiny of an audience demanding the exposure of her body, supposedly to "prove" that she was a woman, but in fact to punish her for daring to speak in public to a "promiscuous" assembly. Freed from slavery as well as the need to embody the dominant cultural aesthetic of feminine purity, Sojourner Truth could present herself as a black woman unabashed by her body's materiality.

Lydia Maria Child's introduction to Jacobs's narrative expresses the concern of white women with a feminine delicacy too easily contaminated by association with the materiality of black women's experience, as much as it suggests a racial division of labor in which white women bore the ideological burden of trying to embody pure womanhood, while black women suffered the harsh materiality of female experience unsoftened by ideology.[4] Child's sponsoring of Jacobs's narrative in order to unveil the "monstrous features" of slavery, especially its component of female sexual slavery, might be read as a response to Stowe's assertion that the successful artist must "draw a veil" over slavery.[5] Child endorses Jacobs in an attempt to divest the white woman reader of the ideological veil that separates her from black women's experience. An unusual instance of a black woman publicly stripping a white woman of her clothing, if not her ideology, occurs in the oral account of the slave woman Cornelia, remembering the spirited resistance of her mother to the physical abuse of a mistress.

> One day my mother's temper ran wild. For some reason Mistress Jennings struck her with a stick. Ma struck back and a fight followed. Mr. Jennings was not at home and the children became frightened and ran upstairs. For half [an] hour they wrestled in the kitchen. Mistress, seeing that she could not get the better of ma, ran out in the road, with ma right on her heels. In the road, my mother flew into her again. The thought seemed to race across my mother's mind to tear mistress' clothing off her body. She suddenly began to tear Mistress Jennings' clothes off. She caught hold, pulled, ripped and tore. Poor mistress was nearly naked when the storekeeper got to them and pulled ma off. "Why, Fannie, what do you mean by that?" he asked. "Why, I'll kill her, I'll kill her dead if she ever strikes me again."[6]

As Sojourner Truth turned the supposed shame of exposing her breasts back onto her brash male accusers and the ladies who were too abashed to look at her body, Fannie's runaway temper turns the slave's degradation back onto her mistress with a gesture intended to shame the white woman who was not too delicate to beat a black woman. The humiliation involved in being publicly stripped seems calculated to deny the white woman the superior status assigned her in the race-gender hierarchy. Fannie's inspired frenzy leads her to attack the white woman's sense of modesty and decorum. This behavior, along with the threat to "kill her dead" if she is beaten again, demonstrates how completely she rejects the idea that her mistress is her superior. Fannie's overt resistance and violent temper initiate a chain reaction of dire consequences affecting her entire family, especially her daughter Cornelia, from whom she is separated after this incident and another violent confrontation with white men hired to punish Fannie with a public flogging.

> Pa heard Mr. Jennings say that Fannie would have to be whipped by law. He told ma. Two mornings afterwards, two men came in at the big gate, one with a long lash in his hand. I was in the yard and I hoped they couldn't find ma. To my surprise, I saw her running around the house, straight in the direction of the men. She must have seen them coming. I should have known that she wouldn't hide. She knew what they were coming for, and she intended to meet them halfway. She swooped upon them like a hawk on chickens. I believe they were afraid of her or thought she was crazy. One man had a long

beard which she grabbed with one hand, and the lash with the other. Her body was made strong with madness. She was a good match for them. Mr. Jennings came and pulled her away. I don't know what would have happened if he hadn't come at that moment, for one man had already pulled his gun out. Ma did not see the gun until Mr. Jennings came up. On catching sight of it, she said, "Use your gun, use it and blow my brains out if you will."[7]

Fannie's open defiance makes her too dangerous to remain on the small farm, so she is hired out and sent away. Her determined resistance also nearly results in her committing infanticide when her master threatens, in addition, to separate Fannie from her youngest child.

"Fannie, leave the baby with Aunt Mary," said Mr. Jennings very quietly. At this, ma took the baby by its feet, a foot in each hand, and with the baby's head swinging downward, she vowed to smash its brains out before she'd leave it. Tears were streaming down her face. It was seldom that ma cried, and everyone knew that she meant every word. Ma took her baby with her.[8]

The mother's subjectivity is underscored by her daughter's oral account, dictated to a Fisk University sociologist around 1929. Through this dictation, Cornelia's memory preserves her mother's small triumphs as a slave, even though both had paid the price of a lengthy separation for Fannie's victories. Indeed, it is only in her mother's absence that Cornelia comes to understand:

Yes, ma had been right. Slavery was chuck full of cruelty and abuse. I was the oldest child. My mother had three other children by the time I was about six years old. It was at this age that I remember the almost daily talks of my mother on the cruelty of slavery. I would say nothing to her, but I was thinking all the time that slavery did not seem so cruel. Master and Mistress Jennings were not mean to my mother. It was she who was mean to them.[9]

Their forced separation changes Cornelia's opinions about slavery and about her mother. It also transforms her own personality, as she emulates her mother and becomes a fighter. Only in Fannie's absence does she decide to "follow [her] mother's example," and only then does it occur to her that the madwoman who had threatened to murder her baby, and had challenged white men to "blow my brains out if you will," was "the smartest black woman" in their community. Stressing her mother's bold intention "to meet [her punishers] halfway," Cornelia is alert to the fugitive "thought [that] seemed to race across [her] mother's mind," as Jacobs's narrative endorses the runaway tongue of slaves her master intended to silence. While the slave narratives employ the trope of writing on the body, with the narrator transformed from a body written upon to a body that writes, Cornelia's illiterate mother Fannie relies upon the spoken word to figuratively brand her child in order to give her some defense against the physical and sexual abuse of slaveholders. "The one doctrine of my mother's teaching which was branded upon my senses was that I should never let anyone abuse me. 'I'll kill you, gal, if you don't stand up for yourself,' she would say. 'Fight, and if you can't fight, kick; if you can't kick, then bite.' "[10]

The older woman's language is situated in the violence of slavery, from which she hopes to protect her daughter by instilling in her the spirit to fight back. Cornelia's retrospection also resorts to the violent imagery of branding. Fannie does not threaten to "kill" her daughter in order to teach her docility, but rather to burn her words into her daughter's memory and impress on her the importance of her message. The harsh words of the mother simultaneously teach the daughter what she can expect as a slave and how to resist it. A continuous tradition of resistance also contextualizes the trope of women's bodies and voices as oppositional or supplemental historical texts, motivating the women of Gayl Jones's novel *Corregidora* (1975) to see their bodies as the means to preserve an oral record of atrocities endured in slavery.[11] Within the folk milieu, the African American mother's persistent practice of a labor-intensive oral transmission and her distrust of the labor-saving technologies of writing and print culture are the result of her systematic exclusion from the discourses of educated people, whom she often has reason to count among her oppressors. The reliance on resistant orality results from the placement of slaves, blacks, women, and the poor at the coercive interface of literacy and orality, with the institutionalization of illiteracy as a mode of "silencing" populations rendered "voiceless" so long as their words are not written, published, or disseminated within a master discourse. It is this effect of discursive silencing that the ex-slave narratives and other abolitionist writings attempted to overcome, producing black speaking subjects within a counterhegemonic discursive practice. The textualization of African American subjectivity makes black voices discursively audible and black speakers discursively visible.

While Harriet Jacobs's literacy was a tremendous source of empowerment, it also exposed her to an even more concentrated dose of the ideology of domesticity than the training she received while living and working in the homes of white women and observing their behavior. Quoting Frances Smith Foster's observation that, in the minds of white women, the black woman's "ability to survive degradation was her downfall . . . since her submission to repeated violations was not in line with the values of sentimental heroines who died rather than be abused," Hazel Carby stresses the role of nineteenth-century literature as a major transmitter of an ideology of womanhood that polarized black womanhood "against white womanhood in the metaphoric system of female sexuality, particularly through the association of black women with overt sexuality and taboo sexual practices."[12]

However, Jacobs is resourceful, almost visionary, in her use of writing to place in dialogue literary and extraliterary resources. From her "loophole of retreat" in the slaveholding South as well as her attic servant's room in the North, she manipulates the ideology of domesticity through successive recombinations of tropes on the home as woman's shelter and prison. In the text, her various confining positions within the sub- and superinteriors of the white household become loopholes in the patriarchal institutions of property, slavery, and marriage, where she gains insight into domestic ideology, allowing her to question and revise the figure of the woman whose interiority is derived from her confinement in domestic space. Thus she is able to link the bondage of slavery with the bonds of marriage and childbearing. Her creative appropriation of literature, which allowed her the latitude to identify herself with Robinson Crusoe the adventurer at the same time that she identified in her bondage with the slave owner Crusoe's native sidekick Friday, suggests that the racial and social ambiguities informing her life developed in her a self-affirming intelligence, a life-affirming empathy, along with a notable capacity for the imaginative transformation and reconstruction of metaphorical and ideological material.[13] Jacobs extends the oral family history she knows through the matrilineal heritage of her maternal grandmother and great-grandmother, in contrast to Frederick Douglass, who constructs himself as the first member of his slave family to acquire a voice. His darker-skinned family members remain symbolically in the dark while he, the master's unacknowl-edged son, becomes enlightened.[14] Within his text they are narratively silent, while his literacy bestows upon him the authority of a narrator.

Harriet Jacobs's narrative, which may be seen as ascribing gender to the generic (male) narrative genre, demonstrates that it is possible to appropriate bourgeois ideology to affirm the humanity of slaves and illiterates—without Douglass's rhetorical conflation of literacy, freedom, and manhood, which reinforces rather than challenges the symbolic emasculation of the male slave and the silencing of the female slave. Because she associates the slave's hu-manity with defiant or subversive speech, resistant behavior, and the ethics of reciprocal relationships, as well as with writing and individual autonomy, Jacobs affirms the humanity of the collectivity of slaves as well as the success-ful fugitive and literate narrator. Jacobs implicitly regards her own narrative voice as the continuation of other voices, especially that of her grandmother, whose story she reiterates in the process of telling her own story.

For Jacobs, literacy serves to record for a reading audience a continuity of experience already constructed and preserved within her family through oral accounts. She credits without question the oral history of her family that her grandmother supplies, while Douglass uses orally transmitted information cautiously, and is suspicious of any fact not verified by a written document. While Jacobs reproduces and extends the story of her family that she had heard all her life from her grandmother, in Douglass's 1845 text the narrator's acquisition of literacy represents a discontinuity, a definite break with the past, signaling the emergence of a new consciousness. He later states in *My Bondage and My Freedom* that his mother in fact was literate. Yet for the purposes of his first narrative, she is represented as holding him in the dark during her occasional night visits before her death. As a slave she is symboli-cally with him "in the night" of ignorance and illiteracy.[15] The narrative is the story of a slave son's resistance to the imposed destiny of a slave woman's offspring, his determination *not* to follow the condition of his mother, but to seek mastery through the instrumental literacy of his father.

In figuring literacy as radical discontinuity, Douglass foregrounds his own emerging subjectivity within the text against the literal and metaphorical dark-ness and silence that envelop other slaves, including members of his own family, who remain narratively silent in his depiction of them. Douglass is perhaps unique in the consistency of this figuration. The bond that he forges between freedom and literacy is managed rhetorically by a narrative silencing of the voices of other slaves; yet this insistent tropology has become, paradoxically, the source of the paradigmatic status of this text within the slave narrative genre. Henry Bibb and William Wells Brown, for instance, are much closer to Jacobs in their acquisition and appreciation of literacy without overvaluing it, and in their use of the narrative voice as an expressive construction of continuity in the face of cultural disruption.[16]

Jacobs's text may be usefully contrasted with Douglass's in her depiction of an instance of the master's punishing a slave. In both cases the slave's punishment may be traced back to a sexual transgression committed by the master. Douglass's Aunt Hester, who has apparently replaced his mother Harriet as the object of the master's lustful desires, is beaten when she defiantly visits her black lover on a neighboring plantation. The master indulges himself in an orgiastic flogging, with the young child Frederick an eyewitness to the "horrible exhibition" of Hester's naked, bleeding body. His harrowing description of the first flogging he ever witnessed employs a balanced rhetoric of repetitions and antitheses as a mimetic device. He flails away at the reader with his language, making the scene disturbingly vivid. The flogging is primarily a visual rather than an aural experience, with Hester's voice unable to affect the master. "No words, no tears, no prayers" move him. All are as ineffective as her "most heart-rendering shrieks." If anything, her voice seems to egg him on: her screams constitute one side of a ghastly, mostly nonverbal, dialogue that Douglass represents as an obscene call and response in which language is debased, and discourse is reduced to "her shrieks and his horrid oaths."[17]

Jacobs serves as "earwitness" to the beating of a man whose wife is among their master's concubines. Jacobs deals more explicitly with the slave woman's sexual subjugation than Douglass, who is always reluctant, in the 1845 *Narrative,* to rely upon information transmitted orally by slaves, which he generally treats as unsubstantiated gossip or "whispered" opinion, inferior to authenticating (written) documents, perhaps anticipating the skepticism of contemporary historians who are reluctant to state that black women were raped in slavery, and who not surprisingly find scarce documentation of sexual abuse in the journals of slaveholders. In addition, Douglass almost silences his Aunt Hester in the stress he lays on the inability of her voice to affect the master who beats her. Hester's speech is not recorded in his narrative. Jacobs concentrates on her own response to the master's violence, rather than on the implacable master, unmoved by the slave's voice and speech.

When I had been in the family [of doctor Flint] a few weeks, one of the plantation slaves was brought to town, by order of his master. It was near night when he arrived, and Dr. Flint ordered him to be taken to the work house, and tied up to the joist, so that his feet would just escape the ground. In that situation he was to wait till the doctor had taken his tea. I shall never forget that night. Never before, in my life, had I heard hundreds of blows fall, in succession, on a human being. His piteous groans, and his "O, pray don't, massa," rang in my ears for months afterwards.[18]

Her textual strategy does not involve the mimetic rhetoric Douglass employs, but a mimesis of quotation and a narrative constructed from collective testimony. Rather than mirror the master's silencing of the slave, rendering the slave as a silent victim, she represents the slave as a speaker in the text, a more dialogic practice of writing. Jacobs gives a voice to the slave specifically to counter the master's attempt to silence the man and his wife, whose fugitive tongues have "run too far" from his control.

> I went into the work house next morning, and saw the cowhide still wet with blood, and the boards all covered with gore. The poor man lived, and continued to quarrel with his wife. A few months afterwards Dr. Flint handed them both over to a slave-trader. The guilty man put their value into his pocket, and had the satisfaction of knowing that they were out of sight and hearing. When the mother was delivered into the trader's hands, she said, "You *promised* to treat me well." To which he replied, "You have let your tongue run too far, damn you!" She had forgotten that it was a crime for a slave to tell who was the father of her child.[19]

Although Jacobs does reinforce the aural with visual proof, the result of her own investigation, she sifts through "conjecture," relying overtly upon the knowledge and speech of slaves to penetrate beyond the official story of a slave whipped for "stealing corn." Through sight and sound she assembles evidence and documents proof of a different crime, which the guilty slave master tries to cover up by selling the victims "out of sight and hearing." Even more consistently than Brown, she not only speaks for oppressed slaves, but gives them a voice in her text. Her narrative does not mimic the silencing of those still in bondage, but endorses the runaway tongue of the slaveholder's victim. "There were many conjectures as to the cause of this terrible punishment. Some said master accused him of stealing corn; others said the slave had quarrelled with his wife, in the presence of the overseer, and had accused his master of being the father of her child. They were both black, and the child was very fair."[20]

Jacobs is aware that she is sheltered not only by the community of slaves and free blacks who do what they can to help her, but also by the white community, which protects her indirectly through the voices of gossip and opinion, fueled by rumors among slaves and the "open-mouthed jealousy of Mrs. Flint." The interconnections between blacks and whites in the community, while often, as in the above instance, resulting in tragedy for the slaves, also potentially empower slaves to influence public opinion about their masters. What slaves say among themselves may be powerful when heard and repeated by influential whites. To protect his reputation in the white community, Flint avoids a public whipping of the domestic servants whose lives are so intimately entwined with his family life.

> [Mrs. Flint] would gladly have had me flogged for my supposed false oath; but . . . the doctor never allowed any one to whip me. The old sinner was politic. The application of the lash might have led to remarks that would have exposed him in the eyes of his children and grandchildren. How often did I

rejoice that I lived in a town where all the inhabitants knew each other! If I had been on a remote plantation, or lost among the multitude of a crowded city, I should not be a living woman at this day.[21]

Within the stifling intimacy of the master's home, violence is more a shameful secret than a public spectacle. Both as master and as man he may hide his sins behind closed doors, while the slave woman whose lover has few opportunities to see her and thus must meet her in the street, lives without privacy, with her emotional life, and her sexual behavior and its consequences, all in plain sight. Jacobs contrasts his power to conceal both his brutality and his sexual affairs, against her own exposed vulnerability to his prying eyes and physical abuse. Under the guise of supervising her morality and protecting the value of his property, the master patrols both the public and private behavior of his slave. As a male he moves freely in the public sphere, and as master and head of his household he controls everyone in sight within the interior of his home. Learning to evade the master's gaze allows her to conduct a secret affair which results in her pregnancy by another white man. The slave girl's attempt to empower herself through an affair with her master's social equal backfires when she discovers how much she values her own reputation. Literacy at first paradoxically increases her sexual vulnerability and desirability as her master begins to conduct a perverse courtship consisting of a one-way correspondence in which he writes lewd propositions to her, slipping the notes into her hands as she performs her chores within the suffocating intimacy of the domestic space. Eventually, as Jacobs grasps the instrumentality of her literacy, the production of an ostensibly private correspondence with her grandmother, intended to be read by her master, becomes a means for Jacobs to outwit her would-be seducer.

While Douglass stresses the definitively heroic and "manly" acts of physically fighting a master and escaping from slavery to become a fugitive headed north to freedom, both oral and written narratives by women concentrate instead on the oral expression of the fugitive thought and the resistant orality of a runaway tongue. Not everyone could physically fight a slaveholder, although the oral tradition offers many examples of slave women resisting masters, and more often mistresses, with physical self-defense. Nor could everyone physically escape from slavery, particularly given the realities of women's role as childbearers and child-care workers, which made escape more difficult for them.

Literacy, the field of bourgeois knowledge, and the technologies it makes possible, Douglass himself recognized, helped white people to define black people as commodities, while providing the means to disseminate a discourse justifying the institution of slavery. But Douglass's text constructs him as an individual acquiring mastery over knowledge as he interiorizes technologies of literacy, while Jacobs's literacy continues to be associated, even in freedom, with the confinement of women and strictures of bourgeois feminine modesty.[22] As a woman, she is caught in the narrative double bind of using her literacy to expose the consequences of her vulnerable sexuality, rather than to attain the mastery identified in Douglass's text with the achievement of manhood.

As the salutation of a letter to Amy Post suggests—"My Dear friend   I steal this moment to scratch you a few lines"—Jacobs's correspondence with Post and her letters to the newspaper, printed under the heading "fugitive," are in one respect—like the narrative itself—pointedly similar to the letters written for a different purpose in her "loophole of retreat."[23] All her writing, even in the free North, falls under the heading of fugitive writing, accomplished in stolen time by a woman who legally remains a fugitive slave until her freedom is purchased by her Northern mistress. In her freedom, the time in which she writes is stolen from her sleep rather than from her master, since her writing occurs in her attic servant's room, after a full day of work for her employers.

Like Harriet Wilson's novel *Our Nig,* Jacobs's writing struggles to overcome the compartmentalization of the bourgeois home, with its parlor, kitchen, servants' quarters, and family living space, which tends to reify the existing relations of domination and exploitation between social classes and genders. As Valerie Smith has suggested, these concrete divisions within the patriarchal household provide the material basis for their respective critiques of "true womanhood" and its ideological limits. Linda's "loophole" (which Hortense Spillers calls her "scrawl space") and Frado's "L-chamber" figure the cramped, hidden spaces in which black women's self-expression moved toward literary production.[24] These writers, conscious of the inaccessibility of literacy to the majority of black women, deploy the trope of orality to represent in their texts a "social diversity of speech types" or "heteroglossia."[25] Thus nonstandard dialects may enter the text as something other than literary minstrelsy, even as the authors themselves are required to demonstrate mastery of standard English. Through their practice of dialogic writing, Jacobs and Wilson (following Stowe and the first black novelist, William Wells Brown) exploit as literary resources discursive conventions familiar to a diversity of speakers, readers, and writers. In Wilson's novel the compartmentalization of the house, which confines the colored servant "in her place" under the supervision of a white mistress herself confined to the domestic sphere, produces a compartmentalized language deployed by the white woman, who speaks like an angel in the parlor but like a "she-devil" in the kitchen, where she disciplines "Nig" with a rawhide kept there for the purpose. Wilson exploits both novelistic convention and the resources of oral invective and sassiness through her manipulation of narrative and dialogue. Wilson's acquisition of a literacy sophisticated enough to produce this novel figures critically as an ellipsis somewhere between author and protagonist, between "Nig" and "Frado," between "I" and "she," as autobiographical materials are placed in dialogue with the slave narrative and the sentimental novel and transformed through the textual operations of fiction. The novel's protagonist, Frado, counters the compartmentalized language of the "two-story white house" with a resistant sassiness, while the narrator appropriates the literate, public, and euphemistic language of the sentimental novel and condemns Mrs. Bellmont for the private, abusive speech she uses, as she-devil of the house, to discipline the colored servant confined with her to the domestic sphere. Because Frado's sass challenges the assumption that her body "belongs" in the kitchen rather than the parlor, or elsewhere, it operates very differently from the so-called sauciness of Stowe's Aunt Chloe in *Uncle Tom's Cabin:*

> "Yer mind dat ar great chicken pie I made when we guv de dinner to General Knox? I and Missis, we come pretty near quarrelling about dat ar crust. What does get into ladies sometimes, I don't know; but, sometimes, when a body has de heaviest kind o' 'sponsibility on 'em, as ye may say, and is all kinder '*seris*' and taken up, dey takes dat are time to be hangin' round and kinder interferin'! Now, Missis, she wanted me to do dis way, and she wanted me to do dat way; and, finally, I got kinder sarcy, and, says I, 'Now, Missis, do jist look at dem beautiful white hands o' yourn, with long fingers, and all a sparkling with rings, like my white lilies when de dew's on 'em; and look at my great black stumpin hands. Now, don't ye think dat de Lord must have meant *me* to make de pie-crust, and you to stay in de parlor? Dar! I was jist so sarcy, Mas'r George."
>
> "And what did mother say?" said George.
>
> "Say?—why, she kinder larfed in her eyes—dem great handsome eyes o' hern; and, says she, 'Well, Aunt Chloe, I think you are about in the right on 't,' says she; and she went off in de parlor. She oughter cracked me over de head for bein' so sarcy; but dar's whar 't is—I can't do nothin' with ladies in de kitchen!"[26]

Although it can justly be said that the author has depicted an act of "signification," or verbal indirection, Stowe's representation of the black woman's sassiness rings false, since Chloe's speech only confirms that the black woman belongs in the kitchen, just as the mistress in the parlor occupies the proper place of a bourgeois white woman. This rendering of a black woman's speech is not an example of a textual representation of resistant orality, but rather an instance of jocular acquiescence, owing more to the conventions of minstrelsy (whites caricaturing blacks who are mocking/"marking" whites) than to African American women's traditional deployment of sass as verbal self-defense. Although the cook indeed knows how to defend herself from the meddling of a well-intentioned mistress, Stowe's evocation of the sassy black woman settles for a comic representation that refuses to construct a complex subjectivity for the black woman who is "a cook . . . in the very bone and center of her soul."[27]

More serious investigations of sass as a form of signification, or verbal self-defense, may be found within African American oral and literate traditions. These accounts frequently demonstrate the ways black women used speech strategically in potentially violent encounters with white women who sometimes felt anxious about their own authority within the patriarchal household. The possibility of a white woman's whipping a slave is raised in Miss Ophelia's disciplining of Topsy for stealing and lying, although Ophelia never actually whips the child. Stowe suggests that Topsy's "wickedness" is the result of her former master's brutality and must be countered by love. Topsy's habit of responding to any accusation with an automatic lie, and perhaps also the verbal inventiveness that made her a popular comic figure, are cured as she is tamed by a Christian education. Similarly, Chloe's comic sassiness in no way challenges the mistress's decorous role as lady of the house.

Stowe's examples of spunk and sassiness do not explore the relationship of sass and invective to violence between servants and mistresses. Violence between women, a significant fact reported in slave testimony, is precluded because the mistress is a "true woman" and because Chloe knows and accepts her place within the patriarchal household, where the white man is master and the white woman is overseer. In this case Mrs. Shelby is too genteel to exercise her authority by cracking the black woman over the head as she "ought" to have done to punish her sauciness. Marie St. Clair, no exemplar of true womanhood, declines to discipline impertinent slaves out of laziness rather than scruples. When it comes to applying the rawhide, neither laziness, Christian uprightness, nor conformity to the ideals of true womanhood stands in the way of Mrs. Bellmont, in Wilson's novel *Our Nig*. She vows incessantly to "strike or scald, or skin" her servant Frado, because of her "impudence."

> James sought his mother; told her he "would not excuse or palliate Nig's impudence; but she should not be whipped or be punished at all. You have not treated her, mother, so as to gain her love; she is only exhibiting your remissness in this matter."
>
> She only smothered her resentment until a convenient opportunity offered. The first time she was left alone with Nig, she gave her a thorough beating, to bring up arrearages; and threatened, if she ever exposed her to James, she would "cut her tongue out."[28]

Mrs. Bellmont, enraged that her son judges her deficient in the virtues of true womanhood and venting her anger on the most convenient target,[29] seems far closer to the mistress of an actual slave woman, Silvia Dubois, whose dictated narrative appeared in 1883.

> [My mistress] was the very devil himself. Why she'd level me with anything she could get hold of—club, stick of wood, tongs, fire-shovel, knife, ax, hatchet; anything that was handiest; and then she was so damned quick about it, too. I tell you, if I intended [to] sass her, I made sure to be off aways. . . . [O]nce she knocked me till I was so stiff that she thought I was dead; once after that, because I was a little saucy, she leveled me with the fire-shovel and broke my pate. She thought I was dead then, but I wasn't.[30]

In the spiritual tradition of Sojourner Truth and Harriet Tubman, both illiterate women who spoke to God and expected God to hear them, and of Nat Turner, who taught himself to read at an early age, and whose famous slave insurrection was precipitated by Turner's reading of "signs in the heavens," black women preachers demonstrated another way to move out of their assigned place within a racist-sexist hierarchy. Nineteenth-century women who pursued a spiritual vocation as itinerant preachers renounced sass, the verbal self-defense of illiterate slave women, in favor of a visionary literacy based on emotionally charged religious experience that confirms the truth of the Bible and empowers them as speakers and writers. As God's chosen spokespersons, Jarena Lee, Zilpha Elaw, and Julia Foote—through their acquisition of spiritually driven literacy and personal communication with God by means of visionary experience—purify their "impudent" tongues of the "sinful" speech in which, like Wilson's Frado, they had indulged as indentured servant girls, separated from their families and growing up under the discipline of white adults.

The fictional Frado affects a partial conversion to Christianity, remaining ambivalent about a religion professed by her "she-devil" mistress. At first she defiantly pursues spiritual training at least partly because her mistress resents any influence that might loosen her own control over her servant's behavior, or cause that servant, even temporarily, to forget "her place." Just as she wedges Frado's mouth shut with a block of wood, Mrs. Bellmont zealously blocks her access to literacy and to Bible-centered religious teaching, insisting that her own style of obedience training is all the education a black child needs. School and church are precisely the institutions that left lasting impressions on Elaw, Foote, and Lee. Apart from their exuberant embrace of Bible study as an intellectually challenging and pleasurable activity, they all seem to have been propelled into religious experience in part because it supplied channels of expression, and emotional contact with kindred spirits, denied them as young servant girls. Their parents were either dead, or unable to rear and educate them because of extreme poverty. These young girls were disciplined at the discretion of their employers, and relied on their own spunk and sass in conflicts with these powerful adult authorities. When, during her term as an indentured servant, Foote was beaten by her white mistress for a transgression she never committed, the child responded by taking the rawhide whip out of the house and cutting it into small pieces, so that it could never be used again.

To such young children, commonly indentured between ages six and twelve, it must have seemed that the authority of masters and mistresses not only superseded that of their own parents, but also, as they began to be influenced by Christianity, that such authority must be compounded by the power of an omniscient God, usually figured as white and male, who could read their innermost thoughts. Stricken by her conscience after telling her employer a lie, Jarena Lee relates, "God . . . told me I was a wretched sinner."[31] Such women had the opportunity to develop both their profound spirituality and a Bible-based literacy, which enabled them to go beyond exhorting sinners to convert and fellow worshipers to keep the faith. Ultimately some of them also claimed the authority of a preacher to "take a text," even when it meant opposing the Pauline restrictions on women's speech espoused by a male-dominated church hierarchy.[32]

While attending a "solemn love feast," Zilpha Elaw, whose mother had died in childbirth after twenty-two pregnancies, took the opportunity to participate in a free expression of emotion, having found a social space in which she could define herself as an expansive soul rather than a circumscribed body.[33] At an outdoor camp meeting that brought worshipers of different races and classes together for a common purpose, she found herself moved to speak, following a profound spiritual experience which freed her to begin her life with a new leaf; the social inscription of her black, female body was erased as she became a blank (white) page to receive God's Word.

> [M]y heart and soul were rendered completely spotless—as clean as a sheet of white paper, and I felt as if I had never sinned in all my life . . . when the prayer meeting afterwards commenced, the Lord opened my mouth in public prayer; and while I was thus engaged, it seemed as if I heard my God rustling in the tops of the mulberry-trees. Oh how precious was this day to my soul![34]

As they reach higher levels of literacy, the study of scripture liberates their "bridled" tongues for preaching and exhorting; through spiritual activity and chaste behavior they attempt to cleanse and purify the black woman's body of the significations acquired through her association in slavery with abusive sexuality. Julia Foote's spiritual autobiography implicitly constructs such a relation between the physical agony of the enslaved mother's body and her daughter's quest for spiritual autonomy and ecstacy. Glorious "heavenly visitations" in which Christ appears to gently strip her body of clothing and wash her in warm water to the accompaniment of "the sweetest music I had ever heard," are spiritual balm for the child who never forgot the story of how her mother had suffered as a slave. Foote's narrative begins significantly with her mother's sexual vulnerability and the painful consequences of her verbal self-defense:

> My mother was born a slave, in the State of New York. She had one very cruel master and mistress. This man, whom she was obliged to call master, tied her up and whipped her because she refused to submit herself to him, and reported his conduct to her mistress. After the whipping, he himself washed her quivering back with strong salt water. At the expiration of a week she was sent to change her clothing, which stuck fast to her back. Her mistress seeing that she could not remove it, took hold of the rough tow-linen undergarment and pulled it off over her head with a jerk, which took the skin with it, leaving her back all raw and sore.[35]

Seeking a figure that could combine the secular representation of a blissful black body, emancipated from the negative social inscriptions of slavery, racism, and sexual exploitation, with the spiritual empowerment of the African American prophetic tradition, Toni Morrison invents a character in *Beloved*, Baby Suggs, an illiterate black woman preacher whose interest in holiness extends beyond the spirit to the body's wholeness. Her eloquent sermons urge black people to love every part of the bodies that white masters and mistresses abused, overworked, injured, and dehumanized. Implicitly problematizing Douglass's linking of literacy and freedom, *Beloved* and Sherley Anne Williams's novel *Dessa Rose* include a critique of literacy as an instrumentality of white male domination, represented in both texts by educators: a schoolteacher whose curriculum includes racist pseudoscience, and a social-climbing tutor who covets the material wealth of the slavocracy he serves.[36]

Yet each also offers an alternative to the binary opposition of predatory literacy and institutionalized illiteracy: the child who takes dictation from an illiterate mother in *Dessa Rose,* and the African American schoolteacher

Lady Jones, who teaches the ex-slave's daughter to read, in *Beloved*. Morrison's slave community's attempt to process unassimilable experience occurs within what is still an oral culture. Sethe, Paul D, and Baby Suggs must orient themselves in a hostile environment without the perceptual apparatus or instrumentalities triumphantly claimed by Douglass. Their individual struggles take place outside the epistemic order of bourgeois society, through processes that Morrison extrapolates by way of her considered appropriation of the African American expressions "disremember" and "rememory," which she employs not as corruptions of the standard English words "remember," "forget," or "memory," but as cultural neologisms invented to refer to ways that African Americans retained specific perceptual habits of their African cultures of origin despite (or because of) their traumatic encounter with an often brutally applied, certainly exclusionary, instrumental literacy.[37]

The writer's text seeks to undo the amputation or erasure of the ancestor's voice and presence in the irrevocable break from primary African orality to institutionalized illiteracy, and restore dignity to black speakers of stigmatized dialects. The nonstandard speech of slaves expressed different cultural perceptions as much as it reflected and often reinforced the power relations of slavery, which were established and maintained in part by means of a predatory and exclusionary practice of literacy. This exclusive literacy produced a correspondent black illiteracy, or what W. E. B. Du Bois called "compulsory ignorance," as well as "the curiosity born of compulsory ignorance, to know and test the power of the cabalistic letters of the white man, the longing to know."[38] The conflation of folklore with ignorance and the persistent, erroneous identification of literacy as the possession of "the white man" are discursive tropes that black writers have always struggled against in their production of literary texts that incorporate the subjugated knowledge of black folk.

Being neither white nor men, black women's possession of literacy and mastery of literate discourses has been especially problematic. African American women writers have often used their texts to "talk back" to texts by white men, white women, and black men in which representations of black women are absent or subordinated to other aims. With her decision to portray the silenced, but not speechless, black ancestor in *Beloved* as an illiterate, pregnant slave woman, Morrison insists on a "herstory" that must be intuited through empathy, as well as a history that can be read, remembered, recorded, and reconstructed by the literate descendants of an illiterate ancestress. Within the oral tradition black women have been anything but silent, unless literally beaten, muzzled, starved, or otherwise suppressed to the point of speechlessness. As for black women writers, if anything, their discursive silencing has been itself a by-product of literacy and of their inability to control the sites and conditions of their own textual production, or ensure it an appropriate reception. The literal bit, muzzle, and whip used to silence the slave woman gave way to the repressive social structures, discursive silencing, and literary oblivion that continued to mute her emancipated descendants, prolonging the discursive effect of black women's silencing even when they not only used their voices to speak, but had also thoroughly interiorized the technology of writing.

Scholars and critics today are unearthing and reevaluating the works of a number of African American women writers: texts that have finally become marketable commodities, having lain dormant for a century, disqualified from serious study by presuppositions about the tradition of African American writing derived from the study of male-authored texts that dominated the black canon until the 1980s. Suspicious scholars excluded both Wilson and Jacobs from the African American canon because of their self-conscious appropriation of nineteenth-century fictional conventions, which were familiar especially to women readers. Similarly Morrison's novel, which mines the resources of the slave narrative tradition while placing an African American woman at its center, has been scorned by at least one African American critic as "sentimental" and "melodramatic," the unfortunate result of the writer's loss of control over her materials owing to a "failure of feeling" he associates with sentimentality.[39] Morrison's literate ghost story has as much, or more, in common with the Gothic as the sentimental tradition. Unquestionably her work self-consciously excavates popular fictional genres associated with traditions of women's writing and oral narrative, as well as the slave narrative. Her deployment of historically gendered generic codes might be compared to Ishmael Reed's use of vaudeville patter or Charles Johnson's use of the tall tale.

While Morrison privileges the point of view of the illiterate protagonist, it is through the figurative possibilities of a written form, the novel, that Morrison imaginatively constructs and validates the perceptual field of the illiterate, offering image after image of a spatiotemporality that is not static, but allows a simultaneity of the present and past, a communication between the dead and the living based on interiorizations of the spoken word: the mother telling stories to a ghost that she has never told her living daughter. Sethe's oral transmission of a legacy of struggle and resistance empowers her daughter Denver to overcome a history of silencing and seek instruction from a literate black woman in their community. In the process Sethe also discovers within half-forgotten memory, through the "rememory" of oral narrative, stories from her own childhood of the mother who had killed every child before Sethe, allowing her alone to live, the child not born of rape.

Writing is a literal inscription on the body of Sethe's African mother, the brand on her breast signifying her violent possession through rape and enslavement. For Sethe, writing is a commodity acquired through prostitution—the word gained in exchange for a mother's body.[40] The concreteness of this inscription (the word "Beloved"—her name is *not* recorded—engraved on the tombstone of the preverbal baby girl) sets the vengeful spirit loose in the haunted house of memory. The ghost is not just embodied but hyperembodied, as it seduces Sethe's lover and becomes pregnant. Beloved emulates the phallic mother's power, as the written word gives a perverse body to the repressed spirit of an oral tradition in which the pain of the child's death and the mother's terror might otherwise be disremembered. Morrison's representation of an illiterate mother, rather than a literate father, implicitly comments on the gaps African American women have discerned, and tried in their own work to bridge, between the male-oriented tradition of the slave narrative genre and the oral folk tradition, which have both been strong influences on the production of African American literature.[41]

The circular, monumental time of primary orality disrupted by slavery and compulsory illiteracy—represented by the ghost in *Beloved*—may be seen on the one hand as covering over all the ruptures and discontinuities that linear historical time, itself a product of writing, is equipped to register. On the other hand, if claims on history implicate the literate slave in the obsessional mastery of linear time, it is through a return to "women's time," which is also "primitive time," that Morrison addresses the power of the pre-Oedipal mother, the power to give or deny life to her child—just as Sherley Anne Williams suggests the power, as mother and as killer, of a woman whose subjectivity is formed outside or at the margins of bourgeois ideological constructions of true womanhood.[42] While slave mothers (as well as their offspring) affirm and stress their life-giving power, Morrison chooses to explore the other aspect of women's power over life by constructing a supernatural character that has access to language, yet mimics the child whose "relation to the pre-oedipal, phallic mother is pre-linguistic, unspoken, and unrepresentable," so as to give an embodied voice to the voiceless maternal semiotic identified here, as in Julia Kristeva's theoretical writing, with both mother and child.[43] For Kristeva, the maternal semiotic comprises the unorganized, presymbolic bodily impulses of the infant's physical interaction with the mother's body.

In Jacobs's account, the exchange of breast milk in nursing binds both the white and black child in a reciprocal relationship which is betrayed by the white child's entry into the patriarchal symbolic of law, property, and inheritance. For Morrison, the theft by the dominant class of that which would nourish a subjugated class, ritualized in the custom of wet-nursing, graphically demonstrates the interactive workings of the slave woman's exploitation. Sethe is exploited both as breeder and as worker, her body's labor producing both milk and ink.[44] The black woman's milk is stolen and, through institutionalized illiteracy, so is her ability to control her discursive representation within a print culture. Her self-definition as mother and human, her ability to operate as a speaking subject, is contradicted by a body of writings constituting a pseudoscientific discourse that helped to rationalize her enslavement. In *Beloved* the maternal semiotic not only is the physical interactions of the individual mother-child dyad, but also becomes, figuratively, an analogue of the relationship, within African American tradition, of the problematic historical opposition of orality and literacy at the point of linguistic imperialism. African languages were lost to the descendants of captive Africans as access to interiorized epistemological constructions, leaving little more than paralinguistic traces in the rhythms of speech, song, and dance. English, therefore, is associated with the symbolic order of law and the enunciation of the ego in language. The *collective racial* maternal semiotic of the novel includes a number of associatively related figures: the preliterate African who dies on the slave ship, the non-English-speaking mother with a brand on her breast, as well as the prelinguistic infant. All these "ghosts" are repressed in the formation of the psyche through insertion into a masculine (white male) symbolic. This process is here made analogous to the slave's internalization of English, literacy, and the symbolic order of Western discursive formations. Yet in any language or semiotic system, something always remains unexpressed—or, in Morrison's own words, "blocked, forgotten, hidden"—whether one operates within primary orality, institutionalized illiteracy, or interiorized literacy.

> When Sethe locked the door, the women inside were free at last to be what they liked, see whatever they saw and say whatever was on their minds.
>   Almost. Mixed in with the voices surrounding the house, recognizable but undecipherable to Stamp Paid, were the thoughts of the women in 124, unspeakable thoughts, unspoken.[45]

In Morrison's novel the unnamed character variously referred to as a witch, a sexually abused young woman, a "crawling already?" baby girl, a dead and buried child, a vengeful ghost, and Sethe's "Beloved," comes to speak not only on the matter and manner of her individual death, but also as ghost/survivor of the harrowing Middle Passage, perverse racial birth canal and mass slaughterhouse. A supernatural and multiplex character—indeed, she operates within the text as a sibyl or medium, emblematic of the fragmentation of the unitary self effected in the multiple personality by extreme abuse, or the ultimate shattering of the ego by death itself—Beloved speaks for "Sixty Million and more" silenced black souls estimated to have died in captivity, including all who lost their lives while trying to escape. The child ghost, whose voice blends and merges with the voices of her living mother and sister, is loosed on the household by the act of inscription and called into embodiment by a challenging male voice. She, Beloved, is made to represent the "disremembered" (repressed, unmentionable, nonexistent) offspring who are voiceless because they either died in infancy, or were never born because African American women who were potential childbearers died while physically resisting slavery, or practiced contraception, abortion, or infanticide to avoid the designated role of breeder. Although the majority of slave women chose to give life, even if it meant that their children would be slaves, Morrison's novel, by stressing the alternative, underscores that motherhood was an active choice, as does Jacobs's narrative.

The slave woman's subjectivity is based upon her self-construction as she who communicates, beyond words, with the dead and the unborn, through her body and through her spiritual commitment to the continuity of generations and the transmission of cultural values. Neither the baby talk of nursing mother to babbling infant, nor the call to and response from a ghost, qualifies as proper discourse within the masculine symbolic order. One is infantile nonsense, a kind of naturalized glossolalia, and the other is evidence of the woman's "hysteria" or the slave's "superstition." The death of the author and the mother's labor in childbirth are conflated in the pregnant child ghost, whose materialization authorizes the collaborative narratives of *Beloved*, in which Morrison puts "his story next to hers."[46] In a writerly yet popular mainstream novel, Morrison merges preoccupations of a Europhallogocentric literary production with the uterocentric tendencies of African American women writers. The exorcism of the malicious ghost set loose by writing is performed by a chorus of black women producing a sound before or beyond words, an indescribable sound to "break the back of words": perhaps moaning, keening, ululating, or panting as in childbirth, when the woman who has chosen to complete a pregnancy is most aware of her human effort to organize and control the rhythmic involuntary contractions of a body in labor.[47] Kristeva's *chora,* a space "anterior to naming," associated with the maternal semiotic, may bear a relationship to Morrison's chorus of mothers unnaming the unspeakable desire that precedes language.[48] Like the unborn child, which has not yet entered culture, the *chora* is a figure of the prelinguistic, yet should not be equated in any simple way with the woman or mother. While conception, pregnancy, childbirth, and lactation continue to be represented as natural events, Maria Mies stresses their importance as cultural activities contributing to a materialist concept of female humanity which seems particularly appropriate to the slave woman, labeled "breeder," who yet managed to transmit coherent cultural values to her offspring.

> [Women] did not simply breed children like cows, but they appropriated their own generative and productive forces, they analysed and reflected upon their own and former experiences and passed them on to their daughters. This means that they were not helpless victims of their bodies' generative forces, but learned to influence them, including the number of children they wanted to have.[49]

Black women's appropriation of materials from African American oral tradition, as well as their interiorization of writing technologies productive of bourgeois subjectivity, are equally products of analysis and reflection upon their own and antecedent experiences passed from mothers to daughters. They were not helpless victims of predatory literacy any more than they were passive or silent victims of their bodies' generative forces or of the abuse of masters and mistresses. On the contrary, they have frequently insisted upon a dialogic writing practice that operates against the tendency of the literate to view the illiterate and the oppressed as "voiceless." In telling the story of her own life to her dead daughter, Sethe is able to communicate with her living daughter and at the same time to recover a forgotten connection to her own mother, a captive African who spoke little or no English. The unspoken (unconstructed) history that has silenced Denver, the living daughter, comes to light (is constructed) when Sethe speaks to the ghost, just as Denver loses her paralyzing fear of leaving the haunted house upon hearing the voice of her dead grandmother.

The stories Beloved solicits are Morrison's way of imagining an oral, spiritual, intuitive analogue of the written, material, empirical history of slavery. In Morrison's text such stories have been pieced together hopefully, like Baby Suggs's color-hungry quilts. For the occasion of writing this novel, haunting tales inspired by words black women have spoken about their lives have been stitched together as provisional fragments, out of which Morrison constructs stories about a ghost that the text assembles and finally unravels, like Sethe's furtively constructed wedding dress. In such "mammy-made" garments our black foremothers wrapped their human dignity, unable to fit themselves and their histories into the ready-made ideologies of true womanhood. *Beloved* may not be "a story to pass on"—it is neither a folktale nor a text to be lightly dismissed—but Morrison's literate ghost story underlines, through its exploration of opposing, interactive forces of rupture and continuity, how difficult and necessary it is that black women construct and pass on personal and collective "herstories." Like Wilson and Jacobs before her, Morrison insists that the oral traditions of slaves and the popular genres appropriated by women speak and write a mother tongue of resistance.

15

The Female Woman: Fanny Fern and the Form of Sentiment

Lauren Berlant

The Lady and the Stereotype

The Life and Beauties of Fanny Fern is an anonymous collection published in 1855, whose purpose was simultaneously to capitalize on and to undercut the vast popularity of Fern's *Ruth Hall*. The editor of *The Life and Beauties* takes Fern's newspaper columns and reprints them with sarcastic commentary, and since Fern's columns themselves were often organized as ironic exegeses of opinions published elsewhere, *The Life and Beauties* sets up a kind of *mise-en-abîme* of gendered irony, a redoubled doubleness that formally embodies the contested conditions of public enunciation under which Fern and many of her sister writers labored and profited. One such entry, on married life, addresses the views of "Sambo." Fern's column is a response to a citation whose origin is the popular lexicon of white, patriarchal America.

> "Sambo, what am your 'pinion 'bout de married life? Don't you tink it de most happiest?"
>
> "Well, I'll tell you 'bout dat ere—'pends altogether how dey enjoy themselves."
>
> "Sambo! Sambo! be quiet! You needn't *always* tell the truth. White folks don't. Just as sure as you do it, you'll lose every friend you have."
>
> "Don't roll up the whites of your eyes at me that way. It's gospel I'm telling you. I promise you I don't go through creation with my eyes shut; and I've found out that good people always tell the truth *when it don't conflict with their interests.* . . . Oh! y-e-s, Sambo, matrimony is a 'blessed institution,' so the ministers say . . . and so everybody says—except those who have *tried it?* So go away, and don't be *wool*gathering. You'll never be the 'Uncle Tom' of your tribe."[1]

The anonymous editor of *The Life and Beauties* uses this column, retitled "Mrs. Farrington on Matrimony," to undermine Fern's critical authority on marriage, since her own history scandalously includes divorce (from her second husband, "Mr. Farrington"). Refuting the "false" Fern with the "true"

Farrington, the editor arrogates the privilege of naming in order to expose her indecorous refusal to submit to patriarchal-domestic identity. Her ventriloquization of Sambo is, by his lights, a further sign of her indiscretion, for in authorizing "Sambo" over "Farrington," she appears shamelessly to have chosen a degraded cross-margin alliance (with an African American stereotype!) over the proper womanly marriage to white masculine authority, here embodied in her former editor, acting *in loco patriarchae.*

It is as though her projection of authority onto the African American stereotype redraws Fern in a kind of miscegenated moral blackface, and makes her a kind of monster. Between Fern and Sambo, we witness the political alliance of vernacular speech, a grotesque idiom of language and the body. The minstrel discourse of Sambo in American culture derives in part from the slaves' dramatic parodies of life in the "big house"[2]; the vulgar speech of Fern occupies an analogously ambiguous relation to the domestic space in which it finds its "subaltern" identity.[3] Sambo and Fern's ironic tap dance thus reverberates far beyond the manifest frame in which marriage turns out to be a disappointment.

Fern's deployment of race and gender stereotypes not only refers to the oft-used woman's rights analogy between white heterosexual women and enslaved African Americans, but also to the current problem of women's professional emergence into capitalist culture. The express motive for producing *The Life and Beauties of Fanny Fern* was to defend Fern's father and especially her brother, N. P. Willis, whose cultural and familial patrimony she caricatures savagely in *Ruth Hall.* These men were pseudofictively savaged in the novel because they let Ruth/Fanny fall between the cracks of patriarchal protection by abandoning her emotionally and financially during her early widowhood. The collective domestic behavior of men in the novel leads Fern to repudiate the patrifocal family as a site of female fulfillment, although she desires intensely to live in a family made up of mothers and daughters. But the men's personal behavior in life and in the novel also points beyond the patriarchal family, to oppressive practices in the public sphere, which emanate in particular from the profession of "letters"[4]: Fern represents newspaper and periodical journalism, as well as book publishing and sales, as another site of gender discipline, where her legitimacy as a journalist is always in question by male culture experts for its nonnormativeness as feminine labor and also for its vulgar feminine content. She in turn constantly aligns her writing with other more typical woman's work: that of housewives, seamstresses, prostitutes. Print capitalism appears to Fern simultaneously utopian and degraded, central to a revolutionary discursive democratization of the national public sphere yet nonetheless the source of revitalized race, gender, and economic exploitation.[5] Considering the tension between democratic and capitalist public sphere practices, this study of Fern means to address locally a larger set of questions, notably: How might the commercial production of a popular feminine discourse be read as a test case in the collaboration of capitalism with social change? How might the case of "women's culture" illuminate the current discussion about how popular genres express both critical and conservative fantasies, operating as sites of consent that enable alliances across antagonistic, or at least different, social positions? And finally, what does it mean that we witness, in this history, a collaboration between the commodity form and the stereotype on behalf of a feminine counterpolitics?

In midnineteenth century America, the popular discourse of feminized "sentimentality" translated the materials of official history and domestic life into the abstract, relatively autonomous realm of "woman's interests," a realm governed by certain immutable "laws." These laws were articulated as part of a set of territorializing social forces, which explicitly served what Fern names the *"public or private—call it by what specious name you will."*[6] Fern understood that the increasingly urbanized, alienated life of industrializing America separated women and men into the separate times and spaces of the public and the domestic, which came to seem naturally gendered by virtue of which sex dominated where.[7] But Fern also sensed, in a more self-reflexive way than did her sentimental peers, that the meaning, the pacing, and the spaces of everyday domestic life were themselves the effect of a new capitalist ethos of personal instrumentalization, where the woman bore the burden of seeing that there would be no affective, no intellectual, no moral, and of course no economic waste.[8] Fern's work in periodical journalism, which asserted the sovereignty of subjective knowledge, aimed to convert the meaning and value of female life in the quotidian: to witness it, to affirm the dignity of its unhistoric acts (often in the face of patriarchal and economic brutality, and extreme isolation within the family and from other women), but also to transform its mind-threatening monotonous and hermetic sameness by proposing her own brand of female soliloquy as a public, collective, and emancipatory form of expressivity and invention, available for any socially silenced subject.[9]

But to foreground Fern's critical function tells only part of a complex story. For her work takes a wide range of advocacy positions within sentimental culture, from the nostalgic maternal to the prophetic feminist. Here I use Fern to explicate how this peculiar popular discourse on women in the second half of the nineteenth century used the expanding cultural resources of industrial capitalism to make women into a "new" consumer group circulating around a subject addressed, and newly empowered, by a female culture industry. It would be more accurate to call this a female "subculture" industry, since the discourse on woman it ratifies is formed around the generic, stereotyped identities that marked women's representation in the dominant culture. Despite some evidence to the contrary, the generic "woman" articulated within the folds of this industry was made to seem dominant, even hegemonic, in American culture—not simply contained in subcultural margins as a "victim/problem,"[10] but also venerated as an "expert" in her moral, maternal capacity to understand and to authorize people in her intimate everyday life and in the texts of women's culture that claimed to represent her experience and her interests as a "woman."[11]

The American Female Culture Industry

The American female culture industry developed a series of generic strategies—which might be called "modes of containment"—whose purpose was to testify to the heretofore "private" trials of womanhood, to demystify patriarchal practices, and to consolidate female collective identity without necessarily abrogating "woman's" loyalty to heterosexual culture. The history of these modes of containment would trace the dialectic between their critical incursions into the patriarchal public sphere on the one hand, and their "sentimental reflex" on the other, which involves the assertion of a feminine value that still exists in a private realm outside social circulation. The sacred aura of this maternally identified site, which is always, as it were, projected ex post facto from a moment of modernity in crisis, hovers as loss and desire over virtually every production of the female culture industry. The most conventional sentimental novels mute their oppositional function, casting the ideals of feminine and masculine self-discipline as moral pedagogy, in an attempt to return to sacred, domestic time: but the larger history of public "women's culture" recasts conventional sentimentality as the ur-instance of collective social practice for bourgeois American women, whose foundational distinguishing mark was to refuse to identify female interest as "political"—that is, interested in obtaining power within the terms of the patriarchal public sphere.[12] In this sense nostalgia for sacred maternal time was redeployed as the imaginary time-space of a feminine counterpolitics. The rising hegemony of urban culture as the site of public fantasy partly made this shift possible.

In sentimental domestic culture the most explicit expression of this elastic "feminine" form is the "complaint"—a generic name applied caustically to Fern's work, but a name she also uses and covets since, through her, the "wail of discontent" silently spoken by the mass of women finds publication.[13] The female complaint is an international mode of public discourse that demonstrates women's contested value in the patriarchal public sphere by providing commentary from a generically "feminine" point of view. It has frequently been deployed against specific nonsexual violences in the political public sphere—for example, in women's antiwar activity. But typically, especially in the American case, the female complaint involves an expression of women's social negation: it is a rich archive of patriarchal oppression, circumscribed by a sense that woman's lack of legitimacy in the public sphere appears virtually inescapable, with the forms of patriarchal sexuality a fact of life so deeply entrenched that they appear natural. The a priori marking of female discourse as *less serious* is paradoxically the only condition under which the complaint can function as an effective political tool: the complaint allows the woman who wants to maintain her privileged alignment with heterosexual culture to speak fearlessly, because the vernacular mode of her discourse assumes the intractability of the conditions of the complaint's production.

The female complaint is thus an aesthetic "witnessing" of injury. Shuttling between a sexual politics that threatens dominant structures of authority and an affirmation of the female speaker's practical powerlessness, it registers the

speaker's frustration, rage, abjection, and/or heroic self-sacrifice in an oppositional utterance that reveals the constraints and contradictions of feminine
desire in its very saying.[14] The appeal of this form for women is, first, in the
therapeutic pleasure of demystifying patriarchy—usually depicted as "men"
in the flesh, as male-identified women, or as impersonal capitalist institutions
like banks and businesses whose operations were manifestly patriarchal. In
this sense the complaint often relies on the bribe of its sentimental reflex,
representing masculinist practices in a feminist way, but accepting as semi-
fixed and even desirable the domestic axes of patriarchal culture in memories
of the mother and dreams of marital bliss.

The design of these strategies had a second purpose, though, apart from
demystifying and perhaps reforming institutional and personal misogyny. Sentimental culture also established a broad audience of women, aiming to stake out
a safe feminine space, a textual habitus in which a set of emotional, intellectual,
and economic styles, knowledges, and practices might be formulated in common and expressed with pleasure. From its inception in the late eighteenth
century, the sentimental abstraction of the values of "woman" from the realm
of material relations meant that interactions among classes, races, and different
ethnic groups also appear to dissolve in their translation into sentimental
semiosis.[15] No matter what my race/class, if I address you as "woman" your
other social positions, and even your particular domestic activity and sexual
practice, dissolve in the simulacrum of generic gendered experience.

Since the midnineteenth century in America, this logic of female legitimation, commodified as a point of identification, has marked public intrafemale
discourse all over the political spectrum—conservative, reform, and radical.
But while the claim to be working for "common" women and women in common was broadly articulated, many popular women writers, among them Fern,
Harriet Beecher Stowe, and Louisa May Alcott, developed a counterstrain
which aimed critically to distinguish "women" in their particularity from
"woman" in her generic purity. Whereas conventional sentimental texts tended
to see the relation between the historical particular and the transcendental
generic woman as a relation of fallen to fulfilled sign, this affiliated mode
tended to characterize these relations of type as fraught with struggle and
socially destructive for women, the family, and society at large. Yet, rather than
deeming these kinds of gender discourse as inertly opposed to each other
because they promote different strategies for transforming normativity, I suggest that they are best viewed dialectically, because they are constituted by the
same terms and are negotiating the same social strains within the category
"woman." The reflexive relation between what we might call pure and critical
sentimentality is, indeed, what has maintained the sentimental intelligibility of
"women's" texts, while they have nonetheless incorporated progressively more
explicit critiques of the patriarchal public sphere in America.

In sum, nineteenth-century sentimental activists of all political persuasions
charged themselves and their sister women with the dual aim of social amelioration and change. By providing consolation of various sorts to the women
whose negation was the fate and the fact of their lives, as well as the passport

to whatever power and pleasure the gender enjoyed, the sentimental agent also aimed to transform the values and practices of domination that went along with life in the patriarchal public and private spheres. Yet it would be hasty to conclude that the war of position in which the female sentimental discoursers were engaged emerged from a basic consensus about what, exactly, they were trying to save.

Clearly, the producers of this discourse were mainly white and identified with casting the racial values of bourgeois domesticity as the cultural given in Victorian America. Our current critical concern with the linkages between sentimentality and American reform movements like abolitionism suggests that this general aspiration toward bourgeois female hegemony in reality had the greater aim of transforming the whole world as we know it; that is to say, we now see these bourgeois women, transformed into a collectivity by way of social praxis and literary production, as extending their spiritual, ideological, and political victory to the downtrodden of races, classes, and genders. Whether one sees this female reformation as contributing to the bathetic self-consumerism of mass society, as Ann Douglas does, or as an energetic feminine refusal to reproduce the structures and values of the patriarchal public sphere, as Jane Tompkins does, or as a pedagogical tool for making hegemonic the self-disciplinary ethos of the bourgeoisie, as Richard Brodhead does, these divergent representations of literary sentimentality presume similar things: first, that female sentimental discourse is interesting only as it engages with the public sphere and, second, that its main urgency was not in representing women per se but in social power as it circulates through the sex/gender system.[16]

Whether dressed up in bloomers or petticoats, then, the female sentimentalists were power transvestites whose sentimentality about female experience would be simply embarrassing, were it really the narcissistic, trivializing realm of value it often appears to be. But in my view female sentimental discourse is a mode of abstraction that has no a priori political implications for the power of women or other marginalized groups whose interests are named as the manifest motives for its deployment. Indeed it often had a more humble but not unrelated function to the positions just sketched out: sentimental ideology served as a structure of consent in which domestically atomized women found in the consumption of popular texts the experience of intimate collective identity, a feminine counterpublic sphere whose values remained fundamentally private.[17]

On Redefining the Female

Lost in this transfiguration of sentimental ideology into a pure "politics" is a theory of the "nonpolitical" feminine subject on whose behalf it was supposedly deployed. The need for such a theory of the "feminine" was central in the national conversation about how even to frame the woman question. By using "feminine," rather than more dignified terms like "gendered" or "female," I mean to evoke a problem of terminology. The protocols under which one discusses what women want have always hinged on the adjudication of antagonistic theories of what women are.[18] Women's sentimental culture, and the industry of productions addressed specifically to the subject of femininity, generated an enormous amount of material explicating the relation between what Fern calls "the female woman" as she appeared to be, and woman as she appeared in her dignified, abstracted dreams of herself.[19] Sometimes, in Fern's words, the woman simply decides to let "life [appear] like the dream that it is."[20] Fern's assertion that woman's realities take place in the spaces of "repose," at night, in the face of suffering and death, of projected and thwarted desire, and in the general rush of detail that overwhelms woman in everyday life, reinforces Douglas's argument that the sentimental world of feminine power/knowledge writes the women as "hothouse products . . . self-announced refugees from history."[21] When life is but a dream, there is no laboring body, no real desire or pain: this is one of the many reasons that death, in much of this literature, is not only the sacred payoff for living a painful life, but is also an attitude the living woman must assume in order to stay sane.

Thus, to appropriate D. A. Miller's account of sentimental masculinity, the feminine woman appears to her critics a deserving recipient of "those mortifying charges (sentimentality, self-indulgence, narcissism) which our culture is prepared to bring against anyone who dwells in subjectivity longer or more intensely than is necessary to his proper functioning as the agent of socially useful work. . . . And those envious charges have at least this much truth in them, that the embarrassing risk of *being too personal* all too often comes to coincide with its opposite in the dismal fate of banality, of *not being personal enough.*"[22] But where Miller's male subject has privileged access to sentimental autobiography, the bourgeois woman of the nineteenth century finds obstacles to autobiography that are historical and political, and therefore psychic. As Miller might have suggested, female self-expression—that is, secular self-expression "as a woman"—was vulnerable to charges of indecency and triviality. But these defamations of character were not simply the disciplinary expressions of a generally instrumentalizing culture, as they are for Miller's emerging bourgeois boy: the bourgeois female impulse to express need, desire, and pleasure unabsorbed by home, church, or the patriarchal dictionary also raised the possibility that "woman," seemingly absorbed in her role as the manager of domestic comforts, somehow had retained a personal subjectivity, an autonomous identity.

Sentimental female autobiography thus raised the possibility that under the "woman" lurked something horrible, a residual "female" whose knowledge and desire were not entirely caught up in the patriarchal domestic economy. For this reason, throughout the century sentimental discoursers struggled over whether the word "female" should be allowed to represent "woman" in the public discourse about her. Historians of American English attribute this struggle to the general desexualization of language, but for female sentimentalists, more than simple "decency" (another taboo word) was at stake. Sarah Josepha Hale, editor of *Godey's Lady's Book,* argued passionately against its use. She convinced the board at what was then called Vassar Female College to drop the word, for this reason: "When used to discriminate between the sexes the word *female* is an adjective; but many writers employ the word as a noun, which, when applied to women, is improper, and sounds unpleasantly, as referring to an animal. . . . It is inelegant as well as absurd."[23]

Noah Webster's and John Walker's dictionaries agree: the noun "female" is a sex noun, and calling a woman a "female" reduces her from her gender to her sex.[24] Agitation around this issue motivated legislators to change the language of the laws they made in order to avoid accidently imputing sexuality or desire to the gender[25]: the word "lady" came into use to distinguish rarefied women from vulgar females.[26] Indeed, when Fern calls a woman a "female woman" she speaks specifically of the worst kind of feminine, feline, male-objectified woman. A "female woman" is a woman who trivializes herself and/or competitively extends this self-negation to other women. "There's more cats than Ferns in the world," she says, "and complimentary notices from a female woman look suspicious. . . . When [such] a woman pats you with one hand you can be morally certain she's going to scratch you with the other."[27] Throughout her career, even after her admission of the value of woman's rights, Fern characterized female duplicity as a present danger. But while theorists like Hale saw the name "female" as a degradation of women's cultural refinement, Fern usually characterizes the "female" in the woman as the mark of her colonization by patriarchal culture: the female woman is first and foremost an animal who has been degraded by her identity within a culture that rewards female stereotypicality. Fern calls these rewards "a relic of barbarism."[28]

Her major response to the lure of the female stereotype is to write countless articles against what she calls the "pattern" or "model" wife, mother, sister—the woman who sees it as her duty and desire to be inevitable, to be true to "form."

> I know scores of bright, intelligent women, alive to their fingertips to every-thing progressive, good, and noble, whose lives, hedged in by custom and conservationism, remind me of that suggestive picture in all our Broadway artist windows, of the woman with dripping hair and raiment, clinging to the fragment of rock overhead, while the dark waters are surging round her feet.[29]

The failure to cultivate intellect, talent, or simply self-expression has a sublime range of effects on women: most parodically, the woman becomes a grotesque slave to surfaces and form, dedicating herself to policing both her own and other women's adherence to rule while often becoming massively hypocritical. Fern's satire of such women includes coquettes, wives who adhere to marriage manuals, and rigidly bluestockinged feminists. Her sarcasm about feminine theatricality might be read as further degradation of women for their fulfillment of type, but by representing overall a wide range of women, Fern marshals evidence against "those conservative old ladies of both sexes, who would destroy individuality by running all our sex in the same mold of artificial nonentity."[30]

Fern's essay "The Other One" plays out in a frenzy of irony the patriarchal logic of female genericization. The column is structured as a response to a male authority's loving nominalization of woman as "the other sex," without whom the world "would be only a dark and cheerless void." Fern responds to this idealizing sentiment by suggesting that, on the contrary, women are actually worthless, a waste of human resources. For women are consumed by their "Mutual Admiration Society; emptying their budget of love affairs; comparing bait to trap victims; sighing over the same rose leaf; sonnetizing the same moonbeam; patronizing the same milliner, and *exchanging female kisses!*"[31] But it turns out that even the erotic intimacy of female identity is sexual policing in disguise; women are so obsessed with being the Other to men that they feign love to mask their mutual scrutiny. Fern pretends to be so disgusted by this sentimental spectacle that she concludes "Oh, there never should be but one woman alive at a time."

But then the essay inverts again, for Fern imagines that the "one" woman alive would be herself. If she were the last remaining woman, Fern imagines that she would turn the tables on men, by making them the generic Other, spectacularly ridiculous in their competition to please her—body, mind, and soul. The "femininity" of "worthless" women is redefined as a name for the way disempowered, delegitimated subjects act. Through this parody of patriarchal practices, the culture of sentimental desire is revealed as an archive of subjugation and distortion. In Fern's view, men who turn women into embodiments of their own love of rule should simply marry men, since the women they imagine are more mannequin than human.[32]

But the affectively colonizing effects of female uni-formalism are much more seriously degrading and penetrating than this satire of manners might suggest. Fern's novella *Fanny Ford,* for example, asks that "God pity her, who, with a great soul, indissolubly bound, must walk ever backward with a mantle (alas! all too transparent), to cover her husband's mental nakedness!"[33] Like the plot of the book itself, Fanny is "bound" to a profligate husband; her pure and innocent belief in human virtue and wifely submission drives her, like so many of Fern's subjects, insane. The debility of women who are virtuously bound to form is not dramatic or sensational, but private and hidden: "Ah! there is no law to protect woman from negative abuse! no mention made in the statute book (which *men frame for themselves*) of the constant dropping of daily discomforts which wear the loving heart away. No allusion to looks or words that are like poisoned arrows to the sinking spirit."[34] Fern calls this kind of marital torture "legal murder," and says its brand of justice is more likely to transgress against than to protect women from the most banal forms of male violence.[35] This petty violation is not simply contained in domestic spaces: Fern's repeatedly expressed wish to wear men's clothes comically refers to the daily degradation of women who happen to walk the street unprotected by the visible arm of a man.[36] So vulnerable are all women to uninvited male mental and physical abuse that Fern links herself and her "common" sisters with prostitutes, who are simply the exaggerated embodiment of the woman who has silently submitted to the sexual economy of patriarchal culture.[37]

I have focused here on the dark side of Fern's distances from sentimental consolation, measured in her enraged sarcasm at the practices and effects of patriarchal man- and womanhood. There are many texts spread throughout her career that validate sentimental ideality in a nonironic sense as well. In texts like "A Word to Mothers," which argues that "a mother's reward is in secret and in silence," she invokes maternal martyrdom as an unfailing index of moral and practical virtue. In texts like "Bogus Intellect" and "Two Kinds of Women," she repeatedly asserts that married women's submission to a domestic regimen must precede any incursions into the public sphere. Old maids and other women forced by circumstances to earn wages have slightly different privileges and obligations, but these are wrought by tragic necessity, not by choice, and involve their own dialectic between radical gender redefinition and sentimental reflexivity—or, to use Fern's language, between "sense as well as freshness, and conversation and repartee as well as dimples and curves."[38] Non-coherent about the value of domestic ideology and woman's rights agitation, Fern has no single position on the woman question—except that she consistently stages the baptism of woman's lot in her continual confrontation with the stereotype to which she must submit, either under duress or spurred on by desire. Her critique of the middle-class embrace of stereotypicality extends to its effects on men as well as women. But her interest is in asserting that, as long as "woman" appears to be "a walking advertisement" for a cultural type, "women" will be immersed in triviality and modes of self-abasement that range from the heroically pathetic to the embarrassing.[39] Fern does not settle on one response to the fact of female humiliation: her perennial task is to testify to the patterned postures women take in public, in their infinite and contradictory variety.

"All Femality is Wide Awake": Fanny Fern's *Fresh Leaves*

Fern's reading of domestic sentimentality acts as an apology and a consolation for the anguish of living under patriarchy, but this critical pose does not align Fern solidly with feminism—or at least authorize her female audience to rupture relations with domestic fantasy. Instead of making simply a complaint against men and male-identified women, Fern carries out the struggle to install female dignity within domestic life by criticizing two disembodied and objective patriarchal forms that define the negativity of women's experience: the dictionary and the nation.

Countless times, à la Becky Sharp, Fern repudiates the patriarchal dictionary, which preserves in panhistorical form the archaic formations of male dominance: its most elaborate incarnation is in the masculine "dictionary on legs," whom Fern exiles from the scene of domestic literature in the introduction to her novel *Rose Clark*.[40] As a metonym for the sum of patriarchal culture, the dictionary itself takes up the space of what women cannot yet say, the silence of subalterns, marked out by their very speech. On the subject of husbands, one of her characters writes, "well—THERE! when I think of THEM, I must wait till a new dictionary is made before I can express my indignation!" On her desire to reinvent clerical definitions of women, she declares that "if I were to swallow a whole dictionary, I couldn't clothe that idea in words!"[41]

Of course women have already swallowed the bitter pill of patriarchal language, so when Fern proclaims that "[a]ll femality is wide awake," she links Margaret Fuller's feminist neologism with granting dignity and expression to the otherwise degraded female libidinousness of woman.[42] "Femality" is a force in excess of the forms of negation and containment that characterize life within the patriarchal abode. Even "pattern" women "exceed" their stereotype[43]: "femality" reroutes female excess from abasement and hypocrisy to a productive and positive vernacular drive, not feminist but celebratory of women's consciousness in a populist appeal.[44] But we must follow carefully the limits of this noun: "femality" is wide awake, but the material conditions of social life lag miserably behind consciousness. Nonetheless, Fern's assertion of women's psychic emergence (which is tied to her own position as a female journalist within a bourgeoning women's culture industry) is a strategic intervention into the impasse of sentimental culture—its representation of feminine ideality, and its renunciation of the female residues not caught up in "type." The invention of a new language, derived from what she calls the "Fern dictionary," will enable Fern as exemplum "to express [her] surplus enthusiasm" and "tumultuous emotions"—to decolonize herself, and so to "forget" strategically the matter of patriarchal culture.[45] "If I wasn't bound to collect their mental skeletons to hang up in my dissecting-room, I should eschew the whole sex," she writes, calling her persona a "female naturalist."[46] Indeed, on occasion she contracts a terrible case of citational amnesia, as when she cannot remember whether the line "*He* for God only, *she* for God in *him*" was written by John Milton or Mother Goose.[47]

But along with revealing the patriarchal quotation marks around the language and culture in which women have assumed distorted "female" identities, Fern's agitation against the dictionary also has a patriotic edge: to repudiate Webster's dictionary as she does repeatedly is to reject the American vernacular so deeply associated with the nation's revolutionary emergence. In Fern's writing, national identity constitutes both the promise and the fraudulence of liberal culture. Her many essays against British and French society champion the common sense that distinguishes American women. But when addressing what her country has done for her, as a woman, Fern measures with her very body the distance between women and citizenship or national personhood. Her columns "Independence" and "A Little Bunker Hill," for example, argue that American rights only refer to "masculine rights,"[48] since women cannot be considered "free" in America, in either the political or the urban public spheres.

"FOURTH OF JULY." Well—I don't feel patriotic. . . . I'm glad we are all free; but as a woman—I shouldn't know it, didn't some orator tell me. Can I go out of an evening without a hat at my side? Can I go out with one on my head without danger of a station-house? Can I clap my hands at some public speaker when I am nearly bursting with delight? Can I signify the contrary when my hair stands on end with vexation? Can I stand up in the cars "like a gentleman" without being immediately invited "to sit down"? Can I get into an omnibus without having my sixpence taken from my hand and given to the driver? Can I cross Broadway without having a policeman tackled to my helpless elbow? Can I go to see anything *pleasant,* like an execution or a dissection? . . . Can I be a Senator, that I may hurry up that millennial International Copyright law? Can I *even* be President? Bah—you know I can't. "*Free!*" Humph![49]

To Fern, citizenship is not an abstract condition or privilege: it is a relay to protection and legitimation under the law and in the public sphere, which includes the world of the arts and the more banal experiences of the body in the marketplace. She focuses not just on the vote, but on laws limiting women's rights as wives and mothers within marriage and in the labor force. She also frequently points out the absurdity of the degree to which society regulates juridically what women wear and what they say. She even argues that the extension of the national promise to women might make the streets safer for women. Finally, she imagines a time when women might speak as abstract citizens, too—as authors protected by copyrights and as national politicians.

In so lampooning and lamenting the bogus promises of American citizenship, Fern finds her strongest link to the rhetoric of nineteenth-century feminism, which derived its first documentary model from the Declaration of Independence. (The Declaration of Sentiments looks exceedingly like a rationalized female complaint, which is perhaps why Fern teasingly refers to the feminist conference at "Sigh-racuse.")[50] In any case, the challenges to American constitutional, juridical, and ideological gender mystification brought by woman's rights activists became, by the 1860s, increasingly central to Fern's thought about what it would take for women to gain dignity in modern America; in addition, transformations in domestic and capitalist attitudes toward the value of women's labor also captured Fern's attention. America justifies in theory a freedom of personality and public trespass as well as a collective politics of consent; in the sum of its practices, however, America becomes the name for the negative space that women like Fern were attempting to occupy, with their minds and voices preceding their actual and juridical bodies. The degree to which the national space signified the barrenness of women's lives is depicted bathetically in "A Business Man's Home; Or, A Story for Husbands," which speaks yet another narrative of silent female martyrdom to husbandly torture and neglect. Fern notes that the house of Mr. and Mrs. Wade is a place of the wife's exile from dignity and pleasure, its white walls vacant, "with the exception of a huge map of the United States in the hall."[51]

Conclusion: Commodity Consciousness

In the concentric spaces of the nation, the home, and the dictionary, Fern identifies the uninhabitable place of American womanhood. In that contested terrain, dominant structures of political legitimation, sexual desire, and personal self-expression appear perversely to undercut the possibility of legitimate "female" agency, although the feminine subject is allowed to choose the contradictions of her constraint, whether they be in the double consciousness of hypocrisy or the self-abasement of martyrdom. As a matter of content, Fern's intervention into these spaces is more radical than that of many sentimental domestics, because she has seen the power of women's culture to deform the women it addresses by enforcing the distance between domestic ideology and everyday life experience. Amnesia permeates the sentimental pieties of domestic fantasy, as women are, in her terms, "bewitched" into forgetting the information about marital and juridical brutality toward women they read and hear about from other women.[52] Such "forgetting" dooms women to repeat their abasement to domestic fantasy.

Fern's insistent vernacular aims to provide a mnemonic, to turn her audience of atomized ladies into a generic woman with "one ear" who will paradoxically recognize her unique female self in Fern's disembodied voice.[53] This voice, which has experienced the banal and the extreme misogyny of American culture, does not tell the one feminine ear to seek out a utopian, revolutionary form of desire nor even, typically, a feminist one; Fern insists instead that women should expect the structure of everyday life *as it is* to pay off on its promise to fulfill the woman, to recognize her specific needs and talents. In thus ranging among domestic and feminist fantasies, Fern shows how the elasticity of sentimental form includes its diverse popular audience—by appealing to the "reality" that all women are generic and therefore misapprehended in their very uniqueness. It is here that we can begin to see the collaboration of the commodity and the stereotype, for being generic becomes the founding condition for the culture of reflection and resistance that marks the history of sentimentality in America.

Nina Baym has suggested that the nineteenth-century American novel reproduced a contradiction in these terms, with respect to the feminine subject. The novel increasingly promotes psychological complexity and depth of character, while insisting that women be drawn to type. The solution of the women's novel was to demonstrate again and again the "education" of a girl to the self-mastery necessary to live the life of typicality.[54] But if the novel does serve this psychojuridical function, it is also an insufficient index to our understanding of the cultural work of sentimentality for women. Fern herself distinguishes between novelistic and journalistic representations of the feminine subject.

Fern's address to her novel readers assumes a different "experience" from that of her weekly consumers. In the preface to *Ruth Hall* she sees the narrative of female emergence from sentimental innocence to a victory within realism as a vehicle of hope for the "tired heart" whose own "continuous story" has been characterized by obstacles similar to that of Ruth/Fanny's.[55] In contrast, in *Fern Leaves* she looks neither for narrative exemplification, personal empowerment through the construction of compelling literary characters, nor for a communal scene of reading in which the performance performs the family in the symbolic time and space of bourgeois self-staging in everyday life. Rather, she looks for punctuated identification: "Some of the articles are sad, some are gay; each is independent of all the others, and the work is consequently disconnected and fragmentary; but, if the reader will imagine me peeping over his shoulder, quite happy should he pay me the impromptu compliment of a smile or a tear, it is possible we may come to a good understanding by the time the book shall have been perused."[56]

Fern wants to elevate women from the mental emptiness and obsessive activity of fashioning daily life. She offers the form for feminine legitimation in the fragment, the detail, the essay, journals—not by rendering women's experience generic, but by expressing the frustration of *being* generic. This mode of female identification allows that one woman's disclosure of the frustrations of everyday life ennobles that of other women; moreover, the complaint installs woman's writing as a part of an ongoing pedagogy about how to negotiate the contested life of femininity. Most important, her witnessing of bourgeois feminine sensibility is here raised to a hermeneutic at the level of the *punctum:* it is the point to which the author and reader of the female sentimental text will return. This is the main form of power/knowledge available to all women, of all classes and races, if only they will consent to consume it. For the women who experience no legitimacy in public, this periodic point of identification is itself the site of value and exchange, far more important and vitalizing than the content of any given column, whether sentimental or sarcastic. By providing a formal structure of identification through the example of her own "personal journalism," the expression of Fern's personality becomes the model for that kind of individuated expression she aims to enable the reader to imagine in herself. Fern thus aims not to change the lives of her audience, but to change their relation to what their minds can do—no longer in retreat from the world, but engaging actively in acute analysis of it. As her character Minnie says, "My mind to me a kingdom is!"[57]

Coda: Strangers in the Night

The archival work of testifying to women's silencing into "stereotype" is also political: it registers the effects of private life and public caricature. But in a world where the abstraction of woman from women, of Sambo from African Americans, is both sign and cause of American disenfranchisement, we can see at least that this mode of abstracting discourse within the female culture industry promotes consciousness as opposed to action, mind and memory versus politics, as a way of naming and containing female excess. It produces as a commodity for women a form of identification whose power derives from its apparent natural superiority to social practice and public exchange. In this mode a cultural discourse about woman—her negation and suffering from her domestic pleasures—tells an open secret about women whose revelation, for the last 150 years, has been the dominant fact of female collective identity in America.

Fanny Fern's brother N. P. Willis was a central figure in the sentimentalization of national culture: he was one of the first publisher-editors of a national newspaper, the *Home Journal,* which introduced to America many of the most conservative male and female ideologues of the "cult of true womanhood," in its pure form an essentialist and ahistorical ethic of female discipline.[58] The *Home Journal* defined itself as national not through affiliation with political parties (which at the time were more regional in focus), but rather through a notion of "society" that diminished the political content of news in favor of less "sectarian" points of cultural convergence. Willis invented "fashion" and recast popular social opinion as national news, driving a wedge between culture and politics.[59] The introduction to the *Journal*'s first number made explicit this intention: "In addition . . . to the entertaining features of the JOURNAL—its narrative, anecdote, humour, poetry and art— we shall give such a summary of news as will make the reader sure that he *loses nothing worth knowing of the world's goings on.*"[60] While late in his career he spoke out against slavery in this newspaper, during the 1840s and 1850s Willis was well known as an apologist for the status quo who desired to displace the divisive issue by constituting the "national" in practices of style and taste. While the regional press of the nation was infused with the political agitations of the abolitionist, woman's rights, and labor movements, segments of the emerging national press invested the elite practices of social caste with a suprapolitical, virtually transcendent value; manners seen through a gauze of morality and patriotism.[61]

Willis's desire to displace political discourse from the center of the social text also motivated practices in his personal life, some of which constituted unfortunate incidents in the lives of two struggling women: his sister Fanny Fern, and Harriet Jacobs, who (as Linda Brent) pseudonymously authored *Incidents in the Life of a Slave Girl* (1861). *Ruth Hall* tells the story of Willis's refusal to publish Fern's writing, while Fern and her children starved in urban tenements. Willis told her that she was too vulgar for his or any journal, and that she lacked the talent to write for a national audience. Ruth waxes bitter at his fictional counterpart's assessment of her provinciality and vows dramatically to make him yet *"proud to claim his sister,"* presumably by finding her own kind of national audience.[62]

At approximately the same time, and in an unrelated life plot, Willis employed as a servant in his home the fugitive slave Harriet Jacobs. He did not overtly support his wife's efforts to protect Jacobs from her Southern owners and also made no attempt to purchase the manumission papers that would enable her to get her freedom. He seems hardly to have recognized her plight at all, although *Incidents* speaks lovingly of the efforts Mrs. Willis (aka "Mrs. Bruce") made on Jacobs's behalf. Jacobs's letters reveal that she intensely mistrusted Willis, writing her narrative in secret, at night, over a period of five years while in his employ.[63] In her previous life as a Southern slave, Jacobs lay entombed in a hollow ceiling, hiding there from her owner for seven years; as a Northern writer she undergoes a similar garreting, away from the cold eye of N. P. Willis. It is extremely ironic that Elizabeth Cady Stanton called *Ruth Hall* a slave narrative, since an authentic slave narrative emerged from such a similar source.[64]

And yet the link between Brent and Fern in Willis, which led to their individual textual fame and legitimacy, also signifies the differences in their struggles to gain freedom and economic autonomy. As Hazel Carby has demonstrated, Brent and other early African American women writers appropriated the conventions of sentimental domesticity as a frame within which to explicate their own brutalized and parodically domestic experiences in slavery.[65] This code-crossing established the protections of sentimental domesticity both as an ideal for which the slave woman yearned and an obstacle to the politicization of white bourgeois women.[66] The very act of speaking "woman to woman" established a common identity at the level of ideality and measured an experiential gap of which consciousness itself was only the necessary but insufficient condition under which social change might take place. Simultaneously a genericizing and a disidentifying gesture, such use of "sentimental womanhood" graphically shows that even when American women apparently speak the same "language" at the same historical "moment," their coarticulation maps out their differences with regard to the privileges and offenses of the dictionary and the nation.

We can see this ambiguity in the juxtaposition of Fern and Jacobs. We might put Fern in a logic of equivalence with Jacobs, because of their mutual violation by Willis and the apolitical sentimental culture he advocates and profits from, even as Fern puts herself in an equivocal position with Sambo, who becomes the "difference" between them. In *The Life and Beauties of Fanny Fern,* a white editor contests a white woman journalist's critical representation of heterosexual life; Fern counters sentimental conventions about women and marriage by deploying a racist stereotype—thus identifying her vernacular knowledge with "Sambo's" in a deeply problematic and ironic gesture of affiliation and racism. In contrast, Jacobs did not have the privilege to stereotype a white woman for the purposes of cultural critique, since to a certain extent it was identification with them that she sought.

The ending of *Incidents in the Life of a Slave Girl* and *Ruth Hall* provide further emblems of the likeness of, and the distance between, the two women sentimentalists. In the conclusion to her tale, Jacobs looks at her own bill of sale and remarks, "I well know the value of that bit of paper; but much as I love freedom, I do not like to look upon it."[67] In contrast, at the end of *Ruth Hall* the text brandishes triumphantly a bank note, worth $10,000, that signifies the finale of Ruth's triumph.[68] Both women have struggled to procure these papers, but while the one denotes the minimal unit of freedom experienced by an American citizen, the other denotes a successful negotiation of the national-capitalist public sphere, a profitable commodification of female pain and heroism in an emerging industry of female cultural workers.

It is more than coincidence that sentimental discourse was the site of convergence for these two differently struggling women. The powerful desire to assert both individual specificity and generic gender identity expresses in polarized form the mental paradoxes that characterize the women represented within the sentimental genres of the female culture industry. Any discussion of this industry needs to address its problematic relation to the racial, classed, and ethnic subjects whose "privileges" as citizens and consumers were strongly contested in American culture; but since, in its own terms, the products of sentimentality aimed to dissolve what appear to be intractable or pseudonatural differences that fix cultural hierarchy, it is also necessary to see how, in its own terms, sentimental discourse figured itself as an emancipatory commodity. And so any investigation of American female sentimental discourse must trace the ambivalent politics of its rhetoric, as it shuttles between profiting by deconstructing dominant stereotypes of woman and passing off generic female self-identity as itself a commodity, a thing to be bought and shared.[69] But sentimentality never reveals its intimacy with commodity culture: sentimental ideology is the public dream work of the bourgeois woman.

Notes

Introduction

The development of this volume was assisted by a conference at Cornell University on April 30–May 2, 1990. We would like to express our thanks to the Society for the Humanities, which housed the conference, and to the many speakers, respondents, organizers, and participants not included in this volume, who very materially enabled both the bodily comfort and the intellectual interrogation needed for productive discourse.

1. Vincent-Buffault goes on to explain: "the tears of sensibility referred to a refined culture of the self. A series of aesthetic, ethical and even medical stakes delineated the limits of this developed sensibility. The fashion which was known as 'sentimentalist' rather jostled this balance and these delicate emotions" (53).

2. *The Sentimental Novel in America, 1789–1860* (Duke University Press, 1940), 358–59, 367–68. In a culture absorbed by "Bloomerism and Transcendentalism, Temperance and Abolition," Brown sees "an exuberant optimism, as jaunty and as expansive as the frontier."

3. George Mosse, *Nationalism and Sexuality: Middle-Class Morality and Sexual Norms in Modern Europe* (University of Wisconsin Press, 1985), 18. For an account of relations between national and natural bodies on the American scene, see Mark Seltzer, *Bodies and Machines* (Routledge, 1992).

4. Lauren Berlant provocatively develops the concept of the "national symbolic" in *The Anatomy of National Fantasy: Hawthorne, Utopia, and Everyday Life* (University of Chicago Press, 1991).

5. Ann Douglas, *The Feminization of American Culture* (Knopf, 1977), 254. Not only does she find that "[s]entimentalism, unlike the modes of genuine sensibility, never exists except in tandem with failed political consciousness," but she goes further: "sentimentalism might be defined as the political sense obfuscated, or gone rancid." Such literal distaste might curiously invoke precisely the bodily response that sentimentality so often encourages.

6. Jane Tompkins, *Sensational Designs: The Cultural Work of American Fiction, 1790–1860* (Oxford University Press, 1985), 160. She claims that "the great subject of sentimental fiction is preeminently a social issue." In short, although scholarship on sentimentality has been wide-ranging and interdisciplinary—literary, social, and cultural historians have all written on the subject—its conceptual terms have been somewhat narrow, in that they have established the (by now) rigidified opposition, to put it crudely, between those *for* it and those *against* it. This volume, it perhaps goes without saying, does not condemn sentiment as culturally disabling, but neither does it simply

endorse it as culturally enabling. Conceiving of sentimentality in gendered as well as racially specific terms, the essays rather examine its cultural trajectory. Other interesting and provocative accounts of nineteenth-century American sentimentality include: Nina Baym, *Woman's Fiction: A Guide to Novels by and about Women in America, 1820–1870* (Cornell, 1978); Nancy Cott, *The Bonds of Womanhood: "Woman's Sphere" in New England, 1780–1835* (Yale University Press, 1977); Barbara Epstein, *The Politics of Domesticity: Women, Evangelism, and Temperance in Nineteenth-Century America* (Wesleyan University Press, 1981); Karen Halttunen, *Confidence Men and Painted Women: A Study of Middle-Class Culture in America, 1830–1870* (Yale University Press, 1982); Blanche Hersh, *The Slavery of Sex: Feminist-Abolitionists in Nineteenth-Century America* (University of Illinois Press, 1978); Mary Kelley, *Private Woman, Public Stage: Literary Domesticity in Nineteenth–Century America* (Oxford University Press, 1984); and Mary Ryan, *Empire of the Mother: American Writing About Domesticity, 1830–1860* (Haworth Press, 1982).

Sentimentality in nineteenth-century America has roots, of course, in eighteenth-century discussions of sensibility, and has correspondences with nineteenth-century cultural productions in England and in Europe. For a history of sentimentality, see Janet Todd, *Sensibility: An Introduction* (Methuen, 1986), who asserts that "the body is a constant communicator" (99). On the eighteenth century see, for instance, David Marshall, *The Surprising Effects of Sympathy: Marivaux, Diderot, Rousseau, and Mary Shelley* (University of Chicago Press, 1988), and Robert Markley, "Sentimentality as Performance: Shaftesbury, Sterne, and the Theatrics of Virtue," in *The New Eighteenth Century*, ed. Felicity Nussbaum and Laura Brown (Methuen, 1987). Drawing on Adam Smith's *The Theory of Moral Sentiments* (1759) in *Sacred Tears: Sentimentality in Victorian Literature* (Princeton University Press, 1987), Fred Kaplan counterposes sentimentality, as expressive of "innate moral sentiment" (and associated with the "man of sentiment," a Victorian hero), to "sensibility," a response to external stimuli (associated with the "man of feeling," the Romantic hero).

7. Pierre Bourdieu, *Distinction: A Social Critique of the Judgment of Taste*, trans. Richard Nice (Harvard University Press, 1984), 170. "The habitus is not only a structuring structure which organizes practices and the perceptions of practices, but also a structured structure: the principle of division into logical classes which organizes the perception of the social world is itself the product of internalization of the division into social classes."

Chapter 1

I would like to thank Joan Hedrick, Margaret Homans, Stephen Lassonde, Joel Pfister, Shirley Samuels, Nancy Schnog, Werner Sollors, Doris Sommer, Martha Viehmann, and Lynn Wardley for their generous and helpful responses to an earlier draft of this essay.

Throughout this essay I have used the term "Indian" rather than "Native American" or "tribal people," because it conforms to the usage in the nineteenth-century texts that I discuss. I am aware, however, that this is something of a compromise.

1. Ann Douglas, *The Feminization of American Culture* (New York, 1977), 6–7, 11, 10, 13, 12, 13, 5, 12, 11, 256, 13.

2. Douglas, *Feminization*, 7, 13.

3. Jane Tompkins, *Sensational Designs: The Cultural Work of American Fiction, 1790–1860* (New York, 1985), 123.

4. Ibid., 12, 126.

5. Ibid., 122, xiv, xvi, xvii, xviii, xiii, xvi.

6. Douglas, *Feminization*, 11.

7. Tompkins, *Sensational Designs*, xiv, 187.

8. Ibid., 217, n. 3.

9. Ibid., 200; Douglas, *Feminization*, 5.

10. Tompkins, *Sensational Designs*, xiv, 200; Douglas, *Feminization*, 12.

11. Douglas, *Feminization*, 9.

12. Tompkins, *Sensational Designs*, xi, 123, and passim.

13. Douglas, *Feminization*, 61 (ellipsis deleted).

14. Ibid., 3, 4, 5.

15. Tompkins, *Sensational Designs*, 122.

16. Patricia Meyer Spacks, *Gossip* (Chicago, 1985), 5.

17. Nina Baym, *Woman's Fiction: A Guide to Novels by and about Women in America, 1820–1870* (Ithaca, N.Y., 1978), 25.

18. Douglas, *Feminization*, 12, 11.

19. Baym, *Woman's Fiction*, 27.

20. Dorothy Sterling, ed., *We Are Your Sisters: Black Women in the Nineteenth Century* (New York, 1984), xiii.

21. Richard Brodhead, "Sparing the Rod: Discipline and Fiction in Antebellum America," *Representations* 21 (Winter 1988): 70, 90–91, 76–77 (ellipsis deleted).

22. Philip Fisher, *Hard Facts: Setting and Form in the American Novel* (New York, 1987), 92, 99, 98, 100.

23. Frederick Douglass, *Narrative of the Life of Frederick Douglass, an American Slave* (1845; New York, 1982), 83–84.

24. Baym, *Woman's Fiction*, 13.

25. Robert Francis Engs, *Freedom's First Generation: Black Hampton, Virginia, 1861–1890* (Philadelphia, 1979), 147. William Roscoe Davis is also reported to have said that "if Negroes don't get any better education than Armstrong is giving them . . . they may as well have stayed in slavery!"; quoted in Engs, 147.

26. Engs, *Freedom's First Generation*, 149–50, 151, 144, 151, 145, 149 (ellipsis deleted), 151, 143.

27. Dexter Fisher, foreword to Zitkala-Ša, *American Indian Stories* (Lincoln, Nebr., 1979), x.

28. Quoted in Melissa Banta and Curtis M. Hinsley, *From Site to Site: Anthropology, Photography, and the Power of Imagery* (Cambridge, Mass., 1986), 105.

29. Douglas, *Feminization*, 10.

30. Lydia Maria Child, *The Mother's Book* (Boston, 1831), 86; quoted in Douglas, *Feminization*, 62.

31. *Catalogue of the Indian Industrial School* (Jamestown, N.Y., 1902), 4; quoted in Lorna M. Malmsheimer, "Imitation White Man: Images of Transformation at the Carlisle Indian School," in *Studies in Visual Communication* 2:4 (Fall 1985): 69.

32. Malmsheimer, "Imitation White Man," 69–70.

33. Fisher, foreword to Zitkala-Ša, *American Indian Stories*, v. Fisher's excellent work in rediscovering, republishing, and contextualizing the life and writing of Zitkala-Ša has been crucial to my own formulation.

34. "Our Indian School," in *Valley Sentinel*, 19 September, 1879; quoted in Malmsheimer, "Imitation White Man," 56–57.

35. Malsheimer, "Imitation White Man," 64.

36. Zitkala-Ša, *American Indian Stories*, 41, 42, 7, 9.

37. Ibid., 39, 27, 34–35, 13.

38. Ibid., 43, 44 (ellipsis deleted).

39. Ibid., 44–45.

40. Ibid., 47–48, 49–50, 50–51.

41. Ibid., 52, 67–68.

42. Ibid., 42.

43. Fisher, foreword to Zitkala-Ša, *American Indian Stories,* vii.

44. Ibid.

45. Zitkala-Ša, *American Indian Stories,* 96–99.

46. Quoted in Banta and Hinsley, *From Site to Site,* 18.

47. Maren Stange, *Symbols of Ideal Life: Social Documentary Photography in America, 1890–1950* (Cambridge, Mass., 1989), 13, 16, 4.

48. Tompkins, *Sensational Designs,* 122; Douglas, *Feminization,* 3.

49. Nancy Armstrong, *Desire and Domestic Fiction: A Political History of the Novel* (New York, 1987), 27.

50. Mary Kelley, *Private Woman, Public Stage: Literary Domesticity in Nineteenth-Century America* (New York, 1984).

51. Armstrong, *Desire and Domestic Fiction,* 255.

Chapter 2

1. *Trial of Lucretia Chapman, otherwise called Lucretia Espos Y Mina, who was jointly indicted with Lino Amalia Espos Y Mina, for the murder of William Chapman, Esq. Late of Andalusia, County of Bucks, Pennsylvania, in the Court of Oyer and Terminer, held at Doylestown, for Bucks, December Term, 1831, continued to February Term, 1832. Prepared for Publication, by William E. Du Bois, Student of Law* (Philadelphia, 1832). Quotes are from pp. 66, 41–42, 43, 48, 40. All subsequent quotes are from this edition. For a concise discussion of the Chapman case, see Ann Jones, *Women Who Kill* (New York: Holt, Rinehart and Winston, 1980), 77–90.

2. Hayden White, "The Value of Narrativity in the Representation of Reality," in W. J. T. Mitchell, ed., *On Narrative* (Chicago: University of Chicago Press, 1981), 23.

3. Paul Ricoeur, quoted in Peter Brooks, *Reading for the Plot: Design and Intention in Narrative* (New York: Vintage Books, 1985), 13.

4. Brooks, *Reading for the Plot,* 6.

5. Hayden White has pointed to the existence of a close relationship between narrativity in general and the law: "But once we have been alerted to the intimate relationship that Hegel suggests exists between law, historicality, and narrativity, we cannot but be struck by the frequency with which narrativity, whether of the fictional or the factual sort, presupposes the existence of a legal system against or on behalf of which the typical agents of a narrative account militate. And this raises the suspicion that narrative in general, from the folktale to the novel, from the annals to the fully realized 'history,' has to do with the topics of law, legality, legitimacy, or, more generally, *authority.*" From "Value of Narrativity," 13.

6. W. Lance Bennett and Martha S. Feldman, *Reconstructing Reality in the Courtroom* (New Brunswick, N.J.: Rutgers University Press, 1981), ch. 1, "Storytelling in the Courtroom," 5 and 9.

7. Though the jury trial dates back to the thirteenth century, it was not until the eighteenth century that it assumed its modern adversarial form with counsel for both

prosecution and defense. In ordinary felony trials before the mideighteenth century, there was thus no voir dire, no opening or closing statements, no formal examination or cross-examination, no evidentiary or procedural motions. The judge served as the main examiner, though the accused, the prosecuting victim, and the various witnesses could be "examined" and "cross-examined" by one another as well, in a haphazardly conversational fashion. See John H. Langbein, "The Criminal Trial Before the Lawyers," *The University of Chicago Law Review* 45:2 (Winter 1978): 263–316; and "Shaping the Eighteenth-Century Criminal Trial: A View from the Ryder Sources," *The University of Chicago Law Review* 50:1 (Winter 1983): 1–136.

8. In the interest of clarity, I treat the case for the prosecution as a whole, though it was presented in pieces by two gentlemen, Mr. Ross and Mr. Reed, for the Commonwealth; though their styles and emphases varied, their central plot line and characterization of Lucretia Chapman were largely in agreement. I will treat the case for the defense, presented by Mr. M'Call and Mr. Brown, in the same fashion.

9. The proof of their guilt, according to the prosecution, lay in their marrying only twelve days after her husband's death, and in Lucretia's letters to Mina after that marriage: "If ever unchecked passion, in a disordered and undisciplined mind, found appropriate language, it is in these singular letters. . . . Every line and every word are traced by passion—passion unchecked and uncontrolled—the very riot of the blood."

10. For a discussion of the symbolic meaning of the confidence man in sentimental culture, see Karen Halttunen, *Confidence Men and Painted Women: A Study of Middle-Class Culture in America, 1830–1870* (New Haven, Conn.: Yale University Press, 1982).

11. The sentence for a woman convicted of petty treason for killing her husband was to be burned alive, though it seems that executioners usually strangled the condemned woman before burning her. See J. H. Baker, "Criminal Courts and Procedure at Common Law, 1550–1800," in J. S. Cockburn, ed., *Crime in England, 1550–1800* (Princeton, N.J.: Princeton University Press, 1977), 15–48; and J. M. Beattie, *Crime and the Courts in England, 1660–1800* (Princeton, N.J.: Princeton University Press, 1986).

12. Her conduct, they argued, was shockingly at odds with her position in life: "It is indeed painful to behold a woman, who had reached the meridian of life, with a family of young and interesting children around her, all dependant, in some measure, upon the good name of their mother for their future reputation, thus surrendering herself to the vilest excesses of criminal indulgence, and becoming a spectacle so odious and debasing to the moral sense of the community" (195).

13. See Nancy F. Cott, "Passionlessness: An Interpretation of Victorian Sexual Ideology, 1790–1850," *Signs* 4 (Winter 1978): 219–36; Carol F. Karlsen, *The Devil in the Shape of a Woman: Witchcraft in Colonial New England* (New York: W. W. Norton, 1987), especially ch. 5; Laurel Thatcher Ulrich, *Good Wives: Image and Reality in the Lives of Women in Northern New England, 1650–1750* (New York: Oxford University Press, 1983), passim.

14. Karlsen, *Devil in the Shape of a Woman*, 87.

15. In arguing that Mina would not have purchased arsenic to murder William Chapman without Lucretia's knowledge, the prosecution observed: "It will not be pretended that he [Mina] was sincere in his profession of love and admiration for a woman of Mrs. Chapman's age and appearance, or that he ever seriously intended to take her to Mexico" (197).

16. Two other circumstances link the Chapman murder trial to seventeenth-century witchcraft accusations. First, the death of the neighbor's poultry linked this murder

case to the many witchcraft cases in which women were accused of performing *maleficia* against their neighbors' livestock. Second, police officers testified that Lucretia Chapman had a bad "police character"; forbidden by judicial procedure from introducing extraneous suspicions concerning her conduct, they generalized that someone would be considered to have a bad police character who was suspected of having stolen goods on her premises, or of being involved in a counterfeiting operation. As Carol Karlsen has demonstrated, witchcraft accusations were frequently linked to charges of theft.

17. Messalina was the notorious Roman empress who was executed in 48 A.D. by order of her husband Claudius I; her name is a byword for lasciviousness and marital incontinence.

18. For a discussion of the sentimental concern for sincere mourning, see my study *Confidence Men and Painted Women*, ch. 5.

19. The third object of this peculiar judicial exorcism was neither a woman nor a servant to the Chapmans. Edwin B. Fanning, the book peddler who lived under the Chapmans' roof during William's final illness, testified that Lucretia neglected her sick husband—refusing to send for physicians, failing to administer medication, driving others from the dying man's bedside—even while she continued to lavish attention upon the boarder Mina. Indeed, before departing from the Chapman home, Fanning left word that he should be summoned, should any suspicions arise about William Chapman's illness. The response of the defense was to heap upon Fanning the rich language of opprobrium reserved for the peddler in a society that remained profoundly suspicious of this avatar of commercialism. Fanning was denominated "the mysterious pedlar," "[t]his eastern mountebank—this peddling bookseller—a fellow, vending his salt-and-water physic [his recommended medication for Chapman], and his milk-and-water literature through the land; one of a wandering tribe, as numerous as the locusts of Egypt, and as great a curse" (173). As a peddler, Fanning was thus proclaimed a fraud, a man of mystery and the occult, and a Jew. Like Mina, he had arrived hungry and penniless at the Chapman home, to be taken under the "fostering care" of the charitable Lucretia Chapman, "and in kind requital for all this, when by the death of her husband, she was left without a protector or a friend, in a strange land, this viper, who had so long coiled in flowery ambush, deliberately attempts stinging her joys to death" (173). But according to the defense, after unleashing rumors "that there were deadly doings in that house," Fanning's actual testimony on the witness stand proved worthless: "He opens his pedlar pack before this court and jury, and while every man stands aghast, with the idea that like Pandora's box, it will pour forth all kinds of evils to afflict the human race, lo, and behold, it presents an empty void!" (173).

20. Karlsen, *Devil in the Shape of a Woman*, 256–57.

21. See Nina Auerbach, *Woman and the Demon: The Life of a Victorian Myth* (Cambridge, Mass.: Harvard University Press, 1982); Mary Poovey, *Uneven Developments: The Ideological Work of Gender in Mid-Victorian England* (Chicago: University of Chicago Press, 1988); Joy S. Kasson, *Marble Queens & Captives: Women in Nineteenth-Century American Sculpture* (New Haven, Conn.: Yale University Press, 1990).

22. See *Supplement to the Trial of Mrs. Chapman, Published by George W. Mentz & Son, Philadelphia. Trial of Lino Amalio Espos Y Mina, for the Murder of William Chapman. Court of Oyer and Terminer, holden at Doylestown, for the County of Bucks, April Sessions, 1832;* bound with the Lucretia Chapman trial. Mina was executed for the crime on 21 June 1832, before a reported crowd of 10,000. After the execution, his alleged "confession" was published under the title *The Confession of*

Mina, the Spaniard, who was executed at Doylestown, Pennsylvania, On the 21st June, 1832, for the Murder of William Chapman, Written by himself in Spanish and translated into English (Doylestown, Pa.: n.p., 1832). In it, Carolino Estradas de Mina charged Lucretia Chapman with the murder of her husband, proclaiming his own perfect innocence. The story in this "confession" does not, however, agree with what Mina had told police officers upon his arrest, according to their testimony during his trial.

23. "It is possible to conclude that it was wise to be female and respectable if one intended to dispose of somebody in the nineteenth century. Middle-class women were literally getting away with murder." Mary S. Hartman, *Victorian Murderesses: A True History of Thirteen Respectable French and English Women Accused of Unspeakable Crimes* (New York: Schocken Books, 1977), 1.

24. As Mary Hartman has observed, evidence is "bound to be" circumstantial "in the very private crime of poisoning"; see *Victorian Murderesses*, 10.

25. See Auerbach, *Woman and the Demon*.

Chapter 3

1. The origins of American antislavery fiction and the extent of its debt to English and French antislavery fiction need further investigation. Extant studies of the genre devote more attention to the novel than to short fiction and children's fiction. See Lorenzo Dow Turner, *Anti-Slavery Sentiment in American Literature Prior to 1865* (1929; reprint, Port Washington, N.Y.: Kennikat Press, 1966); Sterling A. Brown, *The Negro in American Fiction* (1937; reprint, Port Washington, N.Y.: Kennikat Press, 1968); Donald E. Liedel, "The Antislavery Novel, 1836–1861" (Ph.D. diss., University of Michigan, 1961); and Jean Fagan Yellin, *The Intricate Knot: Black Figures in American Literature, 1776–1863* (New York: New York University Press, 1972), and *Women and Sisters: The Antislavery Feminists in American Culture* (New Haven, Conn.: Yale University Press, 1989). Richard Hildreth's *The Slave, or Memoirs of Archy Moore* (1836) is generally considered the first American antislavery novel. Yet Lydia Maria Child's antislavery stories for children antedate Hildreth's novel, and a few antislavery stories appeared in early numbers of Garrison's weekly *The Liberator* (e.g., "A Dream" and "Another Dream" by "T.T.," 2 and 30 April 1831, pp. 53, 70). I have also found a fictional didactic dialogue entitled "The Harmans," signed "Margaret," in Benjamin Lundy's *Genius of Universal Emancipation* (13 November 1829, pp. 76–77). Other early examples of antislavery narrative (though closer to fact than to fiction) are Maria Weston Chapman's "Pinda" and "A Tale of Endeavor," published in the ephemeral abolitionist journal *The Monthly Offering* and reprinted in the *National Anti-Slavery Standard* (29 October and 5 November 1840, pp. 84, 85). My research to date reveals significant differences between men's and women's antislavery fiction: in men's, slave rebellion tends to be the central theme, while the sexual exploitation of slave women is peripheral; in women's, the reverse is true. The present article is partly drawn from ch. 14 of my book in progress, *"The First Woman in the Republic": A Cultural Biography of Lydia Maria Child*, to be published by Oxford University Press.

2. See Blanche Glassman Hersh, *The Slavery of Sex: Feminist-Abolitionists in America* (Urbana: University of Illinois Press, 1978).

3. I am indebted for this insight to Annette Kolodny's brilliant comments on the contrasting theses of my paper on "Slavery's Pleasant Homes" and of Gary Sue Goodman's paper "Secret Sympathy: Autobiography in the Anti-Slavery Fiction of Caroline

Healey Dall," at the session chaired by Susan Koppelman, "Feminist Abolitionists/ Abolitionist-Feminists—Black and White," National Women's Studies Association Conference, Seattle, June 1985.

4. Lydia Maria Child, "Slavery's Pleasant Homes. A Faithful Sketch," *The Liberty Bell* 4 (1843): 147–60.

5. For a more extensive analysis of the novel, see the introduction to Lydia Maria Child, *нововок and Other Writings on Indians,* ed. Carolyn L. Karcher (New Brunswick, N.J.: Rutgers University Press, 1986).

6. Review of Lydia Maria Child, *Hobomok, A Tale of Early Times, North American Review* 19 (July 1824): 263; Jared Sparks, "Recent American Novels," *North American Review* 21 (July 1825): 87.

7. For accounts of Child's literary career, see Patricia G. Holland, "Lydia Maria Child as a Nineteenth-Century Professional Author," *Studies in the American Renaissance,* ed. Joel Myerson (Boston: Twayne, 1981), 157–67; and Carolyn L. Karcher, "Lydia Maria Child," *Dictionary of Literary Biography: American Short Story Writers Before 1880,* ed. Bobby Ellen Kimbel (Detroit: Gale Research Company, 1988), 43–53. For biographies of Child see Helene Baer, *The Heart Is Like Heaven: The Life of Lydia Maria Child* (Philadelphia: University of Pennsylvania Press, 1964); Milton Meltzer, *Tongue of Flame: The Life of Lydia Maria Child* (New York: Thomas Y. Crowell, 1965); and the biographical sketch in Patricia G. Holland, Milton Meltzer, and Francine Krasno, ed., *The Collected Correspondence of Lydia Maria Child, 1817–1880, Guide and Index to the Microfiche Edition* (Millwood, N.Y.: Kraus Microform, 1980), 23–38.

8. Cooper's *The Last of the Mohicans* (1826) and *The Wept of Wish-ton-Wish* (1829) raise the possibility of intermarriage only to reject it. Sedgwick's *Hope Leslie* (1827) depicts a lasting interracial marriage, though not in a very flattering light. Sedgwick does explore another alternative to race war, however—an alliance between Indian and white women. For a brief comparison of these novels with *Hobomok,* see my introduction to the Rutgers reprint edition of *Hobomok,* xxxv–xxxvii.

9. *Juvenile Miscellany,* n.s. 5 (September 1830, January 1831): 81–94, 285–99. See also "Mary French and Susan Easton," *Juvenile Miscellany,* 3d ser., 6 (May 1834): 186–202. Although "The Harmans" antedates these stories, it is closer to the didactic dialogue than to actual fiction. Child's earliest antislavery story for adults, "Malem-Boo. The Brazilian Slave," appeared in her antislavery gift book *The Oasis* (Boston, 1834), 21–40, a forerunner of *The Liberty Bell.* Set in Africa and Brazil and oriented toward refuting stereotypical misconceptions about Africa that served to rationalize slavery as a means of "rescuing" Blacks from savagery in Africa, "Malem-Boo" escapes most of the limitations of women's antislavery fiction. It does not, however, work effectively as a vehicle for mobilizing public opinion against *American* slavery.

10. Lydia Maria Child, *An Appeal in Favor of That Class of Americans Called Africans* (Boston, 1833).

11. For excellent histories of the campaign to suppress public discussion of the slavery question, see Russel B. Nye, *Fettered Freedom: Civil Liberties and the Slavery Controversy, 1830–1860* (1963; reprint, Urbana: University of Illinois Press, 1972); and Leonard L. Richards, *"Gentlemen of Property and Standing": Anti-Abolition Mobs in Jacksonian America* (New York: Oxford University Press, 1971).

12. See the review of "Mrs. Child's 'Appeal' " in *The Liberator* of 14 December 1833, p. 200, praising the book's "forcible, conclusive reasoning" and "appearance of extensive research," and describing it as "a powerful auxiliary to the Anti-Slavery cause" and as "an armory well stored with weapons of approved temper to arm [the

antislavery advocate] for combat." A roll call of the leaders who credited the "forma-tive influence" of "Mrs. Child's Appeal" with recruiting them into the antislavery movement provides another gauge of the book's historical importance: the influential Unitarian minister William Ellery Channing, hitherto a fence-straddler; the fiery ora-tor Wendell Phillips, henceforth second only to Garrison in prominence; the Massachu-setts Senator Charles Sumner, largely responsible for the legislative victories of Recon-struction; and the militant ex-minister Thomas Wentworth Higginson, commander of one of the first black regiments during the Civil War. See Higginson, *Contemporaries*, vol. 2 of *The Writings of Thomas Wentworth Higginson* (Boston: Houghton, Mifflin, 1900), 123.

13. Child, *Appeal*, 19.

14. Katharine Du Pre Lumpkin, *The Emancipation of Angelina Grimké* (Chapel Hill: University of North Carolina Press, 1974), 15–16, 171–72; see also Yellin's fine analysis of Angelina Grimké's deep identification with slave women, *Women and Sisters*, ch. 2.

15. [Theodore Dwight Weld, Angelina Grimké Weld, and Sarah Grimké], *American Slavery As It Is: Testimony of a Thousand Witnesses* (1839; reprint, New York: Arno Press and the *New York Times*, 1969), 53.

16. Lumpkin, *Emancipation*, 220–25.

17. Grimké Weld, *American Slavery*, 53–54.

18. Although Child did not read the *Journal* until its publication in 1863, she must have heard a good deal about its contents. Child's letters report a detailed conversa-tion with the Sedgwicks about Kemble in December 1838, and no doubt there were many more, as the Sedgwicks frequently visited Elizabeth's mother in Northampton, where Child was residing during the very period when Kemble was writing her *Journal* and sharing it with Elizabeth and other friends. At Elizabeth Sedgwick's suggestion, Child wrote to Kemble in 1841, urging her to publish the *Journal* in the *National Anti-Slavery Standard*, which Child was then editing. See LMC to Ellis Gray Loring and Louisa Gilman Loring, 5 December 1838, in *Lydia Maria Child: Selected Letters, 1817–1880*, ed. Milton Meltzer, Patricia G. Holland, and Francine Krasno (Amherst: University of Massachusetts Press, 1982), 95–96, and 340, headnote. Also LMC to Ellis Gray Loring, 27 July 1841, and LMC to Oliver Johnson, 22 August 1863, in Child's *Collected Correspondence*, ed. Holland, Meltzer, and Krasno, 10/244, 56/1499.

19. Frances Anne Kemble, *Journal of a Residence on a Georgian Plantation in 1838–1839*, ed. John A. Scott (1863; reprint, New York: New American Library, 1975). See Scott's Introduction, xli–liii.

20. Kemble, *Journal*, 222.

21. Kemble paid a heavy price: her husband dragged her through the mud in one of the century's most notorious divorce trials, and deprived her of her daughters, in accordance with nineteenth-century custody laws (Introduction, *Journal*, xliv–xlv). The quotation is from Grimké Weld, *American Slavery*, 53.

22. Kemble, *Journal*, 269.

23. Dall, "The Inalienable Love," *The Liberty Bell* 15 (1858): 87.

24. I have quoted Child's explanation of why she returned once more to fiction in 1867, when she wrote her novel *A Romance of the Republic*, intended to "undermine [racial] *prejudice*"; see LMC to Francis George Shaw, 28 July 1867, *Collected Corre-spondence*, 67/1789.

25. "ARCHY MOORE," LMC to William Lloyd Garrison, *The Liberator*, 18 March 1837, reproduced in *Collected Correspondence*, 5/118.

26. See Child's letters to her sister-in-law, Lydia Bigelow Child, about *Archy Moore*

and about her own efforts to write an antislavery novel, 17 January 1837 and 2 April 1837, *Selected Letters,* 60 and 65. The manuscript of that novel appears to have been destroyed.

27. For analyses of the "tragic mulatto" theme and the problems it raises, see Jules Zanger, "The 'Tragic Octoroon' in Pre-Civil War Fiction," *American Quarterly* 18 (Spring 1966): 63–70; Sterling Brown, *The Negro in American Fiction,* 45–46; Barbara Christian, *Black Women Novelists: The Development of a Tradition, 1892–1976* (Westport, Conn.: Greenwood Press, 1980), 22–23; Alice Walker, *In Search of Our Mother's Gardens: Womanist Prose* (New York: Harcourt Brace Jovanovich, 1983), 290–312; and Yellin, *Women and Sisters,* 71–74.

28. LMC to Maria Weston Chapman, 1 December [1841], *Collected Correspondence,* 12/292.

29. These features, in my view, clearly distinguish "Slavery's Pleasant Homes" from the typical "tragic mulatto" narrative. Hence I cannot agree with Yellin in classifying it as such (*Women and Sisters,* 71–74).

30. Child, *Appeal,* 201.

31. Child, *Appeal,* 205; "The Slave Murders," *National Anti-Slavery Standard,* 23 June 1842. This editorial refers to the earlier incident while commenting on a similar case that has just been reported.

32. "Diabolical Wickedness, to Which a Citizen of Boston Was a Party," *The Liberator,* 11 August 1832, p. 127. Quotations are from Child's paraphrases of the *Liberator* story in the *Appeal* (206) and the *National Anti-Slavery Standard,* cited in n. 31. A comparison of the three accounts reveals Child's evolution toward greater freedom of expression in sexual matters. Garrison's article in *The Liberator* is much more explicit than Child's version of the story in the *Appeal,* where she merely says that the overseer "compelled" the women to "remain as long as he thought proper" (206). In the *Standard,* Child supplies the details she had earlier censored from Garrison's account.

33. Child, *Appeal,* 206.

34. "Diabolical Wickedness," *The Liberator,* 11 August 1832, p. 127.

35. "Horrible Events!" and "The Slave Murders," *Standard,* 23 June 1842, pp. 10–11.

36. See "Annette Gray" and "Follow the North Star," *Standard,* 22 July 1841, pp. 26–27, and 21 July 1842, pp. 26–27. I have put the names in quotation marks because they are fictitious.

37. "Peculiar Traits of Southern Life—Condition of Woman—Her Strange Seclusion—True and False Civilization—Southern Chivalry," *Portsmouth Journal,* reprinted in *Standard,* 8 December 1842, p. 108. Child generally sent in her contributions to *The Liberty Bell* by December 1, since the volume had to be published in time for the pre-Christmas fair. The *Portsmouth Journal* article had probably arrived at the *Standard* office well before Child reprinted it. She often held articles for several weeks, when space constraints prevented her from inserting them.

38. See for example George Fitzhugh, *Sociology for the South, or the Failure of Free Society* (1854; reprint, New York: Burt Franklin, n.d.), 297. Child entitled her 1860 antislavery tract, which juxtaposed proslavery rhetoric of this kind with slave laws and examples of slave abuse, *The Patriarchal Institution.*

39. See Lydia Maria Child, *The History of the Condition of Women, in Various Ages and Nations,* 2 vols. (Boston, 1835), 1:2, 24, 45, on the Hebrews' payment of bride prices, the Babylonians' auctioning off of marriageable girls, and the Circassians' sale of disobedient wives into slavery.

40. I am using the term "romance" in the sense that Child uses it, not in the sense

established by Hawthorne. I do not mean to claim that "Slavery's Pleasant Homes" is an example of literary realism, as defined by Howells. Nevertheless, I would like to suggest that antislavery fiction may be profitably examined as one of the sources or precursors of literary realism, which recent critics have traced back to midnineteenth-century women writers. See, for example, *Provisions: A Reader from 19th-Century American Women,* ed. Judith Fetterley (Bloomington: University of Indiana Press, 1985), 10–11.

41. "Slavery's Pleasant Homes," *The Liberty Bell* 4 (1843): 147. All subsequent page references to the story will be given parenthetically in the text.

42. I am indebted to Lucy Freibert for this analysis of Child's imagery. It should be noted that the image of the "dark carnation" represents a departure from the model of the near-white heroine. Rosa's skin color is described as "transparent brown," resembling "claret [seen] through a bottle in the sunshine" when she blushes (148).

43. "Annette Gray" and "Follow the North Star," *Standard,* 22 July 1841, pp. 26–27, and 21 July 1842, pp. 26–27.

44. A scene parallel to the one between Marion and Rosa also occurs in Harriet A. Jacobs's *Incidents in the Life of a Slave Girl. Written by Herself,* ed. Jean Fagan Yellin (1861; reprint, Cambridge, Mass.: Harvard University Press, 1987). Here is how Jacobs describes the reactions of her mistress, Mrs. Flint, when "Linda" tells of the advances the master has been making to her: "As I went on with my account her color changed frequently, she wept, and sometimes groaned. She spoke in tones so sad, that I was touched by her grief. . . . She felt that her marriage vows were desecrated, her dignity insulted. . . . She pitied herself as a martyr; but she was incapable of feeling for the condition of shame and misery in which her unfortunate, helpless slave was placed" (33). Child edited this narrative and helped Jacobs to find a publisher for it.

45. Child leaves it ambiguous whether Frederic or George is the father of Rosa's child. In either case the pregnancy would still be the result of illicit sex, since Child makes it clear that George and Rosa's marriage is informal (slave marriages were not legally recognized).

46. In "Benito Cereno" (1855), Melville appends the legal deposition of the master, which the Spanish court has used to convict the slave rebels; in *Billy Budd,* he appends a newspaper account in "a naval chronicle of the time, an authorized weekly publication," whose version represents a complete distortion of the story he has narrated (ch. 29).

47. Dall, "The Inalienable Love," *The Liberty Bell* 15 (1858): 87.

48. The phrase "delicate-nerved, ladies" is from an article in *The Liberator* entitled "Slavery as it is," 12 June 1840, p. 93, which attacks the view that it is indelicate for women to engage in antislavery work.

49. LMC to Lucy Searle, 4 February 1861, *Collected Correspondence,* 47/1282.

50. LMC to John Greenleaf Whittier, 4 April 1861, *Selected Letters,* 378. The political climate of 1860–61 was almost as hostile to abolitionism as in the 1830s, and much more hostile than during the 1840s and 1850s. Once again, antiabolitionist mob violence raged in Northern cities, as the same elites that had fomented the riots of the 1830s renewed their assault in the wake of Lincoln's election victory. By stamping out abolitionism, Northern elites hoped to conciliate the South, prevent Southern states from carrying out their threats to secede, and avert civil war.

51. Brown lifted whole passages from "The Quadroons" in chapters 4 and 8 of *Clotel.* His plagiarism (which he eliminated from subsequent editions of the novel) betrays both his discomfort with the white-invented tragic mulatto theme and his understanding of its strategic value in appealing to white readers. See William Edward

Farrison, *William Wells Brown, Author and Reformer* (Chicago: University of Chicago Press, 1969), 224, 228, 325; Yellin, *The Intricate Knot,* 172; and Carolyn L. Karcher, "Lydia Maria Child's *A Romance of the Republic:* An Abolitionist Vision of America's Racial Destiny," in *Slavery and the Literary Imagination: Selected Papers from the English Institute, 1987,* ed. Deborah E. McDowell and Arnold Rampersad (Baltimore: The John Hopkins University Press, 1989), 101, n. 6.

52. The quotation is from the headnote to "The Quadroons" in Susan Koppelman, ed., *The Other Woman: Stories of Two Women and a Man* (Old Westbury, N.Y.: Feminist Press, 1984), 2.

Chapter 4

I would like to thank Larry Moore and Shirley Samuels for their comments on earlier drafts. Research for this work was funded in part by an Albert J. Beveridge Grant of the American Historical Association and an NEH Summer Institute Fellowship at the Johns Hopkins University.

1. Lawrence Martin, "The Genesis of *Godey's Lady's Book,*" *The New England Quarterly* 1 (1928): 52.

2. The major reference remains Frank Luther Mott, *A History of American Magazines,* vol. 1: 1741–1850 (New York, 1930), 580–94. In passing, Ann Douglas mentions fashion plates à la Godey in most magazines of the period; see *The Feminization of American Culture* (New York, 1977), 229. Recent works on Sarah Josepha Hale and Godey's magazine include Gail Caskey Winkler, "Influence of *Godey's Lady's Book* on the American Woman and Her Home: Contributions to a National Culture (1830–1877)" (Ph.D. diss., University of Wisconsin, 1988), and Angela Marie Howard Zophy, "For the Improvement of My Sex: Sarah Josepha Hale's Editorship of *Godey's Lady's Book,* 1837–1877" (Ph.D. diss., Ohio State University, 1978). See also Glenda Gates Riley, "The Subtle Subversion: Changes in the Traditional Image of the American Woman," *The Historian* 32 (1970): 210–27; Ruth E. Finley, *The Lady's of Godey's: Sarah Josepha Hale* (Philadelphia, 1931); Isabelle Webb Entrikin, *Sara Josepha Hale and Godey's Lady's Book* (Lancaster, Pa., 1946).

Laura McCall provides a content analysis of the magazine based on coding sheets for 234 female characters of 120 stories in " 'The Reign of Brute Force Is Now Over': A Content Analysis of *Godey's Lady's Book,* 1830–1860," in *Journal of the Early Republic* 9 (Summer 1989): 217–36. An expanded version of her content analysis appears in Laura McCall, "Symmetrical Minds: Literary Men and Women in Antebellum America" (Ph.D. diss., University of Michigan, 1988). For McCall, nineteenth-century magazines were neither visual nor frivolous; "Reign of Brute Force," 224, n. 15.

On the question of sentimental literature, see Nina Baym, *Woman's Fiction: A Guide to Novels by and About Women in America, 1820–1870* (Ithaca, N.Y., 1978); Mary Kelley, *Private Women, Public Stage: Literary Domesticity in Nineteenth-Century America* (New York, 1984); Glenna Mathews, *"Just a Housewife": the Rise and Fall of Domesticity in America* (New York, 1987), 42–44; Kathryn Kish Sklar, *Catharine Beecher: A Study of American Domesticity* (New York, 1976).

3. Mary Poovey's *Uneven Developments: The Ideological Work of Gender in Mid-Victorian England* (Chicago, 1988) offers a provocative account of instabilities and unevenness embodied in representations of gender.

4. Douglas, *Feminization*. Douglas's unambiguous approach recalls the Frankfurt School's critique of mass culture. See Max Horkheimer and Theodor W. Adorno, "The Culture Industry: Enlightenment as Mass Deception," *Dialectic of Enlightenment* (1944; translated by John Cumming; New York, 1982), 120–67. For the tenets of the nineteenth-century opposition to popular women novelists, see Henry Nash Smith, "The Scribbling Women and the Cosmic Success Story," *Critical Inquiry* 1 (September 1974): 47–49; John T. Frederick, "Hawthorne's Scribbling Women," *New England Quarterly* 48 (1975): 231–40.

5. On fiction and women readers, see Jane Tompkins, *Sensational Designs: The Cultural Work of American Fiction, 1790–1860* (New York, 1985); Mary Kelley, *Private Women*, and "The Sentimentalists: Promise and Betrayal in the Home," *Signs* 4 (Spring 1979): 434–46; Nina Baym, *Woman's Fiction*, and *Novels, Readers, and Reviewers: Responses to Fiction in Antebellum America* (Ithaca, N.Y., 1984); Cathy N. Davidson, *Revolution and the Word: The Rise of the Novel in America* (New York, 1986).

6. The economic and political system remained unchanged and the death of Little Eva did not hinder the working of slavery, despite Lincoln's admiration for Stowe. Studies of the death of Little Eva include Ann Douglas, "The Legacy of American Victorianism: The Meaning of Little Eva," *Feminization*, 3–12; and Jane Tompkins, "Sentimental Power: *Uncle Tom's Cabin* and the Politics of Literary History," *Sensational Designs*, 122–46.

7. Here I am applying to print culture the concept of a "separate sphere" which was part of the ideology of domesticity in nineteenth-century America. A true woman was to provide moral influence in the private space of the home, while the public sphere and the immoral marketplace remained the province of men. An ideology of subservience and domesticity was deeply intertwined with the separation of public and private spheres, male and female worlds. The concept of "feminization" is from Barbara Welter, "The Feminization of American Religion, 1800–1860," *Dimity Convictions: The American Woman in the Nineteenth Century* (Athens, Ohio, 1976), 83–102, and Douglas, *Feminization*.

8. Bertha Monica Stearns describes several predecessors to *Godey's*, in the tradition of the British *Lady's Magazine*. See "Early New England Magazines for Ladies," *New England Quarterly* 2 (1929): 420–57; "Before *Godey's*," *American Literature* 2 (1930): 248–55; "Early Philadelphia Magazines for Ladies," *Pennsylvania Magazine of History and Biography* 64 (1940): 479–91; "New England Magazines for Ladies, 1830–1860," *New England Quarterly* 3 (1930): 627–56. See also Martin, "Genesis of *Godey's*," 41–70. On English ladies' magazines, see Alison Adburgham, *Women in Print: Writing Women and Women's Magazines from the Restoration to the Accession of Victoria* (London, 1972), and Kathryn Shevelow, *Women and Print Culture: The Construction of Femininity in the Early Periodical* (London, 1989).

9. Stearns, "Early Philadelphia Magazines," 480, 488, 490.

10. For instance, fashion engravings were eventually added to *Graham's American Monthly Magazine of Literature, Art and Fashion*, which had incorporated *The Casket*. On giftbooks, see my "Reading as Beholding: The Representation of Ladyhood in Giftbooks, 1830–50," unpublished paper presented at the 1990 Berkshire Conference on the History of Women.

11. Martin, "Genesis of *Godey's*," 56.

12. The long history of illustrations in print includes successive phases, from the production of images for the poor and illiterate to images for refined taste. Crude and exquisite qualities of images came to reflect the social strata of the public.

Nineteenth-century illustrations particularly denoted the emergence of the middle classes both in Europe and in America. The technique of steel engraving was perfected in 1818 and proved adaptable to the industrialization of printing. See Gordon N. Ray, *The Illustrator and the Book in England from 1790 to 1914* (New York, 1976); Basil Hunnisett, *Steel-Engraved Book Illustration in England* (London, 1980); Michel Melot, *L'Illustration: histoire d'un art* (Paris, 1984), 130. See also Lucien Febvre and Henri-Jean Martin, *The Coming of the Book: The Impact of Printing, 1450–1800* (London, 1976).

13. For a discussion of the social meaning of fashion in nineteenth-century America, see Karen Halttunen, *Confidence Men and Painted Women: A Study of Middle-Class Culture in America, 1830–1870* (New Haven, Conn., 1982). Halttunen analyzes the antebellum shift from romantic dress to sentimental dress and the ideal of simplicity. She examines the antebellum social conventions of dress and the acceptance of fashion as a necessary evil in a society established on the promise of social mobility. While Halttunen takes for granted the representation of fashion in *Godey's Lady's Book* as evidence of changes in dress and its social meaning, this chapter considers the historical specificity of figures in women's magazines.

14. For a provocative discussion of composite text and the interactions between image and text, see W. J. T. Mitchell, *Iconology: Image, Text, Ideology* (Chicago, 1986), and his "Visible Language: Blake's Wond'rous Art of Writing," in *Romanticism and Contemporary Criticism,* ed. Morris Eaves and Michael Fischer (Ithaca, N.Y., 1986), 46–95; and three articles by Louis Marin: "Mimésis et description," *Word & Image* 4 (January–March 1988): 25–34; "On Reading Pictures: Poussin's Letter on *Manna,*" *Comparative Criticism: A Yearbook* 4 (1982): 3–18; "Toward a Theory of Reading in the Visual Arts: Poussin's *The Arcadian Shepherds,*" in *The Reader in the Text: Essays on Audience and Interpretation,* ed. Susan R. Suleiman and Inge Crosman, (Princeton, N.J., 1980), 293–324. See also Meyer Schapiro, *Words and Pictures: On the Literal and the Symbolic in the Illustration of a Text* (The Hague, 1973).

15. This was also true of the English ladies' magazines of the 1790s. See Adburgham, *Women in Print,* 206.

16. The concept of "residual culture" is from Raymond Williams, "Base and Superstructure in Marxist Cultural Theory," *Problems in Materialism and Culture* (London, 1980), 31–49.

17. Back cover advertisement, *Godey's* 1853.

18. Adburgham, *Women in Print,* 205.

19. *Godey's,* August 1839, p. 95.

20. *Godey's Lady's Book,* May 1839, p. 239. See also Robert Kunciov, ed., *Mr. Godey's Ladies: Being a Mosaic of Fashion and Fancies* (New York, 1971), 2. The shift from an auratic art to a postauratic art occurred with the advent of photography in the late nineteenth century. See Walter Benjamin, "The Work of Art in the Age of Mechanical Reproduction," *Illuminations: Essays and Reflections,* ed. Hannah Arendt (New York, 1969), 17–51.

21. Backcover advertisement, *Godey's,* September 1851. Mott, *History of American Magazines,* 593.

22. Nancy F. Cott, *The Bonds of Womanhood: "Woman's Sphere" in New England, 1780–1835* (New Haven, Conn., 1977), 115.

23. J. G. Chapman, *The American Drawing-Book: A Manual for the Amateur, and Basics of Study for the Professional Artist* (New York, 1847), 8; "Our Artists," *Harper's New Monthly Magazine* 28 (1864): 242.

24. The concept of "civilization of the hand" is from Roland Barthes, "Image, raison, déraison" in *L'Univers de l'Encyclopédie,* ed. Roland Barthes, Robert Mauzi, and Jean-Pierre Seguin (Paris, 1964).

25. Barbara Welter, "The Cult of True Womanhood: 1820–1860," *American Quarterly* 18 (Summer 1966): 151–74. For the question of leisure and conspicuous consumption, see Thorstein Veblen, *The Theory of the Leisure Class* (New York, 1899).

26. Louis Marin, "Poussin's *The Arcadian Shepherds,*" 301.

27. Barbara Welter argues that "women in the first half of the nineteenth century took Christianity and molded it to their image and likeness" (*Dimity Convictions,* 102). The concept of "tongue snatcher" is from Claudine Herrmann, *Les Voleuses de langue* (Paris, 1976), or in translation by Nancy Kline, *The Tongue Snatchers* (Lincoln, 1989).

28. *Godey's,* April 1852, p. 298.

29. Halttunen, *Confidence Men and Painted Women,* 157.

30. Before theater staging became widespread, books of theater proved a success in eighteenth-century Europe. See Wolfgang Baumgart, "Der Leser als Zuschauer: Zu Chodowieckis Stichen zur Minna von Barnhelm," in *Die Buchillustration im 18. Jahrhundert* (Heidelberg, 1980), 13–25.

31. *Godey's,* February 1852, p. 170.

32. Cott, *Bonds of Womanhood;* Carroll Smith-Rosenberg, "The Female World of Love and Ritual: Relations Between Women in Nineteenth-Century America," *Signs* 1 (1975), reprinted in *Disorderly Conduct: Visions of Gender in Victorian America* (New York, 1985), 53–76.

33. Mary H. Blewett's study *Men, Women, and Work: Class, Gender, and Protest in the New England Shoe Industry, 1780–1910* (Urbana, Ill., 1988) discusses how working women defended their rights as domestic mothers and daughters. Their consciousness as workers in production was intertwined and in conflict with the family values of artisan culture. See also her article "Women Shoeworkers and Domestic Ideology: Rural Outwork in Early Nineteenth-Century Essex County," *New England Quarterly* 60 (1987): 403–28. Christine Stansell also analyzes the support for an ideology of domesticity among New York City working men who wanted to protect their wives and daughters from a system of exploitation they themselves were enduring. See *City of Women: Sex and Class in New York, 1789–1860* (New York, 1986). Class distinction among antebellum women is the subject of Gerda Lerner, "The Lady and the Mill Girl: Changes in the Status of Women in the Age of Jackson, 1800–1840," reprinted in Nancy F. Cott and Elizabeth A. Fleck, eds., *A Heritage of Her Own: Toward a New Social History of American Women* (New York, 1979), 182–96.

34. *Voice of Industry,* 3 December 1847, cited in Philip S. Foner, ed., *The Factory Girls: A Collection of Writings on Life and Struggles in the New England Factories of the 1840s* (Urbana, Ill., 1977), 93.

35. On antebellum women's associations, see in particular Nancy F. Cott, *The Bonds of Womanhood;* Mary P. Ryan, *Cradle of the Middle Class: The Family in Oneida County, New York, 1790–1865* (New York, 1981); Barbara Leslie Epstein, *The Politics of Domesticity: Women, Evangelism, and Temperance in Nineteenth-Century America* (Middletown, Conn., 1981).

36. Martin, "Genesis of *Godey's,*" 65.

37. For a broader discussion of antebellum prescriptions of ascetic reading and critique of pleasurable reading, see my "Changes in the Word: Reading Practices in Antebellum America" (Ph.D. diss., Cornell University, 1992), especially ch. 6.

38. Critics of Louis Godey referred to the magazine as "Godey's Bible" or "God-ey's

Bible." See John Tebbel, *The American Magazine: A Compact History* (New York, 1969), 50.

39. Neil Harris has described how Americans began to regard the visual arts as moral and religious tools that could serve political purposes. See *The Artist in American Society: The Formative Years, 1790–1860* (Chicago, 1966), 148. A Philadelphia Unitarian minister, the Rev. William H. Furness, provides a good example of the new faith in the moral power of art; see *An Address Delivered Before the Art-Union of Philadelphia in the Academy of Fine Arts* (Philadelphia, 1848).

40. For a discussion of the clergy's attitudes toward the visual arts, see John Dillenberger, *The Visual Arts and Christianity in America: the Colonial Period Through the Nineteenth Century* (Chico, Cal., 1984), and Diane Apostolos-Cappadona, "The Spirit and the Vision: The Influence of Romantic Evangelicalism on Nineteenth-Century American Art" (Ph.D. diss., George Washington University, 1988), especially 101–9.

41. Welter, *Dimity Convictions;* Douglas, *Feminization;* Sylvia D. Hoffert, " 'A Very Peculiar Sorrow': Attitudes Toward Infant Death in the Urban Northeast, 1800–1860," *American Quarterly* 39 (1987): 601–16; and Sylvia D. Hoffert, *Private Matters: American Attitudes Toward Childbearing and Infant Nurture in the Urban North, 1800–1860* (Urbana, Ill., 1989).

42. Alice B. Neal, "The Coquette," *Godey's,* March 1851, p. 149. The engraving was by W. E. Tucker from an original drawing made expressly for *Godey's* by John Gilbert of London. "The Constant" is another story by Alice B. Neal, published with a plate in *Godey's,* January 1851, p. 5.

43. *Godey's,* February 1845, pp. 49, 60; S. J. Hale, "New Year at Home," *Godey's,* January 1840, pp. 1–4.

44. On the depiction of cottages, see Neville Thompson, "Tools of Persuasion: The American Architecture Book of the Nineteenth Century," in *The American Illustrated Book in the Nineteenth Century,* Gerald W. R. Ward, ed. (Winterthur, Del., 1987), 137–69. On furnishing designs and needlework, see Winkler, "Influence of Godey."

45. *Godey's,* August 1845, p. 84.

46. See Martin, "Genesis of *Godey's,*" 55–56. Sarah J. Hale had also accepted the publication of fashion plates in her *Ladies' Magazine* as a means of exhibiting the domestic life.

47. *Godey's,* February 1840, p. 96.

48. For the importance of objects, see Colleen McDannell, *The Christian Home in Victorian America, 1840–1900* (Bloomington, Ind., 1986); David Jaffee, "One of the Primitive Sort: Portrait Makers of the Rural North, 1760–1860," in *The Countryside in the Age of Capitalist Transformation: Essays in the Social History of Rural America,* Steven Hahn and Jonathan Prude, eds. (Chapel Hill, N.C., 1985), 103–38; Remy G. Saisselin, *The Bourgeois and the Bibelot* (New Brunswick, N.J., 1984).

49. Colleen McDannell argues that Catholic women of Philadelphia read *Godey's,* because there was no Catholic journal available; see *Christian Home,* 55, 103.

50. Ralph Waldo Emerson, *Journals,* April 1852, in Joel Porte, ed., *Emerson in His Journals* (Cambridge, Mass., 1982), 433.

Chapter 5

This paper owes much to the thoughtful readings and generous advice of Sharon Cameron and Larzer Ziff; and to Alexandra Halasz, Elizabeth Hanson, Joe Harrison,

Marcie Frank, and of course Benigno Sánchez-Eppler, who challenged and encouraged me through more drafts than any of us want to remember.

1. Lydia Maria Child, *Anti-Slavery Catechism* (Newburyport, Mass., 1836), 17.

2. Ibid., 16.

3. On the simple level of events, the intersections between antebellum feminism and abolition are legion. The Grimké sisters, antislavery lecturers of the 1830s, were the first women to give public lectures before "mixed" or "promiscuous" audiences, and Angelina Grimké was the first American woman to speak before a legislative body. Censured for such unfeminine activity, they increasingly addressed the issue of woman's rights within their antislavery discourse. In the 1830s and 1840s, Susan B. Anthony and Lucy Stone worked as paid agents of the American Anti-Slavery Society, lecturing on both abolition and woman's rights. Elizabeth Cady Stanton and Lucretia Mott first met at the World's Anti-Slavery Convention of 1840 in London, at which the female delegates were refused seats; legend has it that the idea of a woman's rights convention—not realized until 1848—was first discussed in the hotel rooms of these excluded women. For varying accounts of the relation between the two movements, see Ellen DuBois, "Women's Rights and Abolition: The Nature of the Connection," in Lewis Perry and Michael Fellman, eds. *Antislavery Reconsidered: New Perspectives on the Abolitionists* (Baton Rouge, La., 1979); Ellen Dubois, *Feminism and Suffrage: The Emergence of an Independent Women's Movement in America, 1848–1869* (Ithaca, N.Y., 1978); Blanch Glassman Hersh, *The Slavery of Sex: Feminist-Abolitionists in America* (Urbana, Ill., 1978); and Gerda Lerner, *The Grimké Sisters from South Carolina: Pioneers for Woman's Rights and Abolition* (New York, 1971).

4. Carroll Smith-Rosenberg, "Puberty to Menopause: The Cycle of Femininity in Nineteenth-Century America," in *Disorderly Conduct: Visions of Gender in Victorian America* (New York, 1985).

5. Included in Aileen S. Kraditor, *Up from the Pedestal: Selected Writings in the History of American Feminism* (Chicago, 1968), 190–91. This fantasy was published as an editorial in the *Herald,* providing the very newsprint it gleefully imagines.

6. Dr. Samuel A. Cartwright, "Diseases and Peculiarities of the Negro Race," *De Bow's Review* (1851), excerpted in James O. Breeden, ed., *Advice Among Masters: The Ideal in Slave Management in the Old South* (Westport, Conn., 1980), 173. Breeden identifies Cartwright as among the "leading scientific spokesmen" of "the campaign to defend the South's sectional interests and to promote southern nationalism" and thus a consciously biased interpreter of anatomy.

7. Lydia Maria Child included these quotations along with many similar items gleaned from the Southern press in *The Patriarchal Institution as Described by Members of Its Own Family* (New York, 1860), 13, 11. She added the italics as a form of commentary. The first quote mentioned here is cited by Child from an advertisement for the runaway slave of Anthony M. Minter (A.M.) in the *Free Press* of Alabama, 18 September 1846. She takes the second from an advertisement posted by John A. Rowland, jailer, to publicize his capture of a presumed runaway in the Fayetteville, N.C. *Observer,* 20 June 1838.

8. Angelina Grimké, *An Appeal to the Women of the Nominally Free States: Issued by an Anti-Slavery Convention of American Women Held by Adjournment from the 9th to the 12th of May 1837* (New York, 1837).

9. For a more general analysis of how the idealization of freedom that characterizes Western thought relies upon the historical and factual presence of slavery, see Orlando Patterson, *Slavery and Social Death* (Cambridge, Mass., 1982).

10. Sarah Grimké, *Letters on the Equality of the Sexes and the Condition of Women:*

Addressed to Mary S. Parker, President of the Boston Female Anti-Slavery Society (Boston, 1838), 13, 75.

11. Elizabeth Cady Stanton to the National Woman's Rights Convention, Cooper Institute, dated Seneca Falls, N.Y., 24 November 1856, included in the appendices of *The History of Woman Suffrage,* ed. Elizabeth Cady Stanton, Susan B. Anthony, and Matilda Joslyn Gage, 6 vols. (New York, 1881), 1:860.

12. Margaret Fuller, "Woman in the Nineteenth Century" (1844), in *Writings of Margaret Fuller,* ed. Mason Wade (New York, 1941), 123.

13. The most famous instance of this turn is Sojourner Truth's refrain "a'n't I a woman" at the Akron woman's rights convention on 29 May 1851.

> "Dat man ober dar say dat womin needs to be helped into carriages, and lifted ober ditches, and to hab de best place everywhar. Nobody eber helps me into carriages, or ober mud-puddles, or gibs me any best place!" And raising herself to her full height, and her voice to a pitch like rolling thunder, she asked, "And a'n't I a woman? Look at me! Look at my arm!" (and she bared her right arm to the shoulder, showing her tremendous muscular power).

For this audience her body makes her argument. "Reminiscences of Frances D. Gage: Sojourner Truth," in Stanton, Anthony, and Gage, *History of Woman Suffrage,* 1:116.

14. *The Liberator,* 7 January 1832, as quoted by Hersh, *Slavery of Sex,* 10–11.

15. Quoted by Hersh, *Slavery of Sex,* 66, from Lucy Stone's letter to Susan B. Anthony dated 11 September 1856.

16. Hersh, *Slavery of Sex,* 16; her figures are taken from the records of the Massachusetts society. Angelina Grimké asserted in 1836 that there were a total of sixty female antislavery societies in the Northern states, though I have found no other evidence to corroborate this figure. *Appeal to the Christian Women of the South* (New York, 1836), 23.

17. Grimké, *Appeal to the Christian Women of the South,* 23. Her list of antislavery handiwork includes card racks and needle books as well as all those items listed in the text. This fairly conservative portrait of female antislavery societies, though accurate in its depiction of the majority of the women involved in antislavery work, does not necessarily characterize all the authors whose stories I will be discussing here, just as it does not fit the Grimkés and other public lecturers and political organizers cited earlier. In particular, Lydia Maria Child and Carolyn Wells Healey Dall saw their fiction as a distinctly political, indeed revolutionary, form of action. Nevertheless, even the most overtly political women plied their needles for the cause, while women lecturers urged this more conventional form of political activity on their female audiences, and less daring women constituted the major readership for all these stories, and wrote many of them as well.

18. There has as yet been no systematic study of the history of antislavery stories. Carolyn Karcher postulates that Child's story "The St. Domingo Orphans," published in her *Juvenile Miscellany* of September 1830, may well initiate the genre. Though antislavery stories appeared in *The Liberator* from 1831 on and in many other antislavery papers, the major forum for their publication was provided by gift books and collections of literature for children, since these permitted more lengthy narrations than most newspapers could afford. The earliest antislavery gift book of which I am aware—*The Oasis* (1834)—was produced by Child; it contained mostly her own stories, accompanying them with two articles by her husband, David Child, and a handful of disparate pieces by abolitionist friends. Later antislavery giftbooks, and most notably *The Liberty Bell* (1839–58), follow this model of female production and control.

Male contributors to such collections, even though they constituted a large percentage of the authors, supplied argumentative pieces and poetry but rarely stories. For example, while two-thirds of the over two hundred contributors to *The Liberty Bell* were men, only two (Edmund Quincy and a presumably male, anonymous "Southron") wrote stories. See Carolyn Karcher, ch. 3 of this volume.

19. Most obvious among these followers is *Liberty Chimes,* published in 1845 by the Ladies Anti-Slavery Society of Providence, R.I. But also see the somewhat more successful gift book *Autographs of Freedom,* edited by Julia Griffith for the Rochester, N.Y., Ladies Auxiliary in 1853 and 1854. Antislavery gift books were also occasionally produced by men. For example, Richard Sutton Rost compiled *Freedom's Gift* (Hartford, Conn., 1840) predominantly as a showcase for William Lloyd Garrison; many of the poems and fictional pieces, however, were contributed by women.

20. A total of fifteen issues of *The Liberty Bell* were published, all except the last (which reprinted some earlier selections) consisting entirely of new material. See Ralph Thompson, "The *Liberty Bell* and Other Anti-Slavery Gift-Books," *New England Quarterly* 7: 1 (March 1934): 154–68. The relation between *The Liberty Bell* and other sale items is nicely illustrated by "An English Child's Notion of the Inferiority of the Colored Population in America," in which a mother recounts her daughter's explanation of the words this five-year-old had stitched on a sampler she was making for the Boston fair. The child sent her sampler, the mother sent this anecdote—presumably accompanied by her own needlework. *The Liberty Bell* 8 (1847): 49.

21. The average of the fair's profits is taken from Jane H. Pease and William H. Pease, "The Boston Bluestocking, Maria Weston Chapman," in *Bound with Them in Chains: A Biographical History of the Anti-Slavery Movement* (Westport, Conn., 1972): 45. Information on the finances of *The Liberty Bell* is from Thompson, "*Liberty Bell* and Other Gift-Books," 158–59. Thompson queries the committee's boast, arguing that many volumes were distributed free of charge and hence at a loss; but even if the committee's figures are inflated, there is no reason to believe that the books were not economically successful, especially considering that the cost of each printing was donated.

22. Quoted by Pease and Pease, "Maria Weston Chapman," 34–35, from a letter by Chapman dated 27 January 1846.

23. The point, of course, is that the sentimentality required by the genre necessarily undermines any aspirations toward realism. For a far more sophisticated and interesting variation on this critique, see Walter Benn Michaels, "Romance and Real Estate," in *The American Renaissance Reconsidered: Selected Papers from the English Institute, 1982–83,* ed. Walter Benn Michaels and Donal Pease (Baltimore, 1985), in which Michaels argues that Stowe's claims to realism mask an essentially romantic belief in inalienable property.

24. Fiction had, of course, long been viewed with suspicion in Puritan America, and the practice of defending tales with the claim that they were "founded on fact" had become, by the eighteenth century, a conventional attribute of all storytelling. Because, however, antislavery stories proposed to alter attitudes and behavior—to change the facts of American slavery—their claims to a factual basis served a double purpose, countering not only the general prejudice against frivolous or decadent fictionality but also the more specific charge that fiction had no bearing on political realities.

25. Harriet Beecher Stowe, *Uncle Tom's Cabin* (New York, 1982), preface, 10; Stowe, *A Key to Uncle Tom's Cabin* in *The Writings of Harriet Beecher Stowe,* 16 vols. (Boston, 1896), 2: 255–56. My evocation of Stowe here, and throughout this paper, is

admittedly opportunistic, as her position within the contemporary critical canon allows me to assume a familiarity with the problematics of her work obviously lacking for most of the other texts I cite. Thus her more accessible and discussed novels provide a way into the issues confronted in their more obscure precursors, and a means of situating these stories within contemporary critical discourse. An implicit assumption in my work, moreover, is that Stowe's achievement needs to be read and evaluated within a genre of antislavery fiction initiated at least two decades before the success of *Uncle Tom's Cabin.*

26. Lydia Maria Child, "Mary French and Susan Easton," *Juvenile Miscellany,* 3rd ser., no. 6 (May 1834): 196.

27. In "*Cage aux folles:* Sensation and Gender in Wilkie Collins's *The Woman in White,*" *Representations* 14 (Spring 1986): 107–36, D. A. Miller argues that the nervous sensations that characterize the reading of sensation novels are associated, within the novels themselves, with femininity. This insight and the implications Miller elaborates from it prove equally suggestive for the similarly gendered weeping that characterizes the reading of sentimental fiction. The gendering of physical response in sentimental and sensation fiction bears, however, somewhat different meanings. For while the feminine nervousness instigated by thrillers produces the confinement and incarceration of femininity, the tears ushered by sentimental fiction flow outward as mechanisms of escape.

28. Analyzing the "power" of *Uncle Tom's Cabin,* Jane Tompkins finds that in sentimental fiction "not words, but the emotions of the heart bespeak a state of grace, and these are known by the sound of a voice, the touch of a hand, but chiefly in moments of greatest importance, by tears." Tompkins is most centrally interested in that "state of grace" expressed by emotions that are themselves spoken through bodily signs. So in her catalogue of scenes marked by weeping, Tompkins defends these tears in terms of the message of "salvation, communion, reconciliation" that they suggest. In contrast, I am concerned here less with what the tears may say than with Stowe's recourse to bodily symptoms as the most efficacious means of saying it. See Jane Tompkins, "Sentimental Power: *Uncle Tom's Cabin* and the Politics of Literary History," in *Sensational Designs: The Cultural Work of American Fiction, 1790–1860* (New York, 1985), 131–32.

29. Harriet Beecher Stowe, *Dred: A Tale of the Great Dismal Swamp,* in *Writings,* 3:190–91.

30. *The Slave's Friend,* a penny monthly for children published in New York by the American Anti-Slavery Society from 1836 to 1838, makes its lessons in reading more explicit. The first article of the first number of the 1837 edition follows a picture of two girls—one black and one white—peering together at a large book with three pages of detailed analysis explaining how to interpret the scene. It concludes by pointing to the dog in the lower corner of the print and informing its young readers that "when you see a dog in a picture like this, it is an emblem, or sign of Fidelity" (3). The signs are sure; one need only learn the vocabulary.

31. Stowe, *Dred,* 247–48.

32. Frances Green, "The Slave-Wife," *Liberty Chimes* (Providence, R.I., 1845), 82.

33. Child, "Mary French and Susan Easton," 202.

34. Child's struggle with this problem can be traced through her revisions of the story as she prepared it for republication in *The Slave's Friend* of 1836. In this later version, "the streak whiter than the rest of [Mary's] face" is replaced by a streak that is "lighter": a substitution that masks the problem but does not really avoid it.

35. One source of difficulty is that black and white have traditionally symbolized the

basic moral dichotomy between good and evil. For antislavery discourse such symbolism is profoundly troubling, frequently resulting in absurdly paradoxical rhetoric in which the positive valuation of the black man is depicted in terms of whiteness. For example, the vignette of the "Apple and the Chestnut" presents a "white man" taunting a "poor colored man" by comparing his own race to an apple and the black to a chestnut. The black man replies with a witticism that, by inverting the intended insult, ultimately deepens it: "O, Massa, what you say is true. The chestnut has dark skin just like poor black man, but its kernel is all white and sweet. The apple, though it looks so pretty, has many little black grains at the heart." Attempting to explain the moral of this exchange, the narrator only intensifies the contradictions: "Now little boys and girls can't be abolitionists until they get rid of all these black grains in their hearts." Such logic suggests that the ability to liberate black people would depend upon first expunging blackness. *Slave's Friend* 1 (February 1836): 3.

36. Eliza Lee Follen, "A Melancholy Boy," *The Liberty Bell* 5 (1844): 94–95.

37. The only notable exception to this trend is Jules Zanger, "The 'Tragic Octoroon' in Pre-Civil War Fiction," *American Quarterly* 18:1 (Spring 1966): 63–70, which discusses some of the strategic uses this figure is put to in abolitionist writing. His most useful insight for my purposes is that the octoroon "represented not merely the product of the incidental sin of the individual sinner, but rather what might be called the result of cumulative institutional sin, since the octoroon was the product of four [*sic*] generations of illicit, enforced miscegenation made possible by the slavery system" (66).

38. Caroline Wells Healey Dall, "Amy," *The Liberty Bell* 10 (1849): 6, 8, 11, 12. In "The Inalienable Love," *The Liberty Bell* 15 (1858), Dall makes this point explicit, asserting that if she were to write her story with the "nervous strength" of the slave's narration, "[a]ll the women in the land would tear the pages out of the fair volume" (87).

39. The opposite, and most conservative, pattern of racial and sexual pairings is demarcated by another frequently told story of miscegenation: one that romanticizes the relation between a white man and a darker woman. In its most prevalent form a beautiful, refined quadroon loves a white gentleman only to lose him through either death or marriage, and this loss entails, in addition to the broken heart shared by all ill-fated lovers, a fall from a life of luxury and endearments into one of slavery and sexual exploitation. I would argue, however, that even in these stories, where the power of the white man and the exclusion of the black man seem most absolute, miscegenation works to interrogate white male supremacy. For these are stories about the unequal positions of men and women within a love relation, where the inherent similarities between the nearly white quadroon and the white woman serve to emphasize the ways in which the quadroon's inability to control her fate is only an extreme example of the victimization of all women in a society that considers love a fair exchange for power.

40. The examples of this last passion are myriad; see especially Harry's incestuous worship of his half sister and mistress Nina Gordon in Stowe's *Dred,* and Jan's rivalry with both the husband and the son of his beloved mistress Maria in Lydia Maria Child's "Jan and Zaida," *The Liberty Bell* 14 (1856): 41–93.

41. Child, *An Appeal in Favor of That Class of Americans Called Africans* (1836; reprint, New York, 1968), 196–97.

42. Not explicitly part of the abolitionist debate, Harriet Wilson's *Our Nig* (1859) does describe such a marriage. The exception is a telling one, for it is finally a black woman, not a white one, who is able to write off the white woman's desire.

43. Green, "Slave-Wife," 87, 94, 103, and 107.

44. Matilda G. Thompson, "Aunt Judy's Story: A Story from Real Life," in *The Child's Anti-Slavery Book* (New York, 1859), 113, 115, 112, 117.

45. I do not mean to deny that abolitionists found the domestication of slavery politically useful, but only to suggest that, despite its strategic efficacy, the practice had costs for women, children, and slaves. For a brilliant analysis of how the strategy worked, see Philip Fisher, "Making a Thing into a Man: The Sentimental Novel and Slavery," *Hard Facts: Setting and Form in the American Novel* (New York, 1985). Fisher argues that the domestication of slavery in *Uncle Tom's Cabin,* and particularly the distillation of the horrors of slavery into the recurring image of the separation and destruction of slave families, perform the cultural work of "making a thing into a man," and so prove efficacious in restructuring popular attitudes toward the slave. The notion of the slave as thing, object, property is replaced in domestic antislavery fiction with the imaginative conception of the slave as person, because this fiction makes the slave familiar by putting him or her within the ordinary and emotionally accessible realm of the family. Furthermore, Fisher points out that setting the destruction of the black slave family within the context of the white slave-owning family makes "the contradiction between the inevitable sentimental nature of the family and the corrosive institution of slavery . . . the central analytic point of Stowe's novel" (101). While agreeing with Fisher's analysis, I would add that the juxtaposition of the institutions of slavery and family also reveals the corrosive dimension of the family itself.

Gillian Brown's article "Getting in the Kitchen with Dinah: Domestic Politics in *Uncle Tom's Cabin,*" *American Quarterly* 36:4 (Fall 1984): 503–23, though prior to the publication of *Hard Facts* and positioned largely in response to Jane Tompkins's evaluation of Stowe's use of domestic values as the source of sentimental power and the ideal replacement for political and commercial power, can also serve as a critique of Fisher on this point, questioning his essentially positive reading of the family. Brown argues that the comparison between slavery and family in *Uncle Tom's Cabin* reveals the economic basis of existing familial relations and therefore that Stowe's utopian vision of a society governed by familial mores is predicated upon a prior restructuring of the family. Stowe, she asserts, "seeks to reform American society not by employing domestic values but by reforming them. . . . Stowe's domestic solution to slavery, then, represents not the strength of sentimental values but a utopian rehabilitation of them, necessitated by their fundamental complicity with the market to which they are ostensibly opposed" (507). The obvious difference between Stowe's work, as Brown interprets it, and that of Coleman and Thompson, is that the latter do not self-consciously embrace the feminist project of rehabilitating domesticity, a fact that makes their unwitting display of the similarities between slavery and family all the more disturbing.

46. Anon., "A Few Words About American Slave Children," in *The Child's Anti-Slavery Book,* 10, 9.

47. Anon., "The Difference Between a Slave and a Child," in *The Child's Book on Slavery; or, Slavery Made Plain* (Cincinnati, 1857), 31.

48. Ibid., 30, 28.

49. See David Brion Davis, *The Problem of Slavery in Western Culture* (Ithaca, N.Y., 1966), especially chs. 6 and 7, both titled "The Legitimacy of Enslavement and the Ideal of the Christian Servant," and ch. 10, "Religious Sources of Antislavery Thought: Quakers and the Sectarian Tradition."

50. For a discussion of this dynamic in antislavery work, see Ronald G. Walters, "Families: The 'Center of Earthly Bliss' and Its Discontents," in *The Antislavery Appeal: American Abolitionism after 1830* (Baltimore, 1976). For a more general discussion, see Smith-Rosenberg's introductions to parts 1 and 2 of *Disorderly Conduct.*

51. See for example the minister Laco Ray consults in "The Slave-Wife," or the whole collection of church apologists for slavery in Stowe's *Dred*. Along with Mrs. Shelby from *Uncle Tom's Cabin*, see, in *The Child's Anti-Slavery Book*, Mrs. Nelson and Mrs. Jennings, who cannot prevent the sale of Mark in "Mark and Hasty"; a less harsh reading of Edith's delicacy might also cast her in this role.

52. Stowe, *Uncle Tom's Cabin*, 415.

53. Tom's soul, however, is not completely disentangled from the commerical realm, for in responding to Legree's taunts, Tom engrafts the New Testament vocabulary of redemption based upon Christ's sacrificial payment onto Legree's assertion that the money he paid for Tom establishes his ownership. In claiming God as his purchaser, Tom excludes himself from the conflict and recasts it as a dispute between masters. See Walter Benn Michaels's discussion of the ways in which Stowe found that the body and even the soul "could not be guaranteed against capitalistic appropriation"; "Romance and Real Estate," 176.

54. C., "A Thought upon Emancipation," in *Liberty Chimes*, 80. I do not want to discredit the heroic potential of slave suicides. Surely the will to take one's own life may be the last, and in some situations perhaps the only, means of expressing a will at all. What is suspect here is not the slave's suicide but the abolitionist's desire for and glorification of such deaths.

Chapter 6

I wish to thank Ann Cvetkovich, Walter Michaels, Jeff Nunokawa, Michael Rogin, Eric Sundquist, and Lynn Wardley, each of whom offered indispensible advice on one of the multitude of earlier drafts of this essay.

1. Brian W. Dippie, *The Vanishing American: White Attitudes and U.S. Indian Policy* (Middletown, Conn.: Wesleyan University Press, 1982), 2. Dippie borrows the phrase from G. Harrison Orians, *The Cult of the Vanishing American: A Century View* (Toledo, Ohio: H. J. Chittenden, 1934).

2. *The Last of the Mohicans; A Narrative of 1757* (Albany, N.Y.: State University of New York, 1983), 6–7. Hereafter, quotations will be taken from this edition and cited parenthetically in the text.

3. In fact, the rise of the cult of the Vanishing American corresponds roughly with the rise of the U.S. government's policy of Indian removal, a massive military campaign of systematic dispossession and effective extermination begun in the late 1820s. According to Francis Paul Prucha in *The Great Father: The United States Government and the American Indians* (Lincoln: University of Nebraska Press, 1984), "[t]he military phase of Indian relations" would not end until the early 1880s (560). Thus we see just how much effort went into effecting the "inevitable."

4. Dr. Amariah Brigham, *Remarks on the Influence of Mental Cultivation and Mental Excitement upon Health*, 2nd ed. (Boston, 1833; reprint, New York: Arno, 1973), 49, 42, 36, 45.

5. Margaret Fuller, *Summer on the Lakes, in 1843* (Boston, 1844), 221, 182.

6. Brigham, *Remarks*, vii, viii.

7. For a relevant discussion of the intersecting rhetoric of domesticity and imperialism, see Amy Kaplan, "Romancing the Empire: The Embodiment of American Masculinity in the Popular Historical Novel of the 1890s," *American Literary History* 2:4 (Winter 1990): 659–90.

8. Catherine Beecher, *Letters to the People on Health and Happiness* (New York, 1855), 8, 10, 8.

9. The criticism on the Leatherstocking tales has played a crucial role in establishing for us a sense of ideological distance between the frontier and the home in nineteenth-century America. Since D. H. Lawrence's famous analysis of Cooper's Leatherstocking series appeared in 1923, Cooper criticism has taken as one of its perennial themes the antifeminine (if not outright misogynist) sensibility compelling Natty Bumppo's flight from the civilized society of women into the savage society of the red man. See, for example, D. H. Lawrence, *Studies in Classic American Literature* (Garden City, N.Y.: Doubleday, 1951), and Leslie A. Fiedler, *Love and Death in the American Novel* (New York: Meridian, 1960).

10. Michel Foucault, *The History of Sexuality,* vol. 1: *An Introduction,* trans. Robert Hurley (New York: Vintage, 1980), 147.

11. Ibid., 136–37, 146.

12. Ibid., 59.

13. D. A. Miller, *The Novel and the Police* (Berkeley and Los Angeles: University of California Press, 1988), viii.

14. Freud writes: "In inverted types, a predominance of archaic constitutions and primitive psychical mechanisms is regularly to be found." See Sigmund Freud, "The Sexual Aberrations," in *Three Essays on the Theory of Sexuality,* trans. and revised by James Strachey (New York: Basic Books, 1962), 12 fn. My belief in the relevance of the Freudian developmental narrative to genocidal thinking grows out of discussions with Jeff Nunokawa about his work on the figure of the doomed male homosexual in British Victorian literature.

15. Beecher, *Letters,* 8.

16. *Emile, or On Education,* trans. Allan Bloom (New York: Basic Books, 1979), 215, 216, 165.

17. Fiedler, *Love and Death,* 189.

18. Henry David Thoreau, *Walden,* in *Walden and Civil Disobedience,* ed. Owen Thomas (New York: Norton, 1966), 72, 68.

19. Ibid., 67 (my italics), 68 (my italics), 70, 68, 71.

20. "Momism" is Rogin's term for a "demonic version of domestic ideology" that expresses anxiety over the "maternal power generated by domesticity." Whereas Rogin discusses momism as a twentieth-century response to the revival of the domestic ideal in the 1950s, I am suggesting that domesticity and its demonic double arose simultaneously in the antebellum period and were mutually reinforcing. See Michael Paul Rogin, "Kiss Me Deadly: Communism, Motherhood, and Cold War Movies," *Representations* 6 (Spring 1984): 6–7.

21. Hannah More, *Strictures on the Modern System of Female Education,* 3rd American ed. (Boston, 1802), 97. My argument here has been influenced by Mark Seltzer's analysis of the deployment of gender in literary naturalism in his article "The Naturalist Machine," in *Sex, Politics, and Science in the Nineteenth-Century Novel,* ed. Ruth Bernard Yeazell (Baltimore: The Johns Hopkins University Press, 1986), 116–47.

22. More, *Structures,* 104, 48.

23. In *White Over Black: American Attitudes Toward the Negro, 1550–1812* (Chapel Hill: University of North Carolina Press, 1968), Winthrop D. Jordan notes that early U.S. ethnographers frequently represented the Native American as "deficient in ardor and virility" (162). Cooper's contemporary Henry Lewis Morgan claimed that "the passion of love was entirely unknown among" among the Iroquois. See Henry Lewis Morgan, *League of the Iroquois* (1851; reprint, New York: Corinth, 1962), 322.

24. My identification of Cora with the middle-class woman is complicated by the fact that, even though she has been raised white, she is in fact a mulatta—a product of the British imperialist effort in the West Indies. It might be more accurate to say that Cora represents the Third World woman through whose agency the colonial power exerts its influence. In Frantz Fanon's analysis of "the colonialist program" in Algeria, "it was the woman who was given the historic mission of shaking up the Algerian man." One could argue that Cora performs a similar function for Uncas. Fanon's analysis appears in *A Dying Colonialism* (New York: Grove, 1965), 39, and is quoted in Kaplan, "Romancing the Empire," 673.

25. Renato Rosaldo, "Imperialist Nostalgia," in *Culture and Truth: The Remaking of Social Analysis* (Boston: Beacon Press, 1989), 70.

26. Amy Kaplan, "Romancing the Empire," 664.

27. The classic statement of this position is, of course, Ann Douglas, *The Feminization of American Culture* (New York: Knopf, 1977). For a more developed critique of claims for the feminization of U.S. culture in this period, see my essay "Novels and Domesticity," in *The Columbia History of the American Novel*, ed. Emory Elliott (New York: Columbia University Press 1991).

28. Richard Brodhead, "Sparing the Rod: Discipline and Fiction in Antebellum America," *Representations* 21 (Winter 1988): 87. Actually, this characterization of maternal love appears in an antebellum publication entitled *Mother's Magazine* which Brodhead quotes; however, it is clear in context that Brodhead regards the quote as an accurate description of maternal authority.

29. Miller, *Novel and Police*, 10; Douglas, *Feminization*, 81.

30. Nancy Armstrong, *Desire and Domestic Fiction: A Political History of the Novel* (New York: Oxford University Press, 1987), 93; Christopher Lasch, *Haven in a Heartless World: The Family Besieged* (New York: Basic Books, 1977), 18.

31. I admit that "obliviousness" is probably too strong a word to use in Armstrong's case. On p. 26 of the introduction to her book, she manifests a good deal of self-consciousness about the gender politics of her own claims, even if she seems not to recognize the way in which they implicate her in the historical discourse she analyzes.

32. Previous feminist critiques of New Historicism include Judith Lowder Newton, "History as Usual?: Feminism and the 'New Historicism,' " in *The New Historicism*, ed. H. Aram Veeser (New York: Routledge, 1989), 152–67, and Carolyn Porter, "Are We Being Historical Yet?" *South Atlantic Quarterly* 87:4 (Fall 1988): 743–86. For reasons I explain in my article "Bio-Political Resistance in Domestic Ideology and *Uncle Tom's Cabin*" (*American Literary History* 1:4 [Winter 1989]: 715–34), I do not endorse the view shared by Newton and Porter to the effect that, by subscribing to a theory which (in Newton's words) "den[ies] the possibility of change and agency" (118), New Historicism disallows the possibility of political resistance.

Chapter 7

1. Francis Bowen, "Philip's *Protection and Free Trade*," *North American Review* 72 (1851): 415.

2. Quoted in Wai-chee Dimock, *Empire for Liberty* (Princeton, N.J.: Princeton University Press, 1989), 18.

3. I am thinking here of Wai-chee Dimock's argument in *Empire for Liberty* that the "expansionist social discourse of antebellum America" is characterized by the

"spatialization of time" (15). This argument is, of course, a version of Myra Jehlen's thesis in *American Incarnation* (Cambridge, Mass.: Harvard University Press, 1986).

4. Maria Cummins, *The Lamplighter* (Boston, 1854), 11.

5. Ibid., 12.

6. Fanny Fern, *Ruth Hall* (New Brunswick, N.J.: Rutgers University Press, 1986), 3.

7. Harriet Beecher Stowe, *Uncle Tom's Cabin* (1852; New York: Harper & Row, 1958), 68. Hereafter cited in the text as *UTC*.

8. The democratizing of portraiture—part, surely, of Stowe's point in choosing the daguerreotype as the form for Tom's representation—began with the publicizing of Daguerre's process in 1839. As other critics have suggested, the long exposure time required by daguerreotypy not only produced a deathlike rigidity in the features of the subject but made the dead the perfect subject. Nathaniel Hawthorne exploits this idea in the portraits of the Pyncheons in *The House of the Seven Gables*—as he does the notion that the daguerreotype exposes the truest, most hidden nature of its subject.

9. Rebecca Harding Davis, *Life in the Iron Mills* (1861; Old Westbury, N.Y.: Feminist Press, 1972), 31. Hereafter cited in the text as *IM*.

10. Quoted in Eric J. Sundquist, *New Essays on Uncle Tom's Cabin* (New York: Cambridge University Press, 1986), 9.

11. Fanny Fern in *Rose Clark,* quoted in Nina Baym, *Woman's Fiction* (Ithaca, N.Y.: Cornell University Press, 1978), 33. Susan Warner insisted that her 1850 bestseller *The Wide, Wide World* was no "novel" but only a "story." Likewise, Fanny Fern refused to "dignify" *Ruth Hall* by calling it a novel.

12. Harriet Beecher Stowe, *The Key to Uncle Tom's Cabin* (1853; New York: Arno Press, 1969), v.

13. Ibid., vi.

14. "The Tartarus of Maids" deploys erudite, "literary" language from the start: Melville's narrator passes through a "Dantean gateway" into a gorge called the "Devil's Dungeon," where the paper mill is located. As horrified as Davis's narrator by the exploitation he witnesses there, Melville's narrator has no difficulty in seeing or recounting what he sees—even when what he sees is his own complicity in the exploitative practices of the mill.

15. See, for example, Maribel W. Molyneaux, "Sculpture in the Iron Mills: Rebecca Harding Davis's Korl Woman," *Women's Studies* 17 (1990): 157–77; Jean Pfaelzer, "Rebecca Harding Davis: Domesticity, Social Order, and the Industrial Novel," *International Journal of Women's Studies* 4 (May–June 1981): 234–44; Tillie Olsen, Biographical Interpretation, *Life in the Iron Mills* (Old Westbury, N.Y.: Feminist Press, 1972), 69–174.

16. George Frederickson, *The Black Image in the White Mind: The Debate on Afro-American Character and Destiny, 1817–1914* (New York: Harper & Row, 1971), especially 51–58.

17. Quoted in Frederickson, *Black Image,* 106–7.

18. Karen Halttunen, *Confidence Men and Painted Women: A Study of Middle-Class Culture in America, 1830–1870:* (New Haven, Conn.: Yale University Press, 1982), 83.

19. As Elizabeth Ammons, Jane Tompkins, and others have argued, Uncle Tom is both infantilized *and* feminized. Likewise, as Jean Pfaelzer has suggested, Hugh Wolfe—whose "sobriquet" is "Molly Wolfe" and whose representative is the korl woman—is both a feminized character and a figure for the female artist: "Rebecca

Harding Davis: Domesticity, Social Order, and the Industrial Novel," *International Journal of Women's Studies* 4 (1981): 234–44. In conjunction with my own, this line of argument suggests that one way to lend "plasticity" to the otherwise intractable mill worker was to associate him with women who, like chattel slaves, were understood by sentimental writers to be infinitely malleable subjects.

20. Halttunen, *Confidence Men*, 192.

21. Jane Tompkins, *Sensational Designs: The Cultural Work of American Fiction, 1790–1860* (New York: Oxford University Press, 1985), 124.

Chapter 8

I thank Lynn Wardley for her astute and very helpful reading.

1. Lydia Maria Child, *Letters from New York* (New York, 1848), 111–12.

2. See Thomas L. Haskell, "Capitalism and the Origins of Humanitarian Sensibility," *American Historical Review* 90 (1985): 339–61, 547–66; and John Ashworth, "The Relationship Between Capitalism and Humanitarianism," *American Historical Review* 92 (October 1987), 813–28. I also have in mind here the collection of works behind the recent discussions of sentimental culture. They include Ann Douglas, *The Feminization of American Culture* (New York: Knopf, 1977); Mary Ryan, *Cradle of the Middle Class: The Family in Oneida County, New York, 1790–1865* (New York: Cambridge University Press, 1981); Jane Tompkins, *Sensational Designs: The Cultural Work of American Fiction, 1790–1860* (New York: Oxford University Press, 1985); Karen Halttunen, *Confidence Men and Painted Women: A Study of Middle-Class Culture in America, 1830–1870* (New Haven, Conn.: Yale University Press, 1982).

3. Harriet Jacobs fully felt the contradictions between the tale she had to tell, and the sentimental language in which she tried to tell it, in *Incidents in the Life of a Slave Girl*, Jean Fagan Yellin, ed. (1861; Cambridge, Mass.: Harvard University Press, 1987).

4. Stuart Blumin, *The Emergence of the Middle Class: Social Experience in the American City, 1760–1900* (New York: Cambridge University Press, 1989). Jean-Christophe Agnew, *Worlds Apart: The Market and the Theater in Anglo-American Thought, 1550–1750* (Cambridge: Cambridge University Press, 1986), 177–87.

5. Jonathan Harrington Green, *Gambling Unmasked! or, The Personal Experiences of the Reformed Gambler, J. H. Green* (New York, 1844), 7–8. On the problem of runaway apprentices, see W. J. Rorabaugh, *The Craft Apprentice from Franklin to the Machine Age in America* (New York: Oxford University Press, 1986), 89–92.

6. Details on Green's early life can be found in *Gambling Unmasked!*, 7–21; and in John Richards, "Discourse on Gambling Delivered in the Congregational Meeting-House at Dartmouth College November 7, 1852" (Hanover, N.H., 1852).

7. J. H. Green, *Twelve Days in the Tombs: or A Sketch of the Last Eight Years of the Reformed Gambler's Life* (New York, 1850); J. H. Green, *An Exposure of the Arts and Miseries of Gambling; Designed Especially as a Warning to the Youthful and Inexperienced Against the Evils of That Odious and Destructive Vice* (Cincinnati, 1843). On the Mississippi Valley, see Joseph Baldwin, *The Flush Times of Alabama and Mississippi* (New York, 1854); George Rogers Taylor, *The Transportation Revolution, 1815–1860* (New York: Holt, Rinehard and Winston, 1951).

8. *Gambling Unmasked!*, 300–312; *Arts and Miseries*, 318–36.

9. *Twelve Days in the Tombs,* 26–46, 178–79.

10. Brian Harrison, *Drink and the Victorians: The Temperance Question in England, 1815–1872* (London: Faber and Faber, 1971), 49–50, 129–32.

11. Sean Wilentz, *Chants Democratic: New York City and the Rise of the American Working Class, 1788–1850* (New York: Oxford University Press, 1984). On the literary aspirations of artisans in a different world, see Jacques Rançière, *La Nuit des prolétaires: archives du rêve ouvrier* (Paris: Fayard, 1981).

12. *Gambling Unmasked!,* 230–37, 277–78; *Arts and Miseries,* 172, 178, 181, 194–96, 202.

13. *Arts and Miseries,* 20, 56.

14. Philip Fisher, *Hard Facts: Setting and Form in the American Novel* (New York: Oxford University Press, 1985), 108.

15. On the Gothic, see Cathy N. Davidson, *Revolution and the Word: The Rise of the Novel in America* (New York: Oxford University Press, 1986), 212–53.

16. Charles Burdett, *The Gambler; or the Policeman's Story* (New York, 1848), vi. See also Osgood Bradbury, *The Gamblers' League; or, The Trials of a Country Maid* (New York, [1857]), and Clarence E. Brown, "The American Gambler Story in the Sentimental Tradition, 1794–1870" (Ph.D. diss., Michigan State University, 1970).

17. *Broadway Journal,* 1 March 1845, pp. 133–34; reprinted in Green, *Twelve Days in the Tombs,* 187–89. We can add Green to the popular figures whose speculations Poe refashioned into investigations of the darker side of human character. See David Reynolds, *Beneath the American Renaissance: The Subversive Imagination in the Age of Emerson and Melville* (New York: Oxford University Press, 1988).

18. *Gambling Unmasked!,* 227–28. "William Wilson" was first published in *Burton's Gentleman's Magazine* in 1839. Poe reprinted it in his *Broadway Journal,* 30 August 1845.

19. *Gambling Unmasked!,* 300, 306.

20. *Twelve Days in the Tombs,* 51–72, 79–80.

21. New York Association for the Suppression of Gambling, *First Annual Report* (New York, 1851), 1.

22. Halttunen, *Confidence Men,* 14–16. Paul Johnson, among others, has explored the ways Protestant evangelism in general, and temperance crusades in particular, helped transform the social and labor relations of early nineteenth-century capitalism. But as Johnson points out, if ministers and reformers were talking about capitalism, they were talking about it in religious ways. Paul Johnson, *A Shopkeeper's Millennium: Society and Revivals in Rochester, New York, 1815–1837* (New York: Hill and Wang, 1978), 6–8, 139.

23. William Alcott, *The Young Man's Guide* (Boston, 1834), 146, 160; J. H. Green, *A Report on Gambling in New York* (New York, 1851), 28.

24. In 1844 Green published a short-lived newspaper in Baltimore, *The Gambler's Mirror,* to teach children the dangers of seeing the home as innocent.

25. New York Association for the Suppression of Gambling, *Constitution and Bye-Laws* (New York, 1850), 2; Allan Stanley Horlick, *Country Boys and Merchant Princes: The Social Control of Young Men in New York* (Lewisburg, Pa.: Bucknell University Press, 1975), 245; *First Annual Report,* 6.

26. *Green's Report Number 1 on Gambling and Gambling Houses in New York* (New York, 1851), 33; *Constitution and Bye-Laws,* 1–16.

27. On Tappan's "benevolent empire" and the business that eventually became R. G. Dun and Company and then Dun and Bradstreet, see Bertram-Wyatt Brown, *Lewis Tappan and the Evangelical War Against Slavery* (Cleveland: Press of Case

Western Reserve University, 1969), 226–44, and in particular 235–37. Green wrote a sort of fictional commentary on Tappan in his most sensational book, *The Secret Band of Brothers, or The American Outlaws* (Philadelphia, 1847). Green's band of fictional gamblers communicated by coded message, leaving elaborate descriptions of men and boys traveling with cash; this information was just what was needed to rob the unwary.

28. *Green's Report Number 1*, 33.

29. *First Annual Report*, 5; *New York Tribune*, 10 May 1851, p. 9. A story reported in the *New York Times* in the late 1860s illustrated just how an antigambling association like Green's could serve as a cover for fraud and blackmail. A brief announcement appeared on 4 May 1868, heralding the opening of an office of a Society for the Suppression of Gambling. On 6 January 1869, the Society claimed receipts of $23,975. They had paid out rent and salaries—the largest, $19,720, to a detective who had found 1,034 trusted employees in gambling houses. Six months later, on 25 June 1870, a "serious charge" was brought against the Society by a woolen merchant who had been duped into believing that his partner gambled. He had given $75 to the reformers, who promised to furnish him the damning particulars. When the charges proved "false and malicious slanders," the merchant sued the Society for obtaining money under "fraudulent representations." See the *New York Times* of 4 May 1868, 9 June 1869, and 20 September 1870.

30. *New York Tribune*, 10 May 1851, p. 9; *New York Herald*, 13 May 1851.

31. Halttunen, *Confidence Men*, 153, 157, 186–87. On the importance of numbers, statistics, and facts in the early nineteenth-century United States and their use by moral reformers, see Patricia Cline Cohen, *A Calculating People: The Spread of Numeracy in Early America* (Chicago: University of Chicago Press, 1982), 116–17, 169–73, 207–11.

32. J. H. Green, *One Hundred Tricks with Cards: Gamblers' Tricks with Cards Exposed and Explained* (New York, 1850); Madeleine B. Stern, "Dick and Fitzgerald," in Madeleine B. Stern, ed., *Publishers for Mass Entertainment in Nineteenth-Century America* (Boston: G. K. Hall, 1980), 103–6. On parlor entertainments, see Halttunen, *Confidence Men*, 153–90.

33. G. B. Zieber launched Green's books at a Northern working-class audience, advertising them throughout the spring of 1847 in the *National Police Gazette* (13 and 20 March, 3, 10, and 17 April 1847). On working-class readers, see Michael Denning, *Mechanic Accents: Dime Novels and Working-Class Culture in America* (London: Verso, 1987), and Dan Schiller, *Objectivity and the News: The Public and the Rise of Commercial Journalism* (Philadelphia: University of Pennsylvania Press, 1981).

34. J. H. Green, "Gambling and Its Consequences, Communicated by J. H. Green, the Reformed Gambler; with an Account of his Phrenological Developments," *American Phrenological Journal* 8 (1846): 49. On phrenology, see Roger Cooter, *The Cultural Meaning of Popular Science* (Cambridge: Cambridge University Press, 1984); John D. Davies, *Phrenology Fad and Science: A Nineteenth-Century American Crusade* (New Haven, Conn.: Yale University Press, 1955); Madeleine B. Stern, *Heads and Headlines: The Phrenological Fowlers* (Norman: University of Oklahoma Press, 1971); and Burton Bledstein, *The Culture of Professionalism: The Middle Class and the Development of Higher Education in America* (New York: Norton, 1976), 23–24.

35. Max Weber, *The Protestant Ethic and the Spirit of Capitalism*, trans. Talcott Parsons (New York: Scribners, 1958), 170, 181.

36. There is a considerable literature on the abstraction of consumption in the twentieth century; see, for example, Arjun Appadurai, *The Social Life of Things* (Cambridge: Cambridge University Press, 1986), 48–51. On gamblers' failure to pro-

duce or to consume, see Henry Ward Beecher, *Seven Lectures to Young Men, on Various Important Subjects* (Indianapolis, Ind., 1844), 104; and Alcott, *The Young Man's Guide,* 145.

37. For an explicit expression of concern about the recreations of wage laborers, see *The Annual Reports* of the Society for the Prevention of Pauperism in New York City, 1818–23.

38. G. J. Barker-Benfield, *The Horrors of the Half-Known Life: Male Attitudes Toward Sexuality in Nineteenth-Century America* (New York: Harper & Row, 1976), 175–96.

39. *Gambling Unmasked!,* 207.

40. Eliphalet Nott, "Address to the Candidates for the Degree of A. B. in Union College, Delivered at the Annual Commencement, July 27th, 1814," *Columbia Magazine* 1 (December 1814): 103.

41. A. O. Hirschman, *The Passions and the Interests: Political Arguments for Capitalism Before its Triumph* (Princeton, N.J.: Princeton University Press, 1977), 41–42, 55, 59–63.

42. E. H. Chapin, *Moral Aspects of City Life: A Series of Lectures* (New York, 1853), 100–101. Chapin repeated his warnings in *A Discourse on the Evils of Gaming* (New York, 1859).

Chapter 9

1. I first learned about this doll from my colleague at Cornell University, Harryette Mullen. I would like to thank Harryette as well as Lauren Berlant, Rick Bogel, Laura Brown, Jonathan Culler, and, especially, Mark Seltzer for assistance with this essay. Research at the American Antiquarian Society was helped by a fellowship from the Northeastern Modern Language Association.

2. This story has been discussed by Carolyn Karcher in a talk on Child at the 1989 American Studies Association convention, and by Karen Sánchez-Eppler in "Bodily Bonds: The Intersecting Rhetorics of Feminism and Abolition," ch. 5 of this volume, who comments that if the "liberating tears" of Mary French "offer . . . a perfect emblem for sentimental fiction's power to emancipate, that emblem includes the recognition that the freedom it offers depends upon the black being washed white" (102). The fear of stolen and disguised children shows up in various narratives. In its first issue *The Liberator* announced, "There were kidnapped during the past year . . . MORE THAN FIFTY THOUSAND INFANTS, the offspring of slave parents!!!!" (1 January 1831). In Mary Pike's sensational novel *Ida May,* the slave trader "stained [the white child's] skin with a sponge . . . until it was the color of a dark mulatto." She is discovered when a fellow slave "took some water to wash ye . . . 'cause yer was *dat* dirty . . . how I did jump when I find *de black wash off!*" Mary Pike [Mary Langdon, pseud.] *Ida May: A Story of Things Actual and Possible* (New York, 1855), 58, 129.

3. The very recourse to "white" interiors indicates the reembodiment of identity— as if the body were turned inside out and relations of body and identity not so much transcended as relocated. It is not new to point out that abolition was predominantly a white enterprise, nor is it, I think, particularly helpful to express retrospective outrage about what now appear as racist assumptons of abolitionists. In looking at both pro- and antislavery writings, I want instead to explore how certain bodies and families get constituted in a fantasy of national identity. See, for instance, the analysis by Ronald

Walters: especially in their use of "family as a metaphor for social harmony . . . the antislavery and Southern proslavery arguments often bore deep similarities"; the desire of proslavery forces for "social, racial and sexual hierarchy" could not, however, fit with the "egalitarian" desire of abolitionists to "reconcile industry with order and morality." Ronald Walters, *The Anti-Slavery Appeal: American Abolitionism after 1830* (The Johns Hopkins University Press, 1976), 148.

The sentimental appeals made by abolitionist works like Stowe's *Uncle Tom's Cabin* were often countered by refutations that opposed industrial slavery in the North to Southern chattel slavery. For example, Caroline Rush's *North and South, or Slavery and Its Contrasts, a Tale of Real Life: "Truth is" Stronger "Than Fiction"* (Philadelphia, 1852), asks readers rhetorically "whether the 'broad-chested, powerful negro,' or the fragile, delicate girl, with her pure white face, is most entitled to your sympathy and tears" (128). In a perverse reversal, the novel presents the sale of a white infant to a Southern planter for $10,000—insisting, perhaps paradoxically, both on the mother's sorrow at her loss and on the tremendous advantage for the child, who will be raised on a Southern slaveholding plantation rather than in a Northern city (where most of its siblings are battered to the point of madness or death): "the bondage of poverty forces a lady to give up her child . . . here is another proof of the slavery that exists in the North" (238).

4. The attention to exterior marks of identity coincided with a fascination with photography, phrenology, pseudoscientific racism, and later eugenics. See, for example, "Science, Polygenesis, and the ProSlavery Argument" in George Frederickson, *The Black Image in the White Mind: The Debate on Afro-American Character and Destiny, 1817–1914* (New York: Harper and Row, 1971).

5. The word "miscegenation" was coined in 1864 by David Croly, in *Miscegenation: The Theory of the Blending of the Races, Applied to the White Man and the Negro.* The earlier term, "amalgamation," implies that the "mixture" produces a new whole, whereas miscegenation emphasizes the mixing of distinct races. The criminalization of interracial relations began in the colonial period: Maryland passed a miscegenation statue in 1661 that made marriage between white women and black men illegal, because it would produce legally free children. Such criminalization continued well after the end of slavery. In *Green v. State* (Alabama, 1877), a black man and a white woman were sent to jail for being married, in the name of preserving marriage and the home. Denying legitimacy to this union, the presiding judge announced, "It is through the marriage relation that the *homes* of a people are created. . . . These homes, in which the virtues are most cultivated and happiness most abounds, are the true *officinae gentium*—the nurseries of the States." Cited in Eva Saks, "Representing Miscegenation Law," *Raritan* 8:2 (Fall 1988): 42, 54. See also the discussion of the republican family and slavery in Michael Grossberg, *Governing the Hearth: Law and the Family in Nineteenth-Century America* (Chapel Hill: University of North Carolina Press, 1985), 134–38.

6. Bruno Latour, *The Pasteurization of France* (Cambridge, Mass.: Harvard University Press, 1988), 169.

7. *The Devil in America* (Philadelphia, 1860), 23. Further references will be included parenthetically in the text preceded by *D.*

8. American political culture, according to Anne Norton, is determined by oppositions such as "white and black, East and West, North and South, man and woman," that reflect "the twinned American inheritance of Enlightenment and Reformation" and "have created a network of meaning through the articulation of difference." Anne

Norton, *Alternative Americas: A Reading of Antebellum Political Culture* (Univ. of Chicago Press, 1986), 3.

9. The satanic destruction of women seems easy:

> To make a fool of her, my plan is this:
> Her first persuade her wrongs are very great . . .
> Without a right to rule, or even vote,
> And thus placed on a level with the slave.
>
> (*D*, 72–3)

In these passages the identification that abolitionist women found with slaves, as they tried to claim their "rights," gets at once mocked and reestablished. There is a varied and still growing literature on the attraction of women to the abolitionist cause. See, for a representative example, Blanche Hersch, *The Slavery of Sex: Feminist-Abolitionists in America* (Urbana: University of Illinois Press, 1978). Other treatments of the subject proceed from the standpoint of either abolition or feminism, therefore of course privileging the perspective they adopt in claiming that abolition was what caused women to ask for their rights, or that abolition was the moral imperative through which women realized that they might have rights. The crisis of this identification, in the nineteenth century as well as today, is the implication that one matters more than another. Most famously, the alliances between woman's rights advocates and abolitionists shattered after the Civil War over the issue of woman's right to vote, which was (typically) opposed to that of the freed (male) slave. Advocacy of the former was presented as a betrayal of the latter. A less public instance was the division of the American Anti-Slavery Society in the 1830s over the inclusion of women as officers, notably the participation of the feisty Abby Kelly.

Shortly after her expulsion from the "old" organization, Abby Kelly wrote to the *National Anti-Slavery Standard* about her outrage that "such imputations to abolitionists, as 'no church,' 'no Bible,' 'no ministry,' 'no marriage,' 'woman out of her sphere,' and 'infidelity' [are made] by those who are sustaining an institution which denies the Bible, the church, the Sabbath, the ministry and marriage, to millions of their fellow countrymen, and throws more than a million American women out of the sphere of humanity, making them beasts of burden." She goes on to celebrate the fact that antislavery societies are not confined to slavery; they modestly promote not only "temperance, moral reform, and the sanctity of the Sabbath," but, in seeking to abolish "[d]runkenness, licentiousness, profaneness, [and] infidelity," seek finally the "[a]bolition of all vice and sin in the land and the world" (*National Anti-Slavery Standard*, 20 May 1841).

In Lydia Maria Child's first signed editorial for the *National Anti-Slavery Standard*, she asks, "Why has woman nothing to do with politics? Is she not bought and sold and brutalized. . . ?" (11 June 1840). Angelina Grimké, the first woman to address any senate in the United States, explained to the Massachusetts legislature in May 1838, "All women have to do with this subject, not only because it is moral and religious, but because it is *political*." For an extended account of woman's political rights and responsibilities and woman's "sphere," see her debate with Catherine Beecher, beginning with Grimké, *Appeal to the Christian Women of the South* (New York, 1836), followed by Beecher, *Essay on Slavery and Abolition with Reference to the Duty of American Females* (Boston, 1837), and ending with Grimké, *Letters to Catherine Beecher* (Boston, 1838), in which Grimké makes the typical claim that "[t]he investigation of the rights of the slave has led me to a better understanding of my own" (114).

10. *The Slave's Friend*, vol. 1 (New York, 1836), 11.

11. Sánchez-Eppler, "Bodily Bonds," 114. Responding to the criticism that sentimental fiction "provides an inappropriate vehicle for educating the public to slavery's real terrors," Sánchez-Eppler argues that its effectiveness derives from its power as "an intensely bodily genre" in which the "tears of the reader are pledged . . . as a means of rescuing the bodies of slaves" (99). Still, she finds problematic sentimental fiction's "reliance on the body as the privileged structure for communicating meaning"; although it usefully "reinscribes the troubling relation between personhood and corporeality that underlies the projects of both abolition and feminism" (103), the certainty of its inscription can be dismantled by miscegenation, which stands "as a bodily challenge to the conventions of reading the body, thus simultaneously insisting that the body is a sign of identity and undermining the assurance with which that sign can be read" (104).

12. His best-selling book, *Fowler's Practical Phrenology,* presented graduated lists of dominant and recessive traits with pictured examples and advice about how to respond to or compensate for inadequacy or overabundance in each instance. Orson Squire Fowler and Lorenzo Niles Fowler, *Phrenology* (1856; reprint, New York: Chelsea House, 1980). See also John D'Emilio and Estelle Freedman, *Intimate Matters: A History of Sexuality in America* (New York: Harper and Row, 1988).

13. After the First National Woman's Rights Convention at Worcester, Mass. (23 October 1850), which included Lucy Stone, Frederick Douglass, Lucretia Mott, William Lloyd Garrison, and Wendell Phillips, the *New York Herald* reported an "[a]wful combination of Socialism, Abolitionism, and Infidelity" (cited in the *National Anti-Slavery Standard,* November 1850). Northern reformers were eager to discuss how tactics from revivals, temperance agitation, and even mesmerism and phrenology could assist them.

14. It may be worth noting here how closely the proslavery critique of the impersonal and insubstantial workings of capitalism gets repeated in, for instance, Marxist critiques of capitalist impersonality. On the proslavery critique of capitalist impersonality, see George Fitzhugh, *Cannibals All! or Slaves Without Masters* ed. C. Vann Woodward (1857; Cambridge, Mass.: Harvard University Press, 1960).

15. A parody of the presidential campaign slogan of John Frémont, nominated for the Republican ticket in 1856: "Free Soil, Free Labor, Free Speech, Free Men, Frémont.

16. "But the pictures! the pictures!! these seem to have been specially offensive. And why, unless it is because they give specially distinct impressions of the horrors of slavery?" *Fourth Annual Report of . . . the Massachusetts Anti-Slavery Society, Jan. 20, 1836* (Boston, 1836), 20. The dissemination of information about abolition especially occupies the Demon of Abolition. He describes how

> The anti-slavery papers multiplied
> Each striving to depict the blackest scenes
> And satiate the public appetite . . .
> And works of fiction too were much employ'd,
> Selecting incidents and coloring well
> Such scenes as might the feelings most affect, . . .
> Thus work'd our lying legions everywhere
> Through papers, pamphlets, sermons, and reviews,
> Through novels, poems, and books made for schools,
> Through teachers, preachers, and professors learn'd,
> Through orators, editors, and statesmen,
> Through societies and in conventions,

> In college walls and legislative halls,
> Till agitation everywhere was felt.
>
> (*D*, 134, 139–40)

This incantation is of course the dark side to the celebration that marks the upswelling of popular sympathy against slavery in the North. The major source for Theodore Weld's *American Slavery As It Is: The Testimony of a Thousand Voices* (Boston, 1842), which helped spur that sympathy, was, however, advertisements in Southern newspapers.

17. *The Slave's Friend*, 96. Hereafter, references will be cited parenthetically in the text, preceded by *SF.*

18. In *The Child and the Republic* (Philadelphia: University of Pennsylvania Press, 1968), Bernard Wishy discusses changes in child-rearing practices along the lines of a move from physical discipline to internalized models. On discipline and character formation in the early republic, see also Richard Brodhead, "Sparing the Rod: Discipline and Fiction in Antebellum America," *Representations* 21 (Winter 1988): 67–96.

19. *Anti-Slavery Alphabet* (Philadelphia, 1846).

20. *The Slave's Friend*, vol. 2 (New York, 1837), 20. The magazine's lessons in reading and diction include what amounts to a dictionary of antislavery. Young readers are taught "Never to call a colored person a NEGRO," and "Never to call a colored *man* a BOY." They are told that "immediatism," or "immediate emancipation"—the unconditional freeing of the slaves, which was at the time still a scandalous suggestion even for the North—"means, *doing a thing right off.*": "If you are a good child, and do your duty, as soon as you know it, you are an immediatist"; while "Gradualism . . . means, doing a thing very slowly. . . . When you don't want to do a thing, you know you ought to do, and must do" (*SF,* 96, 97, 105, 106).

21. See, for example, Eric Sundquist's introduction to *Frederick Douglass: New Literary and Historical Essays* (Cambridge: Cambridge University Press, 1990), 8–11, for discussions of reading and reform in Douglass.

22. He asked this while guiding children in a Chatham Street chapel meeting. See Walters, *The Anti-Slavery Appeal*, 91–110, for an analysis of the involvement of abolition with antebellum concepts of the importance of women and children in reform.

23. In a series of significant articles, the historian Thomas Haskell argues that abolition depended upon a certain style of responsibility derived from capitalism. He claims that "abolition was part of a broader effort to tame the market by setting limits to the pursuit of self-interest"; see "Convention and Hegemonic Interest in the Debate over Anti-slavery," *American Historical Review* 92:4 (October 1987): 550. He further asserts that the market functions as an "agency of social discipline" for "education and character modification"; see "Capitalism and the Origins of Humanitarian Sensibility," *American Historical Review* 90:3 (June 1985): 864.

24. They comment that, under slavery, "[e]very year, 100,000 infants—a large proportion the offspring of pollution and shame—are born, and doomed to horrors of bondage." *Annual Report of Board of Managers of New England Anti-Slavery Society, Jan. 9, 1833* (Boston, 1833), 17, 14. More typical is this protest: "We saw [slaves] held incapable of contracting even marriages, and liable to have that relation, at any moment, set at nought . . . we saw men putting those asunder whom God had joined together—tearing the husband from the wife—the wife from the husband—the parent from the child—yea, even the sucking babe from the bosom of his mother." *A Full Statement . . . to the Committee of the Legislature of Massachusetts . . . Respecting Abolitionists and the Anti-Slavery Society* (Boston, 1836), 4.

25. *Annual Report . . . of New England Anti-Slavery Society, Jan. 9, 1833*, 19.

26. *The Family and Slavery* (Cincinnati, n.d.), 23, and Henry Wright in *The Liberator*, 7 March 1838, both cited in Walters, *Anti-Slavery Appeal*, 92, 95.

27. Stephen Pearl Andrews, *Love, Marriage, Divorce, and the Sovereignty of the Individual* . . . (New York, 1853), 85; cited in Walters, 93.

28. [John Humphrey Noyes?] "Slavery and Marriage: A Dialogue" (1850), 8, 13, 9. This discussion of course parodies the women/slaves debate (referred to in n. 3 above). For a good contextual explanation of Noyes and the Oneida colony (1848–1879), see D'Emilio and Freedman, *Intimate Matters*, 118–20. See also the discussion by Ann Braude in *Radical Spirits: Spiritualism and Women's Rights in Nineteenth-Century America* (Boston: Beacon, 1989). She cites the medium Mrs. Julia Branch declaring at the Rutland Free Convention of 1858 that "the slavery and degradation of woman proceed from the institution of marriage" (71).

The call for woman's rights was also connected to slavery by Southerners. The proslavery novelist Caroline Rush attacks "that most horrible of all slaveholders, the tyrannical husband": "If you want to see slavery, in its worst form—the slavery that . . . holds in lifelong chains its wretched victims, you have only to visit the homes of many married people. . . . How many women are irrevocably tied to men. . . . Oh! freedom, thou art a jewel." Her narrator explains; "(. . . I will say, in this parenthesis, where our masters can't see it, Oh! fellow women, stand up for your rights and don't obey: don't yield up every thought to your owners.) The laws of slavery are all formed for the man and against the woman." [Caroline E. Rush], *North and South, or Slavery and Its Contrasts* (Philadelphia, 1852), 163–65.

29. For a discussion of the family in slavery, see Eugene Genovese, " 'Our Family, White and Black': Family and Household in the Southern Slaveholders' World View," and Catherine Clinton, " 'Southern Dishonor': Flesh, Blood, Race, and Bondage," both in *In Joy and in Sorrow: Women, Family, Marriage in the Victorian South, 1830–1900* (New York: Oxford University Press, 1991). Catherine Clinton comments that "both the sexual dynamics of slavery and the racial dynamic of sexuality" must be considered in treating slavery as a "distinctive system of *reproduction* in the plantation South" (53). Genovese cites the proslavery argument: "Slavery *in the family* will be their happiest condition" (79). The proslavery advocate John Fletcher asserted that "we are the property of the great family of man, and are under obligations . . . to the national community of which we form a part, and so on down to the distinct family of which we are a member." John Fletcher, *Studies on Slavery, in Easy Lessons* (1852; reprint, Miami: Mnemosyne Publishing, 1969), 182–83. In answering the question of how a family could hold its members as property, he explained, "if a man has absolute property in himself, he must surely have the right to alienate that property" (85).

30. Richard Hildreth, *The Slave; or Memoirs of Archy Moore* (Boston, 1836) 1:4, 5, 14. Orlando Patterson proposes that Southerners' attraction to chivalry (and, perhaps, their interest in the French Revolution) was because of, and not in spite of, their system of slavery: *Slavery and Social Death: A Comparative Study* (Cambridge, Mass.: Harvard University Press, 1982), 94–97.

31. See, for instance, Frederick Douglass for a typical assertion that "Slavery does away with fathers, as it does away with families." *My Bondage and My Freedom* (1855; Urbana-Champaign: University of Illinois Press, 1987), 38. However, see also Herbert Gutman, *The Black Family in Slavery and Freedom* (New York: Pantheon, 1976), for an analysis of how tenacious were both marital and family bonds.

32. Hildreth, *The Slave*, 1:20, 21, 22.

33. Eva Saks comments: "The taboo of too different (amalgamation/miscegenation) is interchangeable with the taboo of too similar (incest), since both crimes rely on a

pair of bodies which are mutually constitutive of each other's deviance, a pair of bodies in which each body is the signifier of the deviance of the other"; "Representing Miscegenation Law," 53–54. For a discussion of the "sensuality" of the "captive body," see Hortense Spillers, "Mama's Baby, Papa's Maybe: An American Grammar Book," *Diacritics*, Summer 1987, 67. For a discussion of how "abolition's sexual propaganda" appeared as the pornography of slavery, see Peter Walker, *Moral Choices: Memory, Desire, and Imagination in Nineteenth-Century American Abolition* (Baton Rouge: Louisiana State University Press, 1978), 288–90.

34. Harriet Beecher Stowe, *Uncle Tom's Cabin* (1851; New York: Bantam, 1981), 240. In the opening act of Dion Boucicault's *The Octoroon*, the grumbling Pete says of the children under his feet, "Guess they neber was born . . . dem black tings never was born at all; dey swarmed one morning on a sassafras tree in the swamp; I cotched 'em": Dion Boucicault, *The Octoroon, or Life in Louisiana* (1861; reprint, Miami: Mnemosyne Publishing, 1969), 3.

35. Hildreth, *The White Slave, or Memoirs of a Fugitive* (Boston, 1852), 304.

36. Hildreth, *The Slave* 2:48–49; 1:6. His sentiments about paternity undergo a further shock when he becomes a father. Like his own father, he is "father of a slave!" The only power he shares with his father is that of murdering his son; while his father has nearly beaten him to death for running away, Archy wants to kill his own son to keep him from being a slave.

37. Lydia Maria Child, *A Romance of the Republic* (Boston, 1867), 352. Further references will be cited parenthetically, preceded by *R*. For a thorough treatment of the novel, see Carolyn Karcher, "Lydia Maria Child's *A Romance of the Republic:* An Abolitionist Vision of America's Racial Destiny," in *Slavery and the Literary Imagination: Selected Papers from the English Institute, 1987*, ed. Deborah McDowell and Arnold Rampersad, 81–103. In Mark Twain's *Pudd'nhead Wilson*, of course, the identity of the exchanged brothers is revealed by their "natal autographs," or fingerprints.

38. Stuart Ewen discusses Holmes in a section called "Skinners of the Visible World," *All-Consuming Images: The Politics of Style in Contemporary Culture* (NY: Basic Books, 1988). Oliver Wendell Holmes called the photograph a "*mirror with a memory*" in "The Stereoscope and the Stereograph" *Atlantic Monthly* (June 1859); reprinted in Beaumont Newhall, ed., *Photography: Essays and Images* (1980) 53–4; cited in Ewen.

39. The issue of recognizing a legislated racial identity is confronted by the only working-class abolitionist in the novel, Joe Bright, who becomes one when he discovers that he's been "passing" for himself. He sees an ad for a "stout mulatto slave, named Joe; has light sandy hair, blue eyes, and ruddy complexion . . . and will pass himself for a white man": " 'By George!' said I, 'That's a description of *me*. I didn't even know before that I was a mulatto.' Well, it's just as bad for those poor black fellows as it would have been for me; but that blue-eyed Joe seemed to bring the matter home" (*R*, 322). Eva Saks comments that the phenomenon of passing, "blacks who passed as white," implies an "ontological corollary: whites who passed as white": Saks, "Representing Miscegenation Law," 41. The Gerald Fitzgerald who gets sold as a slave discovers himself to be, as he is finally informed, "unmixed white." The other Gerald, Rosa's son, has to "take the case home to myself" (*R*, 382) when he learns of what might be called his "mixed white" identity. In this novel's disturbing proliferation of applied identities, identities and identifications (with others, with oneself) are almost obsessively reenacted.

40. In his brief essay "The Declaration of Independence," Jacques Derrida notes that the act of declaring "we are and ought to be free and independent" constitutes the self

that can make the declaration. What is left out of the Declaration of Independence—and, it has been argued, what makes it incomplete—are the passages on slavery excised by the Continental Congress. *New Political Science* 15 (1986): 7–15.

41. The narrator comments that nothing "made this favored band of colored people forgetful of the brethren they had left in bondage" (*R*, 401). Yet they serve Rosa's children, who don't know that they could be legally claimed as slaves. It is important to note here that I am not accusing Lydia Maria Child of racism: she sacrificed as much as, if not more than, any other white abolitionist (see ch. 3 of this volume). Still, the question of the "transformation into a gentleman" leads to a difficult issue of the novel—the question of how its antislavery impulse retains traces of the subtle racism we have seen informing earlier reform efforts. When Tulipa, the black slave of Rosa's father, is discovered, "her own little episode of love and separation, of sorrow and shame, was whispered only to Missy Rosy" (*R*, 379). We do not hear her story after she is stolen by Mr. Bruteman. The romance of the republic is not her romance—she is not only not a subject in this narrative, but she is quickly returned to a state of servitude, being reemployed as a domestic by Rosa (*R*, 398).

Rosa's other former servants have "places provided for them, either in the household, or in [her husband's] commercial establishment. Their tropical exuberance made him smile . . . he said to his wife. . . . 'It really seemed as if we were landing on the coast of Guinea with a cargo of beads' " (*R*, 398). As Northern reformers, they still find themselves using the labor of others; furthermore, that Rosa's identity as a slave descended from quite different acts of landing on the coast of Guinea seems forgotten, as they imagine themselves to be missionaries colonizing a dark continent.

42. For an elaboration of both realizations of and resistances to this idea see Elizabeth Fox-Genovese, *Within the Plantation Household: Black and White Women in the Old South* (Chapel Hill: University of North Carolina Press, 1989).

Chapter 10

1. Henry James, *William Wetmore Story and his Friends* (Boston: Houghton, Mifflin, 1903), 2:76.

2. Mary Douglas, *Purity and Danger: An Analysis of the Concept of Pollution and Taboo* (New York: Praeger, 1966), 120–24.

3. See Samuel A. Roberson and William H. Gerdts, " '. . . so undressed, yet so refined . . .' The Greek Slave," *The Museum* 17 (Winter–Spring 1965): 1–29.

4. Frances Trollope, *A Visit to Italy* (London, 1842), 1:144–45. See Sylvia Crane, *White Silence: Greenough, Powers, and Crawford, American Sculptors in Nineteenth-Century Italy* (Coral Gables, Fla.: University of Miami Press, 1972), 196.

5. Isaiah Townsend to Hiram Powers, 4 November 1841, Hiram Powers Archives, National Museum of American Art, Smithsonian Institution, Washington, D.C., quoted in Donald Martin Reynolds, *Hiram Powers and His Ideal Sculpture* (New York: Garland Publishing, 1977), 135.

6. Hiram Powers to Col. John Preston, 7 January 1841, Hiram Powers Archives, quoted in Reynolds, *Hiram Powers,* 137–38.

7. Greek captive women from the chorus in Shelley's verse play *Hellas.* See Percy Bysshe Shelley, *Hellas: A Lyrical Drama,* ed. Thomas J. Wise (1822; reprint, London: Reeves and Turner, 1886).

8. Malek Alloula, *The Colonial Harem* (Minneapolis: University of Minnesota Press, 1986).

9. Julius Mattfeld, *A Hundred Years of Grand Opera in New York, 1825–1925: A Record of Performances* (1927; reprint, New York: AMS Press, 1976), 81.

10. See the description of this novel in Steven Marcus, *The Other Victorians: A Study of Sexuality and Pornography in Mid-Nineteenth-Century England* (New York: Basic Books, 1966), 197–216.

11. See Reynolds, *Hiram Powers,* 262–67, 279–90, for a discussion of Ingres's influence on Powers.

12. See Georges Wildenstein, *The Paintings of J. A. D. Ingres* ([London]: Phaidon Publishers, 1954), 210, 213.

13. See *Statues de chair, sculptures de James Pradier (1790–1852)* (Geneva: Musée d'Art et d'Histoire, 17 October 1986–2 February 1986; Paris: Musée du Luxembourg 28 February–4 May 1986), 131–33.

14. Edward Strahan [Earl Shinn], *The Art Treasures of America* (1879; reprint, New York: Garland Publishing, 1977), 1:140.

15. Ibid., 135.

16. On the Venus of Cnidus, see Roberson and Gerdts, *"The Greek Slave,"* 7.

17. Reynolds, *Hiram Powers,* 148–49.

18. For Powers's discussion of his model, see C. Edwards Lester, *The Artist, the Merchant, and the Statesman, of the Age of the Medici, and of Our Own Times* (New York, 1845), 2:190–93.

19. Quoted in ibid., 1:86–88.

20. In 1836 Dewey could only say about the Apollo Belvedere, "I am paralyzed by this wonderful work, so often as I see it. I sit down and gaze upon it, in a sort of revery, and do not know but I sometimes say aloud, 'Oh! Heaven!'—for really it is difficult to resist exclamations and tears." Orville Dewey, *The Old World and the New* (New York, 1836), 2:108.

21. Orville Dewey, "Powers' Statues," *The Union Magazine of Literature and Art* 1 (October 1847): 160–61.

22. William Gerdts, *The Great American Nude: A History in Art* (New York: Praeger, 1974), 40–41, 44–45, and following.

23. Kendall B. Taft, "Adam and Eve in America," *Art Quarterly* 23 (Summer 1960): 171–79.

24. Nathalia Wright, *Horatio Greenough: The First American Sculptor* (Philadelphia: University of Pennsylvania Press, 1963), 71–75.

25. For example, the pamphlet published in Philadelphia was *Powers' Statue of the Greek Slave, Exhibiting at the Pennsylvania Academy of the Fine Arts* (Philadelphia, 1848). Virtually identical pamphlets were published in New York, Boston, and New Orleans.

26. In James Joyce's novel, *Ulysses,* Leopold Bloom takes advantage of a similarly safe environment to inspect the private parts of classical statues.

27. Peter Gay, "Victorian Sexuality: Old Texts and New Insights," *American Scholar* 49 (Summer 1980): 377.

28. Peter Gay, *The Bourgeois Experience, Victoria to Freud,* vol. 1: *The Education of the Senses* (New York: Oxford University Press, 1984), 396–98.

29. Augustin Duganne, "Ode to the Greek Slave, Dedicated to the Cosmopolitan Art and Literary Association," *The Cosmopolitan Art Association Illustrated Catalogue, 1854* (New York, 1854), 25.

30. For comments on Pygmalion, see Clara Cushman in *Neal's Saturday Gazette,* quoted in *Powers' Statue of the Greek Slave,* 18. The poem is L.E.'s "To Powers' 'Greek Slave,' " *The Cosmopolitan Art Journal* 2 (March and June 1858): 68.

31. See Linda Hyman, "*The Greek Slave* by Hiram Powers: High Art as Popular Culture," *College Art Journal* 35 (Spring 1976): 216–23.

32. Suzanne Kappeler, *The Pornography of Representation* (Minneapolis: University of Minnesota Press, 1986).

33. E. Anna Lewis, "Art and Artists of America: Hiram Powers," *Graham's Magazine* 48 (November 1855), 399. Clara Cushman, from *Neal's Saturday Gazette,* quoted in *Powers' Statue of the Greek Slave,* 18.

34. Augustin Duganne, "Ode to the Greek Slave," 25.

35. James Freeman Clarke, "The Greek Slave," quoted in Roberson and Gerdts, "*The Greek Slave,*" 18.

36. H.S.C. in *The Knickerbocker Magazine,* quoted in *Powers' Statue of the Greek Slave,* 19.

37. One critic demanded, "[H]ow can she stand thus serene and erect, when the sanctity of her nature is outraged by this exposure? Where is the bending and shrinking of her form, that expression in every feature and every limb of her unutterable agony, which should make the gazer involuntarily to turn away his eyes. . . ?" W.H.F., "Art Review, The Greek Slave," *The Harbinger,* 24 June 1848, p. 62. But another writer rebuked this critic in a later edition of the same journal, saying that a "cry of anguish would be a very poor subject for a work of art, and . . . the artist would naturally choose the serene moment following, when the triumph of the spirit was revealed in Godlike resignation." John S. Dwight, "The Greek Slave," *The Harbinger,* 8 July 1848, p. 78.

38. James Freeman Clark, quoted in Roberson and Gerdts, "*The Greek Slave,*" 18.

39. Henry Tuckerman, "The Greek Slave," *New York Tribune,* 9 September 1847, quoted in *Powers' Statue of the Greek Slave,* 12.

40. Sigmund Freud, "On Narcissism: An Introduction," *The Standard Edition of the Complete Psychological Works of Sigmund Freud,* ed. James Strachey (London: The Hogarth Press and the Institute of Psycho-Analysis, 1957), 14:88–89.

41. Bram Dijkstra has commented on the theme of female narcissism in nineteenth-century European and American art. He discounts claims for women's spirituality as part of a repressive misogyny that constituted a "cultural war on women." It should be evident that I view the cultural matrix as more complex and conflicted. Bram Dijkstra, *Idols of Perversity: Fantasies of Feminine Evil in Fin-de-Siècle Culture* (New York: Oxford University Press, 1986).

42. Stephen Nissenbaum, *Sex, Diet, and Debility in Jacksonian America* (Westport, Conn.: Greenwood Press, 1980).

43. Carroll Smith-Rosenberg and Charles Rosenberg, "The Female Animal: Medical and Biological Views of Woman and Her Role in Nineteenth-Century America," *Journal of American History* 60 (September 1973): 332–56. See also John S. Haller, Jr., and Robin M. Haller, *The Physician and Sexuality in Victorian America* (New York: W. W. Norton, 1974).

44. *The Art Journal* 12 (London, 1850), 56.

45. Nancy Cott, "Passionlessness: An Interpretation of Victorian Sexual Ideology," *Signs: A Journal of Women in Culture and Society* 4 (1978): 219–36.

46. See Sheila Ryan Johansson, "Sex and Death in Victorian England: An Examination of Age- and Sex-Specific Death Rates, 1840–1910," in Martha Vicinus, ed., *A Widening Sphere: Changing Roles of Victorian Women* (Bloomington: Indiana University Press, 1977), 163–81. See also Allan M. Brandt, *No Magic Bullet: A Social History of Venereal Disease in the United States Since 1880* (New York: Oxford University Press, 1985).

47. E. Anna Lewis, "Art and Artists of America: Hiram Powers," *Graham's Magazine* 48 (November 1855): 399.

48. W. H. Coyle, "Powers' Greek Slave," *Detroit Advertiser,* quoted in Roberson and Gerdts, *"The Greek Slave,"* 18.

49. James Freeman Clark, quoted in Coyle, "Powers' Greek Slave," 18.

50. Vivien Greene, "Hiram Powers's *Greek Slave,* Emblem of Freedom," *American Art Journal* 14 (Autumn 1982): 31–39.

51. *Punch* 20 (1851): 236.

52. *Cosmopolitan Art Journal* 1 (June 1857): 132.

53. *New-York Evening Express,* quoed in ibid., 133.

54. See Teresa de Lauretis, *Alice Doesn't: Feminism, Semiotics, Cinema* (Bloomington: Indiana University Press, 1984), especially chs. 2 and 5.

55. Claude Lévi-Strauss, *The Elementary Structures of Kinship* (Boston: Beacon Press, 1969). See the discussion of this idea in Teresa de Lauretis, *Alice Doesn't,* 18–22.

56. Clara Cushman, from *Neal's Saturday Gazette,* in *Powers' Statue of the Greek Slave,* 18.

57. Henry Tuckerman, *Book of the Artists: American Artist Life* (New York, 1870), 25.

58. Henry Tuckerman, "The Greek Slave," quoted in *Powers' Statue of the Greek Slave,* 12.

59. See the debate over *The Greek Slave* in *The Harbinger.* W.H.F., "Art Review: The Greek Slave," *The Harbinger,* 24 June 1848, p. 62, criticized the sculpture. It was defended by John S. Dwight, "Art Review: The Greek Slave in Boston," *The Harbinger,* 8 July 1848, pp. 77–78.

60. Quoted in David H. Wallace, *John Rogers, the People's Scultpure* (Middletown, Conn.: Wesleyan University Press, 1967), 70.

61. *Power's Statue of the Greek Slave,* 3.

62. Lydia Sigourney, "Powers's Statue of the Greek Slave," in *Poems* (New York, 1860), 112.

63. Elizabeth Barrett Browning, "Hiram Powers' 'Greek Slave,' " *Poems, 1850,* in *The Complete Works of Elizabeth Barrett Browning,* ed. Charlotte Porter and Helen A. Clarke (New York: Thomas Y. Crowell, 1900), 3:178.

64. Quoted in ibid., 16.

65. W. H. Coyle, quoted in Roberson and Gerdts, *"The Greek Slave,"* 17.

66. For measurements, see *American Art in the Newark Museum* (Newark, N.J.: The Newark Museum, 1981), 415. The Newark version was the one given away by the Cosmopolitan Art Association in 1855 and 1858; it was the third replica made, and identical to the one displayed at the Crystal Palace. For the engraving in question, see George Baxter, *Baxter's Gems of the Great Exhibition* (London, 1854).

67. *New York Courrier and Enquirer,* quoted in *Cosmopolitan Art Association Illustrated Catalogue, 1854,* 26.

68. Ibid., 26.

Chapter 11

1. Mary E. Bryan, "How Should Women Write?" (1860), reprinted in *Hidden Hands: An Anthology of American Women Writers, 1790–1870,* ed. Lucy Freibert and Barbara White (New Brunswick, N.J.: Rutgers University Press, 1985), 369.

2. Ibid., 370.

3. Ibid., 371.

4. Ibid., 373.

5. Freibert and White, *Hidden Hands,* 103.

6. Annette Kolodny, *The Land Before Her: Fantasy and Experience of the American Frontiers, 1630–1860* (Chapel Hill: University of North Carolina Press, 1984), 163. Similarly, Freibert and White conclude that frontier novels by women as well as by their male colleagues "served as a form of expiation" (*Hidden Hands,* 104).

7. See Sister Mary Michael Welsh, *Catherine Maria Sedgwick* (Washington: Catholic University of America, 1937), 25; Mary Kelley, Introduction to *Hope Leslie* (New Brunswick, N.J.: Rutgers University Press, 1987), x–xi. Kelley here provides a particularly good historical background and an insightful introduction to the text. All references to *Hope Leslie* are from this text.

8. Ann Douglas (Wood), in "The 'Scribbling Women' and Why They Wrote" (*American Quarterly* 23 [Spring 1971]: 5–13) apparently takes Sedgwick's disclaimers at face value, asserting that "in fact cooking was the only accomplishment to which [Sedgwick] admitted to being vain." But as Kelley's sensitive reading suggests, Sedgwick's relationship to her work was more serious than she was comfortable admitting to publicly—a fact that probably amplified her discontent as a female author in a male-dominated establishment. Kelley traces Sedgwick's anxiety throughout the testing period of each new book, through which it becomes clear that Sedgwick took her writing and her reputation as an author very seriously, despite her nonchalant assurances to family and friends. See Mary Kelley, *Private Woman, Public Stage: Literary Domesticity in Nineteenth-Century America* (New York: Oxford University Press, 1984).

9. Quoted in Welsh, *Sedgwick,* 67. See also Kelley, *Hope Leslie,* 290.

10. See Susan H. Armitage, "Women's Literature and the American Frontier: A New Perspective on Frontier Myth," in *Women Writers and the West,* ed. L. L. Lee and Merrill Lewis (Troy, N.Y.: Whiston, 1979); Leland S. Person, Jr., "The American Eve: Miscegenation and Feminist Frontier Fiction," *American Quarterly* 37 (1985): 669–85; Glenda Riley, *Women and Indians on the Frontier, 1825–1915,* (Albuquerque: University of New Mexico Press, 1984); Lillian Schlissel, *Women's Diaries of the Westward Journey* (New York: Schocken Books, 1982). The work of Kolodny and Persons in particular has been formative to my essay.

11. As Mary Kelley's notations to the Rutgers edition of *Hope Leslie* attest, Sedgwick read widely in preparation for her fictionalization of colonial new England, drawing apparently on diverse sources.

12. The political dimensions of Hope Leslie's behavior in this respect have often been overlooked or sentimentalized by the novel's critics. Michael Davitt Bell's analysis of *Hope Leslie* ("History and Romance Convention in Catherine Sedgwick's *Hope Leslie,*" *American Quarterly* 22 [1970]: 213–21), characterizes the novel's heroine as thoroughly "conventional," used by Sedgwick in a "conventional" way, to personify her "view of the essential movement of American history." Suzanne Gossett and Barbara Bardes, in their essay "Women and Political Power in the Republic: Two Early American Novels" (*Legacy* 2 [Fall 1987]: 13–30), astutely counter that Bell's formulation is limited in that it fails to "consider what it means to embody the spirit of American history in a woman who breaks laws" (29, n. 29). They argue that Hope Leslie's illegal actions speak powerfully to the fact that "a woman may be driven by her sense of political powerlessness to undertake civil disobedience" (21).

13. As Mary Kelley notes, the epigraph is taken from John Robinson, quoted in William Bradford's *History of Plymouth Plantation* (New York: Scribner's, 1908), 41, 357.

14. James Fenimore Cooper, *The Last of the Mohicans*, (1826; New York: Bantam, 1981), 23.

15. I owe this insight to Shirley Samuels, in private correspondence to me, 12 September 1989.

16. See Kappeler's brilliant and polemic study, *The Pornography of Representation* (Minneapolis: University of Minnesota Press, 1986).

17. It might plausibly be argued that Sedgwick is here proposing simply to reverse the historical record, to replace one voice with another rather than to create a dialogue. I would like to point out, however, that the quoted sentence is attributed to Everell, who has been "touched" by Magawisca and whose position is obviously partial at this point. Rather, I think Sedgwick's larger point is that any version at all is an interested version; thus the inherent necessity of constructing history out of a dialogue.

18. Tzvetan Todorov, *The Conquest of America: The Question of the Other*, trans. Richard Howard (New York: Harper and Row, 1984), 157.

19. Todorov, *Conquest*, 252.

20. Albert Memmi, *The Colonizer and the Colonized* (Boston: Beacon Press, 1965), 20.

21. Of course we must also note that her most heroic action serves to save her beloved for Hope Leslie.

22. Todorov, *Conquest*, 190.

23. Quoted from Robert Montgomery Bird's *Nick of the Woods*, (1837; New Haven: New College and University Press, 1967), 236. This novel provides a fully developed, psychologically intriguing (and bloody) reading of the Anglo–American cultural phenomenon of Indian-hating.

24. *Vacuum domicilium*, a justificatory principle for British dominion, argued that the colonists had a right to any lands left agriculturally undeveloped by the Native Americans. For a characteristic discussion, see John Winthrop's "Reasons to Be Considered for Justifying the Undertakers of the Intended Plantation in New England . . ." reprinted in *Massachusetts Historical Society Proceedings* 8 (1864–1865): 420–25.

25. The narrative shortly after notes the "little garden patches" of "the savages," in which were planted "beans, pumpkins and squashes; the seeds of the vegetables, according to an Indian tradition, (in which we may perceive the usual admixture of fable and truth,) having been sent to them, in the bill of a bird, from the south-west, by the Great Spirit" (86). Here again we see the careful maintenance of what Edward Said, in *Orientalism* (New York: Vintage, 1979), 12) has termed "relational superiority"—through which Anglo–Americans can contradict themselves without surrendering the position of authority.

26. I am of course referring to Annette Kolodny's important work, *The Land Before Her*, in which Kolodny explores the less aggressive and heretofore ignored visions of frontier women, who projected garden metaphors, rather than those of rape and conquest, onto the American wilderness. In her preface, Kolodny observes: "I have long ceased to lament the absence of adventurous conquest in women's fantasies before 1860 and have come now to regret men's incapacity to fantasize tending the garden" (xiii).

Chapter 12

For their helpful comments, I thank Ann Fabian, Inderpal Grewal, Dorothy Hale, Cara Hood, Lora Romero, and Shirley Samuels.

1. Harriet Beecher Stowe, *Uncle Tom's Cabin, Or, Life Among the Lowly* (Columbus, Ohio: Charles E. Merrill, 1959). Page numbers to this edition will be given in parentheses in the text.

2. Catharine E. Beecher, *A Treatise on Domestic Economy, For the Use of Young Ladies at Home and School* (1843; reprint, New York: Schocken, 1977), 12–14. Gillian Brown makes the strongest case for this view in *Domestic Individualism: Imagining Self in Nineteenth-Century America* (Berkeley: University of California Press, 1990), 13–38.

3. John W. Blassingame, *The Slave Community: Plantation Life in the Antebellum South*, rev. and enl. (New York: Oxford University Press, 1979), 40–41. W. E. B. Du Bois, "The Religion of the American Negro," *New World* 9 (December 1900): 618.

4. Mechal Sobel, *The World They Made Together: Black and White Values in Eighteenth-Century Virginia* (Princeton, N.J.: Princeton University Press, 1987), 223–24, 233. On the sentimental domestication of death, see Ann Douglas, "Heaven Our Home: Consolation Literature in the Northern United States, 1830–1880," in *Death in America*, ed. David E. Stannard (Philadelphia: University of Pennsylvania Press, 1975), 49–68. See also Ann Douglas, *The Feminization of American Culture* (New York: Knopf, 1977), and Karen Halttunen, *Confidence Men and Painted Women: A Study of Middle-Class Culture in America, 1830–1870* (New Haven, Conn.: Yale University Press, 1982), 124–52. On Emmanuel Swedenborg's idea of heaven, see Colleen McDannell and Bernard Lang, *Heaven: A History* (New York: Vintage Books, 1990), 181–227. Ann Braude discusses black and white spiritualism in *Radical Spirits: Spiritualism and Women's Rights in Nineteenth-Century America* (Boston: Beacon Press, 1989), 28–31.

5. Douglas, *Feminization*, 271. W. E. B. Du Bois, *The Forum* (February 1929): 182–183.

6. Albert J. Raboteau, *Slave Religion: The "Invisible Institution" in the Antebellum South* (New York: Oxford University Press, 1978), 278. Raboteau helpfully summarizes the debate over the existence of Africanisms or survivals, as exemplified in the argument between Melville J. Herscovits and E. Franklin Frazier; see Raboteau, *Slave Religion*, 48–87; Melville J. Herscovits, *The Myth of the Negro Past* (Boston: Beacon Hill Press, 1958); and E. Franklin Frazier, *The Negro Church in America* (New York: Schocken Books, 1964). See also Blassingame, *Slave Community*, 109–10; Eugene D. Genovese, *Roll, Jordan, Roll: The World the Slaves Made* (New York: Vintage Books, 1976); Herbert G. Gutman, *The Black Family in Slavery and in Freedom, 1750–1925* (New York: Vintage Books, 1976); *Africanisms in American Culture*, ed. Joseph E. Holloway (Bloomington: University of Indiana Press, 1990); and Jon Butler, *Awash in a Sea of Faith: Christianizing the American People* (Cambridge, Mass.: Harvard University Press, 1990), 151–63.

7. Harriet Beecher Stowe, *The Key to Uncle Tom's Cabin* (Boston, 1853), 27–28.

8. William Pietz, "The Problem of the Fetish, I," *Res* 9 (Spring 1985): 5, 7. Pietz notes that the earliest fetish discourse concerned witchcraft and the control of female sexuality (6). David Simpson's *Fetishism and Imagination: Dickens, Melville, Conrad* (Baltimore: The Johns Hopkins University Press, 1982) offers a compelling account of the meaning of fetishism to the Romantic imagination and the Protestant mind.

9. Horace Bushnell, *Christian Nurture* (1861; reprint, New Haven: Yale University

Press, 1947), 175. Most of *Christian Nurture* appeared first as *Views of Christian Nurture* in 1847. Catharine E. Beecher, *Miss Beecher's Housekeeper and Healthkeeper* (New York, 1876), 462. David Handlin, *The American Home: Architecture and Society, 1815–1915* (Boston: Little, Brown, 1979), 10, 40.

10. Richard H. Brodhead, "Sparing the Rod: Discipline and Fiction in Antebellum America," *Representations* 21 (Winter 1988): 67–69. Stowe's account of her novel's composition is in Annie Fields, "Days with Mrs. Stowe," in *Critical Essays on Harriet Beecher Stowe,* ed. Elizabeth Ammons (Boston: G. K. Hall, 1980), 294.

11. On the bodily nature of the American sentimental genre, see Brodhead, "Sparing the Rod," 67–96; Karen Sánchez-Eppler, "Bodily Bonds: The Intersecting Rhetorics of Feminism and Abolition," ch. 5 of this volume; and Lora Romero, "Bio-Political Resistance in Domestic Ideology and *Uncle Tom's Cabin,*" *American Literary History* (Winter 1989): 715–54. On sentimentalism's early relation to physiological studies, see G. S. Rousseau, "Nerves, Spirits, Fibres: Towards the Origin of Sensibility," in *Studies in the Eighteenth Century,* vol. 3, ed. F. R. Brissenden (Canberra: Australian National University Press, 1975), 137–57. The best work on the career of sentimentalism is David Marshall, *The Surprising Effects of Sympathy: Marivaux, Diderot, Rousseau, and Mary Shelley* (Chicago: University of Chicago Press, 1988), 1–8 and passim. On sentimentality as the mark of health, see Jan Goldstein, *Console and Classify: The French Psychiatric Profession in the Nineteenth Century* (Cambridge: Cambridge University Press, 1987), 118. On the view of sentimentality as a female pathology, see Emily Apter, "Splitting Hairs: Female Fetishism and Postpartum Sentimentality in the Fin de Siècle," in *Eroticism and the Body Politic,* ed. Lynn Hunt (Baltimore: The Johns Hopkins University Press, 1991), 167. My interest in the anthropomorphized objects in the sentimental novel is not unique; Ann Douglas examines domestic animism in *Feminization,* 240–71. Jane Tompkins defends the "sentimental power" of domestic objects in *Sensational Designs: The Cultural Work of American Fiction, 1790–1860* (New York: Oxford University Press, 1985), 122–46. And in an argument describing Stowe's refinement of the logic of possessive individualism, Gillian Brown defines Stowe as the practitioner of a "sentimental fetishism," which Brown identifies as an empathetic, anti-acquisitive strategy. Brown sees Stowe indirectly revising, and chiefly reversing, Marx's account of commodity fetishism in the effort to remove objects entirely from the exchange values of market culture. See Brown, *Domestic Individualism,* 39–60.

12. James Baldwin, "Everybody's Protest Novel," in Ammons, *Critical Essays,* 92. Helen Waite Papashvily, "All the Happy Endings," in *Hidden Hands: An Anthology of American Women Writers, 1790–1870,* ed. Lucy M. Freibert and Barbara White (New Brunswick, N.J.: Rutgers University Press, 1985), 376.

13. On the racist implications of a sentimental aesthetics, see the argument of Sánchez-Eppler, ch. 5 of this volume; see also Brown, *Domestic Individualism,* 39–60. On sentimentalism as a mode of containment, see Lauren Berlant, "The Female Complaint," *Social Text* 19/20 (Autumn 1988): 237–59. On the "antebellum spiritual hothouse," see Butler, *Awash in a Sea of Faith,* 225.

14. Dolf Sternberger, *Panorama of the Nineteenth Century* (New York: Urizen Books, 1977), 60–62. On Stowe's collection of baby clothes, see Charles Edward Stowe, *Life of Harriet Beecher Stowe Compiled from Her Letters and Journals* (Boston, 1890), 123–4.

15. Brown, *Domestic Individualism,* 50.

16. Hortense Spillers, "Changing the Letter: The Yokes, the Jokes of Discourse, or, Mrs. Stowe, Mr. Reed," in *Slavery and the Literary Imagination,* ed. Deborah A.

McDowell and Arnold Rampersad (Baltimore: The Johns Hopkins University Press, 1989), 27. Harriet Beecher Stowe, *Key,* 28, 27.

17. Calvin Stowe is quoted in Charles Edward Stowe, *Life of Harriet Beecher Stowe* (Boston, 1889), 420. On Stowe's supernatural activities and the middle-class interest in spiritualism, see Howard Kerr, *Mediums, and Spirit-Rappers, and Roaring Radicals: Spiritualism in America, 1850–1900* (Urbana: University of Illinois Press, 1972), 100–125; and Charles Beecher, *Spiritual Manifestations* (Boston, 1879). On Stowe and Brontë, and on Stowe's personal interest in unconverted souls, see Howard Kerr, "The Blessed Dead: Transformation of Occult Experiences in Harriet Beecher Stowe's *Oldtown Folks,"* in *Literature and the Occult: Essays in Comparative Literature,* ed. Luanne Frank (Arlington: University of Texas, 1977), 174–87.

18. Stowe, *Key,* 30.

19. On conjure, see Blassingame, *Slave Community,* 109–10.

20. Mark Seltzer discusses Stowe's "everyday animism" in his essay on property, persons, and literary realism, "Physical Capital: *The American* and the Realist Body," in *New Essays on the American,* ed. Martha Banta (Cambridge: Cambridge University Press, 1987), 132. On Quakers and witchcraft allegations, see Carol F. Karlsen, *The Devil in the Shape of a Woman: Witchcraft in Colonial New England* (New York: Vintage Books, 1989), 120–25.

21. Stowe is quoted in Charles H. Foster, *The Rungless Ladder: Harriet Beecher Stowe and New England Puritanism* (Durham, N.C.: Duke University Press, 1954), 106.

22. Ruth H. Bloch, "American Feminine Ideals in Transition: The Rise of the Moral Mother, 1785–1815," *Feminist Studies* 4 (June 1978): 105; Kathryn Kish Sklar, "Victorian Women and Domestic Life: Mary Todd Lincoln, Elizabeth Cady Stanton, and Harriet Beecher Stowe," in *The Public and the Private Lincoln,* ed. Cullom Davis et al. (Carbondale: Southern Illinois University Press, 1976), 20–37. Catharine Beecher, *Miss Beecher's Housekeeper and Healthkeeper* (New York, 1876), 462.

23. Horace Bushnell, *Christian Nurture,* 175. On the importance of neo-Lamarckian thought in the nineteenth-century United States, see George Stocking, Jr., *Race, Culture, and Evolution: Essay in the History of Anthropology* (Chicago: University of Chicago Press, 1982), 234–69.

24. Horace Bushnell, *The Census and Slavery* (Hartford, 1860), 12; hereafter cited as *Census* in parentheses in the text. George M. Fredrickson links Bushnell with the Christian racists and imperialists of the late nineteenth century; see *The Black Image in the White Mind: The Debate on Afro-American Character and Destiny, 1817–1914* (New York: Harper and Row, 1972), 155–57.

25. Quoted in Blassingame, *Slave Community,* 100.

26. Fisher, *Hard Facts,* 103.

27. On the maternal patriarch, see David Leverenz, *The Language of Puritan Feeling: An Exploration in Literature, Psychology, and Social History* (New Brunswick, N.J.: Rutgers University Press, 1980), 142–43. Jean-Jacques Rousseau, *Emile, or, On Education,* with intro., trans., and notes by Allan Bloom (New York: Basic Books, 1979), 37, 44. On Marie as the "partial product of patriarchal education," see Romero, "Bio-Political Resistance," 722.

28. Sternberger, *Panorama,* 39–52. Stowe subscribed to the theory of "climactic racial determinism," believing that the North American continent was "set aside by the laws of ethnology for the exclusive use of the white race." This idea was offered among the (scientific) rationales for black expatriation; see Fredrickson, *Black Image,* 146, 145–52. On female evangelical "ethnologists" on foreign missions, see Joan Jacobs

328   *Notes to Pages 212–215*

Brumberg, "Zenanas and Girlless Villages: The Ethnology of American Evangelical
Women, 1870–1910," in *The Journal of American History* 69:2 (September 1982): 347–
71; I thank Elizabeth Abrams for directing me to this essay. On white European
captives in Arabic cultures, see also Blassingame, *Slave Community*, 49–65.

29. See Halttunen, *Confidence Men and Painted Women*, 4–6 and passim; and
Charles E. Rosenberg, *The Cholera Years: The United States in 1832, 1849, and 1866*
(Chicago: University of Chicago Press, 1962).

30. Karen Haltunnen, "Gothic Imagination and Social Reform: The Haunted
Houses of Lyman Beecher, Henry Ward Beecher, and Harriet Beecher Stowe," in *New
Essays on Uncle Tom's Cabin,* ed. Eric. J. Sundquist, (Cambridge: University of Cam-
bridge Press, 1986), 107–34.

31. Emerson is quoted in David S. Reynolds, *Faith in Fiction: The Emergence of
Religious Literature in America* (Cambridge, Mass.: Harvard University Press, 1981),
13. On the Oriental tale as a visionary and often subversive mode in the literature of
the early republic, and on its absorption into other genres, see Reynolds, 13–68.

32. On the Lake Pontchartrain meetings and the Laveaus, see Zora Neale Hurston,
Mules and Men (New York: Harper and Row, 1970), 239–60; Raboteau, *Slave Religion,* 79–80; Mechal Sobel, *Trabelin' On: The Slave's Journey to an Afro-Baptist Faith*
(Westport, Conn.: Greenwood Press, 1979), 49–50; and Jessie Gaston Mulira, "The
Case of Voodoo in New Orleans," in Holloway, ed., *Africanisms in American Culture,*
34–68. Sobel points out that the third Marie Laveau (b. 1827), the "most important
voodoo practitioner in North America," also regarded herself as a "good Catholic"
(50). On the fusion of Madonna and Christ in the Victorian cultural imagination, see
Colleen McDannell, *The Christian Home in Victorian America, 1840–1890* (Blooming-
ton: Indiana University Press, 1986), 130. On Eva's identification with Christ, see
Elizabeth Ammons, "Stowe's Dream of a Mother-Savior: *Uncle Tom's Cabin* and
American Women Writers Before the 1920s," in Sundquist, ed., *New Essays,* 162–70.

33. Alan Bewell, "An Issue of Monstrous Desire: *Frankenstein* and Obstetrics,"
The Yale Journal of Criticism 2 (Fall 1988): 109.

34. Douglas, *Feminization,* 2. Sternberger argues for the idea of the sentimental
genre as a "form of viewing" *Panorama,* 52.

35. Stowe is quoted in E. Bruce Kirkham, *The Building of Uncle Tom's Cabin*
(Knoxville: University of Tennessee Press, 1977), 66–67.

36. Marshall, *Surprising Effects of Sympathy,* 5.

37. Ralph Waldo Emerson, *The Journals and Miscellaneous Notes of Ralph Waldo
Emerson,* ed. William H. Gilman et al. (Cambridge, Mass.: Harvard University Press,
1960), 2:9, 8. For a striking passage in which Eva's silent, melodramatic gestures are
viewed as if through a parted proscenium, see her exchange with Topsy, and St. Clare's
mimetic response (II.92–93).

38. Christopher Crowfield [Harriet Beecher Stowe], *Household Papers and Stories*
(Boston: Houghton Mifflin, 1896), 100.

39. Oliver Smith, *The Domestic Architect* (Buffalo, 1857), iii.

40. Fowler is quoted in McDannell, *Christian Home,* 24. See also Orson Fowler,
Hereditary Descent (New York: Fowler, 1843), 218, 226.

41. Handlin, *American Home,* 17. On hair art, see also McDannell, 99.

42. See Catharine Beecher, *A Treatise on Domestic Economy, for the Use of
Young Ladies at Home and at School* (New York, 1843); Catharine E. Beecher and
Harriet Beecher Stowe, *The American Woman's Home* (1869; Hartford, Conn.: The
Stowe-Day Foundation, 1975). On the decoration, mechanization, and reformation
of the American home, see Siegfried Giedion, *Mechanization Takes Command: A*

Contribution to Anonymous History (1848; New York: Norton, 1969); Dolores Hayden, *The Grand Domestic Revolution: A History of Feminist Designs for American Homes, Neighborhoods, and Cities* (Cambridge, Mass.: MIT Press, 1983); and Witold Rybczynski, *Home: A Short History of an Idea* (New York: Penguin Books, 1986), 123–61.

43. Louis Prang, quoted in Neil Harris, *Cultural Excursions: Marketing Appetites and Cultural Tastes in Modern America* (Chicago: University of Chicago Press, 1990), 320.

44. Simpson, *Fetishism and Imagination,* 4–38.

45. Adolph Loos, "Ornament and Crime," in Ludwig Munz and Gustav Kunstler, *Adolph Loos: Pioneer of Modern Architecture* (New York: Praeger, 1966), 226.

46. Braude, *Radical Spirits,* 76–81.

47. Cathy N. Davidson, "Photographs of the Dead: Sherman, Daguerre, Hawthorne," in *The South Atlantic Quarterly* 89:4 (Fall 1990): 682; Alan Trachtenberg, *Reading American Photographs: Images as History: Matthew Brady to Walker Evans* (New York: Hill and Wang, 1989), 14; Kerr, *Mediums,* 110; and Walter Benjamin, "The Work of Art in the Age of Mechanical Reproduction," in *Illuminations: Essays and Reflections,* ed. Hannah Arendt (New York: Schocken Books, 1969), 219–53.

48. Charles W. Chesnutt, *The Wife of His Youth* (1899; reprint, Ann Arbor: University of Michigan Press, 1968).

49. Raboteau, *Slave Religion,* 276.

50. Charlotte Perkins Gilman, *Women and Economics: The Economic Factor Between Women and Men as a Factor in Social Evolution* (1898; New York: Harper and Row, 1966), 69 (hereafter cited as *WE* in parentheses in the text); and Gilman, *The Home: Its Work and Influence* (Chicago: University of Illinois Press, 1972) (hereafter cited as *Home* in parentheses in the text).

51. On Gilman and Ward, see Mary A. Hill, *Charlotte Perkins Gilman: The Making of a Radical Feminist, 1860–1896* (Philadelphia: Temple University Press, 1980), 263–71. The most helpful studies of the ideological components of Gilman's aesthetic reform remain Hayden, *Grand Domestic Revolution,* 183–205, and Roger B. Stein, "Artifact as Ideology: The Aesthetic Movement in Its American Cultural Context," in *In Pursuit of Beauty: Americans and the Aesthetic Movement,* ed. Doreen Bolger Burke et al. (New York: The Metropolitan Museum of Art, Rizzoli, 1987), 43–48.

52. Charlotte Perkins Gilman, *The Yellow Wallpaper* (1892; Brooklyn, N.Y.: The Feminist Press, 1973), 20; hereafter cited as *YW* in parentheses in the text.

53. Nancy F. Cott, *The Bonds of Womanhood: "Woman's Sphere" in New England, 1780–1835* (New Haven, Conn.: Yale University Press, 1977), 68.

54. John S. Haller and Robin M. Haller, *The Physician and Sexuality in Victorian America* (Urbana: University of Illinois Press, 1974), 144. For a different reading of the narrator's peculiar triumph, see Walter Benn Michaels, *The Gold Standard and the Logic of Naturalism: American Literature at the Turn of the Century* (Berkeley: University of California Press, 1987), 3–28.

55. Naomi Schor, *Reading in Detail: Aesthetics and the Feminine* (New York: Methuen, 1987), 11–22 and passim.

56. Melissa Meyer and Miriam Shapiro, "Waste Not, Want Not: An Inquiry into What Women Saved and Assembled," *Heresies* 4 (1978): 66–69; Emily Apter, "Splitting Hairs," in Lynn Hunt, ed., *Eroticism and the Body Politic,* 175–76; Mary Kelly, *Post-Partum Document* (London: Routledge and Kegan Paul, 1985), xvi.

57. Raymond Williams, *Problems in Material Culture* (London: Verso, 1980), 128. See also June Howard, *Form and History in American Literary Naturalism* (Chapel Hill: University of North Carolina Press, 1975), 34–47, and Fisher, *Hard Facts,* 17, 125–26.

Chapter 13

1. W. E. B. Du Bois, "Mencken," *Crisis* 34 (October 1927): 276. For an example of the negative readings of the tragic mulatta, see Gwendolyn Brooks's afterword to Pauline Hopkins, *Contending Forces: A Romance Illustrative of Negro Life North and South* (Carbondale: Southern Illinois University Press, 1978), 403–9, where Brooks laments, "Pauline Hopkins had, and this is true of many of her brothers and sisters, new and old, a touching reliance on the dazzles and powers of anticipated integration."

2. For a compelling argument on the use of mulatto figures, see Hazel V. Carby, *Reconstructing Womanhood: The Emergence of the Afro-American Woman Novelist* (New York: Oxford University Press, 1987), 88–91, 140.

3. Peter Brooks, *The Melodramatic Imagination: Balzac, Henry James, Melodrama, and the Mode of Excess* (New York: Columbia University Press, 1985), 4.

4. Frances E. W. Harper, *Iola Leroy, or Shadows Uplifted*, with an introduction by Frances Smith Foster (1892; New York: Oxford University Press, 1988), 263. Future references to this work will hereafter be cited in the text. Both Frances Harper and Pauline Hopkins are among the black women writers whose work has recently been collected and reissued in Oxford University Press's Schomburg Library of Nineteenth-Century Black Women Writers, general editor, Henry Louis Gates, Jr.

5. On a similar genre crossing race, sexuality, and nationalism, see Doris Sommer, "Irresistible Romance: The Foundational Fictions of Latin America," in Homi K. Bhabha, ed., *Nation and Narration* (New York: Routledge, 1990), 71–98.

6. Robert A. Bone, *The Negro Novel in America,* rev. ed. (New Haven, Conn.: Yale University Press, 1965), 24–25; Judith R. Berzon, *Neither White Nor Black: The Mulatto Character in American Fiction* (New York: New York University Press, 1978), 109. Though I quibble with Hazel Carby, hers is a brilliant book on this whole nexus of issues; see *Reconstructing Womanhood,* 61, 145. Richard Yarborough, "Introduction" to Pauline E. Hopkins, *Contending Forces: A Romance Illustrative of Negro Life North and South* (New York: Oxford University Press, 1988), 37, 41.

7. Fredric Jameson, *The Political Unconscious: Narrative as a Socially Symbolic Act* (Ithaca, N.Y.: Cornell University Press, 1981), 139, 171. Peter Brooks's work on melodrama should also be cited here as another important exception to the ahistorical tendency of melodrama studies; Brooks's views have very much influenced my own. See *his Melodramatic Imagination.*

8. W. E. B. Du Bois, *The Souls of Black Folk: Essays and Sketches* (1903; reprint, New York: New American Library, 1969), 45.

9. Benedict Anderson, *Imagined Communities: Reflections on the Origin and Spread of Nationalism* (London: Verso, 1983), 16, 140. Anderson specifies that the novel helps to create imagined communities because of the technical possibilities of simultaneity it offers through Benjamin's "homogeneous empty time" (30).

10. The term "romantic racialist" is George M. Fredrickson's; see *The Black Image in the White Mind: The Debate on Afro-American Character and Destiny, 1817–1914* (New York: Harper and Row, 1971), 97–129, 288–90, 322–30. Titles of the fiction I allude to: Harriet Beecher Stowe, *Uncle Tom's Cabin* (1852); George Washington Cable, *The Grandissimes* (1880); Kate Chopin, "Desiree's Baby," "La Belle Zoraide"; William Wells Brown, *Clotelle* (1864); Charles Chesnutt, *The House Behind the Cedars* (1900); Nella Larsen, *Passing* (1929).

11. On the etymology of "mulatto" and its cultural meanings, see Winthrop D. Jordan, *White over Black: American Attitudes Toward the Negro, 1550–1812* (1968; reprint, Baltimore: Penguin, 1969), 169. On Southern "muleology," see Joel William-

son, *New People: Miscegenation and Mulattoes in the United States* (New York: The Free Press, 1980), 73, 92, 96.

12. "Editorial and Publishers' Announcements," *Colored American Magazine* 1 (May 1900): 603.

13. See Hazel V. Carby, "Introduction" to *The Magazine Novels of Pauline Hopkins* (New York: Oxford University Press, 1988), xiv. The Harper quote is from *Iola Leroy*, 262–63.

14. Daniel Patrick Moynihan, *The Negro Family: The Case for National Action* (Washington, D.C.: Government Printing Office, 1965), 134. The historian Wilson J. Moses notes in *The Golden Age of Black Nationalism, 1850–1925* (New York: Oxford University Press, 1978) that "Frazier's influences on Daniel Patrick Moynihan are so obvious and so often commented upon that we need only mention them here," but goes on to add that Moynihan's ideas on the black family are "ultimately traceable" to a less obvious source: the black nationalist Alexander Crummell, a pioneer in sociological approaches to the race problem (81).

15. See my *Dark Twins: Imposture and Identity in Mark Twain's America* (Chicago: University of Chicago Press, 1989), and *Mark Twain's Pudd'nhead Wilson: Race, Conflict, and Culture* (Durham, N.C.: Duke University Press, 1990).

16. See Shelley Fisher-Fishkin, *From Fact to Fiction: Journalism and Imaginative Writing in America* (New York: Oxford University Press, 1985), 84. The public "unveiling" of this letter, long known to the Mark Twain scholarly community, was made in an editorial in the *New York Times* on the occasion of the centenary of *Huckleberry Finn*'s publication.

17. The Morgan manuscript of *Pudd'nhead Wilson* is in the J. Pierpont Morgan Library, New York. References to this work, hereafter MMS, will be cited in the text.

18. I take my language here directly from Henry Nash Smith, *Mark Twain: The Development of a Writer* (Cambridge, Mass.: Harvard University Press, 1962), reprinted in Sidney E. Berger, ed., *Pudd'nhead Wilson and Those Extraordinary Twins* (New York: Norton, 1980), 248–49.

19. ["The Man With the Negro Blood,"], four manuscript pages (Box 37), The Mark Twain Papers, Bancroft Library, University of California, Berkeley.

20. "Which Was It?" in John S. Tuckey, ed., Mark Twain, *Which Was the Dream? and Other Symbolic Writings of the Later Years* (Berkeley and Los Angeles: University of California Press, 1968), 179–429. Future references will be cited in the text.

21. Notebook 18, typescript, p. 19, The Mark Twain Papers, Bancroft Library, University of California, Berkeley.

22. Hortense J. Spillers, "Mama's Baby, Papa's Maybe: An American Grammar Book," *Diacritics* 17:2 (Summer 1987): 67.

23. Pauline Hopkins, *Of One Blood, Or, The Hidden Self*, in *The Magazine Novels of Pauline Hopkins*, 520. Future references to this work will be cited in the text.

24. My whole discussion here and throughout the Hopkins section is deeply indebted to Anderson's work in *Imagined Communities* (especially ch. 4, "Old Empires, New Nations"), and to his recent unpublished paper, "Holy Perversions: Nationalism in Last Wave and Creole Novels," delivered at the Nationalisms and Sexualities Conference, Center for Literary and Cultural Studies, Harvard University, June 1989.

25. This is the title of a series of documentary articles by A. Kirkland Soga that ran concurrently with *Of One Blood* in the *Colored American Magazine*.

26. As with her depiction of mulattoes and octoroons, Hopkins's use of the language of blood has been the subject of some debate among her readers. See Richard Yarborough's introduction to *Contending Forces*, xxxiv–xxxv.

27. "The Study of the Negro Problems," *The Annals of the American Academy of Political and Social Science* 11 (January 1898): 1–23; quoted in Dan S. Green and Edwin D. Driver, eds., *W. E. B. Du Bois on Sociology and the Black Community* (Chicago: University of Chicago Press, 1978), 72.

28. *Dusk of Dawn: An Essay Toward an Autobiography of a Race Concept* (New York: Harcourt, Brace, 1940), 94; future references to this work will be cited in the text. "Criteria of Negro Art," *Crisis* 32 (October 1926): 290–97.

The sense of the divided career promulgated by the man himself has provided the major structure to most general studies of Du Bois. See, for example, Arnold Rampersad, *The Art and Imagination of W. E. B. Du Bois* (Cambridge, Mass.: Harvard University Press, 1976), 48–67.

29. *The Philadelphia Negro: A Social Study* (Philadelphia: University of Pennsylvania Press, 1899), 1; future references to this work, abbreviated as *PN,* will be cited in the text. "The Atlanta Conferences," *Voice of the Negro* 1 (March 1904): 88; *Dusk of Dawn,* 64. On Du Bois's relation to the developing field of sociology, see "Introduction," Green and Driver, eds., *W. E. B. Du Bois on Sociology and the Black Community,* 1–48; Elliot Rudwick, "W. E. B. Du Bois as Sociologist," in *Black Sociologists: Historical and Contemporary Perspectives,* ed. James E. Blackwell and Morris Janowitz (Chicago: University of Chicago Press, 1974), 25–55.

30. *The Philadelphia Negro,* 1; *The Negro American Family,* ed. W. E. B. Du Bois (New York: Negro University Press, 1908), 9. Future references to this latter work will be cited in the text.

31. Rampersad, *Art and Imagination,* 52.

32. *Darkwater: Voices from Within the Veil* (New York: Harcourt, Brace, 1921), 517. Future references to this work will be cited in the text. The black woman Du Bois quotes here is Anna Julia Cooper, *A Voice from the South* (1892).

33. Samuel L. Clemens to Francis Wayland, 24 December 1885, in the private collection of Nancy and Richard Stiner; quoted in Fisher-Fishkin, *From Fact to Fiction,* 84.

34. As an indication of the slipperiness of what exactly constitutes "race" in literature, it is notable that *The Hazeley Family* was included on Du Bois's bibliography in *The Negro American Family* and yet has recently been described as a portrayal of a family that is "racially indeterminate." See Barbara Christian's introduction to A. E. Johnson, *The Hazeley Family* (New York: Oxford University Press, 1988), xxvii–xxviii.

35. Hortense J. Spillers, "Mama's Baby, Papa's Maybe," 77–80.

36. "The Study of the Negro Problems," quoted in Green and Driver, eds., *W. E. B. Du Bois on Sociology and the Black Community,* 71–72.

Chapter 14

1. Eric J. Sundquist, ed., *New Essays on Uncle Tom's Cabin*(Cambridge: Cambridge University Press, 1986).

2. Jane Tompkins, *Sensational Designs: The Cultural Work of American Fiction, 1790–1860* (New York: Oxford University Press, 1985).

3. Joanne Braxton, "Harriet Jacobs' *Incidents in the Life of a Slave Girl:* The Redefinition of the Slave Narrative Genre," *The Massachusetts Review,* Winter 1986.

4. "I am well aware that many will accuse me of indecorum for presenting these pages to the public: for the experiences of this intelligent and much-injured woman

belong to a class which some call delicate subjects, and others indelicate. This peculiar phase of Slavery has generally been kept veiled; but the public ought to be made acquainted with its monstrous features, and I willingly take the responsibility of presenting them with the veil withdrawn. I do this for the sake of my sisters in bondage, who are suffering wrongs so foul, that our ears are too delicate to listen to them." Lydia Maria Child, "Introduction" to Harriet A. Jacobs, *Incidents in the Life of a Slave Girl,* ed. Jean Fagan Yellin (Cambridge, Mass.: Harvard University Press, 1987), 3–4. Originally self-published by Child in Boston, 1861.

5. Harriet Beecher Stowe, *The Key to Uncle Tom's Cabin* (1854; Salem, N.H.: Ayer, 1987), 1. "The writer acknowledges that the book [*Uncle Tom's Cabin*] is a very inadequate representation of slavery; and it is so, necessarily, for this reason—that slavery, in some of its workings, is too dreadful for the purposes of art. A work which should represent it strictly as it is would be a work which could not be read; and all works which ever mean to give pleasure must draw a veil somewhere, or they cannot succeed."

6. Bert James Loewenberg and Ruth Bogin, eds., *Black Women in Nineteenth-Century American Life* (University Park: Pennsylvania State University Press, 1976), 50.

7. Ibid., 51.

8. Ibid., 52.

9. Ibid., 50.

10. Ibid., 49.

11. Gayl Jones, *Corregidora* (Boston: Beacon Press, 1975).

12. Hazel Carby, *Reconstructing Womanhood* (New York: Oxford University Press, 1987), 32. Frances Smith Foster, *Witnessing Slavery: The Development of Ante-bellum Slave Narratives* (Westport, Conn.: Greenwood Press, 1979), 131.

13. Jacobs, *Incidents,* 115.

14. Frederick Douglass, *Narrative of the Life of Frederick Douglass, an American Slave,* ed. Benjamin Quarles (1845; Cambridge, Mass.: Harvard University Press, Belknap Press, 1979).

15. Ibid., 25.

16. Gilbert Osofsky, *Puttin' on Ole Massa: The Slave Narratives of Henry Bibb, William Wells Brown, and Solomon Northup* (New York: Harper and Row, 1976).

17. Douglass, *Narrative,* 28–30.

18. Jacobs, *Incidents,* 13.

19. Ibid., 13.

20. Ibid., 13.

21. Ibid., 35.

22. I have adapted Ong's concept of writing as a technology that restructures consciousness as literacy is "interiorized," along with Lowe's concept of "bourgeois perception," as the dominant mode of subjectivity prevalent in print culture. Walter J. Ong, *Orality and Literacy* (New York: Methuen, 1982). Donald Lowe, *The History of Bourgeois Perception* (Chicago: University of Chicago Press, 1982).

23. Jacobs, *Incidents,* 234.

24. Valerie Smith, "Loopholes of Retreat: Architecture and Ideology in Harriet Jacobs's *Incidents in the Life of a Slave Girl,*" in *Reading Black, Reading Feminist,* ed. Henry Louis Gates, Jr. (New York: Penguin Books/Meridian, 1990), 212–26. Hortense Spillers, "Mama's Baby, Papa's Maybe: An American Grammar Book," *Diacritics 17* (1987): 65–81.

25. Mikhail Bakhtin, *The Dialogic Imagination,* trans. Caryl Emerson and Michael

Holquist, ed. Michael Holquist (Austin: University of Texas Press, 19810, 262–63. See also Mae Gwendolyn Henderson, "Speaking in Tongues: Dialogics, Dialectics, and the Black Woman Writer's Literary Tradition," in *Changing Our Own Words,* ed. Cheryl Wall (New Brunswick, N.J.: Rutgers University Press, 1989).

26. Harriet Beecher Stowe, *Uncle Tom's Cabin* (1852; New York: Harper & Row/ Harper Classics, 1965), 26–27.

27. Ibid., 22.

28. Harriet E. Wilson, *Our Nig; or Sketches from the Life of a Free Black,* ed. Henry Louis Gates, Jr. (1859; New York: Vintage Books/Random House, 1983), 72.

29. Ibid., 47.

30. Loewenberg and Bogin, *Black Women, 45.*

31. William L. Andrews, *Sisters of the Spirit: Three Black Women's Autobiographies of the Nineteenth Century* (Bloomington: Indiana University Press, 1986), 27.

32. Ibid., 1–22.

33. For Elaw the camp meeting functions similarly to the "Clearing" in Toni Morrison's novel *Beloved.* It is a site of spiritual empowerment for black people, and particularly black women. While Elaw exalts the soul above the despised earthly body, Morrison reinscribes the camp meeting as a scene in which a black woman preacher, "Baby Suggs, Holy," a self-called preacher whose voice rings through the Clearing, powerfully exhorts newly emancipated black men, women, and children to reclaim their broken, unloved, and abused bodies. Toni Morrison, *Beloved* (New York: Plume/ New American Library, 1987), 86–89.

34. Andrews, *Sisters of the Spirit,* 67.

35. Ibid., 166.

36. My reading is informed by that of Deborah E. McDowell, "Negotiating Between Tenses: Witnessing Slavery after Freedom—*Dessa Rose,*" in *Slavery and the Literary Imagination,* ed. Deborah E. McDowell and Arnold Rampersad (Baltimore: The Johns Hopkins University Press, 1989), 144–63.

37. Morrison, *Beloved,* passim.

38. William E. B. Du Bois, *The Souls of Black Folk,* in *Three Negro Classics,* ed. John Hope Franklin (1903; New York: Discus/Avon Books, 1965), 217.

39. While feminist scholarship has in some instances made possible complex critical readings of sentimental literature as a genre exploited by socially conscious women writers, sentimentality—and for that matter feminism itself—continue to be regarded by both male and female critics as suspect contaminants by which feminized modes of thinking and writing threaten masculine/universalist norms that have long been implicit in standards of literary criticism and value. In a review of *Beloved,* Stanley Crouch seems to conflate sentimentality and melodrama with feminism in order to censure Toni Morrison. He complains that this novel "is designed to placate sentimental feminist ideology, and to make sure that the vision of black women as the most scorned and rebuked of the victims doesn't weaken. . . . *Beloved* reads largely like a melodrama lashed to the structural conceits of the miniseries. . . . Morrison almost always loses control. She can't resist the temptation of the trite or the sentimental. . . . [T]o render slavery with aesthetic control demands not only talent but the courage to face the ambiguities of the human soul, which transcend race. Had Toni Morrison that kind of courage, had she the passion necessary to liberate her work from the failure of feeling that is sentimentality, there is much that she could achieve." Stanley Crouch, "Aunt Medea," *Notes of a Hanging Judge* (New York: Oxford University Press, 1990), 202–9.

40. African American women novelists Morrison, Sherley Anne Williams, Gloria

Naylor, Gayl Jones, Alice Walker, and Octavia Butler have all contemplated the conundrum that the African American literary tradition is, in a sense, founded on the bodies of raped and mutilated ancestors, whose bodies are literally inscribed by the scars of slavery and sexual abuse, or whose illiteracy motivates their offspring to acquire an empowering literacy.

41. The folk tradition itself is sometimes identified primarily with male speech, as in Hurston's novel *Their Eyes Were Watching God,* as opposed to her study of African American folklore, *Mules and Men,* in which women and men participate as equals in the "lying sessions."

42. Julia Kristeva, "Women's Time," in *Feminist Theory,* ed. Nannerl O. Keohane; Michelle Z. Rosaldo, and Barbara C. Gelpi (Chicago: University of Chicago Press, 1982), 33–35. See also Julia Kristeva, *Desire in Language: A Semiotic Approach to Literature and Art* (New York: Columbia University Press, 1980).

43. Elizabeth Grosz, *Sexual Subversions* (London: Allen and Unwin, 1989), 87.

44. Anne E. Goldman, "I Made the Ink": (Literary) Production and Reproduction in *Dessa Rose* and *Beloved,*" *Feminist Studies* 16 (Summer 1990): 313–30.

45. Morrison, *Beloved,* 199.

46. 44. Ibid., 273.

47. It was Molly Hite, in a 1989 discussion sponsored by the Cornell University Society for the Humanities, who first suggested to me that the sounds made by the chorus of women, all mothers, who participate in the exorcism/psychodrama/communal ritual at the conclusion of *Beloved,* might resemble the extralinguistic utterances of a woman in labor. This works well with Barthes's notion of "the grain of the voice," which he describes as "the materiality of the body speaking its mother tongue," the intimate associations among mother, body, tongue, voice, and speech constituting the discursive grain of Morrison's text. Roland Barthes, *Image-Music-Text,* trans. Stephen Heath (New York: Hill and Wang, 1977), 182. In their conscious and collaborative manipulation of this collective noise, the women all participate in the unbirthing of Beloved. The ghost child's hysterical pregnancy is terminated as she is spirited back into the unconscious, destined to be forgotten, the memory of her existence repressed by the Christian women who briefly perform the rite of a coven of witches in dispatching her back to the spirit world.

48. Kristeva, *Desire in Language,* 133.

49. Maria Mies, Veronika Bennholdt-Thomsen, and Claudia von Werlhof, *Women, the Last Colony* (London: Zed Books, 1988), 74.

Chapter 15

1. Anon., *The Life and Beauties of Fanny Fern* (New York, 1855), 162–63.

2. Joseph Boskin, *Sambo: The Rise and Demise of an American Jester* (New York: Oxford University Press, 1986).

3. Through the word "subaltern," I cite Gayatri Chakravorty Spivak, "Can the Subaltern Speak?" in *Marxism and the Interpretation of Culture,* edited and with an introduction by Cary Nelson and Lawrence Grossberg (Urbana: University of Illinois Press, 1988), 271–313. I do not, however, mean to minimize the differences between the situation of the bourgeois white woman of the American mid-nineteenth century and the colonial situation of the subjects of Western imperialism in India. Yet we can see international linkages in the "narrow epistemic violence" that plots the impossibility of unencumbered public female speech and the strategies of indirection that work

as a "floating buffer zone" (285). We can see that, caught in the space between being a "descriptive" hegemonic class and a discursive projection of a "transformative" class, the female sentimentalists of the nineteenth century occupy an affiliated moment in American culture. "Whether or not they themselves perceive it . . . their text articulates the difficult task of rewriting its own conditions of impossibility as the conditions of its possibility" (285).

4. Fern's father and brother were publisher/editors of controversial religious and secular journals. So coextensive is Fern's familial genealogy with the history of American letters that James Parton's contemporary biography of Fern considers her less as a product of familial identity than as an event in the annals of American popular journalism. Fern was that, indeed: the first American woman to have her own regular newspaper column and, not coincidentally, one of the earliest modern media stars, whose essays and books were accompanied by extensive advertising campaigns that proclaimed their popularity prior to their publication.

5. Susan Geary posits Fern's personal and symptomatic centrality to women's emergence via print into forms of capitalist publicity. She casts *Ruth Hall* as the first best-seller whose popularity was generated in advance by a massive advertising campaign. See "The Domestic Novel as a Commercial Commodity: Making a Best Seller in the 1850s," *Papers of the Bibliographical Society of America* 70 (1976): 365–93. Nina Baym provides the foundational casting of American "women's novels" in terms of the commodity form, arguing that the texts derive their value and intelligibility by adhering to a standard plot, and demonstrating the centrality of practical (professional, not political) considerations to the women authors' participation in the marketplace. See *Woman's Fiction: A Guide to Novels by and About Women in America, 1820–1870* (Ithaca, N.Y.: Cornell University Press, 1978).

6. Fern, "The 'Coming' Woman," in *Ruth Hall and Other Writings,* (1854; New Brunswick, N.J.: Rutgers University Press, 1986), 310.

7. For an incisive overview of the public-private debate and its accompanying practice of gendered (de)territorialization in the American nineteenth century, see Mary P. Ryan, *Women in Public: Between Banners and Ballot, 1825–1880* (Baltimore: The Johns Hopkins University Press, 1990).

8. In her insertion of the essentialist spaces of sentimental difference into the places of urban domestic modernity, Fern is identifiably a "realist," in Fredric Jameson's sense: one who produces "this whole new spatial and temporal configuration itself: what will come to be called "daily life," the *Alltag,* or, in a different terminology, the "referent"—so many diverse characterizations of the new configuration of public and private spheres or space in classical or market capitalism." See Fredric Jameson, "The Realist Floor-Plan," in *On Signs,* ed. Marshall Blonsky (Baltimore: The Johns Hopkins University Press, 1985), 373–83; quotation from 374. On the oppositional capacities and practices of this new capitalized space, see Michel de Certeau, *The Practice of Everyday Life,* trans. Steven Randall (Berkeley: University of California Press, 1984), and Andrew Ross, "The Everyday Life of Lou Andreas-Salomé: Making Video History," in Richard Feldstein and Judith Roof, eds., *Feminism and Psychoanalysis* (Ithaca, N.Y.: Cornell University Press, 1989), 142–63.

9. Fern frequently registers her rage at how the isolation and monotony of women's lives threatens them mentally, in the direction of insanity or psychic dullness. One might think that the lunatic asylums were filled with ordinary women, so frequently do her tales mention female insanity. *Ruth Hall* tells the story of Ruth's one female friend, Mary Leon, whose marriage to an unsympathetic husband reveals that the "privilege" of the bourgeois wife is to be intimate with forms of male domination

that lead to insanity and death (chs. 25 and 54). For journalistic discussions and depictions of the mental toll wrought by the dreary routine of women's everyday lives, see these pieces by Fern: "Blackwell's Island No. 3," *Ruth Hall and Other Writings,* 306–9; "Tyrants of the Shop," ibid., 339–40; "A Postscript to a Sermon," ibid., 356–58; "Helen, the Village Rose-Bud," in *The Life and Beauties,* 190–99; "Horace Mann's 'Opinion,' " ibid., 111–12; "Thorns for the Rose," in *Fern Leaves from Fanny's Port-folio* (Auburn, N.Y., 1853), 49–58; "A Word to Mothers," ibid., 234–35; "Fanny Ford," *Fresh Leaves* (New York, 1857), 114–209; "The Bride's New House," *Ginger-Snaps* (New York, 1870), 16–24; "Delightful Men," ibid., 44–52.

10. I cite here the inspiring analysis of minoritization put forth by Paul Gilroy, *'There Ain't No Black in the Union Jack': The Cultural Politics of Race and Nation* (London: Hutchinson, 1987), 26.

11. David Reynolds argues that the women sentimentalists really were not tremendously popular. That they *seemed* to be dominating the hearts, minds, and purses of the American reading public is, however, crucial testimony to the rupture in patriarchal expectations that even the most ideologically conservative of these women writers acheived. David S. Reynolds, *Beneath the American Renaissance: The Subversive Imagination in the Age of Emerson and Melville* (New York: Alfred A. Knopf, 1988), 338.

12. For the paradigmatic powerful reading of women's sentimental politics, see Jane P. Tompkins, *Sensational Designs: The Cultural Work of American Fiction, 1790–1860* (New York: Oxford University Press, 1985). Its particular complex abolitionist incarnation is documented by Jean Fagan Yellin, *Women and Sisters: The Antislavery Feminists in American Culture* (New Haven, Conn.: Yale University Press, 1989).

13. See, for example, *The Life and Beauties,* 27, 219; *Ginger-Snaps,* 82.

14. This paragraph draws from my essay "The Female Complaint," *Social Text* 19/20 (Fall 1988): 237–59.

15. Nancy Armstrong makes this argument in *Desire and Domestic Fiction: A Political History of the Novel* (New York: Oxford University Press, 1987).

16. These three axes of interpretation dominate the current discussion of the meaning of American sentimental literary culture. For their strongest representatives, see Richard Brodhead, "Sparing the Rod: Discipline and Fiction in Antebellum America," *Representations* 21 (Winter 1988): 67–96; Ann Douglas, *The Feminization of American Culture* (New York: Avon Books, 1977), and Ann D. Wood, "The 'Scribbling Women' and Fanny Fern: Why Women Wrote," *American Quarterly* 23 (1971): 3–24; and Tompkins, *Sensational Designs.* Diverse in their methods, contentious in their findings, in conjunction they nonetheless reveal a common problem of *reading* bourgeois women's culture: it seems that the more literary an account is, the more likely it is to be embarrassed by excesses of textual sentiment, and the more motivated it is to rationalize excess in the normative languages of political life. This defensiveness can be located historically in the American academic tradition of pathologizing and belittling women's culture as bad, irrational writing about banality.

There are notable exceptions to this critical custom. Nina Baym, in *Woman's Fiction,* argues for the women writers' value, characterizing them as cultural agents who transformed the disgrace surrounding women's entrance into the public sphere of print capitalism into an opportunity for expressive emancipation and economic independence. Yellin's *Women and Sisters* reads the use of feminine iconography in the American political imagination as an index of the interface between the cultural work of female abolitionist, African American, and nationalist authors. Karen Sánchez-Eppler speaks powerfully about the contradictions of cross-race and cross-class identification between white sentimental workers and their African American object-referents; see ch. 5 of this volume. "Bodily Bonds: The Intersecting Rhetorics of Feminism and Abolition." Extremely interesting evidence suggesting the uneven development of literary sentimentality and other forms of bourgeois expression—with literature lagging behind the more performative forms of journalism and theater—is provided by Karen Halttunen, *Confidence Men and Painted Women: A Study of Middle-Class Culture in America, 1830–1870* (New Haven, Conn.: Yale University Press, 1982).

17. Rita Felski, in *Beyond Feminist Aesthetics: Feminist Literature and Social Change* (Cambridge, Mass.: Harvard University Press, 1989), suggests that women's gender-reflexive literary incursions into the public sphere of discourse are rooted in twentieth-century feminist practice; her analysis of the feminist use of confession to establish an intimate public sphere is excellent. But a far broader range of women participated in the production of this sphere in America, in the nineteenth century, as has been established by Mary Kelley, *Private Woman, Public Stage: Literary Domesticity in Nineteenth-Century America* (New York: Oxford University Press, 1984), and Nancy Walker, *A Very Serious Thing: Women's Humor and American Culture* (Minneapolis: University of Minnesota Press, 1988). For studies about British women writers that also help establish this discursive prehistory, see Terry Lovell, *Consuming Fictions* (London: Verso, 1987), and Armstrong, *Desire and Domestic Fiction*.

18. The history over the struggle to define "woman" in the political public sphere s told by Denise Riley, *"Am I That Name?": Feminism and the Category of "Women" in History* (Minneapolis: University of Minnesota Press, 1988).

19. Fern, "Praise from a Woman," *The Life and Beauties*, 80.

20. Fern, *Fern Leaves*, 73.

21. Douglas, *Feminization*, 223.

22. D. A. Miller, *The Novel and the Police* (Berkeley: University of California Press, 1988), 193.

23. H. L. Mencken, *The American Language*, Supplement I (New York: Alfred A. Knopf, 1945), 652. See also the discussion in H. L. Mencken, *The American Language* (New York: Alfred A. Knopf, 1937), 303, which more explicitly links "female" to the American vernacularization of proper British speech.

24. John Walker, *The Rhyming Dictionary of the English Language*, revised and enlarged by Lawrence H. Davidson, (1775; New York: E. P. Dutton, 1936), 79; Noah Webster, *An American Dictionary of the English Language*, revised and enlarged by Chauncey A. Goodrich (Springfield, Mass., 1840), 446.

25. William A. Craigie and James R. Hulbert, eds., *A Dictionary of American English*, vol. 2 (Chicago: University of Chicago Press, 1940), 954.

26. In addition to the choice between female and woman, "lady" appeared to designate at least one kind of feminine subject not vulnerable to the linguistic equation of female animality with female subjectivity: women's organizations appeared like "the *Ladies'* Association for Educating *Females*." See Mencken, *The American Language*, Supplement I, 653.

27. Fanny Fern, "Praise from a Woman," *The Life and Beauties*, 80.

28. Fern, *Ginger-Snaps*, 13.

29. Fern, *Ginger-Snaps*, 72–73.

30. Fern, "Where Have I Been, and What Have I Seen?," in *Ruth Hall and Other Writings*, 295.

31. Fern, "The Other One," in *Life and Beauties*, 277–78. See also "Amiable Creatures," *Ruth Hall and Other Writings*, 310–11.

32. Fern, "Two Kinds of Women," *Ginger-Snaps*, 128.

33. Fern, "Fanny Ford," *Fresh Leaves*, 122.

34. Fern, "Our Nelly," *The Life and Beauties*, 268.

35. See also Fern's "Thorns for the Rose," "Mary Lee," and "Edith May; or, The Mistake of a Life-Time," in *Fern Leaves*, 49–58, 83–88, 108–13; and "Delightful Men" and "Blue Monday" in *Ginger-Snaps*, 43–52 and 70–73.

36. Fern, "The 'Coming' Woman," "A Law More Nice Than Just [I and II]," *Ruth Hall and Other Writings*, 309–10, 299–304; and "Summer Travel," *Fresh Leaves*, 56–58.

37. Fern, "Blackwell's Island No. 3," in *Ruth Hall and Other Writings*, 308–9.

38. Susan B. Anthony's appropriation of Fern's article "The Old Maid of the Period" signifies perfectly the problem raised by the complaint's ideologically elastic form. In her essay "Homes of Single Women," Anthony quotes Fern at length on how woman's rights have enabled a new type of woman to emerge who is self-sufficient and not dependent on any husband for her upkeep or her pleasure. But Anthony's quotation from Fern elides without ellipsis many feminizing passages of Fern's text which describe, for example, how the modern old maid has "two dimples in her cheek, and has a laugh as musical as a bobolink's song. She wears . . . cunning little ornaments around her plump throat . . . and her waist is shapely, and her hands have sparkling rings, and no knuckles; and her foot is cunning, and is prisoned in a bewildering boot" (147). Susan B. Anthony, "Homes of Single Women (October 1877)," in *Elizabeth Cady Stanton and Susan B. Anthony: Correspondence, Writings, Speeches*, edited and with a critical commentary by Ellen Carol DuBois, foreword by Gerda Lerner (New York: Schocken Books, 1981), 148–49; Fern, "The Old Maid of the Period," *Ginger-Snaps*, 146–48.

39. Fern, "Rules for Ladies," *The Life and Beauties*, 283.

40. Fanny Fern, *Rose Clark* (New York, 1856), iii–iv; quoted in Baym, *Woman's Fiction*, 32–33.

41. Fern, "Always Speak the Truth," in *The Life and Beauties*, 141; "A Woman with a Soul," *The Life and Beauties*, 169. See also *Ruth Hall and Other Writings*, 101, 146, 229.

42. Fern, "Was n't You Caught Napping?" in *Fern Leaves*, 380.

43. Ibid., 380–81.

44. Fuller's use of "femality" emphasizes "woman's" role as a harmonizer of disparate elements and an inspiration for labor and art. Fern's appropriation of this term adds "consciousness" to the mix of renewing and purifying activity that distinguishes woman in Fuller's view; it emphasizes agency, emergence, practice. See Margaret Fuller, *Woman in the Nineteenth Century* (1845; New York: Norton, 1971), 114–15.

45. Fern, "Horace Mann's 'Opinion,' " in *The Life and Beauties*, 112.

46. Fern, "Mrs. Jupiter's Soliloquy, Taken Down in Short-Hand.—by Fanny Fern," in *The Life and Beauties*, 205.

47. Fern, "The Private History of Didymus Daisy, Esq.—by Fanny Fern," in *The Life and Beauties*, 121.

48. Fern, "A Little Bunker Hill," *Fern Leaves*, 275.

49. Fern, "Independence," in *Ruth Hall and Other Writings*, 314–15.

50. Fern, "A Little Bunker Hill," 346.

51. Fern, "A Business Man's Home; Or, A Story for Husbands," *Fresh Leaves*, 16–17.

52. Fern, "Aunt Hetty on Matrimony," *Fern Leaves*, 376–79.

53. Fern, *Ruth Hall and Other Writings*, 224.

54. Nina Baym, *Novels, Readers, and Reviewers: Responses to Fiction in Antebellum*

America (Ithaca, N.Y.: Cornell University Press, 1984), 99–105. See also Baym, *Woman's Fiction,* "Introduction and Conclusions," 11–21.

55. Fern, "Preface: To the Reader," *Ruth Hall and Other Writings,* 3.

56. Fern, "Preface," *Fern Leaves,* vi.

57. Fern, "Minnie," *Fern Leaves,* 282.

58. See Brodhead, "Sparing the Rod."

59. David Simpson points out that while Willis pioneered in popularizing the transcription of vernacular speech into writing, he used the vernacular mainly to install comic class discriminations within the field of popular letters. Fern uses sentimental discourse more archly, both insisting on its populist authenticity and writing parodies of it. David Simpson, *The Politics of American English, 1776–1850* (New York: Oxford University Press, 1986), 144.

60. Cortland P. Auser, *Nathaniel P. Willis* (New York: Twayne Publishers, 1969), 125.

61. Trenchant testimony to Willis's retrogressive cultural and political practices is available, for example, in Lydia Maria Child, *Lydia Maria Child: Selected Letters, 1817–1880,* ed. Milton Meltzer and Patricia G. Holland (Amherst, Mass.: University of Massachusetts Press, 1982). Child not only lambasts Willis for focusing on "mere external things" (298) like the "*American world of fashion*" exemplified in Mrs. Lincoln's fashionable foreign bonnets, while "oppressed millions must groan on" (396); she also asserts that "[t]he *Home Journal* is not *violently* pro-slavery, but it is very *insidiously* and *systematically* so. The *New York Herald,* the *Day Book,* and the *Home Journal,* are announced by the Jeff. Davis organs to be the *only* Northern papers that the South can securely *trust*" (378).

62. Fern, *Ruth Hall and Other Writings,* 116.

63. Jean Fagan Yellin, "Written by Herself: *Harriet Jacobs' Slave Narrative,*" *American Literature* 53 (1981): 481–83. In *Incidents,* Mrs. Willis is called Mrs. Bruce.

64. Susan Phinney Conrad, *Perish the Thought: Intellectual Women in Romantic America, 1830–1860* (New York: Oxford University Press, 1976), 173.

65. Hazel V. Carby, *Reconstructing Womanhood: The Emergence of the Afro-American Woman Novelist* (New York: Oxford University Press, 1987), 45–61.

66. On the privileges of sentimental domesticity, and its always alienated status for African American women, see Hortense J. Spillers, "Mama's Baby, Papa's Maybe: An American Grammar Book," *Diacritics* (Summer 1987): 76–80.

67. Linda Brent, pseud. (Harriet Jacobs), *Incidents in the Life of a Slave Girl,* ed. Jean Fagin Yellin (1861; Cambridge, Mass.: Harvard University Press, 1987), 200.

68. Fern, *Ruth Hall and Other Writings,* 209.

69. Perhaps Fern is mindful of this irony of colonized consciousness, when she initiates her first book with this disclaimer: "And, such as it is, it must go forth; for 'what is written, is *written,*' and—stereotyped." *Fern Leaves,* v.

Contributors

Lauren Berlant, who teaches at the University of Chicago, is author of *The Anatomy of National Fantasy: Hawthorne, Utopia, and Everyday Life,* and other essays on the cultural and sexual politics of American nationality. This essay is part of an ongoing project about the sentimental identity of American "women's culture," titled *The Female Complaint.*

Ann Fabian teaches American studies and history at Yale University. She is the author of *Card Sharps, Dream Books & Bucket Shops: Gambling in 19th-century America,* and is currently at work on a book on personal narratives.

Susan Gillman is associate professor of literature at the University of California, Santa Cruz. She is working on a study of race relations entitled *The American Race Melodrama, 1870–1910.*

Karen Halttunen is professor of history at the University of California, Davis. She is the author of *Confidence Men and Painted Women: A Study of Middle-Class Culture in America, 1830–1870,* and is at work on a study of murder and the Gothic imagination in American culture.

Carolyn L. Karcher is associate professor at Temple University, author of *Shadow over the Promised Land: Slavery, Race, and Violence in Melville's America,* and editor of Lydia Maria Child's *Hobomok and Other Writings on Indians.* She is currently finishing a cultural biography of Child, to be titled *"The First Woman in the Republic."*

Joy Kasson is Bowman and Gordon Gray professor of American studies and English at the University of North Carolina at Chapel Hill. Her most recent work, *Marble Queens and Captives: Women in Nineteenth-Century American Sculpture,* was published in 1990 by Yale University Press.

Amy Schrager Lang is associate professor of American studies in the Graduate Institute of Liberal Arts at Emory University. The author of *Prophetic Woman: Anne Hutchinson and the Problem of Dissent in the Literature of New England,* she is at work on a book entitled *Negotiating the Border: The Social Vocabularies of American Fiction, 1848–1877.*

Isabelle Lehuu, assistant professor of history and American studies, St. Michael's College, is working on an historiographical essay on American culture and intellectual history to be published by the *Centre d'Etudes Nord-Americaines* of the *Ecole des Hautes Etudes en Sciences Sociales* in Paris.

Harryette Mullen, who teaches English at Cornell University, is currently completing *Gender and the Subjugated Body,* a study of tropes of embodiment in the African American slave narrative tradition. Her next project, *Visionary Literacy,* is a study of cultural syncretism in African American visionary art and literature.

Dana Nelson teaches American literature, women's studies, and cultural studies at Louisiana State University. She has recently published *The Word in Black and White* and is currently working further on the intersection of race and gender.

Lora Romero is an assistant professor of English at the University of Texas at Austin. She has published several articles on domesticity and the antebellum novel and is finishing a book entitled *Domestic Fictions: A Rereading of the American Renaissance.* Her essay won the Forester Prize for the best article published in *American Literature* in 1991.

Shirley Samuels teaches American literature at Cornell University. She has written the forthcoming *Romances of the Republic: Politics and the Family in Antebellum American Writing.*

Karen Sánchez-Eppler, assistant professor of American studies and English, Amherst College, has written *Touching Liberty: Abolition, Feminism, and the Politics of the Body,* forthcoming from the University of California Press, and is presently working on the ties between mesmerism, psychotherapy, and women's suffrage in the late nineteenth-century literary imagination.

Lynn Wardley is a member of the Department of English and American Literature and Language at Harvard; she has published in *American Literary History* and *English Literary History* and is finishing a book titled "Civilizing House: From American Sentimentalism to American Naturalism."

Laura Wexler, assistant professor of women's studies and American studies at Yale University, has written a book on contemporary photography, *Pregnant Pictures,* forthcoming from Routledge.

Index

Green, Jonathan Harrington, 144–56, 310nn.17,27
An Exposure of the Arts and Miseries of Gambling, 146–48
One Hundred Tricks with Cards, 153
The Secret Band of Brothers, or The American Outlaws, 310n.27
Greenough, Horace, 174, 179
Chanting Cherubs, 179
Griffith, D. W., 223, 226
Griffith, Julia, 301n.19
Griggs, Sutton, 223
Grimké, Angelina, 61–63, 94–95, 97–98, 299n.3, 300n.17, 314n.9
American Slavery As It Is: The Testimony of a Thousand Witnesses, 61–63, 315n.16
An Appeal to the Christian Women of the South, 300n.17, 314n.9
Letters to Catherine Beecher, 314n.9
Grimké, Sarah, 61, 95, 97
American Slavery As It Is: Testimony of a Thousand Witnesses. See Grimké, Angelina

Hale, Sarah Josepha, 74, 76, 81–83, 86, 88–89, 271–72
Hall, James, 201
Halttunen, Karen, 6, 153, 213, 296n.13, 337n.16
Handlin, David, 205, 215
Harper, Francis, 223, 226, 242
Iola Leroy; or Shadows Uplifted, 223, 242
Harper's, 28
Harper's Bazaar, 33
Harper's Monthly, 128
Harris, Neil, 298n.39
Harrison, Katherine, 49
Hartman, Mary S., 289nn.23,24
Haskell, Thomas, 316n.23
Havens, Rensselaer N., 152
Hawthorne, Nathaniel, 14, 73, 126, 292n.40, 308n.8
The House of the Seven Gables, 308n.8
Higginson, Thomas Wentworth, 290n.12
Hildreth, Richard, 63–64, 167, 289n.1, 318n.36
The Slave; or, Memoirs of Archy Moore, 63–64, 167–68, 289n.1, 318n.36
The White Slave, 168
Hirschman, Albert O., 155
Hite, Molly, 335n.47
Holmes, Oliver Wendell, 169
Homans, Margaret, 30
Home Journal, 279, 340n.61
Hooker, Isabella Beecher, 14

Hopkins, Pauline E., 221, 223–26, 231–36, 241–43
Contending Forces: A Romance Illustrative of Negro Life North and South, 221, 224, 234–35, 242
Of One Blood, Or, the Hidden Self, 226, 231–36
Howells, William Dean, 5, 292n.40
Hubbard, William, 195, 196
Hunt, William Holman, 56
"The Awakening Conscience," 56
Hurston, Zora Neale, 335n.41
Mules and Men, 335n.41
Their Eyes Were Watching God, 335n41

Imitation of Life, 243
Ingres, Jean-Auguste-Dominique, 175–76
Odalisque with Slave, 175–76

Jacobs, Harriet A., 8, 71, 244–54, 260–61, 264, 279–80, 293n.44, 309n.3, 332n.4
Incidents in the Life of a Slave Girl, 71, 245, 249–53, 279–80, 293n.44, 309n.3, 332n.4
James, Henry, 172
Jameson, Fredric, 196, 224, 336n.8
Jane Eyre, 55
Jarves, James Jackson, 185
Johnson, A. E., 242
The Hazeley Family, 242
Johnson, Charles, 260
Johnson, Paul, 310n.22
Jones, Gayl, 249, 334n.40
Jordan, Winthrop D., 306n.23
Juvenile Anti-Slavery Society of Rhode Island, The, 165
Juvenile Miscellany, The, 59–60, 106, 300n.18

Kaplan, Amy, 126
Kaplan, Fred, 284n.6
Kappeler, Suzanne, 180, 196
Karcher, Carolyn, 300n.18, 312n.2
Karlsen, Carol, 48, 55, 288n.16
Kasebier, Gertrude, 34, 36
Kelley, Mary, 12, 38, 200, 323nn.8,11, 338n.17
Kellogg, Miner, 179
Kelly, Abby, 314n.9
Kelly, Mary, 219
Kemble, Fanny, 61–62, 68, 291nn.18,21
Journal of a Residence on a Georgian Plantation in 1838–1839, 62, 291n.18
Kinmont, Alexander, 138, 220
Knickerbocker Magazine, The, 181
Kolodny, Annette, 192, 324n.26
Kristeva, Julia, 261, 263